Guide to C# and Object Orientation

Springer
London
Berlin
Heidelberg
New York
Barcelona
Hong Kong
Milan
Paris
Singapore
Tokyo

John Hunt

Guide to C# and Object Orientation

 Springer

John Hunt
JayDee Technology Ltd, www.jaydeetechnology.co.uk

British Library Cataloguing in Publication Data
A catalogue record for this book is available from the British Library

Library of Congress Cataloging-in-Publication Data
Hunt, John, 1964-
   Guide to C# and Object Orientation / John Hunt.
      p. cm.
   Includes bibliographical references and index.
   ISBN 1-85233-581-5 (alk. paper)
      1. C# (Computer program language) I. Title.

QA76.73.C154 H86 2002
005.13'3--dc21   2002021063

ISBN 1-85233-581-5 Springer-Verlag London Berlin Heidelberg
A member of BertelsmannSpringer Science+Business Media GmbH
http://www.springer.co.uk

First published 2002

Typeset by Ian Kingston Editorial Services, Nottingham, UK
Printed and bound at The Cromwell Press, Trowbridge, Wiltshire
34/3830-543210 Printed on acid-free paper SPIN 10863476

This book is dedicated to my mother, Maureen Hunt

Preface

The aim of this book is to provide current practitioners with an introduction not only to C#, but also to the object-oriented model upon which C# is based and to elements of the .NET environment most relevant to C#. The presentation of the object-oriented model upon which C# builds is essential, as it is not possible to move from languages such as C and Pascal to C# without also moving to object orientation. This is indeed the problem with many C# books: they teach you only the language, and mostly ignore object orientation (or at best devote a single chapter to this). In many ways it is object orientation that is harder to learn (the C# syntax is relatively small and straightforward). In addition, C# was designed from the ground up to work with the .NET framework, and an understanding of that framework and how C# relates to it is essential for any real world development. Thus this book also considers the use of various aspects of the .NET framework from C# as well as the C# language itself.

The chapters are listed below and are divided into seven parts. You are advised to work through Parts 1 and 3 thoroughly in order to gain a detailed understanding of object orientation. Parts 2 and 4 introduce the C# language. You may then dip into other chapters as required. For example, if you wish to hone your C# skills then the chapters in Part 6 will be useful, whereas if you wish to gain an overview of object-oriented design then you may prefer to read Part 7. However, if you wish to discover the delights of graphical user interfaces in C#, then you should read Part 5 next.

Content Summary

Part 1: Introduction to Object Orientation

Chapter 1: Introduction to Object Orientation

This chapter introduces the range of concepts and ideas that make up object technology. It presents the background that led to the acceptance of object orientation as a mainstream technology and discusses the pedigree of the C# language.

vii

Chapter 2: Elements of Object Orientation

This chapter provides a more formal definition of the terminology introduced in Chapter 1. It also considers the advantages and disadvantages of an object-oriented approach compared with more traditional procedural approaches.

Part 2: Introduction to the C# Language

Chapter 3: Why Object Orientation?

This chapter presents the motivation behind the OO model and compares and contrasts simple implementations in languages such as C and Pascal with how they would be achieved in an OO language (such as C#).

Chapter 4: Constructing an Object-Oriented System

A typical problem for many people when being introduced to a new approach is that they understand the terminology and the concepts but not how to use them. This chapter aims to alleviate this problem by presenting a detailed worked example of the way in which an object-oriented system may be designed and constructed. It does so without reference to any particular language, so that language issues do not confuse the discussion.

Chapter 5: An Introduction to C#

This chapter provides some background on the history of C# and the development environments which are available to support it (such as the .NET Framework SDK and Visual Studio .NET as well as the GNU .NET project). It also considers some of the tools that you will encounter.

Chapter 6: A Little C#

This chapter introduces the C# syntax, and examines the structure of a basic C# application.

Chapter 7: C# Classes

This chapter considers classes, instances, methods and variables. These are the basic building blocks of any object-oriented program and in particular of a C# program.

Chapter 8: Structs and Enumerations

In this chapter we look at two data-oriented features of the C# language. The first is the `struct` construct, used for representing data only structures. The second are enumerations, which are useful for defining specific sets of values that may have a specific order associated with them.

Chapter 9: Interfaces

This chapter introduces the concept of an interface and looks at how C# defines them. It also considers how classes in C# can implement interfaces.

Chapter 10: C# Constructs

This chapter presents further details of the C# language, including numbers, operators, variables and message passing. This chapter also looks at assignments, literals and variables and operations.

Chapter 11: Characters and Strings

In this chapter we consider how characters and strings are represented, created, manipulated and compared.

Chapter 12: An Example C# Class

This chapter presents you with a detailed worked example of software development in C#. This example presents a very simple class definition that uses only those concepts that have been introduced at this stage. The intention is to illustrate how the constructs and language elements can be combined in a real (if simple) application.

Part 3: C# and Object Orientation

Chapter 13: Classes, Inheritance and Abstraction

This chapter considers how you should use inheritance, abstraction and classes in C#. It considers the role of classes and when to create subclasses and define abstract classes.

Chapter 14: Encapsulation and Polymorphism

This chapter considers how to achieve encapsulation in C#. It considers how the visibility of methods and variables can be modified. It presents packages and how they are defined and used. It also discusses issues associated with the polymorphic appearance of C#.

Chapter 15: Nested Classes

Nested classes and their use are discussed in this chapter.

Chapter 16: Arrays in C#

In this chapter we consider how arrays are created, manipulated and accessed in C#.

Chapter 17: The Collections API

C# contains a set of classes for building standard data types such as lists, dictionaries, queues and stacks. This chapter provides a comprehensive description of the collections class framework.

Chapter 18: An Object-Oriented Organizer

This chapter presents a detailed example application constructed using the ArrayList class. The application is an electronic personal organizer that contains an address book, a diary (or appointments section) and a section for notes. The remainder of this chapter describes one way of implementing such an organizer. At the end of this chapter is a programming exercise.

Part 4: Further C#

Chapter 19: Control and Iteration

This chapter introduces control and iteration in C#.

Chapter 20: Attributes and Versioning

In this chapter we consider C# attributes and the use of versioning within classes and inheritance.

Chapter 21: Delegates

Delegates specify a contract between a caller and an implementor of some functionality. They can be used to provide a callback mechanism in C# and are used extensively in event handling.

Chapter 22: Exception Handling

In C# exceptions are objects; thus to throw an exception you must first make an instance of an exception class. This chapter considers exceptions and how to create, throw and handle them. It also discusses defining new exceptions by creating subclasses.

Part 5: Graphical User Interfaces

Chapter 23: Graphical User Interfaces

This chapter looks at how to construct windows (Windows Forms) and generate GUIs.

Chapter 24: Event Handling

This chapter considers the C# event handling model.

Chapter 25: The JDEdit Application

This chapter describes a detailed worked example of how to construct a user interface for a simple editor.

Part 6: C# Development

Chapter 26: Streams and Files

This chapter discusses how to obtain information on files and directories and how to read and write data via streams.

Chapter 27: Serialization

This chapter explains how objects can be stored to file and restored from file using serialization. This provides a very basic persistent object system for C#.

Chapter 28: Sockets in C#

This chapter introduces TCP/IP sockets and their implementation in C#.

Chapter 29: Data Access

In this chapter we consider in more detail the data access-oriented classes in C#. We look at how the OLE DB class operates and use a simple Microsoft Access database to illustrate this. We then look at the SQL specification classes, the ODBC classes and the use of ADO.

Chapter 30: Remoting in .NET

This chapter introduces remoting in C#.

Chapter 31: Concurrency

This chapter describes the concurrency mechanism of C#. That is, it describes the way in which C# implements threads.

Chapter 32: Using C# in ASP .NET

This chapter discusses how C# can be used with the ASP .NET services in the .NET framework.

Chapter 33: Web-Based User Interfaces

In this chapter we will look at the creation of Web-based user interfaces using the System.Web.UI namespace.

Chapter 34: XML and C#

XML is a major topic in today's computing world. This chapter introduces XML to the reader and presents a description of the DOM API for creating, manipulating and searching XML documents. Two example programs illustrate the ideas presented.

Chapter 35: C# Style

This chapter aims to promote readable, understandable, concise and efficient C# code.

Chapter 36: C# Roundup

This chapter discusses a variety of topics that a C# practitioner should be aware of, such as memory management, compiler directives etc.

Chapter 37: The .NET Environment

This chapter describes the .NET concept and the role of C# within it.

Part 7: Object-Oriented Design

Chapter 38: Object-Oriented Analysis and Design

This chapter introduces the concepts of object-oriented analysis and design. It reviews a number of the more popular techniques, such as OOA, OMT, Objectory and Booch. It also briefly considers the unification of the OMT and Booch notations.

Chapter 39: The Unified Modeling Language

The Unified Modeling Language (UML) is a third generation object-oriented modelling language which adapts and extends the published notations used in the Booch, OMT and Objectory methods. UML is intended to form a single, common, widely used modelling language for a range of object-oriented design methods (including Booch, Objectory and OMT). It should also be applicable to a wide range of applications and domains. This chapter summarizes the UML notation.

Chapter 40: The Unified Process

This chapter discusses the influential design method referred to as the Unified Process. It summarizes the main phases of the Unified Process using the UML notation.

Obtaining Source Code Examples

The source code for the examples in this book is available on the Web at http://www.guide-to-csharp.net/). Each chapter has its own directory within which the class files are listed individually. The source code has all been tested using the .NET Framework SDK Beta 2. As new versions of C# are released all examples will be tested against them. Any changes necessitated by a new release will be noted at the above Web site.

Typographical Conventions

In this book, the standard typeface is Minion; however, source code is set in Letter Gothic (for example, a = 2 + 3;). A bold font indicates C# keywords, for example:

```
public class Address : Object {. . .}
```

Acknowledgements

I would like to thank my wife Denise for having the patience to let me write this book and the wisdom to keep encouraging me. I would also like to thank my colleagues for suffering me while I kept throwing pieces of the manuscript of this book at them for comments. In particular, I would like to thank Jolene Lewis, Liz Osborne, Tim Cairnes, Dave Owen and Steve Mabbort.

John Hunt

Contents

Part 2 Introduction to the C# Language

Part 3 C# and Object Orientation

Part 7 Object-Oriented Design

Part 1

Introduction to Object Orientation

Chapter 1

Introduction to Object Orientation

1.1 Introduction

This book is intended as an introduction to object orientation for computer science students or those actively involved in the software industry. It assumes familiarity with standard computing concepts, such as stacks and memory allocation, and with a procedural language, such as C. From this background, it provides a practical introduction to object technology using C#, one of the newest and best pure object-oriented languages available.

This book introduces a variety of concepts through practical experience with an object-oriented language. It also tries to take you beyond the level of the language syntax to the philosophy and practice of object-oriented development.

In the remainder of this chapter, we will consider the various programming paradigms which have preceded object orientation. We will then examine the primary concepts of object orientation and consider how they enable object orientation to be achieved.

1.2 Programming Paradigms

Software construction is still more of an art than a science. Despite the best efforts of many software engineers, software systems are still delivered late, over budget and not up to the requirements of the user. This situation has been with us for many years. Indeed, the first conference to raise awareness of this problem was the NATO Software Engineering Conference of 1968, which coined the term *software crisis*. Since then a variety of programming paradigms have been developed explicitly to deal with this issue or have been applied to it.

A programming paradigm embodies a particular philosophy. These philosophies usually represent an insight which sets a new type of best practice. For a programming language to support a particular paradigm, it must not just allow adoption of the paradigm (you can use object-oriented programming techniques in assembler, but would you want to?), it must also actively support implementations based on the paradigm. This usually means that the language must support constructs which make development using that paradigm straightforward.

The major programming paradigms which have appeared in computer science can be summarized as follows:

- *Functional* Lisp is the classic example of a functional language, although by no means the only one (ML is a very widely used functional language). These languages place emphasis on applying a function (often recursively) to a set of one or more data items. The function then returns a value – the result of evaluating the function. If the function changes data items, this is a side effect. There is limited support for algorithmic solutions which rely on repetition via iteration. The functional approach turned out to be an extremely useful way of implementing complex systems for early AI researchers.
- *Procedural* Pascal and C exemplify procedural languages, which attempt to move to a higher level than the earlier assembler languages. The emphasis is on algorithmic solutions and procedures which operate on data items. They are extremely effective, but software developers still encounter difficulties. This is partly due to the increased complexity of the systems being developed. It is also because, although high-level procedural languages remove the possibility of certain types of error and increase productivity, developers can still cause problems for themselves. For example, the interfaces between different parts of the system may be incompatible, and this may not become obvious until integration or system testing.
- *Modular* In languages such as Modula-2 and Ada, a module hides its data from users. The users of the module can only access the data through defined interfaces. These interfaces are "published" so that users know the definitions of the available interfaces and can check that they are using the correct versions.
- *Object-oriented* This is the most recent "commercial" programming paradigm. The object-oriented approach can be seen as taking modularization a step further. Not only do you have explicit modules (in this case, objects), but these objects can inherit features from one another. We can of course ask "Why another programming paradigm?". The answer to this lies partly in the failure of many software development projects to keep to budget, remain within time-scales and give the users what they want. Of course, it should not be assumed that object orientation is the answer to all these problems; it is just another tool available to software developers.

This book attempts to introduce the object-oriented programming paradigm through the medium of an object-oriented programming language. It assumes that the majority of readers have a background in at least one procedural language (preferably a C-like language) and compares and contrasts the facilities provided by an object-oriented language with a procedural language.

Object orientation, even though it is quite different in many ways from the procedural approach, has developed from it. You should therefore not throw away all that you have learned using other approaches. Many of the good practices in other languages are still good practices in an object-oriented language. However, there are new practices to learn, as well as new syntax. It is much more than a process of learning a new syntax – you have a new philosophy to learn.

1.3 Revolution Versus Evolution

In almost every area of scientific endeavour there are periods of evolution followed by periods of revolution and then evolution again. That is, some idea or theory is held to be "accepted" (not necessarily true, but at least accepted). The theory is refined by successive experiments, discoveries etc. Then the theory is challenged by a new theory. This new theory is typically held by a small set of extremely fervent believers. It is often derided by those who are staunch supporters of the existing theory. As time continues, either this new theory is proved wrong and disappears, or more and more people are drawn to the new theory until the old theory has very few supporters.

There are many examples of this phenomenon in science: for example the Copernican theory of the Earth orbiting the Sun, Einstein's theory of relativity and Darwin's theory of evolution. Men such as Darwin and those who led him to his discoveries were revolutionaries: they went against the current belief of the times and introduced a new set of theories. These theories were initially derided, but have since become generally accepted. Indeed, Darwin's theories are now being refined further. For example, Darwin believed in a mechanism of fertilization of an egg derived from an old Greek theory (pangenesis). Every organ and tissue was assumed to produce granules which combined to make up the sex cells. Of course, we now believe this to be wrong and it was Darwin's own cousin, Francis Galton, who helped to disprove the pangenesis theory. It is unlikely that we will enter a new revolutionary phase which will overturn the theory of evolution; however, Einstein's theory of relativity is already being challenged.

Programming paradigms provide another example of this cycle. The move from low-level to high-level programming was a revolution (and you can still find people who will insist that low-level machine code programming is best). Object orientation is another revolution, which is still happening. Over the past 10 years, object orientation has become much more widely accepted and you will find many organizations, both suppliers and users of software, giving it lip service. However, you will also find many in the computer industry who are far from convinced. A senior colleague of mine recently told me that he believed that object orientation was severely over-hyped (which it may be) and that he really could not see the benefits it offered. I hope that this book will convince him (and others) that object orientation has a great deal to offer.

It is likely that something will come along to challenge object-oriented programming, just as it challenges procedural programming, as the appropriate software development approach. It is also likely that a difficult and painful battle will ensue, with software suppliers entering and leaving the market. Many suppliers will argue that their system always supported approach *X* anyway, while others will attempt to graft the concepts of approach *X* onto their system. When this will happen or what the new approach will be is difficult to predict, but it will happen. Until then, object orientation will be a significant force within the computer industry.

1.4 Why Learn a New Programming Paradigm?

The transition from a procedural viewpoint to an object-oriented viewpoint is not always an easy one. This prompts the question "Why bother?". As you are reading this book you must at least be partly convinced that it is a good idea. This could be because you have noticed the number of job advertisements offering employment for those with object-oriented skills. However, that aside, why should you bother learning a new programming paradigm?

I hope that some of the reasons will become clear during your reading of this book. It is worth considering at least some of the issues at this point.

1.4.1 Software Industry Blues

There is still no silver bullet for the problems in the software industry. Object-oriented technology does not remove the problems of constructing complex software systems, it just makes some of the pitfalls harder to fall into and simplifies traditionally difficult problems. However, difficulties in software development are almost inevitable; many of them arise due to the inescapable intangibility of software and not necessarily all by accident or poor development methods.

We should not, however, just throw up our hands and say "Well if that's the case, it's not my fault". Many of the problems which beset our industry relate to some deficiency in how programmers build software today. For example, if a software development project runs late, then adding more people to it is likely to make matters worse rather than get the project back on time.

Object technology is not the first attempt at addressing these issues. However, past attempts have met with mixed success for a number of reasons, some of which we consider below.

Modularity of Code

Traditional, procedural systems, typically relied on the fact that not only would the data they were using not change, for example, its type, but the way in which they obtained that data would not alter. Invariably, the function (or functions) that used the data also obtained the data. This meant that if the way in which data was accessed had to change, all the functions which used that data had to be re-written. If you have attended any sort of software engineering course, you will say that what was required was a function to obtain the data. This function could then be used in many different places. However, such application specific functions tend not to get used in "real world" systems for several reasons:

- *Small subroutines are too much effort.* Although many people talk about reusable code, they often mean relatively large code units. Small functions of one, two or three lines tend to be defined by a single programmer and are rarely shared amongst a development team, let alone several development teams.
- *Too many subroutines leads to too little reuse.* The larger the number of subroutines available, the less likely that they will be reused. It is very difficult to search through a code library of small subroutines trying to find one that does what you want. It is often much quicker to write it yourself!
- *It may not be obvious that a function is reusable.* If you are a programmer working on one part of a system, it may not be obvious that the function you are writing is of generic use. If a function is small then it is not identified by the designer as being a useful reusable component.

Ability to Package Software

Another issue is the way in which programming languages package up software for reuse. Many systems assume that the software should be partitioned into modules which are then integrated at compile-time. Such fixed compile-time integration can be good for some types of problem, but in many cases it is too inflexible. For example, while this approach can ensure that the modules being reused are compatible, developers may not know until run-time which modules they wish to use, and therefore some form of run-time binding is necessary.

Unix pipes and filters are examples of software systems which can be bound at run-time. They act as "glue", allowing the developer to link two or more programs in sequence together. However, in this case there is absolutely no error protection. It is quite possible to link two incompatible systems together.

What would be really useful would be a combination of these features: that is, the ability to specify either compile-time or run-time binding. In either case, there should be some form of error checking to ensure that you are integrating compatible modules. An important criterion is to avoid the need for extensive recompilation when, for example, just one line is altered. Finally, such a system should, by definition, enforce encapsulation and make packaging of the software effortless.

Flexibility of Code

In early procedural languages, for example C or Pascal, there was little or no flexibility. More recent procedural languages have introduced some flexibility but need extensive specification to achieve it. The result is internal flexibility at the cost of interface overheads, for example in Ada. Object technology allows code flexibility (and data flexibility) with little overhead.

1.4.2 The Advantages Claimed for Object Orientation

There are a range of benefits which can be identified for object-oriented programming languages. Not all of these are unique to object-oriented technology, but that does not matter; we are talking about the good things about object orientation here:

- *Increased code reuse* Languages such as Java encourage reuse. Every time you specify that one class inherits from another (which you do all the time in Java), you are involved in reuse. In time, most developers actively look to see where they can restructure classes to improve the potential for reuse. As long as this is not taken too far, it is an extremely healthy thing to do.
- *Data protection for little effort* The encapsulation facilities provided as part of the language protect your data from unscrupulous users. Unlike languages such as Ada, you do not have to write reams of specification in order to achieve this protection.
- *Easier integration with encapsulation* As users of an object cannot access the internals of the object, they must go via specified interfaces. As these interfaces can be published in advance of the object being implemented, others can develop to those interfaces knowing that they will be available when the object is implemented.
- *Easier maintenance with encapsulation* This point is really a variation on the last one. As users of an object must use the specified interfaces, as long as the external behaviour of these objects remains the same the internals of the object can be completely changed. For example, an object can store an item of data in a flat file, read it from a sensor or obtain it from a database; external users of the object need never know.
- *Simplified code with polymorphism* With polymorphism, you do not need to worry about exactly what type of object is available at run-time as long as it responds to the message (request for a method to be executed) that you send it. This means that it is a great deal easier to write reusable, compact code than in many other languages.

- *More intuitive programming* It has been argued that object orientation is a more intuitive programming paradigm than other approaches, such as procedural programming. This is because we tend to perceive the world in terms of objects. We see dials, windows, switches, fuel pumps and automated teller machines (ATMs). These objects respond to our use in specific ways when we interact with them. For example, an ATM requires a card, a PIN etc., in a particular sequence. Of course, those of us who have programmed before bring with us a lot of baggage, including preconceptions of what a program should be like and how you develop it. I hope that this book is about to turn all that on its head for a while, before putting everything back together again.

1.4.3 What Are the Problems and Pitfalls of Object Orientation?

No programming language is without its own set of problems and pitfalls. Indeed, part of the skill in becoming fluent in a new programming language is learning what the problems are and how to avoid them. In this section, we concentrate on the criticisms usually levelled at object orientation.

Lots of Confusing Terminology

This is a fair comment. Object orientation is littered with new terms and definitions for what appears to have been defined quite acceptably in other languages. Back in the early 1970s, when Smalltalk, one of the very first object-oriented programming languages, was being researched, many of the terms we now take for granted were already quite well established. It would be reasonable to assume that even if the inventors of the language liked their own terminology, early users would have tried to get it changed.

One possible answer is that in the past (that is, during the early and mid-1980s) object-oriented languages, such as Smalltalk, tended to be the preserve of academic and research institutions. (Indeed, I was introduced to my first object-oriented language while working on a research project at a British university during 1986–87.) It is often the case that academics enjoy the mystique that a language with terminology all of its own can create. By now, it is so well established in the object-oriented culture that newcomers just have to adapt.

The important point to remember is that the concepts are actually very simple, although the practice can be harder. To illustrate this, consider Table 1.1, which attempts to illustrate the parallels between object-oriented terminology and procedural terminology.

These approximations should not be taken too literally as they are intended only to help you visualize what each of the terms means. I hope that, by the end of the book, you will gain your own understanding of their meaning.

Table 1.1 Approximate equivalent terms.

Procedural term	Object-oriented term
Procedure	Method
Procedure call	Message
Non-temporary data	Instance variable
Records and procedures	Objects

Yet Another Programming Paradigm to Master

In general, people tend to like the things they are used to. This is why many people buy the same make of car again and again (even when it gives them trouble). It is also why computer scientists refuse to move to a new word processor, editor, operating system or hardware. Over the years, I have had many "discussions" with people over the use of LaTeX versus Word versus WordPerfect, the merits of Emacs versus vi, of Unix versus Mac, or of Windows versus Linux. In most cases, the issues raised and points made indicate that those involved in the discussions (including me) are biased, have their own "hobby horse" to promote and do not understand fully the other approach.

Object orientation both benefits and suffers from this phenomenon. There are those who hold it up almost like a religion and those who cast it aside because it is so different from what they are used to. Many justify this latter approach by pointing out that procedural programming has been around for quite a while now and many systems are successfully developed using it. This is a reasonable statement and one which promotes the status quo. However, the fact that object orientation is a new software paradigm, quite different from the procedural paradigm, should not be a reason for rejecting it.

Object orientation explicitly encourages encapsulation (information hiding), promotes code reuse and enables polymorphism. Most procedural languages have attempted to present these advantages as well; however, they have failed to do so in such a coherent and concise manner. Ada, for example, is not only a large cumbersome language, it requires an extensive specification to be written to enable two packages to work together. Any error in these specifications and the system does not compile (even if there are no errors or incompatibilities in the code). Ada95 has introduced the concept of objects and classes, although for most object technology practitioners the way in which it has done this is both counterintuitive and unwieldy.

Many Object-Oriented Environments Are Inefficient

Historically, object-oriented development environments have been inefficient, processor-intensive and memory hungry. Such environments tended to be designed for use on powerful workstations or mini-computers. Examples of such environments include Lisp Flavors (which even required specialist hardware, e.g. the Symbolics Lisp machine), Self and Smalltalk-80 (the forerunner of VisualWorks, a commercial Smalltalk development environment). These machines were expensive, sometimes non-standard and aimed at the research community.

With the advent of the PC, attempts were made to rectify this situation. For example, Smalltalk/V was designed specifically to run on the PC, and the first version of Smalltalk that I used was on a 286 PC. C# in particular possesses many features that are designed for efficiency; thus an object-oriented language and the environments required to run those languages may not be excessive.

Although 64 Mbyte of RAM is advisable on many of these systems, any Pentium III machine or above provides ample performance. The issue of additional RAM is not large; RAM can be purchased at reasonable rates and many industry pundits predict that 256 Mbyte (and more) will soon become the industry standard. Indeed, systems are now emerging which assume that a user has access to larger amounts of memory; for example, Microsoft's Visual Studio .NET requires a minimum of anything from 64 Mbyte to 192 Mbyte to run, depending on which version of Windows it is being used on.

C++ and object-oriented versions of Pascal (such as Delphi) are no more memory or processor intensive than any non-object-oriented language. However, it is worth noting that these languages do not offer the same level of support for the programmer as, for example, C#, Java and Smalltalk. In particular, they do not provide automatic memory management and garbage collection.

Pedigree of Object-Oriented Languages

In the horse or dog breeding world, the pedigree of an animal can be determined by considering its ancestry. Whilst you cannot determine how good a language is by looking at its predecessors, you can certainly get a feel for the influences which have led to the features it possesses. The current set of commercial object-oriented languages have all been influenced to a greater or lesser extent by existing languages.

C# is no exception, as it inherits features from other languages, and C++ and Java can be seen as having a particularly strong lineage (whatever may be said publically). Of course C++ and Java were not the first object-oriented languages created. Indeed both of these languages owe a big debt to earlier languages, such as Smalltalk, Lisp, Objective-C and, before them all, Simula (which is, at most, object-based).

The extent to which a language can be considered to be a *pure* object-oriented language (i.e. one which adheres to object-oriented concepts consistently) as opposed to a *hybrid* object-oriented language (i.e. one in which object-oriented concepts lie alongside traditional programming approaches) tends to depend on its background.

A pure object-oriented language supports only the concept of objects. Any program is made up solely of interacting objects which exchange information with each other and request operations or data from each other. This approach tends to be followed by those languages which most directly inherit features from Simula (C++ is a notable exception). Simula was designed as a language for discrete event simulation. However, it was influenced by many of the features from ALGOL 60 and was effectively the first language to use the concepts which we now describe as object-oriented. For example, it introduced the concepts of classes, inheritance and polymorphism.

The language which inherits most directly from Simula is Smalltalk. This means that its ALGOL heritage is there for all to see in the form of structured programming constructs (although the syntax may, at first, seem a little bizarre). It is a pure object-oriented language in that the only concepts supported by the language are object-oriented. It also inherits from Lisp (if not syntax, then certainly the philosophy). This means that not only does it not include strong typing, it also provides dynamic memory management and automatic garbage collection. This has both benefits and drawbacks, which we will discuss at a later stage. In contrast Eiffel, another pure object-oriented language, attempts to introduce best software engineering practice, rather than the far less formal approach of Lisp. Self is a recent, pure object-oriented language which is still at the research stage.

Many language designers have taken the *hybrid* approach. That is, object-oriented constructs have either been grafted onto, or intermixed with, the existing language (for example, C++). In some cases, the idea has been to enable a developer to take advantage of object orientation when it appears appropriate. In other situations, it has eased the transition from one approach to another. The result has often been less than satisfactory. Not only does it mean that many software developers have moved to their new object-oriented language believing that it is just a matter of learning the new syntax (which it is not), they have written procedural programs in which objects are limited to holding data, believing that this is sufficient (which it is not). It is really only safe to move to a hybrid language once you have learnt about object technology using a pure object-oriented language.

1.5 Fundamentals of Object Orientation

The object-oriented programmer's view of traditional procedural programming is of procedures wildly attacking data which is defenceless and has no control over what the procedures do to it (the rape and pillage style of programming). In contrast, object-oriented programming is viewed as polite and well-behaved data objects passing messages to one another, each data object deciding for itself whether to accept the message and how to interpret what it means.

The basic idea is that an object-oriented system is a set of interacting objects which are organized into classes. Figure 1.1 illustrates a simplified cruise control system from a car. It shows the objects in the system, the links between the objects and the direction in which information flows along these links. The object-oriented implementation of this system would mirror this diagram exactly. That is, there would be an object representing each box; between the boxes, there would be links allowing one object to request a service from, or provide information to, another. For example, the cruise control electronic control unit (ECU) might request the current speed from the speed sensor. It would then use this information when asking the throttle to adjust its position. Notice that we do not talk about functions or procedures which access information from data structures and then call other functions and procedures. There is no concept such as the ECU data structure and the ECU main program. This can be a difficult change of emphasis for some people and we shall try to illustrate it further below.

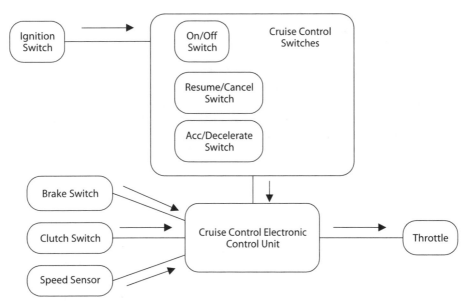

Figure 1.1 A cruise control system as a set of objects.

The aim of object-oriented programming is to shift the focus of attention from *procedures that do things to data* to *data which is asked to do things*. The task is not to define the procedures which manipulate data but to define data objects, their attributes and the way in which they may be examined or changed. Data objects (and procedures) can communicate with other data objects only through narrow, well-defined channels.

1.6 The Basic Principles of Object Orientation

- *Encapsulation or data hiding* Encapsulation is the process of hiding all the details of an object that do not contribute to its essential characteristics. Essentially, it means that what is inside the class is hidden; only the external interfaces can be seen by other objects. The user of an object should never need to look inside the box!
- *Inheritance* Objects may have similar (but not identical) properties. One way of managing (classifying) such properties is to have a hierarchy of classes. A class inherits from its immediate parent class and from classes above the parent (see the hierarchy in Figure 1.3). The inheritance mechanism permits the common characteristics of an object to be defined once but used in many places. Any change is thus localized.

  If we define a concept *animal* and a concept *dog*, we do not have to specify all the things which a dog has in common with other animals. Instead, we inherit them by saying that *dog* is a **subclass** of *animal*. This feature is unique to object-oriented languages; it promotes (and achieves) huge amounts of reuse.
- *Abstraction* An abstraction denotes the essential characteristics of an object that distinguish it from all other kinds of object and thus provides crisply defined conceptual boundaries, relative to the perspective of the viewer. That is, it states how a particular object differs from all others.
- *Polymorphism* This is the ability to send the same message to different instances which appear to perform the same function. However, the way in which the message is handled depends on the class of which the instance is an example.

An interesting question to ask is "How do languages such as Ada, C and Lisp relate to the four concepts above?". An obvious issue is related to inheritance. That is, if we define a concept *animal* and we then define a concept *dog*, we do not have to specify all the things that a dog has in common with other animals. Instead, we inherit them by saying that a dog is a **subclass** of animal. This feature is unique to object-oriented languages; it promotes (and achieves) huge amounts of reuse. The next four sections expand on each of these basic principles in more detail

1.7 Encapsulation

Encapsulation or data hiding has been a major feature of a number of programming languages; Modula-2 and Ada both provide extensive encapsulation features. But what exactly is encapsulation? Essentially, it is the concept of hiding the data behind a software "wall". Those outside the wall cannot get direct access to the data. Instead, they must ask intermediaries (usually the owner of the data) to provide them with the data.

The advantage of encapsulation is that the user of the data does not need to know how, where, or in what form the owner of the data stores that data. This means that if the owner changes the way in which the data is stored, the user of the data need not be affected. The user still asks the owner for the data; it is the data owner that changes how the request is fulfilled.

Different programming languages implement encapsulation in different ways. For example, Ada enables encapsulation using packages which possess both data and procedures. It also specifies a set of interfaces which publish those operations the package wishes to make available to users of the package. These interfaces may implement some operations or provide access to data held within the package.

Object-oriented languages provide encapsulation facilities which present the user of an object with a set of external interfaces. These interfaces specify the requests to which the object will respond (or, in the terminology of object orientation, the requests which the object will understand). These interfaces not only avoid the need for the caller to understand the internal details of the implementation, they actually prevent the user from obtaining that information. Users of an object cannot directly access the data held by an object as it is not visible to them. In other words, a program that calls this facility can treat it as a black box; the program knows what the facility's external interfaces guarantee to do, and that is all it needs to know.

It is worth pointing out a difference between the object-oriented approach and the package approach used in Ada. In general, a package is a large unit of code providing a wide range of facilities with a large number of data structures (for example, the TextIO package). In an object-oriented language, the encapsulation is provided at the object level. While objects may well be as large and as complex as the typical Ada package, they are often much smaller. In languages such as C# and Java, where (virtually) everything is an object, the smallest data and code units also naturally benefit from encapsulation. You can attempt to introduce the same level of encapsulation in Ada, but it is not natural to the language.

Figure 1.2 illustrates the way in which encapsulation works within an object-oriented language. It shows that anything outside the object can only gain access to the data the object holds through specific interfaces (the black squares). In turn, these interfaces trigger

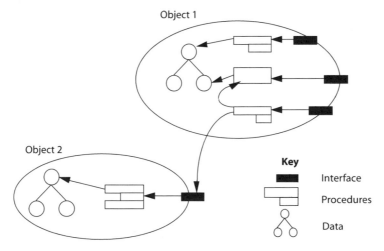

Figure 1.2 Object structure and interaction.

procedures which are internal to the object. These procedures may then access the data directly, use a second procedure as an intermediary or call an interface to another object.

1.8 Inheritance

A class is an example of a particular type of thing (for example, *mammal* is a class of *animal*). In the object-oriented world, a class is a definition of the characteristics of that thing. Thus, in the case of mammals, we might define that they have fur, are warm-blooded and produce live young. Animals such as dogs and cats are then instances of the class mammal. This is all quite obvious and should not present a conceptual problem for anyone. However, in most object-oriented languages (Self is an exception) the concept of the class is tightly linked to the concept of inheritance.

Inheritance allows us to state that one class is similar to another class, but with a specified set of differences. Another way of putting it is that we can define all the things which are common about a class of things, and then define what is special about each sub-grouping within a subclass.

For example, if we have a class defining all the common traits of mammals, we can define how particular categories of mammals differ. The duck-billed platypus is a quite extraordinary mammal that differs from other mammals in a number of important ways. However, we do not want to define all the things that it has in common with other mammals. Not only is this extra work, but we then have two places in which we have to maintain this information. We can therefore state that a duck-billed platypus is a class of mammal that does not produce live young. Classes allow us to do this.

An example which is rather closer to home for most computer scientists is illustrated in Figure 1.3. For this example, we assume that we have been given the job of designing and implementing an administration system for a small software house that produces payroll, pensions and other financial systems. This system needs to record both permanent and temporary employees of the company. For temporary employees, we need to record their department, the length of their contract, when they started and additional information which differs depending on whether they are contractors or students on an industrial placement. For permanent employees, we need to record their department, their salary, the languages and operating systems with which they are familiar and whether they are a manager. In the case of managers, we might also want to record the projects that they run.

Figure 1.3 illustrates a class hierarchy diagram for this application. It shows the classes we have defined and from where they inherit their information.

- *Inheritance versus instantiation* Stating that one class is a specialized version of a more generic class is different from saying that something is an example of a class of things. In the first case, we might say that *developer* is one category of employee and *manager* is another. Neither of these categories can be used to identify an individual. They are, in effect, templates for examples of those categories. In the second case, we say that "John" is an example of a developer (just as "Chris", "Myra" and "Denise" may also be examples of developers). "John" is therefore an instance of a particular class (or category) of things known as developers. It is important to get the concept of specializing a class with a subclass clear in your mind. It is all too easy to confuse an instance of a class with a subclass.

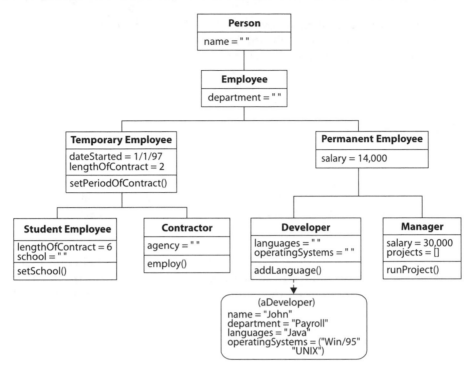

Figure 1.3 n e ample of inher itance

- *Inheritance of common information* We place common concepts together in a single class. For example, all people have a name and all employees have a nominated department (whether they are permanent or temporary). All temporary employees have a start date, whether they are contractors or students. In turn, all classes below Employee inherit the concept of a department. This means that not only do all Managers and Developers have a department, but "John" has a department, which in this case is "Payroll".

- *Abstract classes* Figure 1.3 defines a number of classes of which we have no intention of making an example: Employee, Permanent Employee and Temporary Employee. These are termed abstract classes and are intended as placeholders for common features rather than as templates for a particular category of things. This is quite acceptable and is common practice in most object-oriented programs.

- *Inheritance of defaults* Just because we have stated that Permanent Employees earn a default salary of £14,000 a year does not mean that all types of employee have that default. In the diagram, Managers have a default of £30,000, illustrating that a class can overwrite the defaults defined in one of its parents.

- *Single and multiple inheritance* In Figure 1.3, we have only illustrated single inheritance. That is, a class inherits from only one other class. This is the case in many object-oriented programming languages, such as Java and Smalltalk. However, other languages, such as C++ and Eiffel, allow multiple inheritance. In multiple inheritance, you can bring together the characteristics of two classes to define a third class. For example, you may have two classes, Toy and Car, which can be used to create a third class Toy-Car. Multiple inheritance is a controversial subject which is still being debated. Those who think it is useful fail to see why other languages do not include it and vice versa. C# does not include multiple inheritance.

1.9 Abstraction

Abstraction is much more than just the ability to define categories of things which can hold common features of other categories of things (for example, Temporary Employee is an abstract class of Contractor and Student Employee). It is a way of specifying what is particular about a group of classes of things. Often this means defining the interface for an object, the data that such an object holds and part of the functionality of that object.

For example, we might define a class DataBuffer which is the abstract class for things that hold data and return them on request. It may define how the data is held and that operators such as put() and get() are provided to add data to, and remove it from, the DataBuffer. The implementation of these operators may be left to those implementing a subclass of DataBuffer.

The class DataBuffer might be used to implement a stack or a queue. Stack could implement get() as *return the most recent data item added*, while Queue could implement it as *return the oldest data item held*. In either case, a user of the class knows that put() and get() are available and work in the appropriate manner.

In some languages, abstraction is related to protection. For example, in C++ and C#, you can state whether a subclass can overwrite data or procedures (and indeed whether it has to overwrite them). In Smalltalk, the developer cannot state that a procedure cannot be overwritten, but can state that a procedure (or method) is a subclass responsibility (that is, a subclass which implements the procedure in order to provide a functioning class).

Abstraction is also associated with the ability to define abstract data types (ADTs). In object-oriented terms these are classes (or groups of classes) which provide behaviour that acts as the infrastructure for a particular class of data type (for example, DataBuffer provides a stack or a queue). However, it is worth pointing out that ADTs are more commonly associated with procedural languages such as Ada. This is because the concepts in object orientation essentially supersede ADTs. That is, not only do they encompass all the elements of ADTs, they extend them by introducing inheritance.

1.10 Polymorphism

Polymorphism is a strange sounding word, derived from Greek,[1] for a relatively simple concept. It is essentially the ability to request that the same operation be performed by a wide range of different types of things. How the request is processed depends on the thing that receives the request. The

---

1   *Polymorphos* means "having many forms".

Figure 1.4 An example of polymorphism.

programmer need not worry about how the request is handled, only that it is. This is illustrated in Figure 1.4.

In this example, the variable MotorVehicle can hold an instance of a MotorVehicle and any subclass of the class MotorVehicle (such as car, MotorBike or Sports etc.). As the class MotorVehicle defines a method drive() they will all respond to that method. However, if each subclass defines its own version of drive() they will each do their own thing. For example, driving a family car might be quite different from driving a motorbike or a sports car. However, developers do not need to worry about these details; they just need to know that they will all support the drive() method (which they will, as they are subclasses of MotorVehicle).

Effectively, this means that you can ask many different things to perform the same action. For example, you might ask a range of objects to provide a printable string describing themselves. If you ask an instance of the Manager class, a compiler object or a database object to return such a string, you use the same interface call (ToString in C#).

The name "polymorphism" is unfortunate and often leads to confusion. It makes the whole process sound rather grander than it actually is. There are two types of polymorphism used in programming languages: overloading and overriding. The difference in name relates to the mechanism that resolves what code to execute.

1.10.1 Overloading Operators

Overloading occurs when procedures have the same name but apply to different data types. The compiler can determine which operator to use at compile-time and can use the correct version.

Ada uses exactly this type of overloading. For example, you can define a new version of the + operator for a new data type. When a programmer uses +, the compiler uses the types associated with the operator to determine which version of + to use.

In C, although the same function, printf, is used to print any type of value, it is not a polymorphic function. The user must specify the correct format options to ensure that a value is printed correctly.

1.10.2 Overriding Operators

Overriding occurs when a procedure is defined in a class (for example, Temporary Employee) and also in one of its subclasses (for example, Student Employee). It means that instances of Temporary Employee and Student Employee can each respond to requests for this procedure (assuming it has not been made private to the class). For example, let us assume that we define the procedure ToString in these classes. The pseudocode definition of this in Temporary Employee might be:

```
public String ToString(){
    return "I am a temporary employee"
}
```

In Student Employee, it might be defined as:

```
public String ToString(){
    return "I am a student employee"
}
```

The procedure in Student Employee replaces the version in Temporary Employee for all instances of Student Employee. If we ask an instance of Student Employee for the result of ToString, we get the string "I am a student employee". If you are confused, think of it this way:

> If you ask an object to perform some operation, then, to determine which version of the procedure is run, look in the class used to create the instance. If the procedure is not defined there, look in the class's parent. Keep doing this until you find a procedure which implements the operation requested. This is the version which is used.

In languages such as Java the choice of which version of the procedure to execute is not determined at compile-time, because the compiler would have to be able to determine the type of object and then find the appropriate version of the procedure. Instead, the procedure is chosen at run-time. The technical term for this process of identifying the procedure at run-time rather than compile-time is called "late binding".

1.11 Summary

In this chapter you have been introduced to the background and history of object orientation. You have explored the main concepts which underpin object orientation and have encountered some of the (sometimes arcane) terminology used. There is a great deal of new information in this chapter which can, at times, appear to make obsolete all that you already know.

The object-oriented view of the world can be daunting for a programmer who is used to a more procedural view of the world. To adjust to this new view of the world is hard (and some never do). Others fail to see the difference between an object-oriented programming language and a language such as Ada (we refer here to the pre-Ada95 version). However, object orientation will become second nature to many once they have worked with object-oriented systems for a while. The key thing is to try things out as you go along and, if possible, have someone around who understands a bit about object orientation – they can often illuminate and simplify an otherwise gloomy network of tunnels.

1.12 Further Reading

There are a great many books available on object orientation. Some of the best known include Booch (1994), Budd (1991), Wirfs-Brock *et al.* (1990) and Cox and Novobilski (1991). An excellent book aimed at managers and senior programmers who want to learn how to apply object-oriented technology successfully to their projects is Booch (1996). Another good book in a similar style is Yourdon (1994).

Other books which may be of interest to those attempting to convince themselves or others that object technology can actually work are Harmon and Taylor (1993), Love (1993) and Meyer and Nerson (1993).

Other places to find useful references are the *Journal of Object-Oriented Programming* (SIGS Publications, ISSN 0896-8438) and the OOPSLA conferences. The OOPSLA conferences are annual worldwide conferences on Object-Oriented Programming: Systems, Languages and Applications. References for the proceedings of some recent conferences are listed at the back of this book. There are also references for the proceedings of the European Conference on Object-oriented Programming (ECOOP).

For further reading on the software crisis and approaches aimed at solving it see Brooks (1987) and Cox (1990). For a discussion of the nature of scientific discovery, refinement and revolution see Kuhn (1962).

Chapter 2

Elements of Object Orientation

2.1 Introduction

This chapter is intended to reinforce what you have already learned. It concisely defines the terminology introduced in the last chapter and attempts to clarify issues associated with hierarchies. It also discusses some of the perceived strengths and weaknesses of the object-oriented approach. It then offers some guidance on the approach to take in learning about objects.

2.2 Terminology

- *Class* A class defines a combination of data and procedures that operate on that data. Instances of other classes can only access that data or those procedures through specified interfaces. A class acts as a template when creating new instances. A class does not hold any data, but specifies the data that is held in the instance. The relationship between a class, its superclass and any subclasses is illustrated in Figure 2.1.
- *Subclass* A subclass is a class that inherits from another class. For example, in the last chapter, Student Employee was a subclass of Temporary Employee. Subclasses are, of course, classes in their own right. Any class can have any number of subclasses.
- *Superclass* A superclass is the parent of a class. It is the class from which the current class inherits. For example, in the last chapter, Temporary Employee was the superclass of Student Employee. In C#, a class can have only one superclass.
- *Instance or object* An instance is an example of a class. All instances of a class possess the same data variables but contain their own data. Each instance of a class responds to the same set of requests.
- *Instance variable* This is the special name given to the data which is held by an object. The "state" of an object at any particular moment relates to the current values held by its instance variables. (In C#, there are also class-side variables, referred to as static variables, but these will be discussed later.) Figure 2.2 illustrates a definition for a class in pseudocode. It includes some instance variable definitions: fuel, mileage and name.

21

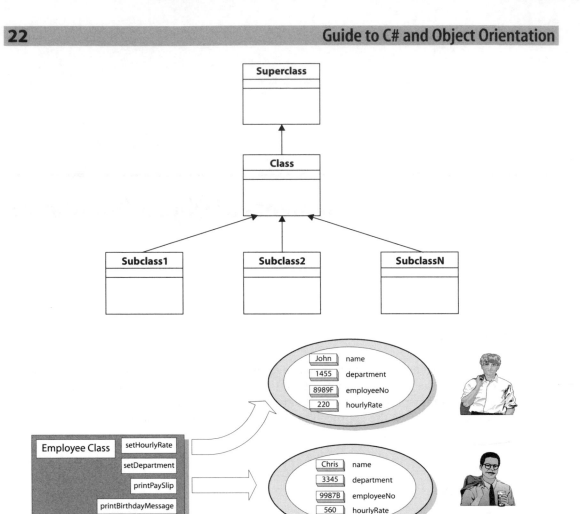

Figure 2.1 The relationship between class, superclass and subclass.

- *Method* A method is a procedure defined within an object. In early versions of Smalltalk, a method was used to get an object to do something or return something. It has since become more widely used; languages such as CLOS and Java also use the term. Two methods are defined in Figure 2.2: one calculates the miles per gallon, while the other sets the name of the car object.

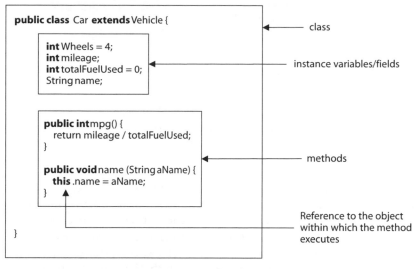

Figure 2.2 A partial class definition.

- *Message* One object sends a message to another object requesting some operation or data. The idea is that objects are polite, well-behaved entities which carry out functions by sending messages to each other. A message may be considered akin to a procedure call in other languages.
- *This* The special (pseudo-) variable, **this**, is a reference to the object within which a method is executing (see Figure 2.2). It enables messages to "this" (the current) object.
- *Single or multiple inheritance* Single and multiple inheritance refer to the number of superclasses from which a class can inherit. C# is a single inheritance system, in which a class can only inherit from one class. C++ is a multiple inheritance system in which a class can inherit from one or more classes.

2.3 Types of Hierarchy

In most object-oriented systems there are two types of hierarchy; one refers to inheritance (whether single or multiple) and the other refers to instantiation. The inheritance hierarchy (or *extends* hierarchy) has already been described. It is the way in which an object inherits features from a superclass.

The instantiation hierarchy relates to instances rather than classes and is important during the execution of the object. There are two types of instance hierarchy: one indicates a *part-of* relationship, while the other relates to a using relationship (it is referred to as an *is-a* relationship).

The difference between an *is-a* relationship and a *part-of* relationship is often confusing for new programmers (and sometimes for those who are experienced in one language but are new to object-oriented programming languages, such as C#). Figure 2.3 illustrates that a student *is-a* type of person whereas an engine is *part-of* a car. It does not make sense to say that a student is *part-of* a person or that an engine *is-a* type of car!

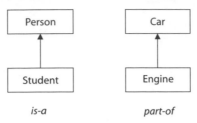

Figure 2.3 *is-a* does not equal *part-of*.

In C#, *extends* relationships are generally implemented by the subclassing mechanism. It is possible to build up large and complex class hierarchies which express these *extends* relationships. These classes express the concept of inheritance, allowing one class to inherit features from another. The total set of features is then used to create an instance of a class. In contrast, *part-of* relationships tend to be implemented using instance variables in C#.

However, *is-a* relationships and classes are not exactly the same thing. For example, if you wish to construct a semantic network consisting of explicit *is-a* relationships between instances you will have to construct such a network manually. The aim of such a structure is to represent knowledge and the relationships between elements of that knowledge, and not to construct instances. The construction of such a network is outside the scope of the subclassing mechanism and would therefore be inappropriate.

If John is an instance of a class Person, it would be perfectly (semantically) correct to say that John *is-a* Person. However, here we are obviously talking about the relationship between an instance and a class rather than a subclass and its parent class.

A further confusion can occur for those encountering C# after becoming familiar with a strongly typed language. These people might at first assume that a subclass and a subtype are essentially the same. However, they are not the same, although they are very similar. The problem with classes, types and *is-a* relationships is that on the surface they appear to capture the same sorts of concept. In Figure 2.4, the diagrams all capture some aspect of the use of the phrase *is-a*. However, they are all intended to capture a different relationship.

The confusion is due to the fact that in modern English we tend to overuse the term *is-a*. We can distinguish between the different types of relationship by being more precise about our

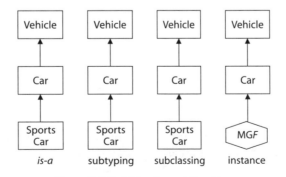

Figure 2.4 Satisfying four relationships.

Table 2.1 Types of *is-a* relationship.

Specialization	One thing is a special case of another
Type	One type can be used interchangeably with another type (substitutability relationship)
Subclassing or inheritance	An implementation mechanism for sharing code and representations
Instantiation	One thing is an example of a particular category (class) of things

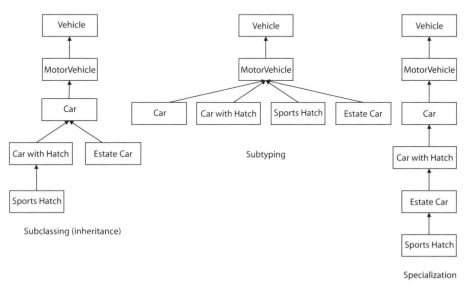

Figure 2.5 Distinguishing between relationships.

definitions in terms of a programming language, such as C#. Table 2.1 defines the relationships illustrated in Figure 2.4.

To illustrate this point, consider Figure 2.5, which illustrates the differences between the first three categories.

The first diagram illustrates the potential relationships between a set of classes that define the behaviour of different categories of vehicle. The second diagram presents the subtype relationships between the categories. The third diagram illustrates a straight specialization set of relationships. Notice that although *estate car* is a specialization of *car with hatch*, its implementation (the subclassing hierarchy) indicates that it does not share any of its implementation with the *car with hatch* class. It is worth noting that type relationships are specifications, while classes (and subclasses) are implementations of behaviour.

2.4 The Move to Object Technology

At present you are still acclimatizing to object orientation. It is extremely important that from now on you do your utmost to immerse yourself in object orientation, object technology and C#. This is because when you first encounter a new language or paradigm, it is all too easy to say that it is not good because you cannot do what you could in some other language or paradigm. We are all subject to the "better the devil you know than the devil you don't" syndrome. If you embrace object orientation, warts and all, at least for the present, you will gain most.

In addition, it is a fact of life that most of us tend to fit in learning something new around our existing schedules. This may mean for example, that you are trying to read this book and do the exercises while still working in C, Visual Basic, Ada etc. From personal experience, and from teaching others about C#, I can say that you will gain most by putting aside a significant amount of time and concentrating on the subject matter involved. This is not only because object orientation is so different, but also because you need to get familiar not only with the concepts but also with and its development environment.

So have a go, take a "leap of faith" and stick with it until the end. If, at the end, you still cannot see the point, then fair enough, but until then accept it.

2.5 Summary

In this chapter, we reviewed some of the terminology introduced in the previous chapter. We also considered the types of hierarchy which occur in object-oriented systems and which can at first be confusing. We then considered the pros and cons of object-oriented programming. You should now be ready to start to think in terms of objects. As has already been stated, this will at first seem a strange way to develop a software system, but in time it will become second nature. In the next chapter we examine how an object-oriented system might be developed and structured. This is done without reference to any source code, as the intention is to familiarize you with objects rather than with C#. It is all too easy to get through a book on Smalltalk, C++, C# etc. and understand the text but still have no idea how to start developing an object-oriented system.

2.6 Exercises

1.   Research what other authors have said about single and multiple inheritance. Why do languages such as Smalltalk and C# not include multiple inheritance?

2.   Look for terms such as class, method, member, member function, instance variable and constructor in the books listed in the further reading section. When you have found them, read their explanation of these terms and write down your understanding of their meaning.

2.7 Further Reading

Suggested further reading for this chapter includes Coad and Yourdon (1991) and Meyer (1988). In addition, all the books mentioned in the previous chapter are still relevant.

Part 2

Introduction to the C# Language

Chapter 3

Why Object Orientation?

3.1 Introduction

The pervious two chapters have introduced the basic concepts behind object orientation and the terminology, and have explored some of the motivation. This chapter looks at how object orientation addresses some of the issues that have been raised with procedural languages. To do this it looks at how a small extract of a program might be written in a language such as C, considers the problems faced by the C developer and then looks at how the same functionality might be achieved in an object-oriented language such as C#. Again, do not worry too much about the syntax you will be presented with: it will be C#, but it should not detract from the legibility of the examples.

3.2 The Procedural Approach

As has already been stated, object orientation provides four things:

1. Encapsulation
2. Abstraction
3. Inheritance
4. Polymorphism

It has been claimed that these four elements combine to provide a very powerful programming paradigm, but why? What is so good about object orientation?

3.2.1 A Naked Data Structure

Consider the following example:

```
record Date {
  int day;
```

```
    int month;
    int year;
}
```

This defines a data structure for recording dates. There are similar structures in many procedural languages, such as C, Pascal and Ada. It is naked because it has no defences against procedures accessing and modifying its contents.

So what is wrong with a structure such as this? Nothing, apart from the issue of visibility? That is, what can see this structure and what can update the contents of the structure? For example, code could set the day to –1, the month to 13 and the year to 9999. As far as the structure is concerned, the information it holds is fine (that is day = 01, month = 13, year = 9999). This is because the structure only knows it is supposed to hold an integer; it knows nothing about dates *per se*. This is not surprising: it is only data.

3.2.2 Procedures for the Data Structure

This data is associated with procedures that perform operations on it. These operations might be to test whether the date represents a date at a weekend or part of the working week. It may be to change the date (in which case the procedure may also check to see that the date is a valid one).

For example:

- isDayOfWeek(date);
- inMonth(date, 2);
- nextDay(date);
- setDay(date, 9, 23, 1946);

How do we know that these procedures are related to the date structure we have just looked at? By the naming conventions of the procedures and by the fact that one of the parameters is data (a record).

The problem is that these procedures are not limited in what they can do to the data (for example the setDay procedure might have been implemented by a Briton who assumes that the data order is day, month and year. However, it may be used by an American who assumes that the date order is month, day, year. Thus the meaning of setDay(date, 9, 23, 1946) will be interpreted very differently. The American views this as 23 September 1946, while the Briton views it as the 9th day of the 23rd month, 1946. In either case, there is nothing to stop the date record being updated with both versions. Obviously the setDay() procedure might check the new date to see that it was legal, but then again it might not. The problem is that the data is naked and has no defence against what these procedures do to it. Indeed, it has no defence against what any procedures that can access it may do to it.

3.2.3 Packages

One possibility is to use a package construct. In languages such as Ada packages are commonplace and are used as a way of organizing code and restricting visibility. For example,

```
package Dates is
  type Date is ...
  function isDayOfWeek(d: Date) return BOOLEAN;
  function inMonth(d: Date, m: INTEGER) return BOOLEAN;
...
```

The package construct now provides some ring fencing of the data structure and a grouping of the data structure with the associated functions. In order to use this package a developer must import the package (for example by using with and uses in Ada). The developer can then access the procedures and work with data of the specified type (in this case Date). There can even be data which is hidden from the user within a *private part*. This therefore increases the ability to encapsulate the data (hide the data) from unwelcome attention.

3.3 Does Object Orientation Do Better?

This is an important question: "Does object orientation do any better" than the procedural approach described above? We will first consider packages, then inheritance.

3.3.1 Packages Versus Classes

It has been argued (to me at least) that a package is just like a class. It provides a template from which you can create executable code, it provides a wall around your data with well-defined gateways etc. However, there are a number of very significant differences between packages and classes.

Firstly, packages tend to be larger (at least conceptually) units than classes. For example, the TextIO package in Ada is essentially a library of textual IO facilities, rather than a single concept such as the class String in C#. Thus packages are not used to encapsulate a single small concept such as Date, but rather a whole set of related concepts (as indeed they are used in C# itself, where they are called namespaces). Thus a class is a finer level of granularity than a package, even though it provides similar levels of encapsulation.

Secondly, packages still provide a relatively loose association between the data and the procedures. A package may actually deal with very many data structures with a wide range of methods. The data and the methods are related primarily via the related set of concepts represented by the package. In contrast, a class tends to closely relate data and methods in a single concept. Indeed, one of the guidelines presented later in this book relating to good class design is that if a class represents more than one concept, split it into two classes.

Thus this close association between data and code and means that the resulting concept is more than just a data structure (it is closer to a concrete realization of an abstract data type). For example:

```
class Date {
  private int day, month, year;
  public bool IsDayOfWeek() {..}
}
```

Anyone using an instance of Date now gets an object which can tell you whether it is a day of the week or not and can hold the appropriate data. Note that the isDayOfWeek() method takes no parameters – it doesn't need to, as it and the date are part of the same thing. This means that users of the Date object will never get their hands on the actual data holding the date (i.e. the integers day, month and year). Instead, they are forced to go via the internal methods. This may only seem a small step, but it is a significant one: nothing outside the object may access the data within the object. In contrast, the data structure in the procedural version is not only held separately from the procedures, the values for day, month or year could be modified directly without the need to use the defined procedures.

For example, compare the differences between an ADA-esque excerpt from a program to manipulate dates:

```
d: Date;
setDay(d, 28);
setMonth(d, 2);
setYear(d, 1998);
isDayOfWeek(d);
inMonth(d, 2);
```

Note that it was necessary first to create the data and then to set the fields in the data structure. Here we have been good and have used the interface procedures to do this. Once we had the data set up we could then call methods such as IsDayOfWeek and InMonth on that data.

In contrast, the C# code uses a constructor to pass in the appropriate initialization information. How this is initialized internally is hidden from the user of the class Date. We then call methods such as IsDayOfWeek() and IsMonth(12) directly on the object date.

```
Date d = new Date(12, 2, 1998);
d.IsDayOfWeek();
d.InMonth(12);
```

The thing to think about here is where would code be defined?

3.3.2 Inheritance

Inheritance is the key element that makes an object-oriented language more than an object-based language. An object-based language possesses the concept of objects, but not of inheritance. Indeed, inheritance is the thing that marks an object-oriented language as different from a procedural language. The key concept in inheritance is that one class can inherit data and methods from another, thus increasing the amount of code reuse occurring as well as simplifying the overall system. One of the most important features of inheritance (ironically) is that it allows the developer to get inside the encapsulation bubble in limited and controlled ways. This allows the subclass to take advantage of internal data structures and methods, without compromising the encapsulation afforded to objects. For example, let use define a subclass of the class Date (the colon is used to indicate inheritance in C#):

```
class Birthday : Date {
  private String name;
  private int age;
  public boolean IsBirthday() {..}
}
```

The method IsBirthday() could check to see whether the current date matched the birthday represented by an instance of Birthday and return true if it does and false if it does not.

Note, however, that the interesting thing here is that not only have I not had to define integers to represent the date, neither have I had to define methods to access such dates. These have both been inherited from the parent class Date.

In addition, I can now treat an instance of Birthday as either a Date or as a Birthday, depending on what I want to do!

What would you do in languages such as C, Pascal or Ada83? One possibility is that you could define a new package, Birthday, but that package would not extend Date; it would have to import Date and add interfaces to it etc. However, you certainly couldn't treat a Birthday package as a Date package.

In a language such as C#, because of polymorphism, you can do exactly that. You can reuse existing code that only knew about Date, for example:

- **public void** Test (Date d) {..}
- t.Test(birthday);

This is because Birthday is indeed a type of Date as well as being a type of Birthday.

You can also use all of the features defined for Date on Birthdays:

- birthday.IsDayOfWeek();

Indeed, you don't actually know where the method is defined. This method could be defined in the class Birthday (in which case it would override that defined in the class Date). However, it could be defined in the class Date (if no such method is defined in Birthday). However, without looking at the source code there is no way of knowing!

Of course you can also use the new methods defined in the class Birthday on instance (objects) of this class. For example:

- birthday.IsBirthday();

3.4 Summary

Classes in an object-oriented language provide a number of features that are not present in procedural languages. Hopefully, by the end of the book you will agree that they are useful additions to the developer's toolbox. If not, give it time; one of the problems that we all face (myself included) is a reluctance to change. To summarize, the main points to be noted from this chapter on object orientation are:

- Classes provide for inheritance.
- Inheritance provides for reuse.
- Inheritance provides for extension of data types.
- Inheritance allows for polymorphism.
- Inheritance is a unique feature of object orientation.
- Encapsulation is a good software engineering feature in object orientation.

Chapter 4

Constructing an Object-Oriented System

4.1 Introduction

This chapter takes you through the design of a simple object-oriented system without considering implementation issues or the details of any particular language. Instead, it illustrates how to use object orientation concepts to construct a software system. We first describe the application and then consider where to start looking for objects, what the objects should do and how they should do it. We conclude by discussing issues such as class inheritance, and answer questions such as "Where is the structure of the program?".

4.2 The Application: Windscreen Wipe Simulation

This system aims to provide a diagnosis tutor for the equipment illustrated in Figure 4.1. Rather than use the wash–wipe system from a real car, students on a car mechanics diagnosis course use

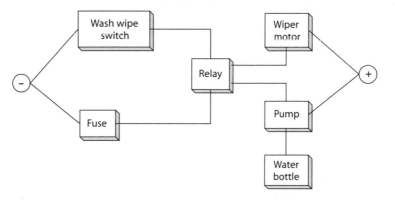

Figure 4.1 The windscreen wash–wipe system.

Table 4.1 System states.

Switch setting	System state
Off	The system is inactive.
Intermittent	The blades wipe the windscreen every few seconds.
Slow	The wiper blades wipe the windscreen continuously.
Fast	The wiper blades wipe the windscreen continuously and quickly.
Wash	The pump draws water from the water bottle and sprays it onto the windscreen.

this software simulation. The software system mimics the actual system, so the behaviour of the pump depends on information provided by the relay and the water bottle.

The operation of the wash–wipe system is controlled by a switch which can be in one of five positions: off, intermittent, slow, fast and wash. Each of these settings places the system into a different state (Table 4.1).

For the pump and the wiper motor to work correctly, the relay must function correctly. In turn, the relay must be supplied with an electrical circuit. This electrical circuit is negatively fused, and thus the fuse must be intact for the circuit to be made. Cars are negatively switched, as this reduces the chances of short circuits leading to unintentional switching of circuits.

4.3 Where Do We Start?

This is often a very difficult point for those new to object-oriented systems. That is, they have read the basics and understand simple diagrams, but do not know where to start. It is the old chestnut: "I understand the example, but don't know how to apply the concepts myself". This is not unusual and, in the case of object orientation, is probably normal.

The answer to the question "Where do I start?" may at first seem somewhat obscure; you should start with the data. Remember that objects are things which exchange messages with each other. The things possess the data that is held by the system and the messages request actions that relate to the data. Thus, an object-oriented system is fundamentally concerned with data items.

Before we go on to consider the object-oriented view of the system, let us stop and think for a while. Ask yourself "Where would I start if I was going to develop such a system in C or Pascal or even Ada?". In most cases, the answer is "With some form of functional decomposition". That is, you might think about the main functions of the system and break them down into sub-functions and so on. As a natural part of this exercise, you would identify the data required to support the desired functionality. Notice that the emphasis would be on the system functionality.

Let us take this further and consider the functions we might identify for the example presented above (Table 4.2). We would then identify important system variables and sub-functions to support the above functions.

Now let us go back to the object-oriented view of the world. In this view, we place a great deal more emphasis on the data items involved and consider the operations associated with them

Table 4.2 System functions.

Function	Description
Wash	Pump water from the water bottle to the windscreen.
Wipe	Move the windscreen wipers across the windscreen.

(effectively, the reverse of the functional decomposition view). This means that we start by attempting to identify the primary data items in the system; next, we look to see what operations are applied to, or performed on, the data items; finally, we group the data items and operations together to form objects. In identifying the operations, we may well have to consider additional data items, which may be separate objects or attributes of the current object. Identifying them is mostly a matter of skill and experience.

The object-oriented design approach considers the operations far less important than the data and their relationships. In the next section we examine the objects that might exist in our simulation system.

4.4 Identifying the Objects

We look at the system as a whole and ask what indicates the state of the system. We might say that the position of the switch or the status of the pump is significant. This results in the data items shown in Table 4.3.

The identification of the data items is considered in greater detail in Part 7. At this point, merely notice that we have not yet mentioned the functionality of the system or how it might fit together; we have only mentioned the significant items. As this is such a simple system, we can assume that each of these elements is an object and illustrate it in a simple object diagram (Figure 4.2).

Notice that I have named each object after the element associated with the data item (e.g. the element associated with the fuse condition is the fuse itself) and that the actual data item (e.g. the condition of the fuse) is an instance variable of the object. This is a very common way of naming objects and their instance variables. We now have the basic objects required for our application.

Table 4.3 Data items and their associated state information.

Data item	States
Switch setting	Is the switch set to off, intermittent, wipe, fast wipe or wash?
Wiper motor	Is the motor working or not?
Pump state	Is the pump working or not?
Fuse condition	Has the fuse blown or not?
Water bottle level	The current water level
Relay status	Is current flowing or not?

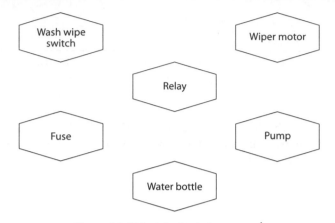

Figure 4.2 Objects in simulation system..[1]

4.5 Identifying the Services or Methods

At the moment, we have a set of objects each of which can hold some data. For example, the water bottle can hold an integer indicating the current water level. Although object-oriented systems are structured around the data, we still need some procedural content to change the state of an object or to make the system achieve some goal. Therefore we also need to consider the operations a user of each object might require. Notice that the emphasis here is on the **users of the object** and what they **require of the object** rather than what operations are performed on the data.

Let us start with the switch object. The switch state can take a number of values. As we do not want other objects to have direct access to this variable, we must identify the services which the switch should offer. As a user of a switch we want to be able to move it between its various settings. As these settings are essentially an enumerated type, we can have the concept of incrementing or decrementing the switch position. A switch must therefore provide a moveUp and a moveDown interface. Exactly how this is done depends on the programming language; for now, we concentrate on specifying the required facilities.

If we examine each object in our system and identify the required services, we may end up with Table 4.4.

We generated this table by examining each of the objects in isolation to identify the services which might reasonably be required. We may well identify further services when we attempt to put it all together.

Each of these services should relate to a method within the object. For example, the moveUp and moveDown services should relate to methods which change the state instance variable within the object. Using a generic pseudocode, the moveUp method within the switch object might contain the following code:

---

1 The hexagonal shape representing instances is based on the structured cloud used in Unified Modeling Language version 0.8, described in Part 7 of this book.

Table 4.4 Object services.

Object	Service	Description
switch	moveUp	Increment switch value
	moveDown	Decrement switch value
	state?	Return a value indicating the current switch state
fuse	working?	Indicate whether the fuse has blown or not
wiper motor	working?	Indicate whether the wipers are working or not
relay	working?	Indicate whether the relay is active or not
pump	working?	Indicate whether the pump is active or not
water bottle	fill	Fill the water bottle with water
	extract	Remove some water from the water bottle
	empty	Empty the water bottle

```
define method moveUp()
  if state == "off" then
    state = "wash"
  elseif state == "wash" then
    state = "wipe"
  endif
end define method
```

This method changes the value of the state variable in switch. The new value of the instance variable depends on its previous value. You can define moveDown in a similar manner. Notice that the reference to the instance variable illustrates that it is global to the object. The moveUp method requires no parameters. In object-oriented systems, it is common for few parameters to be passed between methods (particularly of the same object), as it is the object which holds the data.

4.6 Refining the Objects

If we look back to Table 4.4, we can see that fuse, wiper motor, relay and pump all possess a service called working?. This is a hint that these objects may have something in common. Each of them presents the same interface to the outside world. If we then consider their attributes, they all possess a common instance variable. At this point, it is too early to say whether fuse, wiper motor, relay and pump are all instances of the same class of object (e.g. a Component class) or whether they are all instances of classes which inherit from some common superclass (see Figure 4.3). However, this is something we must bear in mind later.

4.7 Bringing it all Together

So far we have identified the primary objects in our system and the basic set of services they should present. These services were based solely on the data the objects hold. We must now consider how to

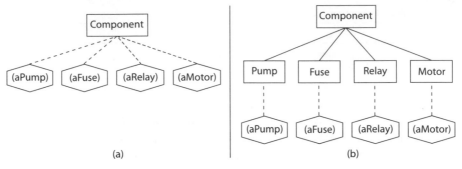

Figure 4.3 Possible classes for components in the simulation.

make our system function. To do this, we need to consider how it might be used. The system is part of a very simple diagnosis tutor; a student uses the system to learn about the effects of various faults on the operation of a real wiper system, without the need for expensive electronics. We therefore wish to allow a user of the system to carry out the following operations:

- change the state of a component device
- ask the motor what its new state is

The moveUp and moveDown operations on the switch change the switch's state. Similar operations can be provided for the fuse, the water bottle and the relay. For the fuse and the relay, we might provide a changeState interface using the following algorithm:

```
define method changeState()
  if state == "working" then
    state = "notWorking"
  else
    state = "working"
  endif
end define method
```

Discovering the state of the motor is more complicated. We have encountered a situation where one object's state (the value of its instance variable) is dependent on information provided by other objects. If we write down procedurally how the value of other objects affect the status of the pump, we might get the following pseudocode:

```
if fuse is working then
  if switch is not off then
    if relay is working then
      pump status = "working"
    endif
  endif
endif
```

This algorithm says that the pump status depends on the relay status, the switch setting and the fuse status. This is the sort of algorithm you might expect to find in a main() program. It links the sub-functions together and processes the data.

In an object-oriented language (such as C#), we do not have a main program in the same way that a C program has. Instead the main() method in C# is an initiating point for an object-oriented system. As it is on the class-side, it can trigger the creation of instances, but it is not itself part of those instances. This can be confusing at first; however, if you think of the main() method in C# as initiating a program that is outside the scope of the main() method, you are fairly close.

In an object-oriented system, well-mannered objects pass messages to one another. How then do we achieve the same effect as the above algorithm? The answer is that we must get the objects to pass messages requesting the appropriate information. One way to do that is to define a method in the pump object which gets the required information from the other objects and determines the motor's state. However, this requires the pump to have links to all the other objects so that it can send them messages. This is a little contrived and loses the structure of the underlying system. It also loses any modularity in the system. That is, if we want to add new components then we have to change the pump object, even if the new components only affect the switch. This approach also indicates that the developer is thinking too procedurally and not really in terms of objects.

In an object-oriented view of the system, the pump object only needs to know the state of the relay. It should therefore request this information from the relay. In turn, the relay must request information from the switches and the fuse.

Figure 4.4 illustrates the chain of messages initiated by the pump object:

1. pump sends a working? message to the relay
2. relay sends a state? message to the switch
   the switch replies to the relay

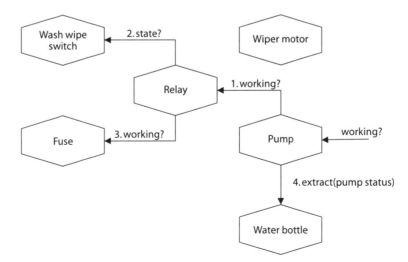

Figure 4.4 Collaborations between the objects for wash operation.

3. relay sends a second working? message to the fuse
      the fuse replies to the relay
      the relay replies to the motor
      if the pump is working, then the pump object sends the final message to the water bottle
4. pump sends a message extract to the water bottle

In Step 4, a parameter is passed with the message because, unlike the previous messages which merely requested state information, this message requests a change in state. The parameter indicates the rate at which the pump draws water from the water bottle.

The water bottle should not record the value of the pump's status as it does not own this value. If it needs the motor's status in the future, it should request it from the pump rather than using the (potentially obsolete) value passed to it previously.

In Figure 4.4, we assumed that the pump provided the service working? which allows the process to start. For completeness, the pseudocode of working? for the pump object is:

```
define method working?()
  begin
    this.status = relay.working().
    if this.status == "working" then
      water_bottle.extract(this.status)
    endif
  end
end define method
```

This method is a lot simpler than the procedural program presented earlier. At no point do we change the value of any variables which are not part of the pump, although they may have been changed as a result of the messages being sent. Also, it only shows us the part of the story that is directly relevant to the pump. This means that it can be much more difficult to deduce the operation of an object-oriented system merely by reading the source code. Development environment for object-oriented languages alleviate this problem to some extent. For example, for C# the Visual Studio .NET environment does overcome this problem to some extent through the use of sophisticated browsers.

4.8 Where is the Structure?

People new to object orientation may be confused because they have lost one of the key elements that they use to help them understand and structure a software system: the main program body. This is because the objects and the interactions between them are the cornerstone of the system. In many ways, Figure 4.4 shows the object-oriented equivalent of a main program. This also highlights an important feature of most object-oriented approaches: graphical illustrations. Many aspects of object technology, for example object structure, class inheritance and message chains, are most easily explained graphically.

Let us now consider the structure of our object-oriented system. It is dictated by the messages which are sent between objects. That is, an object must possess a reference to

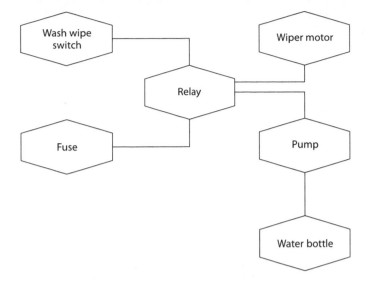

Figure 4.5 Wash–wipe system structure.

another object in order to send it a message. The resulting system structure is illustrated in Figure 4.5.

In C#, this structure is achieved by making instance variables reference the appropriate objects. This is the structure which exists between the instances in the system, and does not relate to the classes, which act as templates for the instances.

We now consider the classes that create the instances. We could assume that each object is an instance of an equivalent class (see Figure 4.6(a)). However, as has already been noted, some of the classes bear a very strong resemblance. In particular, the fuse, the relay, the motor and the pump share a number of common features. Table 4.5 compares the features (instance variables and services) of these objects. From this table, the objects differ only in name. This suggests that they are all instances of a common class such as `Component` (see Figure 4.6(b)). This class would possess an additional instance variable to simplify object identification.

If they are all instances of a common class, they must all behave in exactly the same way. However, we want the pump to start the analysis process when it receives the message `working?`, so it must possess a different definition of `working?` from fuse and relay. In other ways, it is very similar to fuse and relay, so they can be instances of a class (say `Component`) and pump and motor can be instances of classes that inherit from `Component` (but redefine `working?`). This is illustrated in Figure 4.6(c). The full class diagram is presented in Figure 4.7.

Table 4.5 Comparison of components.

	fuse	*relay*	*motor*	*pump*
Instance variable	state	state	state	state
Services	working?	working?	working?	working?

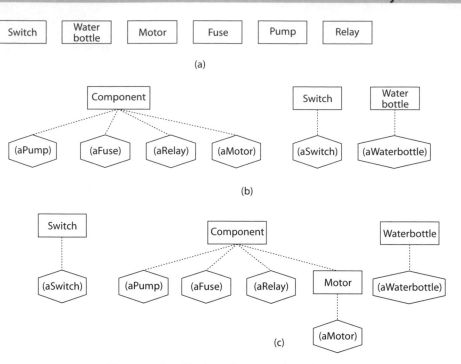

(a)

(b)

(c)

Figure 4.6 Possible class inheritance relationships.

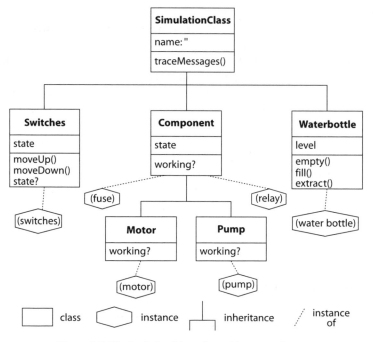

Figure 4.7 The final class hierarchy and instance diagram.

4.9 Summary

In this chapter, you have seen how a very simple system can be broken down into objects. These objects combine to provide the overall functionality of the system. You have seen how the data to be represented determines the objects used and that the interactions between objects determine the structure of the system. You should also have noted that objects and their classes, methods and instance variables are identified by more of an evolutionary process than in languages that are not object-oriented.

4.10 Exercises

1. Take a system with which you are familiar and try to break it down into objects. Carry out a similar set of steps to those described above. Do not worry about how to implement the objects or the classes. Use whatever representation best fits your way of working to describe what the methods do (pseudocode or a programming language, such as C or Pascal, if you prefer). You can even use a flow chart if you are most comfortable with that. It is very important that you try to do this, as it is a useful exercise in learning to think in terms of objects.

4.11 Further Reading

A good place to start further reading on building object-oriented systems is with the first few chapters of Rumbaugh *et al.* (1991). In addition, Wirfs-Brock *et al.* (1990) is an excellent, non-language-specific introduction to structuring object-oriented systems. It uses a rather simplistic approach, which is ideal for learning about object-oriented system design but is not generally applicable. This is not a problem, as what you want to do at the moment is to get the background rather than specific techniques. Another good reference for further reading is Yourdon (1994).

Chapter 5

An Introduction to C#

5.1 Introduction

C# is a new programming language. There have only been a few programming languages introduced in the last 10 years that have had the impact that C# has had: Java, another object-oriented language, is the obvious example. In this chapter I will try to provide some background on the C# language, what the motivations behind C# are and how it fits into the grand scheme of things (from Microsoft's point of view as well as with respect to existing languages).

5.2 Background

First we need to (briefly) consider the .NET environment. .NET is Microsoft's new environment for software development on Windows-based machines. Some have pushed it as an environment for developing Web-based services (which it certainly is), but it is more than that: it is a new way for Windows applications to be designed, built, deployed and run. Rather than just updating the existing tools and languages (and so making them even more complex), Microsoft has started from the ground up with .NET. The aim was to create a development environment within which most programming tasks can be easily accomplished. A major component of .NET is the C# programming language.

C# (pronounced C-Sharp, just like in musical notation) is a new language for software development on Windows-based machines. It is heavily integrated with the .NET environment and is intended as an alternative to the main previous languages, Visual C++ and VB. It builds very heavily on Visual C++ and (let's be honest) Java. It is, however, its own language, and whilst borrowing from both adds new features (and again let's be honest: nothing is new under the Sun!).

Of course, one thing that has counted against Microsoft in the past has been its tendency to try to make everything it produces proprietary, and to restrict access to the inner details of its world. Possibly to counter this Microsoft has put the key .NET technologies forward as a standard. As part of this, C# was submitted for standardization to ECMA in late 2000. The ECMA (http://www.ecma.ch/), founded in 1961, is a vendor-neutral international standards organization committed to driving industry-wide adoption of information and communications technologies. The idea behind this (at least from the standards organization's point of view) is that this should make it possible for anybody who wishes to implement C# programming tools on any platform to do so. Microsoft has also submitted a subset of the Microsoft .NET Framework, called the Common Language Infrastructure (CLI), to ECMA. This could also make it possible for other vendors to implement the CLI on a variety of platforms (whether this actually happens or not we shall have to wait and see). The C# Language Specification and the Common Language Infrastructure were approved by the ECMA General Assembly on 13 December 2001 (see `http://www.ecma.ch/ecma1/STAND/ecma-334.htm` and `http://www.ecma.ch/ecma1/STAND/ecma-335.htm`.

An interesting point to note is that when C# and the Common Language Infrastructure were submitted they were actually submitted by Hewlett-Packard and Intel Corporation as well as by Microsoft.

5.3 What Is C#?

C# can be viewed from a number of perspectives; in this it differs from many other programming languages, which can only be viewed as a programming language and nothing else. However, C# is more than just a programming language. Below we consider some of the ways to classify C#:

- *An object-oriented programming language* C# certainly provides the syntax and semantics of an object-oriented language. It is supported by a compiler that takes programs written in C# and produces code that can be executed by the .NET runtime environment (more on this later). As for the C# language itself, it is rather compact, unlike languages such as Ada, which are very large.
- *A programming environment* I refer here to the presence of the system-provided classes (often referred to as the .NET Classes) rather than any particular development environment. Unlike many languages (including traditional C++), C# has associated with it a large (and fairly standard) set of classes. These classes make C# very powerful and promote a standard development style. You spend most of your time extending the "system" rather than programming from scratch. In a number of cases, these classes provide facilities that are considered part of the language in Ada, C and Pascal. The result is that C# is anything but a small programming system.
- *An operating environment* The operating environment is the Common Language Runtime (CLR) in which all C# programs execute (actually it goes wider than C# and incorporates the other .NET languages as well). This is C#'s run-time environment, which handles memory allocation and deallocation, references, flow of control, interaction with other .NET elements etc.
- *The language of Web Services* C# (and .NET) have received huge hype as the language which will bring the .NET framework and the associated Web Services alive. However, in many ways C# is just an object-oriented language. There is no particular reason why C# should be any better as a Web language than Smalltalk or any other interpreted object-oriented language, such as Objective-C or Eiffel. Indeed, Visual Basic or Visual C++ could just as easily be made

the language to leverage the .NET framework (and indeed Microsoft has extended each to work with the .NET framework, creating VB.NET and Managed C++). However, *C# has been designed specifically with the .NET framework in mind, and hence is very well structured for writing code that will be compiled for .NET*. It is also a green field language, in that it did not need to take into account any previous incarnations that might lead to the incorporation of legacy features in the language. It could also learn a few tricks from Java and C++ which it could use to its advantage (see later).

Thus it is quite possible to say that C# is a programming language, a set of extensible classes, an operating environment or even a Web development tool. It is, in fact, all of these.

5.4 Objects in C#

Almost everything in C# is an object; for example, strings, arrays, windows and even exceptions can be objects. Objects, in turn, are examples of classes of things; for example, the string "John Hunt" is an object of the class String. Thus, to program in C#, you define classes, create instances and apply operations to classes and objects.

However, unlike languages such as Smalltalk, which are considered pure object-oriented languages, C# also has standard types (such as ints, floats and bools) and procedural programming statements. This hybrid approach can make the transition to object orientation simpler. In some languages, such as C++, this can be a disadvantage, as the developer can avoid the object-oriented nature of the language. However, C# has no concept of a procedural program; instead, everything is held within an object (even the procedural elements).

5.5 Commercial Versions of C#

At present the only vendor of a C# compiler is Microsoft itself; however, there is no reason why this should be the case. Indeed, there is already a project to take C# and port it to Linux. This is very exciting and would mean that C# programs would have the potential to be cross-platform. In theory, there is no reason why this should not be the case (C# compiles to an intermediate language which, like Java, could be interpreted by run-time environments ported to different platforms). However, in practice, because C# can exploit the whole of the .NET framework and the .NET classes, this would mean that the .NET framework would need to be ported to a new operating system (hardly something that Microsoft will be pushing!). The result is that it is likely that C# will make the move, but I suspect .NET will not (at least not in any major way).

5.6 The C# Environment

C# is different from other previous Microsoft languages that you may have used in that, when you write C# code, it does not execute on your host machine, even when it is compiled. Instead, it

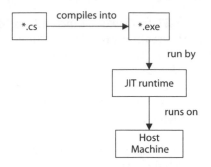

Figure 5.1 C# run-time environment.

executes in a virtual machine, which in turn executes on your host computer. This is because your C# code is compiled into an Intermediate Language (IL). This IL code is then run using a JIT run-time. A JIT is a Just-In-Time compiler that converts the IL code into an executable form the first time that code is encountered. All subsequent calls to that code can then use the dynamically generated native code.

This can look a little confusing at first sight, as the C# compiler (csc) appears to generate a .exe file. However, if you refer to these executables as "managed executables" that will be "managed" by your run-time environment then you are not far off the mark.

As an example of what is actually going on, take a look at Figure 5.1. In this figure we compile our C# program into the IL form using the C# compiler (called csc). When we execute this a JIT run-time system is used to run it on the host machine.

5.7 Comparing C# to Java and C++

Although if you read any of the material from Microsoft you will not find any reference to Java there, C# owes a very big debt to both Java and C++. Many of the ideas in C# can be found in these languages. Indeed, C# uses the same syntax as Java for comments, flow of control commands and exception handling, while 46 of its 50 keywords and 47 of its 56 operators are similar or identical to their Java counterparts. However, this does not mean that C# is Java or indeed that it is just an extension to C++. As an exercise of interest to the reader, the similarities with C++ and Java are listed in Table 5.1. Note that in the table, C++ relates to the original C++ language and not to the extensions provided by Microsoft for C++ in the .NET framework.

As stated earlier C# is not Java and it is not C++; indeed, C# introduces a number of new concepts itself, summarized in Table 5.2.

Each of the features described in this section relating to C# will be explained in more detail later in this book. However, what you should take from this is that C# has things in common with both C++ and Java, as well as introducing some new features.

Table 5.1 Comparison of features in Java, C# and C++.

Feature	Java	C#	C++
Object-oriented programming language	Yes	Yes	Yes
Single inheritance	Yes	Yes	No
Single class hierarchy root	Yes	Yes	No
Automatic memory management	Yes	Yes	No
Reusable components and information on how to use and deploy	Yes	Yes	No
A large library of base components	Yes	Yes	No
Web page development framework	Yes	Yes	No
Database access framework	Yes	Yes	No
Middleware and application integration	Yes	Yes	No
Inner/nested classes	Yes	Yes	No
Interfaces	Yes	Yes	No
Templates	No	No	Yes
Goto statement	No	Yes	Yes
Enumerated types	No	Yes	Yes
Operator overloading	No	Yes	Yes
Destructors	No	Yes	Yes
Compiler directives	No	Yes	Yes
Header files	No	No	Yes

Table 5.2 New features in C#.

Features	Description
Unified type system	Primitive data types inherit from parent object, dispensing with need for wrapper classes like Int for integers or Double for doubles.
Rich parameter-passing syntax	in, out, ref and params allow for easier interfacing with other languages and systems.
Delegate functions	References to functions are. made type-safe and secure
Structs	Similar to classes, except that they cannot inherit and they are value types. Structs are used to optimize code performance.
Properties	Simplify the syntax of getting and setting single-field values in a class.
Indexers	Simplify the syntax for getting at an array of object values.
Attributes	Assign run-time values based on compilation steps.

5.8 C# Keywords

Table 5.3 presents all the C# keywords. Do not worry about what they mean too much at the moment; we will be covering all of them during the course of this book.

Table 5.3 C# keywords.

abstract	base	bool	break	byte
case	catch	char	checked	class
const	continue	decimal	default	delegate
do	double	else	enum	event
explicit	extern	false	finally	fixed
float	for	foreach	goto	if
implicit	in	int	interface	internal
is	lock	long	namespace	new
null	object	operator	out	override
params	private	protected	public	readonly
ref	return	sbyte	sealed	short
sizeof	static	string	struct	switch
this	throw	true	try	typeof
uint	ulong	unchecked	unsafe	ushort
using	virtual	void	while	

5.9 Where to Get More Information

There are numerous places on the Web that can provide useful information for the C# developer. Some of these are:

- http://msdn.microsoft.com/vstudio/technical/articles/Csharpintro.asp
- http://www.microsoft.com/net/default.asp: .NET Platform home site
- http://www.csharphelp.com/:   CSharpHelp.Com
- http://www.c-sharpcorner.com/:   C# Corner
- http://www.csharptoday.com/:   CSharpToday.Com
- http://www.codehound.com/csharp/:   Code Hound C# Search Engine
- http://www.csharp-station.com/:   C# Station
- http://www.cshrp.net/:   CShrp.Net
- http://www.csharpindex.com/:   CSharpIndex.Com

Chapter 6

A Little C#

6.1 Introduction

In the last chapter, you learned a little about the history of C# and the C# development environment. In this chapter, you encounter the C# language, the command line compiler and running C# programs from a command prompt.

Just to get you started, we will add two numbers together. First we do it in a procedural language, such as Pascal:

```
int a, b, c;
a := 1;
b := 2;
c := a + b;
```

This says something like, "create three variables to hold integer values (call them a, b and c). Store the value 1 into variable a and 2 into variable b. Add the two numbers together and save the result into the third variable, c". Now we look at how we could write the same thing in C#:

```
int a, b, c;
a = 1;
b = 2;
c = a + b;
```

As you can see, this looks basically the same (apart from the use of = rather than :=). Thus, as you can see from this, if you have used most of the current crop of high-level languages you are likely to be familiar with some of the syntax of C# already.

6.2 Setting Up the Development Environment

As was discussed in the last chapter, there are two ways to obtain the C# compiler. The first is as part of the .NET SDK (which contains a compiler for C# (among other things)). The second is as part of the Visual Studio. NET environment. In this chapter (and for most of the rest of this book) we will focus on using the command line compiler provided with the .NET SDK.

The C# compiler must be able to obtain information about the classes, interfaces and structs being used by any program it is compiling. To do this it will automatically obtain information about system-provided classes and interfaces etc. from the mscorlib.dll file; however, it must be told where to find any other classes (for example those created by yourself or another developer). This can be done from the command line by passing in the appropriate .dll to the compiler. For the time being we will not need to do this, but we will come back to this later in the book.

Once you have installed the .NET SDK you should now have available to you the C# compiler, which is provided as the csc command on the command line.

6.3 Compiling and Executing C#

```
using System;
class Hello
{
  public static void Main()
  {
    Console.WriteLine("Hello World");
  }
}
```

Type in the program above very carefully to ensure that the syntax is correct. At this point, do not worry about what it means; we are only trying to get to grips with the tools provided by the .NET SDK. Once you have typed in the text, save it to a file called:

Hello.cs

Ensure that you use exactly the same capitalization as above. Next bring up a command line prompt. How you do this depends on the environment you are using. For example, in Linux it may involve opening an XTERM; on Windows 95 or NT you may need to bring up the DOS prompt; on a Windows 2000 or XP machine you will need a command prompt. You can then compile your C# program, using the csc command:

> csc Hello.cs

If it compiles successfully, it generates a Hello.exe file that contains the Intermediate Language (IL) codes. For example, on a Windows 2000 machine, the compilation and the directory listing looks like Figure 6.1.

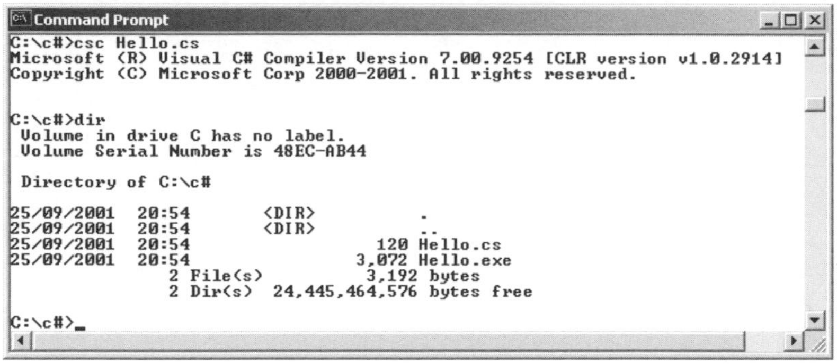

Figure 6.1 Running a C# program.

You can run the .exe program directly from the command line:

```
C:\c#>Hello
Hello World
C:\c#>
```

Congratulations! You have now written, compiled and run your first C# application.

So what have we got here? Firstly you are using the System namespace (using System;). This is a bit like an import or include in other languages, in that it makes the classes in the System namespace available to your program. There are very many useful classes in the System namespace; however, we are using it here because it provides the Console class. This class allows us to write a line of text to the console. In this case we use it to write the string "Hello World" to the console.

Our C# program also defines a single class, called Hello, that contains a single method. In this case it is the Main method. The Main method is the starting point for any C# application. In this case our Main method merely requests that the Console class print out a string (it will do more later in the book!).

In fact, there are two versions of the Main method: one that takes no parameters (the version used here) and one that takes an array of parameters (the command line arguments), which we will look at later.

So what you have here is a class called Hello, which provides a single method Main that uses the class Console from the System namespace to print out the message "Hello World"! Obviously this is a very simple program, but it exhibits all the fundamental features of much larger C# programs.

6.4 Summary

You have just written a C# program, used the C# compiler and executed the results. You are now ready for the C# language itself!

Chapter 7

C# Classes

7.1 Introduction

This chapter presents an introduction to classes in the C# programming language. As such, it discusses the concept of classes and instances and how they are defined, presents methods and method definitions, and considers dynamic binding. More information on classes in C# will be provided in later chapters.

7.2 The Basics of the Language

All C# programmers make extensive use of the existing classes even when they write relatively trivial code. For example, the following version of the "Hello World" program reuses existing classes rather than just using the language (do not worry too much about the syntax of the definition or the parameters to the Main method – we will return to them later):

```csharp
using System;
class HelloWorld
{
  public static void Main (String [] args) {
    if (args.Length > 0) {
      String name = args[0];
      if (name.EndsWith("Hunt")) {
        Console.WriteLine("Hello {0}", name);
      }
      else
      {
        Console.WriteLine("Hello World");
      }
    }
  }
```

```
    else
    {
      Console.WriteLine("Usage: HelloWorld <name>");
    }
  }
}
```

In this example, I have reused the String class to represent the string "John Hunt" and to find a substring in it using the message EndsWith(). Some of you may say that there is nothing unusual in this and that many languages have string-handling extensions. However, in this case, it is the string contained within name which decides how to handle the EndsWith() message and thus whether it contains the substring "Hunt". That is, the data itself handles the processing of the string! What is printed to standard output thus depends on which object receives the message. These features illustrate the extent to which existing classes are reused: you cannot help but reuse existing code in C# – you do so by the very act of programming. The result of running this program is illustrated in Figure 7.1.

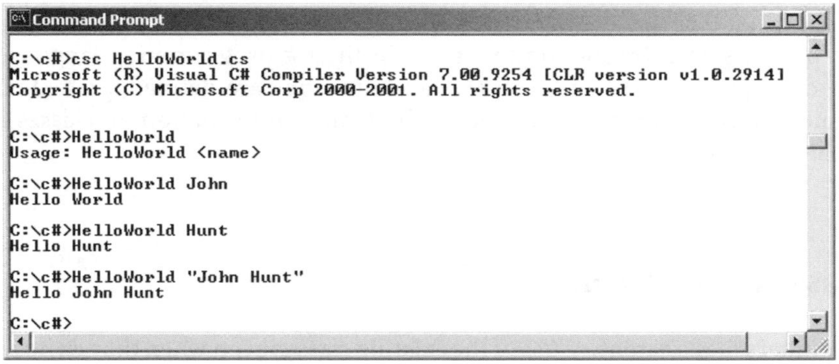

```
C:\c#>csc HelloWorld.cs
Microsoft (R) Visual C# Compiler Version 7.00.9254 [CLR version v1.0.2914]
Copyright (C) Microsoft Corp 2000-2001. All rights reserved.

C:\c#>HelloWorld
Usage: HelloWorld <name>

C:\c#>HelloWorld John
Hello World

C:\c#>HelloWorld Hunt
Hello Hunt

C:\c#>HelloWorld "John Hunt"
Hello John Hunt

C:\c#>
```

Figure 7.1

Notice that in this example of a C# class we have used a main method that takes some parameters. These parameters are the command line arguments in an array of Strings (we will come back to arrays in more detail later). However, the point to note if you are coming to C# from a language such as C or C++ is that the array knows how long it is (the code asks the String array for its Length).

As well as possessing objects and classes, C# also possesses an inheritance mechanism. This feature separates C# from object-based languages, such as Ada, which do not possess inheritance. Indeed, we have already used inheritance twice, as both the Hello class in the last chapter and the HelloWorld class in this chapter have automatically extended the class Object. This means that these classes automatically obtain all the features of Object (such as the method ToString()) without any additional work from us!

Inheritance is very important in C#. It promotes the reuse of classes and enables the explicit representation of abstract concepts (such as the class CollectionBase – the abstract parent of all strongly typed collections), which can then be turned into concrete concepts (such as the class XmlElementAttributes). It is also one of the primary reasons why C# is so successful as a rapid application development tool – you inherit much of what you want and only define the ways in which your application differs from what is already available.

7.2.1 Some Terminology

We now recap some of the terminology introduced in Part 1 of this book, explaining it with reference to C#.

In C# programs, actions or operations are performed by passing *messages* to and from objects. An object (the *sender* of the message) uses a message to request that a procedure (referred to in C# as a *method*) be performed by another object (the *receiver* of the message). Just as procedure calls can contain parameters, so can messages.

C# is a typed language; however, the typing relates to the class of an object (or the interface that a class implements or a struct – we will return to this later) rather than its specific type. Thus, by saying that a method can take a parameter of a particular class, you actually mean that any instance of that class (or one of its subclasses) can be passed into that method.

7.2.2 The Message-Passing Mechanism

The C# message-passing mechanism is somewhat like a procedure call in a conventional language:

- The point of control moves to the receiver; the object sending a message is suspended until it receives a response.
- The receiver of a message is not determined when the code is created (at *compile-time*); it is identified when the message is sent (at *run-time*).

This *dynamic* (or *late*) binding mechanism is the feature which gives C# its polymorphic capabilities (see Chapter 1 for a discussion of polymorphism). Although a very powerful feature, polymorphism can inhibit the performance of a programming language as the run-time environment must look up methods at run-time, which limits the amount of inlining that a compiler can perform. However, C# extends the concepts of polymorphism compared with a language such as Java, in that consideration has been given to ways of improving run-time performance compared with a language that always assumes late binding.

7.2.3 The Statement Terminator

In C#, the majority of statements terminate with a semi-colon (;):

```
Console.WriteLine("Hello World");
```

7.3 Classes

A class (along with the struct) is the basic building block in C#. Classes act as *templates* which are used to construct instances. Classes allow programmers to specify the *structure* of an object (e.g. its instance variables) and the function of an object (i.e. its methods) separately from the object itself.

This is important, as it would be extremely time-consuming (as well as inefficient) for programmers to define each object individually. Instead, they define classes and create *instances* of the classes.

7.3.1 Class Definitions

In C#, a class definition has the following format:

```
access-modifier class nameOfClass : SuperClass {
  scope static type classVariable;
  scope type instanceVariable;
}
```

You need not remember this format precisely, as the meanings of the various parts of the class definition are explained later in the book. Indeed, the above is far from complete, but it illustrates the basic features. The following code is an example of a class definition:

```
using System;

class Person : Object {
  private int age = 0;
  public String name = "Bob";
}
```

This code defines a new class, Person, which is a subclass of the Object class (all classes extend Object by default; it is stated here only as an illustration). The new class possesses two *instance variables* called name and age. It has no class variables and no methods.

Notice that the age instance variable contains a value of type int (this is a basic data type), while the instance variable name possesses an object of the class String. Both variables are initialized: age to zero and name to the string "Bob".

Classes are not just used as templates. They have three further responsibilities: holding methods, providing facilities for inheritance and creating instances.

7.3.2 Classes and Messages

When a message is sent to an object, it is not the object which possesses the method but the class. This is for efficiency reasons: if each object possessed a copy of all the methods defined for the class then there would be a great deal of duplication. Instead, only the class possesses the method definitions. Thus, when an object receives a message, it searches its class for a method with the name in the message. If its own class does not possess a method with the appropriate name, it goes to the superclass and searches again. This search process continues up the class hierarchy until either an appropriate method is found or the class hierarchy terminates (with the class Object). If the hierarchy terminates, an error is raised.

If an appropriate method is found, then it executes *within the context of the object*, although the definition of the method resides in the class. Thus, different objects can execute the same method at the same time without conflict.

Do not confuse methods with instance variables. Each instance possesses its own copy of the instance variables (as each instance possesses its own state). Figure 7.2 illustrates this idea more clearly.

7.3.3 Instances and Instance Variables

In C#, an *object* is an *instance* of a *class*. All instances of a class share the same responses to messages (methods), but they contain different data (i.e. they possess a different "state"). For example, the instances of class Point all respond in the same way to messages inquiring about the value of the *x*-coordinate, but they may provide different values.

The class definition consists of variable declarations and method definitions. The state of each instance is maintained in one or more instance variables.

Figure 7.2 contains five instances of the class Person. Each instance contains copies of the instance variable definitions for name and age, thus enabling them to have their own values for these instance variables. In contrast, each instance references the single definition for the method birthday, which is held by the class.

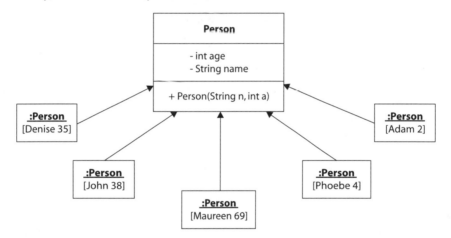

Figure 7.2 Multiple instance variables but a single method.

7.3.4 Classes and Inheritance

It is through classes that an object inherits facilities from other types of object. That is, a subclass inherits properties from its superclass. For example, the Person definition above is a subclass of Object. Therefore, Person inherits all the methods and instance variables that were defined in Object (except those that may have been overwritten in Person).

Subclasses are used to refine the behaviour and data structures of a superclass. It should be noted that Java supports single inheritance while some of the object-oriented languages (most notably C++) support multiple inheritance. Multiple inheritance is where a subclass can inherit from more than one superclass. However, difficulties can arise when attempting to determine where methods are executed. C# introduces the concept of *interfaces* to overcome one of the most significant problems with single inheritance. C# interfaces are discussed later in the book.

An Example of Inheritance

To illustrate how single inheritance works, consider Figure 7.3. There are three classes: Class1 is a subclass of Object, Class2 is a subclass of Class1 and Class3 is a subclass of Class2.

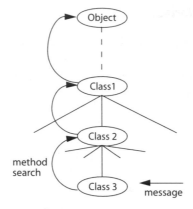

Figure 7.3 Class inheritance in C#.

When an instance of Class3 is created, it contains all the instance variables defined in classes 1 to 3 and class Object. If any instance variable has the same name as an instance variable in a higher class, then the Class3 instance uses the instance variable definition from the nearest class. That is, Class3 definitions take priority over Class2 and Class2 definitions take priority over Class1 etc.

We can send an instance of Class3 a message requesting that a particular method is executed. Remember that methods are held by classes and not by instances. This means that the system first finds the class of the instance (in this case Class3) and searches it for the required method. If the method is found, then the search stops and the method is executed. However, if the method is not found, then the system searches the superclass for Class3, in this case Class2. This process is repeated until the method is found. Eventually, the search through the superclasses may reach the class Object (which is the root class in the C# system). If the required method is not found here, then the search process terminates and the doesNotUnderstand: method in the class Object is executed instead. This method raises an exception stating that the message sent to the original instance is not understood.

This search process is repeated every time a message is sent to the instance of Class3. Thus, if the method which matches the original message sends a message to itself (i.e. the instance of Class3), then the search for that method starts again in Class3 (even if it was found in Class1).

The Yo-Yo Problem

The process described above can pose a problem for a programmer trying to follow the execution of the system by tracing methods and method execution. This problem is known as the Yo-Yo problem (see Figure 7.4) because, every time you encounter a message which is sent to "this" (the current object), you must start searching from your own class. This may result in jumping up and down the class hierarchy.

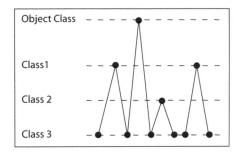

Figure 7.4 The Yo-Yo Problem.

The problem occurs because you know that the execution search starts in the current instance's class, even if the method which sends the message is defined in a superclass of the current class. In Figure 7.4, the programmer starts the search in Class3, but finds the method definition in Class1; however, this method sends a message to "this" which means that the programmer must restart the search in Class3. This time, the method definition is found in the class Object, etc. Even with the browsing tools provided, this can still be a tedious and confusing process (particularly for those new to C#).

7.3.5 Instance Creation

A class creates an instance in response to a request, which is handled by a constructor. It may be confusing, but classes can possess class-specific methods and class instance variables. These are often referred to as class-side (or static) methods and variables, and they can respond to a message as an instance would.

A programmer requests a new instance of a class using the following construct:

```
new ClassName();
```

Any parameters that need to be passed into the class can be placed between the parentheses. They are then passed on to an appropriate constructor. Constructors possess the same name as the class and are used to initialize a new instance of the class in an appropriate manner (you do not need to know the details of the process). The whole of this process is referred to as instantiation. An example of instantiating the class Person is presented below:

```
new Person("John Hunt", 37);
```

The class Person receives the message new which causes the class method new to generate a new instance of the class, with its own copy of the instance variables age and name (see Figure 7.5). The name of the instance is "John Hunt" and the age is set to 37.

The issue of classes having methods, some of which are intended for an instance of the class, and some of which are intended for the class, is not as complicated as it may at first seem, not least because the language syntax used with C# tends to keep the two *sides* of classes pretty well distinct. To aid this, when developing most programmers define the class side before defining the instance side of the class. Some of the tools now available for C# also make this separation distinct and simplify the whole development process.

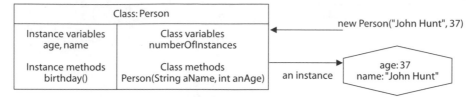

Figure 7.5 Instance creation.

In an attempt to make it clearer, here are some definitions:

- *Instance variables* are defined in the class, but a copy is maintained in each instance, which has its own value.
- *Class (or static) variables* are defined in the class, with a single copy maintained in the class.
- *Instance methods* are defined in the class, with a single copy maintained in the class, but they are executed within the context of an object.
- *Class (or static) methods* are defined in the class, with a single copy maintained in the class and executed within the context of the class.

The accessibility of these variables and methods depends on whether the programmer has made them public, private or protected. Some of these concepts are considered in greater detail later.

7.3.6 Constructors

A constructor is not a method but a special operator which is executed when a new instance of a class is created. Depending on the arguments passed to the class when the instance is generated, a different constructor can be called. For example, a class may need to have three fields initialized when it is instantiated. However, the programmer may allow the user of the class to provide one, two or three values. This can be done by defining constructors which take one, two or three parameters.

The syntax for a constructor is:

```
class classname {
    scopeofconstructor classname ( ... parameters ...) {
    ... statements ...
    }
}
```

By default, every class has a single constructor with no parameters. However, as soon as you define a constructor, the default constructor is no longer available.

7.3.7 Static Constructors Blocks

A class can also possess a static constructor, which initializes the values to be held in class variables. This is useful if the initial values are not straightforward literals, but are related to some function (which may depend on other values held within the system).

```
class className {
  class variable definitions ....
  static classname () {
    ... static initialization statements ....
  }
}
```

Static constructors cannot call methods which may throw an exception back to the message sender (in this case, the static constructor) unless they explicitly handle the exception.

Static constructors are only run when the class is first loaded into the system (and before any instances of that class are created). They are therefore only run once, and this is not under the control of the programmer.

The compiler cannot catch cyclic loops between classes caused by static constructors. Thus the result can be unpredictable and depends on the point at which the cycle occurred and the class variables which were set. For example, assume that class A's initialization block calls a class method in class B. Class B is then loaded into the system; however, its initialization block calls a class method in class A. At this point, class A's initialization block has not completed and the correct functioning of its class methods may depend on class variables which have yet to be initialized.

7.3.8 Finalize Methods

In C#, memory is managed automatically for you by the C# Runtime. You do not therefore have to destroy objects or reclaim the memory they use. However, there is a C# facility which allows you to execute a special method (referred to as a destructor method) when the Runtime reclaims (or collects as garbage) an object. Note that "destructor" is probably the wrong name for this method, as it is not to be used to destroy the object itself. Instead it is intended to be used to perform some form of housekeeping role just before an object is to be garbage collected. Therefore the programmer has no control over when this method will be called (or even if it will be called at all).

As just mentioned, these destructor methods are typically used for application-specific housekeeping and are not intended as destroy methods (which you may have seen in other languages such as C++).

You define a destructor method in the following way:

```
~classname(){
  ...
}
```

Notice that the method has the same name as the class preceded by a ~.

Above we stated that the programmer has no control over when (or even if) a destructor will be called. However, in some cases we want an object's resources to be reclaimed sooner than "the next time the garbage collector gets around to running". In C# objects can indicate that they hold some useful and in-demand resource that needs to be reclaimed by implementing the IDisposable interface. Interfaces will be covered in more detail later; for the moment, accept that any class implementing an interface must implement all the methods in that interface. In the case of the interface IDisposable, it defines a single method Dispose(). This method has the same role as the destructor, but there are some additional rules that need to be applied to the Dispose() method. If either its base class or any of the other resources it holds implement IDisposable, it needs to call Dispose() on them so that they also get the chance to clean up their resources. After it does this it calls GC.SuppressFinalize() so that the garbage collector won't bother to execute the deconstructor for this object. For example, we might extend the Person example presented earlier with a Dispose method thus:

```csharp
using System;
class Person : IDisposable {
  private int age = 0;
  public String name = "Bob";
  public Person (String name, int age) {
    this.name = name;
    this.age = age;
  }

  public void Dispose()
  {
    Console.WriteLine("Tidying up");
    GC.SuppressFinalize(this);
  }
  public static void Main() {
    Person p = new Person("John", 37);
  }
}
```

If you do use an object that implements the IDisposable interface, then it is important to make sure that the method Dispose() is called when you no longer require the object's resources. Thus you might have code that does this:

```csharp
Person p = new Person("John", 37);
//....
p.Dispose();
p = null;
```

Notice that we have both called the Dispose method and reset the variable referring the Person object to null. In fact, this sort of thing is so common that C# provides a short cut for doing this via the using statement:

```csharp
using System;
class Person : IDisposable {
  private int age = 0;
  public String name = "Bob";
  public Person (String name, int age) {
    this.name = name;
    this.age = age;
  }
```

```
  public void Dispose()
  {
    Console.WriteLine("Tidying up");
    GC.SuppressFinalize(this);
  }
  public static void Main() {
    using (Person p = new Person("John", 37))
    {
    //... do something with p
    }
  }
}
```

7.3.9 Supplied Classes

There are very many classes in any C#/.NET environment. Depending upon how you have obtained a C# compiler you may have documentation provided via a .NET documentation browser or within Visual Studio .NET. However, you only need to become familiar with a very few of them. The remaining classes provide facilities that you often use without even realizing it.

7.4 Method Definitions

Methods provide a way of defining the behaviour of an object, i.e. what the object does. For example, a method may change the state of the object or it may retrieve some information. A method is the equivalent of a procedure in most other languages. A method can only be defined within the scope of an object. It has a specific structure:

```
access control modifier ReturnType MethodName (args) {
  /* comments */
  local variable definitions
  statements
}
```

The *access control modifier* is one of the keywords that indicate the visibility of the method. The ReturnType is the type of the object returned, for example, String or int. **MethodName** represents the name of the method and args represents the types and names of the arguments. These arguments are accessible within the method.

7.4.1 The Comments Section

The /* comments */ section describes the operation performed by the method and any other useful information. Comments cannot be nested in C#, which can be awkward if you wish to comment out some code for later. For example, consider the following piece of C#:

```
/*
x = 12 * 4;
/* Now calculate y */
y = x * 23;
*/
```

The C# compiler reads this as a comment, followed by the code y = x * 23;, followed by the end of another comment. This causes an error. However, C# has another type of comment. You can instruct the C# compiler to ignore everything until the end of the line, using the // indicator:

```
x = 12 * 4;
// Now calculate y
y = x * 23;
```

7.4.2 The Local Variables Section

In the local variable definition section, you define variables that are local to the method. These variables are typed and can appear anywhere in the method definition.

```
birthday()
int newAge = 0;
...
```

7.4.3 The Statements Section

The statements section represents any legal set of C# statements that implement the behaviour of the method.

7.4.4 The Return Operator

Once a method has executed, an answer can be returned to the sender of the message. The value returned (whether an object, a basic type or an instance of a subclass) must match the return type specified in the method definition. The return expression in Java is the last expression executed in a method, although it need not be the last expression in the method.

The C# keyword to return a value is return (just as in C and Java):

```
if (x == y)
  return x;
else
  return y;
```

In this case, the value of x or y is returned, depending upon whether x and y are equal or not.

7.4.5 An Example Method

Let us examine a simple method definition in C#. We wish to define a procedure to take in a number, add 10 to it and return the result.

```csharp
public int AddTen (int aNumber) {
  int result = 0;
  result = aNumber + 10;
  return result;
}
```

Although the format may be slightly different from code that you have been used to, it is relatively straightforward. If you have C or C++ experience you might think that it is exactly the same as what you have seen before. Be careful with that idea – things are not always what they seem!

Let us look at some of the constituent parts of the method definition. The method name is AddTen. Notice that every method name is followed by (), whether or not it takes parameters. If it does, then the parameters are placed within the parentheses. In this case, the method has one parameter, called aNumber, of the basic type int. Just as in any other language, the parameter variable is limited to the scope of this method. The method also defines a temporary variable, result, also of the basic type int and limited to the scope of this method.

Variable names are identifiers that contain only letters and numbers and must start with a letter (the underscore, _, and the dollar sign, $, count as letters). Some examples are:
anObject MyCar totalNumber $total

A capitalization convention is used consistently throughout C#, and most C# programmers adhere to this standard:

- *Private variables* (i.e. instance or temporary variables) start with a lower-case letter.
- *Shared variables* (e.g. class-side variables) start with an upper-case letter.
- *Constructors, methods and classes* always start with an upper-case letter.

Another convention is that if a variable or method name combines two or more words, then you should capitalize the first letter of each word, from the second word onwards, e.g. DisplayTotalPay or studentName.

7.4.6 Static Fields and Methods

Object-oriented languages often have the concept of class or static methods and variables. Class or static members are not part of any particular instance or object, but rather are part of the class as a whole. These can be used for housekeeping roles or for behaviour that is not part of any particular instance of that class. Things that are static are not able to access the contents of the instances (such as static methods accessing instance variables). To place something on the class the keyword static is used. For example:

```csharp
using System;

class Person
```

```csharp
{
    // Static variable
    public static int count = 0;

    // private instance variables
    public String name;
    // A constructor
    public Person (String name)
    {
        this.name = name;
        count = count + 1;
    }

    // A property
    public String Name
    {
        get
        {
            return name;
        }
        set
        {
            name = value;
        }
    }

    public static void Main()
    {
        Person p1 = new Person("John");
        Console.WriteLine(Person.count);
        Person p2 = new Person("Denise");
        Console.WriteLine(Person.count);
    }
}
```

In the above example, each time a new instance of the class Person is created the class side static variable count is incremented. Thus the result of running this code is:

```
C:\c#>Person
1
2
```

However, it is not only data but also methods that can be made static. For example, we could have had a static method to provide access to the value of count. This method would have looked like:

```csharp
using System;

class Person
{

  // Static variable
  private static int count = 0;

  public static int GetCount() {
    return count;
  }

  // private instance variables
    public String name;
    // A constructor
    public Person (String name)
    {
      this.name = name;
      count++;
    }

    // A property
    public String Name
    {
      get
      {
        return name;
      }
      set
      {
        name = value;
      }
    }

    public static void Main()
    {
      Person p1 = new Person("John");
      Console.WriteLine(Person.GetCount());
      Person p2 = new Person("Denise");
      Console.WriteLine(Person.GetCount());
    }
}
```

The result of executing this program is once again 1, 2. However, we have now provided a controlled way of accessing the value of count. In addition, only the class Person can modify the value of count, as it is now private to the class. We will come back to access modifiers later in this book.

7.4.7 Constants

Most programming languages allow the developer to specify that some value is a constant, and C# is no exception. The keyword const is used to indicate that a variable should be treated as a constant. Making something constant also implies that the field is a static member rather than an instance member. However, for a value to be a constant, its value must be something that can be written as a constant. This limits the types of constants to the built-in (or basic) types that can be written as literal values. As an example:

```csharp
using System;

class Person
{
  // Two constants
  public const int maxAge = 115;
  public const int minAge = 0;
  // private instance variables
    private int age = 0;
    public String name = "Bob";
    // A constructor
    public Person (String name, int age)
    {
      this.name = name;
      this.age = age;
    }

    public static void Main()
    {
      Person p = new Person("John", 37);
      Console.WriteLine("Min age is {0} max age is {1}",
        Person.minAge,
        Person.maxAge);
    }
}
```

7.4.8 Read-Only Fields

In the last section we noted that constants can only be provided for values that can be initialized using literals (such as literals of built-in values). That is, a constant's value must be determined at compile-time and not at run-time. Because of this there are many situations where it is not possible to use constants. To overcome this, C# provides read-only fields. Read-only fields are defined using the readonly keyword. This allows a member's value to be set in a constructor or an initializer, but it does not allow the value to be changed after this. Thus it is possible to write:

```csharp
using System.Drawing;

class Colourizer
{
  public static readonly Color Selected;
  public static readonly Color Go;
  public static readonly Color Edited;

  static Colourizer()
  {
    Selected = Color.Blue;
    Go = Color.Green;
    Edited = Color.Red;
  }
}

class Test
{
  public static void Main()
  {
    Color sel = Colourizer.Selected;
  }
}
```

Note that Color is defined in the System.Drawing namespace.

7.4.9 Properties and Indexers

One of the uses of methods is to provide an interface between an object's internal data and the outside world. Such a method, often termed an accessor method, retrieves the value of an instance variable and makes it available to other objects. For example, the class Person has two instance variables: age and name. The method getAge returns the age of an employee. Thus in response to the message GetAge(), this method is executed and the value of the person's age is returned to the object sending the message.

In this situation the person's age is held explicitly. An equally valid internal representation for a Person would be to have an instance variable, dateOfBirth. The method GetAge() would need to calculate the age as the difference between the date of birth and the current date.

Notice that this would change the implementation of Person, but there would be no change as far as any other object in the system is concerned. This illustrates the encapsulation possible with C# (and other object-oriented programming languages).

In fact, this sort of thing is so common that C# provides for it explicitly with properties and indexers. A property (for a single value) or an indexer (for an array of values) allows a statement block to be specified to perform the access, while still allowing the field or array usage. The big advantage of this is that it abstracts the user of the set and get methods (compared with languages such as Java), allowing the user of the class to treat the "property" as a high-level element of the object. For example:

```csharp
using System;

class Person
{

  // private instance variable for the property
  public String name;
  // A constructor
  public Person (String name)
  {
    this.name = name;
  }

  // A property
  public String Name
  {
    get
    {
      return name;
    }
    set
    {
      name = value; // Note value holds new value
    }
  }

  public static void Main()
  {
    Person p = new Person("John");
    Console.WriteLine("Person was {0}", p.Name);
    p.Name = "John Hunt";
    Console.WriteLine("Person is now {0}", p.Name);
  }
}
```

The effect of compiling and running this class is:

```
C:\c#>Person
Person was John
Person is now John Hunt
```

Chapter 8

Structs and Enumerations

8.1 Introduction

In this chapter we look at two data-oriented features of the C# language. The first is the struct construct, used for representing data-only structures. The second is enumerations, which are useful for defining specific sets of values that may have a specific order associated with them.

8.2 Structs in C#

In C#, as well as being able to define classes (reference types), it is also possible to define value types (called structs). A value type is a data structure that is defcleared on the stack (in a similar manner to an int or float), whereas reference types are declared on the heap. In turn, variables that hold objects hold a reference to them, whereas variables that hold value types hold the value directly.

In general you would normally use structs (value types) for elements that are essentially just data, whereas virtually everything else would be defined via classes. Structs also have the advantage of being more efficient than classes (as they are on the stack and accessed directly rather than via a reference).

However, structs have a number of limitations on their behaviour. Firstly, you cannot use them in inheritance. That is, a struct cannot extend any class or struct, nor can any class extend a struct. Structs behave as though they extend the class Object; however, in practice they do not (although they do automatically extend the class System.ValueType, but this is hidden from you).

The syntax for a struct is:

```
access-modifier struct nameOfStruct {
... struct details ...
   }
```

For example, the following listing defines a struct for holding addresses:

```csharp
using System;

public struct Address {
  public int number;
  public String street;
  public String town;
  public String postCode;

  public Address (int n, String s, String t, String p) {
    number = n;
    street = s;
    town = t;
    postCode = p;
  }

  public override String ToString()
  {
    String result = "";
    result += number + ", " + street + ", " + town + ", " + postCode;
    return result;
  }
}

public class Test
{
  public static void Main() {
    Address a = new Address(10, "High Street", "Bath", "BA1 3ER");
    Console.WriteLine(a);
  }
}
```

The result of compiling and running this program is:

```
C:\c#>Address
10, High Street, Bath, BA1 3ER
```

This program defines a struct that holds an int (for the house number) and three strings for the street name, the town and the postcode. It also defines a ToString method so that it can be printed in a tidy manner. The struct also defines a single constructor that takes an initial value for the four variables.

Structs are created using the keyword new, as for classes. Thus the Main method creates a new struct and then prints out the result.

8.3 Initialization of Structs

One interesting aspect of structs is that you do not actually need to use the keyword new to create a struct. This is because they are not reference types. That is, if I define a class Family and have an instance variable Person p in it, it will be initialized to null. This is because it is a reference type and p will hold an address of an instance of Person. However, if in this class I have an instance variable of type int, this variable will automatically hold the value 0 directly (it is a value type).

In a similar way, if I create a variable of a struct (say Address) it directly holds that struct. If I do not create a new example of this struct then the struct it holds is the zero initialized version. For example, the Address will hold zero for the house number and the strings will be empty strings. Of course, we can assign values to the fields in the struct, but we do not need to in order to create a zero struct. For example, we could modify the example program presented earlier to be:

```
public class Test
{
  static Address b;
  public static void Main() {
    Address a = new Address(10, "High Street", "Bath", "BA1 3ER");
    Console.WriteLine(a);
    Console.WriteLine(b);
    b.number = 20;
    b.street = "Walston Road";
    b.town = "Oxford";
    b.postCode = "OX1 6TG";
    Console.WriteLine(b);
  }
}
```

The result of compiling and running this program is:

```
C:\c#>Address
10, High Street, Bath, BA1 3ER
0, , ,
20, Walston Road, Oxford, OX1 6TG
```

Note that we had to make the variable b part of the class; this is because local variables are not initialized by default.

8.4 Structs and Constructors

The fact that a struct can be zero initialized, as described in the previous section, has some implications for the definition of constructors within a struct. If you could define a default zero parameter constructor in a struct then it would be possible to initialize the variables of the struct to values other than their zero settings. As this is not what would be expected, C# does not allow you to define zero parameter constructors on structs. You can define any number of constructors in a struct as long as they take a parameter.

This also goes further, in that it is not possible to initialize the fields in a struct. For example we *cannot* write:

```
int number = 30;
```

8.5 Immutable Structs

In some cases you may wish to define a struct that is considered immutable. That is, once it is created it is not possible to change its value. To do this the fields in the struct should not be public. Rather, they should always be accessed via accessor methods. If the result of running an accessor method is that the value of the struct should change, then a new struct should be created as the result of the method.

8.6 Enumerations

Enumerations are a common programming language construct. They allow the developer to define a set of values that have an order (implicit or explicit). They also limit the set of values that can be taken. For example, we could define an enumeration of the days of the week. This would allow us to use values such as Monday, Tuesday etc., and to test whether Monday was less than or greater than Tuesday etc. Variables would be able to be defined to be of the type of the enumeration and would be limited to holding whatever values were defined inside the enumeration.

The syntax for an enumeration is:

```
access-modifier enum nameOfEnumeration {
... value details ...
}
```

For example, to define an enumeration for the days of the week we could define:

```
using System;

public enum DaysOfWeek {
    Monday,
    Tuesday,
    Wednesday,
    Thursday,
    Friday
}
```

```
public class Test
{
  public static void Main() {
    DaysOfWeek day = DaysOfWeek.Monday;
    Console.WriteLine(day);
  }
}
```

The effect of compiling and running this program is:

```
C:\c#>Test
Monday
```

Notice that we have not given any specific values to the days of the week; nor have we said how they should be printed. Also note that the last item in the enumeration can optionally have a trailing ",". This is probably good style, but has been omitted in the above example.

We now know that the variable day can only ever hold the values in the DaysOfWeek enumeration; thus it cannot hold the values 23, Sunday etc. We can also compare two variables of type DaysOfWeek to see which comes first in the week. For example, we could extend the Main method thus:

```
public class Test
{
  public static void Main() {
    DaysOfWeek day1 = DaysOfWeek.Monday;
    Console.WriteLine(day1);
    DaysOfWeek day2 = DaysOfWeek.Wednesday;
    Console.WriteLine(day1 < day2);
  }
}
```

8.7 Enumeration Foundations

Each enumeration type is actually built on top of an existing type. By default, all enumerations are built on ints. That is, the number of entries cannot exceed the possible values for an int – which is pretty large and therefore rarely an issue. However, the valid base types on which an enumeration can be built are byte, sbyte, short, ushort, int, unit, long and ulong. If space is of concern it is possible to specify that an enumeration is derived from a type other than an int. For example, to save space, the type could be derived from a byte. If an int does not provide sufficient values, then a long could be used.

To specify the base type for an enumeration you specify the underlying type by following the enumeration name by a colon and the type. For example:

```
public enum DaysOfWeek : byte {
  Monday,
```

```
    Tuesday,
    Wednesday,
    Thursday,
    Friday
}
```

This indicates that DaysOfWeek should be derived from the byte type, and thus can have only 127 possible values – which is more than enough for our days of the week enumeration type.

8.8 Initialization of Enumeration Values

At this point you may be wondering what values the items within the enumeration have? By default they are integers numbered from zero. Thus in our days of the week example, our previous definition is exactly equivalent to the following:

```
public enum DaysOfWeek : byte {
    Monday = 0,
    Tuesday = 1,
    Wednesday = 2,
    Thursday = 3,
    Friday = 4
}
```

The above listing illustrates how initial values can be given to the items in an enumeration. As it happens, these are the default values; however, you can use any values you wish. The one condition on this is that you should set the first member of the enumeration to the value zero. The significance of this will be highlighted later; however, C# does not enforce it. Thus it is quite legal to write:

```
public enum DaysOfWeek : byte {
    Monday = 10,
    Tuesday = 1,
    Wednesday = 2,
    Thursday = 3,
    Friday = 4
}
```

The result of running the Main method is now:

```
C:\c#>Test
Monday
False
```

It is also possible to initialize the members of the enumeration based on other members in the enumeration. For example:

```
public enum DaysOfWeek : byte {
  Monday = 0,
  Tuesday = Monday + 10,
  Wednesday = Tuesday + Monday,
  Thursday = Wednesday + (2 * 3),
  Friday = 100
}
```

8.9 Zero and Enumerations

It is always possible to assign and test an enumeration against the value zero. For example, it is quite legal to write:

```
DaysOfWeek d = 0;
```

or

```
if (day == 0) { ... }
```

Zero is the only integer for which this is true. Any other value must be cast to the enumeration type (which will check that it is a valid value). For example, if Tuesday has the value 1, then we could write:

```
d = (DaysOfWeek)1;
```

This would set d to the DaysOfWeek value Tuesday.

The reason for the ability to use the literal zero directly is that it is a convenient way to initialize enumerated types. It is also the reason why you should always define the default value in your enumeration with the value zero.

8.10 Bit Flag Enumerations

Enumerations can also be used to define bit flags or masks. As bit-based enumerations can be used to perform bitwise logical operations (such as 'OR'ing) you can use an attribute to indicate that the enumeration holds a bit flag. This is done in the manner illustrated below:

```
using System;

[Flags]
enum PrintFlag : uint
{
  Empty = 0,
```

```
  Text = 0x00000001,
  Image = 0x00000010,
  Combined = 0x00000011,
  All = 0xFFFFFFFF
}

public class Test
{
  public static void Main() {
    PrintFlag f1 = PrintFlag.Text;
    PrintFlag f2 = PrintFlag.Image;
    Console.WriteLine( f1 | f2);
  }
}
```

In this example, the attribute [Flags] allows designers and browsers to present bit-oriented enumerations in a different way from standard enumerations. The result of running this example is:

```
C:\c#>Test
Combined
```

8.11 System Support for Enumerations

When you create an enumeration type in C# you also get some support for this type from the Runtime environment. You have already seen in the previous examples that we do not need to define how a member of an enumerated type should be printed. This is handled for us. Thus when we print out the value of day of type DaysOfWeek then we get Monday displayed (not the underlying integer).

As well as the ability to print a value for an enumeration we can also get hold of all its values, obtain the enumeration member for a value based on a string, see if a specific value is defined in an enumeration, obtain its underlying type etc. This functionality is provided by the class Enum in the System namespace. The following program illustrates some of the facilities of this class:

```
using System;

public enum DaysOfWeek : byte {
  Monday,
  Tuesday,
  Wednesday,
  Thursday ,
  Friday
}

public class Tester
{
```

```
    public static void Main() {

      Console.Write("Underlying type: ");
      Console.WriteLine(Enum.GetUnderlyingType(typeof(DaysOfWeek)));

      Console.WriteLine("\nThe members of the enumeration are:");
      foreach (String s in Enum.GetNames(typeof(DaysOfWeek))) {
        Console.WriteLine(s);
      }

      Console.WriteLine("\nThe values of the enumeration are:");
      foreach (byte b in Enum.GetValues(typeof(DaysOfWeek))) {
        Console.WriteLine(b);
      }

      DaysOfWeek day1 = (DaysOfWeek)Enum.Parse(typeof(DaysOfWeek), "Monday");
      Console.WriteLine("\nGenerated form Parse method {0} ", day1);

      Console.WriteLine("\nChecking isDefined?");
      bool def = Enum.IsDefined(typeof(DaysOfWeek), (byte)1);
      Console.WriteLine("is 1 defined ? {0} " , def);
    }
}
```

The result of compiling and running this program is:

```
C:\c#>Tester
Underlying type: System.Byte
The members of the enumeration are:
Monday
Tuesday
Wednesday
Thursday
Friday

The values of the enumeration are:
0
1
2
3
4

Generated form Parse method Monday

Checking isDefined?
is 1 defined ? True
```

Chapter 9

Interfaces

9.1 Introduction

This chapter discusses interfaces in C#. Interfaces act like a specification. This specification can then be used by classes as a contract between a user and a supplier of some functionality. The user of that functionality need not know anything about who implemented that functionality or how it was implemented. In turn, the provider of that functionality need not know anything about where it is to be used.

To illustrate this idea, consider the power socket in your wall. This socket does not know what you are going to plug into it. it could be a computer, a video recorder or a toaster (or many other electrical devices). In turn, the computer, video recorder or toaster need know nothing about what is behind the socket. They are just provided with electricity. What both need to know is the specification of the socket: that is, whatever it is a two- or three-pin socket; whether it has round or square pins; which pin is positive and which is negative; etc. As long as the creator of the socket and the creator of the plug that goes into that socket were working to the same specification, then both should be happy. An interface is like that specification.

An interface defines the methods that an implementing class must provide. It specifies what the parameters to that method are, what its return type is and what its name is (i.e. it specifies the method signature). It does no more than that – no implementation details are provided. The implementing class can then provide the details.

9.2 Interface Definitions

The C# interface construct is essentially a skeleton that specifies the protocol that a class must provide if it implements that interface. That is, it indicates the methods that must be available from any class that implements that interface. The interface itself does not define any functionality. The format for an interface is:

```
access-modifier interface interface-name : super-interfaces {
    static variable definitions
```

85

```
    method headers ...
}
```

The following interface specifies that any class implementing the IOrganizer interface must provide Add, Get and Remove methods. In addition, it specifies that the Get method should return a string and that the Remove method should return a bool. The interface also specifies the parameters for the methods:

```
public interface IOrganizer {
  public abstract void Add(String string, Date date);
  public abstract String Get(Date date);
  public abstract bool Remove(String string);
}
```

It is not necessary to define these methods as being abstract because they are abstract by default. Notice that you cannot define a class-side (static) method in an interface, as they cannot be abstract.

A naming convention used throughout C# is also illustrated here – an interface name often starts with an 'I' to denote that this is an interface.

9.3 Interfaces Versus Abstract Classes

It may appear at this point that an interface is the same as an abstract class. However, they differ in a number of ways:

- An interface cannot, by definition, provide any functionality. An abstract class can provide default functionality.
- Any class can implement one (or more) interfaces. A class can inherit from only one parent class.
- Interfaces are a compile-time feature; they influence the static analysis of the program being compiled. Abstract classes involve run-time issues associated with method selection, execution etc.
- An abstract class can inherit from an existing class. An interface abstracts a class from which it inherits.
- An interface can extend one or more interfaces by adding new protocols. A class cannot extend an interface (it can only implement it, or "fill it out").

9.4 Implementing an Interface

A class may implement one or more interfaces. To do this the name of the interface or interfaces is listed after a colon following the class name. That is, the syntax is:

```
access-modifier classname : interface-name <, interface-name> {
   ... class body ...
}
```

For example, if we wish to define an interface for a type of reference work we might define:

```
public interface IReference {
   void AddTitle(String t);
   void AddAuthor(String a);
   void AddDate(String d);
}
```

This could then be implemented by classes such as Article, Manuscript or Book. For example:

```
using System;

public interface IReference {
   void AddTitle(String t);
   void AddAuthor(String a);
   void AddDate(String d);
}

public class Book : IReference {
   private String author;
   private String title;
   private String date;

   public Book() {
   }

   public Book(String a, String t, String d) {
      AddTitle(t);
      AddAuthor(a);
      AddDate(d);
   }
   public void AddTitle(String t) {
      title = t;
   }
   public void AddAuthor(String a) {
      author = a;
   }
   public void AddDate(String d) {
      date = d;
   }
   public override String ToString()
```

```
  {
    String result = "";
    result += author + ", " + title + ". " + date;
    return result;
  }
}

public class Test
{
  public static void Main() {

    IReference ref1 = new Book("John Hunt", "Guide to C#", "2002");
    Console.WriteLine(ref1);
    ref1 = new Book();
    ref1.AddAuthor("Denise Cooke");
    ref1.AddTitle("Essential XML Fast");
    ref1.AddDate("2001");
    Console.WriteLine(ref1);
  }
}
```

Note that ref1 is of type IReference and not of type Book. Thus once we have created the object we never refer back to its actual class.

9.5 Using Interfaces

In addition to acting as a contract with a class that specifies what that class (and its subclasses) must provide, an interface can also be used as a type specifier. This means that you can specify an interface and then to use it to specify the type of object which a variable can hold. Thus you can define an interface that is implemented by classes in completely different hierarchies. A method parameter, for example, can take instances of both those class hierarchies and only instances of those class hierarchies:

```
public class Bozo {
  ...
  public void Add (IOrganizer temp) {
    ...
  }
}
```

This means that the method Add can take an instance of any class which implements the IOrganizer interface.

9.6 Multiple Inheritance and Interfaces

Interfaces can also inherit from more than one interface. Thus, for example, we could define an interface IRecords that extends three other interfaces:

```
public interface IRecords : IWorkers, IEmployers,
      IClonable {
  ...
}
```

When an interface extends more than one super interface the result is that the union of all the methods in the parent interfaces and the current interface must be implemented by the implementing class.

9.7 Implementing Interfaces and Extending a Superclass

It is common to want to implement one or more interfaces at the same time as extending a super class. This can be done in C# by listing the super class and then any interfaces following the : after the class name. Note that the interfaces must come after the superclass separated by commas. For example:

```
using System;

public interface IReference {
  void AddTitle(String t);
  void AddAuthor(String a);
  void AddDate(String d);
}

public class Manuscript {
  protected String title;
  public void addTitle(String t) {
    title = t;
  }
}

public class Book : Manuscript, IReference {
  private String author;
  private String date;

  public Book() {
  }

  public Book(String a, String t, String d) {
```

```
      AddTitle(t);
      AddAuthor(a);
      AddDate(d);
    }

  public void AddAuthor(String a) {
    author = a;
  }
  public void AddDate(String d) {
    date = d;
  }
  public override String ToString()
  {
    String result = "";
    result += author + ", " + title + ". " + date;
    return result;
  }
}

public class Test
{
  public static void Main() {
    IReference ref1 = new Book("John Hunt", "Guide to C#", "2002");
    Console.WriteLine(ref1);
    ref1 = new Book();
    ref1.AddAuthor("Denise Cooke");
    ref1.AddTitle("Essential XML Fast");
    ref1.AddDate("2001");
    Console.WriteLine(ref1);
  }
}
```

In this example the class Book now extends the class Manuscript and implements the interface IReference. That means that instances of the class Book can now be treated as an Object, as a Book, as a Manuscript or as an IReference thing!

Also note that the method AddTitle is inherited by the class Book (it does not define it directly). This is quite acceptable – the implementing class must implement all the methods in the interface either directly or through inheritance!

9.8 Method Hiding

In some cases a class may implement an interface, but you only want the methods specified by the interface to be available when the object is treated as being of the interface's type. That is, if a method AddExtra is defined in the interface IList and it should only be used when the implementing object is treated as an IList, then you can hide AddExtra except when the object is viewed as an IList. This is done by prefixing the method name with the name of the interface that specified it. This is referred to as explicit implementation. For example:

```
using System;
using System.Collections;

interface IList
{
  void AddExtra(Object obj);
}

class Employee : IList
{
  private int id;
  private String name;
  private ArrayList list = new ArrayList();
  public Employee(int i, String s)
  {
    id = i;
    name = s;
  }

  void IList.AddExtra(Object obj)
  {
    list.Add(obj);
  }

  public override String ToString()
  {
    String result = "";
    result += id + ", " + name + ": " + list;
    return result;
  }
}

public class Test
{
  public static void Main() {
    Employee e = new Employee(23, "John");
    IList il = (IList)e;
    il.AddExtra("Hunt");
    //e.AddExtra("Hunt");
    Console.WriteLine(e);
  }
}
```

In the above listing the method AddExtra is prefixed with the name of the interface that defines it. The only way that the program compiles is if any instance of the class Employee is first cast to the IList type (as is done in the Main method). If you comment out the two lines:

```
IList il = (IList)e;
il.AddExtra("Hunt");
```

and uncomment the line

```
e.AddExtra("Hunt");
```

and tried to compile the resulting file you would find that the compiler would generate an error message indicating that Employee does not implement the method AddExtra!

9.9 Interfaces and Structs

Just as classes can implement interfaces, structs can implement interfaces. The syntax is very similar and we will look at an example in a moment. However, you should note that interfaces assume that they are being used with reference types and that structs are used to define value types. Thus there is a boxing operation (see Chapter 10) that takes place whenever a struct is cast to an interface.

The syntax for defining that a struct implements an interface is:

```
access-modifier struct struct-name : interface {
... struct declaration ...
}
```

For example:

```
using System;

public interface IReference {
  void AddTitle(String t);
  void AddAuthor(String a);
  void AddDate(String d);
}

public struct Article : IReference {
  String author;
  String date;
  String title;

  public void AddTitle(String t) {
    title = t;
  }
```

```
    public void AddAuthor(String a) {
      author = a;
    }
    public void AddDate(String d) {
      date = d;
    }
    public override String ToString()
    {
      String result = "";
      result += author + ", " + title + ". " + date;
      return result;
    }
  }

public class Test
{
  public static void Main() {
    IReference ref1 = new Article();
    ref1.AddAuthor("Denise Cooke");
    ref1.AddTitle("Essential XML Fast");
    ref1.AddDate("2001");
    Console.WriteLine(ref1);
  }
}
```

Chapter 10

C# Constructs

10.1 Introduction

This chapter presents more of the C# language. It considers the representation and use of numbers. It also discusses assignments, literals and variables and operations.

10.2 Data Types

In C# there are essentially two types of data; value types and reference types. Value types are data types that are allocated on the stack (or allocated inline in a structure). Reference types in turn are data types that are allocated on the heap. In practical terms, this means that basic or built-in types such as integers are value types while all objects are reference types; that is, a variable holds the value 37 directly, but has a reference (or pointer) to an object. This is illustrated below:

```
int I = 37;
Person p = new Person("John", 37);

I 37
p *-> Person Object
```

10.3 Numbers and Numeric Operators

10.3.1 Numeric Values

Numbers in C# can be examples of basic types, such as int, short or double. C# also provides the programmer with the choice of using signed or unsigned integers. In some situations it is necessary to be able to treat a basic type as if it were an object. This is because some data structure objects can only hold objects. In these situations a wrapper is used to make the basic type appear like an object. This process is known as boxing (while the reverse process is known as unboxing). Boxing and unboxing can happen automatically and allow the developer to treat any type of value as if it were an object. This is extremely useful. For example:

```
using System;
class HelloWorld
{
  public static void Main()
  {
    Console.WriteLine("John is {0}", 37);
  }
}
```

In the above example the integer 3 is boxed and the `Int32.ToString()` method is used to box the integer.

Just as in most programming languages, a numeric value in C# is a series of numbers which may or may not have a preceding sign and may contain a decimal point:

```
25 -10 1996 12.45 0.13451345 -3.14
```

In line with recent programming language standards (such as Java), C# explicitly specifies the number of bytes which must be used for data types, such as `short`, `int`, `long`, `float` and `double` (Table 10.1).

The C# language designers' purpose in specifying the number of bytes to use for each data type was to enhance the interoperability of code written in C# with other languages within the .NET environment.

As an example of using these types, see the program below:

Table 10.1 Standard numbers of bytes for numeric data types.

Type	Bytes	Stores
byte	1	Unsigned byte
sbyte	1	Signed byte
short	2	Signed short
ushort	2	Unsigned short
int	4	Signed integer
uint	4	Unsigned integer
long	8	Signed integer
ulong	8	Unsigned integer
float	4	Floating point numbers
double	8	Double precision floating point numbers
decimal	8	Fixed precision number

```
using System;

public class Number
{
  public static void Main()
  {
    byte b = 10;
    sbyte sb = -10;
    short s = -127;
    ushort us = 127;
    int i = -3000;
    uint ui = 3000;
    long l = -12345678;
    ulong ul = 12345678;
    float f = 6400.15F;
    double d = 123456789.12345657689;
    decimal dec = 25.13M;
    char c = 'a';
    Console.WriteLine(
      "byte {0}, sbyte {1}, short {2} ushort {3}",
      b, sb, s, us);
    Console.WriteLine(
      "int {0}, uint {1}, long {2} ulong {3}",
      i, ui, l, ul);
    Console.WriteLine(
      "float {0}, double {1}, decimal {2} char {3}",
      f, d, dec, c);
  }
}
```

Notice that for the float and decimal types we have had to append an F and an M respectively to the end of the literal. This is because real number literals default to double as their type. As both float and decimal could lead to loss of information when a double is converted to either of them, it is necessary to indicate to the compiler that they should be treated as a float (F) or a decimal (M).

The result of running this program is illustrated in Figure 10.1.

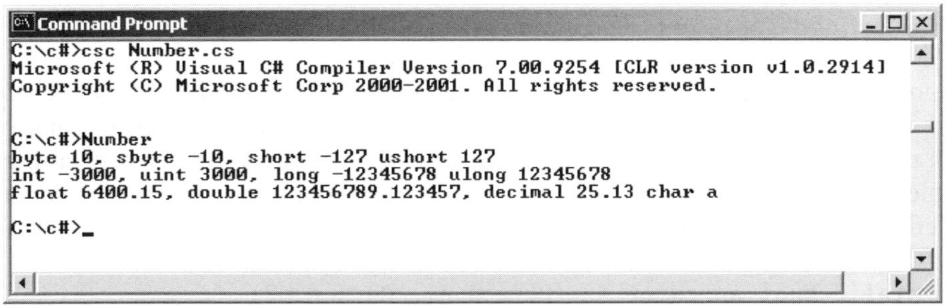

```
Command Prompt                                                    _ |□| x|
C:\c#>csc Number.cs
Microsoft (R) Visual C# Compiler Version 7.00.9254 [CLR version v1.0.2914]
Copyright (C) Microsoft Corp 2000-2001. All rights reserved.


C:\c#>Number
byte 10, sbyte -10, short -127 ushort 127
int -3000, uint 3000, long -12345678 ulong 12345678
float 6400.15, double 123456789.123457, decimal 25.13 char a

C:\c#>_
```

Figure 10.1

10.3.2 Built-In Arithmetic Operators

In general, the arithmetic operators available in C# are the same as in any other language. There are also comparison functions and truncation functions (see Table 10.2).

Table 10.2 Basic numeric operators.

+	addition	==	equality
–	subtraction	<	less than
*	multiplication	>	greater than
/	division	!=	inequality
%	remainder	<=	less than or equal to
++	increment	>=	greater than or equal to
--	decrement		

In addition, C# provides a class called Math in the System namespace. This class, which is a subclass of Object, provides the usual range of mathematical operations (see Table 10.3). All these methods are class (or static) methods available from the class Math. You do not have to create an instance of the class to use them. The class Math also provides a number of useful constants, such as PI.

Table 10.3 Mathematical functions provided by Math.

max	maximum	min	minimum
ceiling	round up	floor	round down
round	round to nearest	sqrt	square root
abs	absolute value	exp	exponential
pow	raises one number to the power of the other	tan	tangent of an angle

There is also a Random class in the System namespace that can be used to generate random numbers. For example:

```
Random r = new Random();
Console.WriteLine(r.Next());
```

10.3.3 User-Defined Operators

In C# it is possible to define operators for classes or structs (see later in this book for structs). These user-defined operators operate in the same way as built-in operators. That is, the + operator can be defined on a class or struct so that an expression such as p1 + p2 is valid and has a meaningful result. For example, in a class it is possible to use the operator keyword to indicate that a static method is actually defining a user-defined operator. For example:

```
public static bool operator == (Person p1, Person p2)
  {
```

```
    if (p1.Name == p2.Name) {
      return true;
    } else {
      return false;
    }
  }
```

Note that the syntax is "operator =="; that is, **operator** immediately followed by the operation to be defined.

10.3.4 Type Operators

In C# there are a number of operators whose sole role is to help the developer work with the type of an object. These are typeof, is and as.

typeof

If you wish to find out the type of an object, you can do this with the typeof operator. This operator is applied to a class to obtain a type object. The type object can then be used to find out information about the class. Another way to do this is to use the GetType() method available on all objects on an instance of a class. For example:

```
using System;

class Person {
  public virtual int GetAge() {
    return 37;
  }
}

public class Test {
  public static void Main() {
    Person p;

    Console.WriteLine(typeof(Person));

    p = new Person();
    Console.WriteLine(p.GetType());
  }
}
```

The result of compiling and executing this program is shown in Figure 10.2.

```
C:\c#>csc Test.cs
Microsoft (R) Visual C# Compiler Version 7.00.9254 [CLR version v1.0.2914]
Copyright (C) Microsoft Corp 2000-2001. All rights reserved.


C:\c#>Test
Person
Person
```

Figure 10.2

is

The is operator can be used to determine whether a particular object *is* an instance of a particular class or whether that instance's class implements an interface. This is usually used as a guard before converting the object to that type with a cast (see later in this book for a description of casting). Below is an example of using the is operator:

```csharp
using System;

class Person {
  public virtual int GetAge() {
    return 37;
  }
}

public class Test {

  public static void Main() {
    Person p = new Person();
    Object o = p;

    Console.WriteLine((o is Person));

  }
}
```

The result of compiling and running this program is the value True. That is, the content of the variable o (a variable of type Object) is really an instance of the class Person.

as

The as operator is very similar to the is operator except that as well as performing the type test of the is operator it also converts the run-time type to the type specified. For example, given the above example we could write:

```csharp
Person q = o as Person;
```

10.4 Assignments

A variable name can refer to different objects at different times. You can make *assignments* to a variable name, using the = operator. It is often read as "becomes equal to" (even though it is not preceded by a colon as in languages such as Ada).

Some examples of assignment statements follow:

```
currentEmployeeIndex = 1;
newIndex = oldIndex;
myName = "John Hunt";
```

Like all C# operators, the assignment operator returns a value. The result of an assignment is the value of that assignment (thus the value of the expression x = 2 + 2; is 4). This means that several assignments can be made in the same statement:

```
using System;

public class Test {

  public static void Main() {
    int a, b, c;
    a = b = c = 1 + 2;
    Console.WriteLine(a);
  }
}
```

Although variables in C# are strongly typed, this typing is perhaps not as strong as in languages such as Pascal and Ada. You can state that a variable is of type Object. As Object is a class, such a variable can possess instances of the class Object or *one of its subclasses*! This means that a variable of type Object which currently holds a string may then be assigned a character or a vector (a type of data structure). This is quite legitimate:

```
using System;

public class Test {

  public static void Main() {
    Object temp;
    temp = "John";
    Console.WriteLine(temp);
  }
}
```

An important point to note is that assignment is by reference when dealing with objects. This means that, in the following example, nextObject, newObject and oldObject all refer to the *same* object (as illustrated in Figure 10.3):

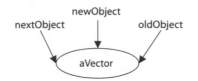

Figure 10.3 The result of a multiple assignment.

```
newObject = oldObject = new ArrayList();
nextObject = newObject;
```

As all three variables point to an instance of a container class (in this case Vector), if an update is made to the contents of any one of the variables, it is made for all three!

10.5 Compound Assignment

In C#, as well as having the standard assignment operator (=), there are also the compound assignment operators that perform some operation and assignment in one go. These compound assignments are comprised of some operator and "=" and are listed in Table 10.4.

Table 10.4

Op	Example	Longhand form
*=	x *= 2;	x = x * 2;
/=	x /= 2;	x = x / 2;
%=	x %= 2;	x = x % 2;
-=	x -= 2;	x = x − 2;

There are also bitwise versions of these operators.

10.6 Variables

10.6.1 Temporary Variables

These variables exist only for the duration of some activity (e.g. the execution of a method). They can be defined anywhere within a method (as long as they are defined before they are used). The definition takes the form of the type (or class) of the variable and the variable name followed by any initialization required:

```
char aChar;
char anotherChar = 'a';
Object anObject;
String myName = "John Hunt";
```

The scope of a temporary variable depends on the context in which it is defined. For example, variables declared at the top level of a method are in scope from the point at which they are declared. However, block variables only have scope for the block within which they are defined (including nested blocks). Loop variables only have scope for the loop within which they are defined. Thus the scope of each of the following variables is different:

```
public int Add (int a, int b) {
  int result = 0;                          r
  for (int i = 0; i < 5, i++) {            ir
    if (a < i) {                           ir
      int total = b;                       tir
      total = total + c * i;               tir
    }                                      ir
  }                                        r
}
```

In the right-hand column, r indicates that result is in scope, i indicates the scope of the loop variable and t indicates the scope of the inner block variable, total.

10.6.2 The this Pseudo-Variable

A pseudo-variable is a special variable whose value is changed by the system, but which cannot be changed by the programmer. The value of a pseudo-variable is determined by the current context and can be referenced within a method.

this is a pseudo-variable which refers to the receiver of a message itself. The search for the corresponding method starts in the class of the receiver. To ensure that your source code does not become cluttered, C# assumes that you mean this object if you just issue a reference to a method. The following statements have the same effect:

```
this.MyName();
MyName();
```

You can use this to pass a reference to the current object to another object:

```
otherObject.AddLink(this);
```

10.6.3 Variable Scope

Temporary variables are only available within the method in which they are defined. However, both class variables and instance variables are in scope (or are visible) at a number of levels. An instance variable can be defined to be visible (available) outside the class or the package, only within the package, within subclasses, or only within the current class. The scope is specified by modifiers that precede the variable definition:

```
public String myName = "John Hunt";
```

10.6.4 Special Values – `true`, `false` and `null`

The `null` value is an object that represents nothing or no object. It is not of any type nor it is an instance of any class (including `Object`). It should not be confused with the null pointer in languages such as C. It really does means *nothing* or *no value*. The other two special values are boolean literals, representing truth and falsehood. It is possible to declare variables to hold boolean values as being of type `bool`, for example:

```
bool flag = true;
```

10.7 Messages and Message Selectors

10.7.1 Invoking Methods

Invoking a method is often referred to as *sending a message* to the object that owns the method. The expression which invokes a method is composed of a receiving object (the receiver), the method name and zero or more parameters. The combination of method name and parameters is often called the message and it indicates to the class of the receiving object which method to execute. Figure 10.4 illustrates the main components of a message expression.

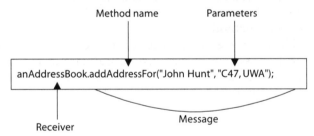

Figure 10.4 The components of a message expression.

The value of an expression is determined by the definition of the method it invokes. Some methods are defined as returning no value (e.g. `void`) while others may return a basic type or object. In the following code, the result returned by the method `marries` is saved into the variable `newStatus`:

```
newStatus = thisPerson.marries(thatPerson);
```

10.7.2 Precedence

The rules governing precedence in C# are similar to those in other languages. Precedence refers to the order in which operators are evaluated in an expression. Many languages, such as C, explicitly specify the order of evaluation of expressions such as the following:

```
2 + 5 * 3 - 4 / 2;
```

C# is no exception. The rules regarding precedence are summarized in Table 10.5. The above expression would be evaluated as:

```
(2 + (5 * 3)) - (4 / 2);
```

Notice that if operators with the same precedence are encountered they are evaluated strictly from left to right. The following table lists the operators in descending order of precedence.

Table 10.5 Operator precedence.

Operators
`(x)  x.y  f(x)  x++  x--  new  typeof  sizeof`
`-  !  ~  +  ++x  --x  (T)x`
`*  /  %`
`+  -`
`<<  >>  (bit shift operators)`
`<  >  <=  >=  is`
`==  !=`
`&`
`^`
`|`
`&&`
`||`
`?  :`
`=  *=  /=  %=  +=  -=  <<=  >>=  &=  ^=  |=`

10.8 Checked and Unchecked Expressions

In many situations there are problems that could arise if the software performs some operation which is illegal. In some cases programming languages always check for such situations (such as overflow exceptions) in other languages they do not check. The reason for not checking is execution speed. C# provides the option for marking a block of code as being checked. Then a compiler switch can be used to turn on or off the checking behaviour. Thus you could have the code checked during testing but unchecked for deployment. To mark a block of code as checked, use the checked keyword followed by the block of code to check:

```
checked
{
... code ...
}
```

10.9 Summary

In this chapter and the previous, you have learnt about classes in C#, how they are defined, how instance variables are specified and how methods are constructed. You have also encountered many of the basic C# language structures.

Chapter 11

Characters and Strings

11.1 Introduction

This chapter considers how strings are represented and manipulated in C#.

11.2 Characters

Characters in C# are 2 bytes in size and based on the Unicode character set. The Unicode character set is a superset of ASCII. It is a superset of ASCII because it represents all of the ASCII character set as well as the characters in other standards, such as Greek or Japanese.

Just like numbers, characters in C# can be either basic types (such as char) or boxed for use as an object. In C#, a single character literal is defined by surrounding it with single quotes:

```
'J' 'a' '@' '1' '$'
```

There are some special characters that represent things such as newline and tab. These are also represented using the "' '" notation but are made up of a "\" and a character. For example '\n' is newline and '\t' is tab.

11.3 Strings

All strings in C# are instances of the class String defined in the System namespace. In turn, the class String is a direct subclass of the Object class. As such, they are made up of individual elements, similar to strings in C. However, this is the only similarity between strings in C and C#. A C# string is not terminated by a null character and should not be treated as an array of characters. It should be treated as an object that responds to an appropriate range of messages (e.g. for manipulating or

Table 11.1 Methods provided by the class String.

CharAt(int index)	Returns the character at position index
CompareTo (String aString)	Compares two strings (optionally ignoring case)
Concat(String s1, String s2)	Concatenates two strings together to generate a third
EndsWith(String s1)	Tests to see if the receiving strings ends with the specified string
Equals(String aString)	Compares to string to see if they are the same value
Insert(int pos, String s)	Insert the string specified at the position indicated
IndexOf (char c)	Returns the first index of the character in the receiving string
StartsWith(String s1)	Checks to see if the receiving string starts with the specified string
Substring (int start, int stop)	Creates substring from start to stop (in the receiving string)
ToLower()	Returns the receiver in lower-case letters
ToUpper()	Returns the receiver in uppe- case letters
Trim()	Removes whitespace from a string

extracting substrings; Table 11.1). For example, a string in C# can tell you how long it is via its Length public instance property.

A string is defined by one or more characters placed between double quotes (rather than the single quotes used for characters):

```
"John Hunt" "Tuesday" "dog"
```

Note that a string containing a single character is not equivalent to that single character:

```
'a' != "a"
```

The string "a" and the character 'a' are, at best, instances of different classes; at worst, one may be an instance and one a basic type. The fact that the string contains only one character is just a coincidence.

To denote that a variable should take an instance of String, define it as being of type String:

```
String aVariable;
aVariable = "John";
```

The "=" operator seen earlier in this chapter as an arithmetic operator has another function – as a string concatenation operation. That is, the "=" operator is overloaded by default. If one or more of the operands to this operator are a string then an attempt to concatenate two strings is carried out. If one of the operands must be converted to a string first then an attempt to do so is made. As an example, see below:

```
String s = "Phoebe " + "Hunt";
```

As an example of working with strings, consider the following code:

```
using System;

public class StringTest
{
    public static void Main() {
     String s1 = "John";
     String s2 = "John Hunt";
     String s3 = "Hunt";
     String s4 = "John";

     String s5 = s1 + " " + s3;
     Console.WriteLine("s1 + s3 => " + s5);

     Console.WriteLine("s2 == s5 " + (s2 == s5));
     Console.WriteLine("s2.Equals(s5) " + s2.Equals(s5));
     Console.WriteLine("s2.StartsWith(s4) " + s2.StartsWith(s4));
     Console.WriteLine("s5.Substring(2, 5) " + s5.Substring(2, 5));

     // Compare is a static method that
     // tests the ordering of the strings
     Console.WriteLine("Compare s1, s2 {0} ", String.Compare(s1, s2));
  }
}
```

Note that the Compare method has the following specification for its return value: a 32-bit signed integer indicating the lexical relationship between the two comparands.

Value	*Meaning*
Less than zero	strA is less than strB
Zero	strA equals strB
Greater than zero	strA is greater than strB

The results of executing this program are presented in Figure 11.1.

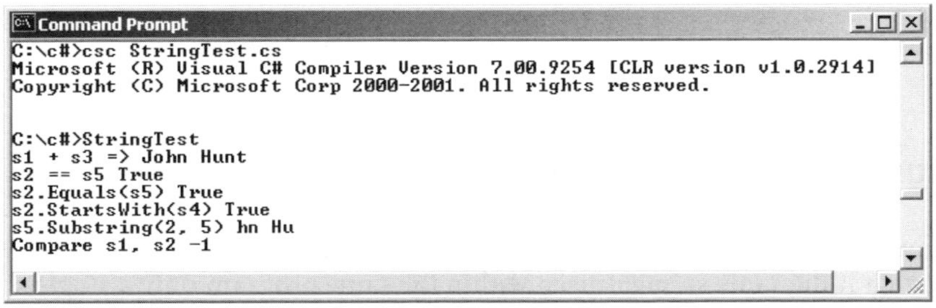

```
C:\c#>csc StringTest.cs
Microsoft (R) Visual C# Compiler Version 7.00.9254 [CLR version v1.0.2914]
Copyright (C) Microsoft Corp 2000-2001. All rights reserved.


C:\c#>StringTest
s1 + s3 => John Hunt
s2 == s5 True
s2.Equals(s5) True
s2.StartsWith(s4) True
s5.Substring(2, 5) hn Hu
Compare s1, s2 -1
```

Figure 11.1

11.4 Converting Objects to Strings

All objects in C# can convert themselves to a string. This is done via the `ToString()` method. The `ToString()` method is defined in the class `Object` and thus all classes in C# either inherit the version of `ToString` in `Object` or define an override for this method. Overriding inherited methods will be considered later in this book. For now, just accept that the syntax of the method needs to be:

```
public override String ToString() {
  ...
  return <result string>
}
```

For example, for the class `Person` I might write:

```
public override String ToString() {
  return name + " " + age;
}
```

If the `Main` method then read:

```
public static void Main()
{
  Person p = new Person("John", 37);
  p.Birthday();
  Console.WriteLine("Person: " + p);
}
```

the end result of running this program would be:

```
C:\c#>Person
In Person constructor
Happy birthday John
You were 37 but now you are 38
Person: John 38
```

11.5 Strings and `StringBuilder`

There are a couple of other points to note about strings. The first is that for efficiency string literals are cached so that if the same string is used within the same program only a single string literal is needed. This is called string interning. This is possible in C# because strings are immutable. That is, once a string is created it cannot be changed. If you concatenate two strings together, for example, you create a third string and the first two strings remain unchanged.

An implication of this is that if you are writing a program that is going to build up a string (say from text in a file) it is much more efficient to use a `StringBuilder` than to continuously concatenate text to a string. This is because a `StringBuilder` is a growable string rather than an immutable string. For example, in the following code a `StringBuilder` is used to build up a string of 200 characters (note that `StringBuilder` can be found in the `System.Text` namespace).

```
using System;
using System.Text;

public class StringTest
{
  public static void Main() {
    StringBuilder sb = new StringBuilder();
    for (int i=0; i < 200; i++) {
      sb.Append("a");
    }
    Console.WriteLine(sb.ToString());
  }
}
```

The result of compiling and executing this program is presented in Figure 11.2.

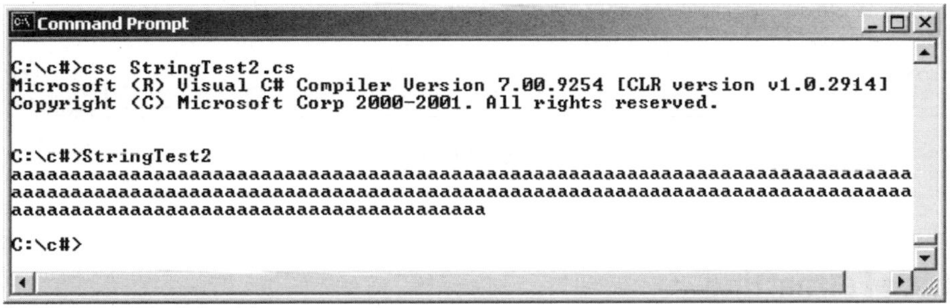

```
C:\c#>csc StringTest2.cs
Microsoft (R) Visual C# Compiler Version 7.00.9254 [CLR version v1.0.2914]
Copyright (C) Microsoft Corp 2000-2001. All rights reserved.

C:\c#>StringTest2
aaaaaaaaaaaaaaaaaaaaaaaaaaaaaaaaaaaaaaaaaaaaaaaaaaaaaaaaaaaaaaaaaaaaaaaaaaaaaaaaa
aaaaaaaaaaaaaaaaaaaaaaaaaaaaaaaaaaaaaaaaaaaaaaaaaaaaaaaaaaaaaaaaaaaaaaaaaaaaaaaaa
aaaaaaaaaaaaaaaaaaaaaaaaaaaaaaaaaaaaaaaaaaaaaa

C:\c#>
```

Figure 11.2

11.6 Regular Expressions

In some situations the simple search-based methods in the `String` class are insufficient. In these situations the regular expression class in the `System.Text.RegularExpressions` namespace can be used. This class, Regex, provides a very powerful method for searching (and replacing) in strings. As a simple example of using the Regex class consider the following:

```
using System;
using System.Text.RegularExpressions;
```

```
public class StringTest3
{
  public static void Main() {
    String s = "John Hunt, Bath";
    Regex r = new Regex(@"Hunt|,");
    Console.WriteLine("Does it match the regular expression? " +
r.IsMatch(s));
    Match m = r.Match(s);
    Console.WriteLine("First match? " + m);
    Console.WriteLine("Second match? " + m.NextMatch());
  }
}
```

This very simple example sets up a Regex object that will match on the string "Hunt" or the character ",". This is then applied to the string "John Hunt, Bath". The results of doing this are then printed out. The results are presented in Figure 11.3.

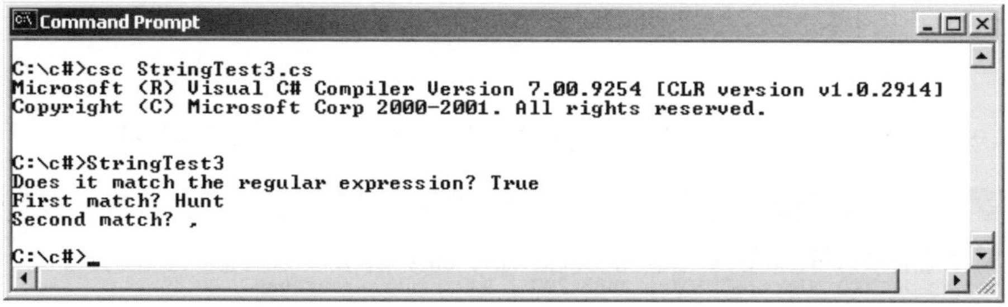

Figure 11.3

11.7 String Formatting

Just as formatting directives can be used with strings in the WriteLine method of the Console class, strings can use the Format method of the String class to create new formatted strings.

The specification of the Format method on the class String is:

```
static string Format(
                 string format,
                 object arg0
                 )
```

This indicates that it is a class-side or static method. Thus you call the method on the class String and obtain a new string back.

The format parameter is embedded with zero or more format specifications of the form { N [, M][: formatString]}, where:

- N is a zero-based integer indicating the argument to be formatted.
- M is an optional integer indicating the width of the region to contain the formatted value, padded with spaces. If the sign of M is negative, the formatted value is left-justified in the region; if the sign of M is positive, the value is right-justified (Figure 11.4).
- formatString is an optional string of formatting codes.

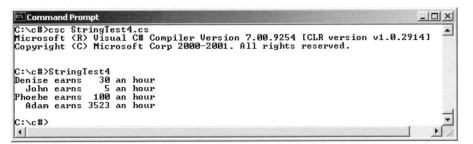

Figure 11.4 Formatting strings.

11.8 String Encoding

Inside C# strings are always represented as combinations of characters in Unicode. However, not all systems use Unicode (indeed most editors, operating systems and programming languages do not use Unicode). Thus it may be necessary to convert between Unicode and other encodings from time to time. The System.Text namespace contains classes that can be used to do such code conversions. A typical example might be to convert between ASCII and Unicode. However, this is done on an array of bytes. Thus it is also necessary to convert a string into an array of bytes that can then be encoded.

Chapter 12

An Example C# Class

12.1 Introduction

You should now be ready to write some C# code, so this chapter takes you through a worked example. It is a very simple example, in which you create a new class, define some instance variables and write a couple of methods.

12.2 Defining a Class

We have already seen examples based around the Person class earlier in this book. However, in this chapter we will work through the Person class, examining how it does what it does. It must record a person's name and age. It must also allow the person to have a birthday (and thus increment the person's age).

The first thing you need to do is define a C# class in a file with the same name as the class. This is just a convention that allows you to identify where your classes are defined – but it is a useful convention. Note that you can define more than one class in a file – the file should then be named after the most significant class.

12.2.1 Creating the Class

1. Create an empty file called Person.cs using your favourite editor. If you have a tool such as Visual Studio .NET, you can use it instead (indeed, it will probably make your life much easier).
2. In the file, define a new class by typing in the following C# code:

```
public class Person {
  private int age = 0;
  private String name = "";
}
```

The above code defines the class Person (by default, it is a subclass of Object) and gives it two instance variables, name and age, which are only accessible from within the class.

3. Compile the class by issuing the following command:

```
> csc Person.cs
```

12.3 Defining a Constructors and Methods

We first define the Main method. We then define a constructor that initializes the instance variables in the appropriate manner.

12.3.1 The Main Method

Every C# application must have at least one Main method where the execution begins. This method creates a new instance of the class and sends it the message birthday:

```
public static void Main () {
  Person p = new Person();
  p.Birthday();
}
```

This is essentially the same as in Chapter 6, so we do not re-analyze it.

12.3.2 The Constructor

As was explained in Chapter 6, a constructor allows parameters to be passed into a class when a new instance is created. However, we are keeping things simple here and relying on the default constructor (which is called with no parameters). The definition of this constructor is presented below:

```
public Person () {
  Console.WriteLine("In Person constructor");

  age = 37;
  name = "John Hunt";
}
```

This constructor prints out a message to the console and then initializes age (as the integer 37) and name (the string "John Hunt"). Once this method has executed, control returns to the point at which the instance was created (in our case, to the main method).

At this point your class definition should resemble that presented below.

```
using System;

class Person
```

```
  {
    // private instance variables
      private String name;
      private int age;

      // A constructor
      public Person (String name, int age)
      {
        Console.WriteLine("In Person constructor");
        this.name = name;
        this.age = age;
      }

      public static void Main()
      {
        Person p = new Person();
        p.Birthday();
      }
  }
}
```

Notice that the instance variable definitions do not need to be at the start of the class. Also note that if you do not provide any constructors then the C# compiler provides a default null parameter constructor for you.

12.3.3 The Properties

Now we can define some properties for accessing the instance variables. These are sometimes called *getter* methods. The two properties to be defined are for name and age. The code for these is presented below:

```
// Name property
public String Name
{
  get
  {
    return name;
  }
  set
  {
    name = value;
  }
}

// Age property
public int Age
{
```

```
  get
  {
    return age;
  }
  set
  {
    age = value;
  }
}
```

12.3.4 The Birthday Method

Having defined the methods that access the private instance variables (notice that nothing outside the class can modify these variables), we now define a method called Birthday:

```
public void Birthday () {
  int oldAge, newAge;
  oldAge = this.Age;
  Console.WriteLine("Happy birthday " + this.Name);
  Console.Write("You were " + oldAge);
  Console.Write(" but now you are ");
  newAge = oldAge + 1;
  this.Age = newAge;
  Console.WriteLine(age);
}
```

This last method prints out a birthday greeting and increments the person's age. It uses the other methods to change the current value of the instance variable age and to print a meaningful message to the user. This type of programming is known as variable-free programming and is considered good style.

Note that the Console class defined in the System namespace has a number of methods on it that are used to print strings, objects and basic types. The two used here are WriteLine and Write. WriteLine prints out the value and a newline, while Write just prints out the value.

12.4 Creating an Instance

You should now execute the C# application you have created. You do this by running the byte code compiled from the file Person.cs on the virtual machine. The result of compiling and running this application in Windows is presented in Figure 12.1.

Executing the .exe generated by the compiler causes an instance of Person to be created, the constructor to be called automatically and the message Birthday to be sent to the new instance.

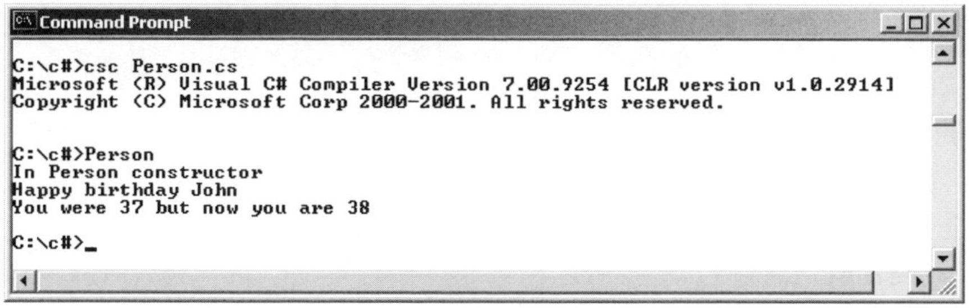

Figure 12.1 Running the Person application.

Once you have done this and are happy with what is happening, try to change the method definitions or add a new instance variable called address and define the appropriate methods for it. The complete Person class definition is presented below.

```csharp
using System;
class Person
{
  // private instance variables
  private String name;
  private int age;

  // A constructor
  public Person (String name, int age)
  {
    Console.WriteLine("In Person constructor");
    this.name = name;
    this.age = age;
  }
  // Name property
  public String Name
  {
  get
    {
      return name;
    }
  set
  {
    name = value;
  }
}

// Age property
public int Age
```

```csharp
{
  get
  {
    return age;
  }
  set
  {
    age = value;
  }
}

public void Birthday () {
  int oldAge, newAge;
  oldAge = this.Age;
  Console.WriteLine("Happy birthday " + this.Name);
  Console.Write("You were " + oldAge);
  Console.Write(" but now you are ");
  newAge = oldAge + 1;
  this.Age = newAge;
  Console.WriteLine(age);
}

public static void Main()
{
  Person p = new Person("John", 37);
  p.Birthday();
}
}
```

Part 3

C# and Object Orientation

Chapter 13

Classes, Inheritance and Abstraction

13.1 Introduction

In this chapter, we consider some of the language features you saw in the last section of the book from an object-oriented point of view. This chapter discusses how you should use classes and what you should, and should not, use them for. It considers how you should use inheritance, abstraction and subclasses and highlights the use of constructors. It also tries to explain the use of (the oft misunderstood) main method.

13.2 Classes Revisited

The following is an incomplete example that illustrates many of the features found in class definitions. It is presented as a reminder without further explanation.

```
public class Person {
  // Define a class variable
  public static int numberCreated = 0;
  // Define an instance variable
  public String name = " ";

  // Define a class method
  public static void IncrementNumberCreated() {
    numberCreated = numberCreated + 1;
  }

  // Define an instance method
  public void SetName(String aName) {
    name = aName;
  }
```

```
...
}
```

Notice that the keyword static illustrates that the following element is on the class side (as opposed to the instance side).

13.2.1 What Are Classes For?

In some object-oriented languages, classes are merely templates used to construct objects (or instances). In these languages, the class definition specifies the structure of the object and a separate mechanism is often used to create the object using this template.

In some other languages (for example Smalltalk-80), classes are objects in their own right; this means that they can not only create objects, they can also hold data, receive messages and execute methods just like any other object. Such object-oriented systems tend to have what is called a rich meta-model built upon the use of metaclasses. A metaclass is a special class, whose sole instance is a class.

An object is an instance of something, so if a class is an object, it must be an instance of something. In the meta-model, a class is an instance of a metaclass. It should be noted that the metaclass concept is probably one of the most confusing parts of the whole of Smalltalk. This is partly due to the names used, but also because almost all of it is hidden from the developer. The developer is therefore only vaguely aware of it (if at all) during development.

C# adopts a position halfway between the two camps. That is, it has a weak meta-model in which classes can respond to messages and to requests for class variable values. However, although C# does not provide the full power of the Smalltalk meta-model, this is not a problem in practice as the Smalltalk meta-model is confusing and most developers never need to use it. The end result is that the C# approach is simpler, cleaner and easier to understand.

Thus, in C#, classes are not objects (in the true sense of the word), but are unique within a program and can:

- create instances
- be inherited by subclasses (and can inherit from existing classes)
- implement interfaces
- have class methods
- have class variables
- define instance methods
- define instance variables
- be sent messages

Objects (or instances), on the other hand, can:

- be created from a class
- have instance variables
- be sent messages
- execute instance methods
- have many copies in the system (all with their own data)

Thus a class is more than just a template for an object: it can also hold data and provide class-specific behaviour. However, if you are confused by most of the above, remember: a class's two primary roles are to define instances and to allow inheritance.

13.2.2 Class-Side Methods

It may at first seem unclear what should normally go in an instance method as opposed to what should go in a class (or static) method when defining a new class. After all, they are both defined in the class. However, it is important to remember that one defines the behaviour of the instance and the other the behaviour of the class (it is a pity that these methods are designated by the keyword static, as it is not obvious to the new programmer what static actually means). Class-side methods should perform only one of the following roles:

- *Instance creation* This role is very important, as it is how you can use a class as the root of an application. It is common to see main methods which do nothing other than create a new instance of the class. For example:

```
public class Account {
  double balance = 0.0;

  public static void Main () {
    Account account = new Account();
  }
... remainder of class definition ...
```

- *Answering enquiries about the class* This role can provide generally useful objects, frequently derived from class variables. For example, they may return the number of instances of this class that have been created.
- *Instance management* In this role, class-side methods control the number of instances created. For example, a class allows only a single instance to be created. Instance management methods may also be used to access an instance (e.g. randomly or in a given state).
- *Documentation* Methods for documentation can be very useful, illustrating how to use the class.
- *Examples* Occasionally, class methods are used to provide helpful examples that illustrate or explain the operation of a class. This is good practice.
- *Testing* Class-side methods can be used to support the testing of an instance of a class. You can use them to create an instance, perform an operation and compare the result with a known value. If the values are different, the method can report an error. This is a very useful way of providing regression tests.
- *Support for one of the above roles*

Any other tasks should be performed by an instance method.

13.2.3 A Class or an Instance

In some situations, you may only need to create a single instance of a class and reference it wherever it is required. A continuing debate ponders whether it is worth creating such an instance or whether it is better to define the required behaviour in class methods and reference the class (which, after all, can be sent messages and have its class variables accessed). Invariably the answer to this is no, for the following reasons:

- Such an approach breaks the object-oriented model. Although this approach has been adopted by numerous object-oriented systems, it is not object-oriented and suggests that the programmer has not fully embraced the object-oriented model.
- The creation of an instance has a very low overhead. This is a key feature in Java and it has received extensive attention.
- You may require more than one instance sometime in the future. If you implement all the code on the class side, you will have to move the methods to the instance side of the class.
- You may be tempted to treat the class as a global reference. This suggests that the implementation has been poorly thought out.
- The use of what is often referred to as the Singleton pattern allows the developer to limit the number of objects created to a single instance and to control access to that instance. this is often done either by a Factory class or via a factory method on the object. An example of a class with a factory method is presented below:

```csharp
using System;
class ActionManager {
  private static ActionManager instance;
  private ActionManager() {}
  public static ActionManager GetInstance() {
    if (instance == null) {
      instance = new ActionManager();
    }
    return instance;
  }
}
public class Test {
  public static void Main() {
    ActionManager am = ActionManager.GetInstance();

    Console.WriteLine(am);

  }
}
```

Note that the constructor for the ActionManager class is private. This stops anything outside of the ActionManager class from creating an instance of the ActionManager. Thus the only way to get an instance of the ActionManager is via the method GetInstance. This method in turn creates a new instance of the class the first time it is called (this technique is often referred to as lazy initialization) and returns it. Each time it is called after that it returns the same instance. This thus guarantees that there is only one instance of the class created per execution of this program.

13.3 Inheritance in Classes

Inheritance is achieved in C# using the : syntax. C# is a single inheritance system, so a C# class can only inherit from a single class, but can, of course, implement zero or more interfaces. The following class definition builds on the class Person presented earlier:

```
public class Student : Person {
  private String subject = "Computer Science";
  public String GetSubject() {
    return subject;
  }
}
```

This class extends the class Person by adding a new instance variable, subject, and a method to access it.

13.3.1 The Role of a Subclass

A subclass modifies the behaviour of its parent class. This modification should refine the class in one or more of these ways:

- Changes to the external protocol, the set of messages to which instances of the class respond.
- Changes in the implementation of the methods, the way in which the messages are handled.
- Additional behaviour that references inherited behaviour.

If a subclass does not provide one or more of the above, then it is incorrectly placed. For example, if a subclass implements a set of new methods, but does not refer to the instance variables or methods of the parent class, then the class is not really a subclass of the parent (it does not extend it).

For example, consider the class hierarchy illustrated in Figure 13.1. A generic (probably abstract) root class has been defined. This class defines a Conveyance that has doors, fuel (both with default values) and a method, startUp, that starts the engine of the conveyance. Three subclasses of Conveyance have also been defined: Dinghy, Car and Tank. Two of these subclasses are appropriate, but one should probably not inherit from Conveyance. We shall consider each in turn to determine their suitability.

The class Tank overrides the number of doors inherited, uses the startUp method within the method fire, and provides a new instance variable. It therefore matches all three of our criteria.

Similarly, the class Car overrides the number of doors and uses the method startUp. It also uses the instance variable fuel within a new method accelerate. It also, therefore, matches our criteria.

The class Dinghy defines a new instance variable sails and a new method setSail. As such, it does not use any of the features inherited from Conveyance. However, we might say that it has extended Conveyance by providing this instance variable and method. We must then consider the features provided by Conveyance. We can ask ourselves whether they make sense within the context of Dinghy. If we assume that a dinghy is a small sail-powered boat, with no

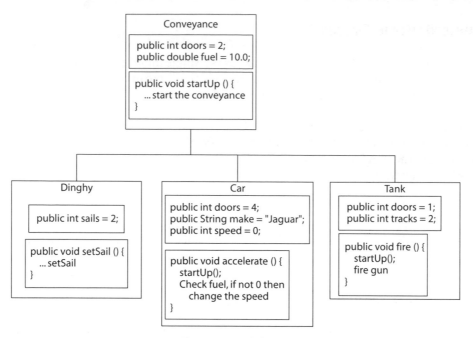

Figure 13.1 Subclasses.

cabin and no engine, then nothing inherited from Conveyance is useful. In this case, it is likely that Conveyance is misnamed, as it defines some sort of a motor vehicle, and the Dinghy class should not have extended it.

The exceptions to this rule are subclasses of Object. This is because Object is the root class of all classes in C#. As you must create a new class by subclassing it from an existing class, you can subclass from Object when there is no other appropriate class.

13.3.2 Capabilities of Classes

A subclass or class should accomplish one specific purpose; it should capture only one idea. If more than one idea is encapsulated in a class, you may reduce the chances for reuse, as well as contravene the laws of encapsulation in object-oriented systems. For example, you may have merged two concepts together so that one can directly access the data of another. This is rarely desirable.

Breaking a class down costs little but may produce major gains in reusability and flexibility. If you find that when you try to separate one class into two or more classes some of the code needs to be duplicated for each class, then the use of abstract classes can be very helpful. That is, you can place the common code into an abstract superclass to avoid unnecessary duplication.

The following guidelines may help you to decide whether to split the class with which you are working. Look at the comment describing the class (if there is no class comment, this is a bad sign in itself). Consider the following points:

- Is the comment short and clear. If not, is this a reflection on the class? Consider how the comment can be broken down into a series of short clear comments. Base the new classes around those comments.
- If the comment is short and clear, do the class and instance variables make sense within the context of the comment? If they do not, then the class needs to be re-evaluated. It may be that the comment is inappropriate, or the class and instance variables inappropriate.
- Look at the instance variable references (i.e. look at where the instance variable access methods are used). Is their use in line with the class comment? If not, then you should take appropriate action.

13.3.3 Overriding Methods

In C# there are a number of limitations to control whether a subclass is allowed to override a method inherited from a parent class. These are:

- The method must be virtual or abstract (see below). If the method is neither of these it cannot be overridden.
- The overridden method must state explicitly that it is intending to override the method defined in the parent class.

To support this the keywords virtual and override are used. They are placed on the method specification before the return type of the method (and so may go before or after the access modifier, such as public).

As an example, consider the following classes:

```csharp
using System;

class Person {
  public virtual int GetAge()
  {
    return 37;
  }
}

class Employee : Person {
  private int age = 40;
  public override int GetAge()
  {
    return age;
  }
}

class Test {
  public static void Main() {
    Employee e = new Employee();
    Console.WriteLine(e.GetAge());
```

```
    }
}
```

When this code is compiled and executed the result is that the value 40 is printed out as the person's age. If either the virtual keyword in the class Person or the override keyword in the class Employee were missed out then the code would not compile.

13.3.4 Restricting a Subclass (Sealed Classes)

You can restrict the ability of a subclass to change what it inherits from its superclass. Indeed, you can also stop subclasses being created from a class. This is done using the keyword sealed. This keyword has different meanings depending on where it is used:

```
public sealed class LaserPrinter : Printer {
```

No element of this class can be extended, so no subclass of LaserPrinter can be created. You can also apply the keyword sealed to methods.

```
public sealed void Handshake() {
```

This states that this method cannot be overridden in a subclass. That is, a subclass cannot redefine Handshake(); it must use the one that it inherits. You can also specify class methods as sealed.

Restricting the ability to overwrite part of, or all of, a class is a very useful feature. It is particularly important where the correct behaviour of the class and its subclasses relies on the correct functioning of particular methods, or the appropriate value of a variable, etc. A class is normally only specified as sealed when it does not make sense to create a subclass of it. These situations need to be analyzed carefully to ensure that no unexpected scenarios are likely to occur. As an example of a sealed class in C#, take a look at the System.String class.

13.4 Abstract Classes

An abstract class is a class from which you cannot create an object. It is missing one or more elements required to create a fully functioning instance. In contrast, a non-abstract (or concrete) class leaves nothing undefined and can be used to create a working instance. You may wonder what use an abstract class is. The answer is that you can group together elements that are to be shared amongst a number of classes, without providing a complete implementation. In addition, you can force subclasses to provide specific methods, ensuring that implementers of a subclass at least supply appropriately named methods. You should therefore use abstract classes when:

- you wish to specify data or behaviour common to a set of classes, but insufficient for a single instance
- you wish to force subclasses to provide specific behaviour

In many cases, the two situations go together. Typically, the aspects of the class to be defined as abstract are specific to each class, while what has been implemented is common to all classes. For example, consider the following class (based loosely on the Conveyance class presented above):

```
using System;

public abstract class Conveyance {
  private int doors = 2;
  protected double fuel = 5.0;
  private bool running = false;
  public void StartUp() {
    running = true;
    ConsumeFuel();
    while (fuel > 0) {
      ConsumeFuel();
    }
  }
  public abstract void ConsumeFuel();
}
```

This abstract class definition means that you cannot create an instance of Conveyance. Within the definition of Conveyance, we can see that the startUp method is defined, but the method ConsumeFuel is specified as abstract and no method body is provided. Any class that has one or more abstract methods is necessarily abstract (and must therefore have the keywords abstract class). However, a class can be abstract without specifying any abstract methods.

Any subclass of Conveyance must implement the ConsumeFuel method if instances are to be created from it. Each subclass can define how much fuel is consumed in a different manner. The following PetrolCar class provides a concrete class that builds on Conveyance:

```
public class PetrolCar : Conveyance {
  public static void Main () {
    PetrolCar p = new PetrolCar();
    p.StartUp();
  }
  public override void ConsumeFuel () {
    fuel = fuel - 1.0;
    Console.WriteLine(fuel);
  }
}
```

The result of executing this class is illustrated below:

```
C:\c#>PetrolCar
4
3
2
```

```
1
0
```

We can also define a `DieselCar` class in which the fuel consumption rate is lower, for example:

```csharp
public class DieselCar : Conveyance {
  public static void Main () {
    DieselCar d = new DieselCar();
    d.StartUp();
  }
  public void ConsumeFuel () {
    fuel = fuel - 0.5;
    Console.WriteLine(fuel);
  }
}
```

However, if all you wish to do is to specify that a set of methods should be defined by a subclass, then you may well be better off defining an interface. Interfaces never contain method bodies, nor do they declare instance variables, thus it is clearer that all you intend to do is to specify a particular protocol to be defined by those classes that implement the interface (see Chapter 6).

13.5 Constructors and Their Use

Constructors should only be used to initialize an instance of a class in an appropriate manner and you should attempt to place all the initialization code in as few constructors as possible. For example, if there is only one initialization process but different numbers or combinations of parameters can be passed to the constructors, then you should define a stack of constructors, each one of which adds some more behaviour. The root constructor should represent the constructor with the most parameters. This should then call the constructor with the next level of parameters setting any data not handled by that constructor itself. The syntax for this is to follow the constructor method signature specification with a ";" and "this(<parameter list>)". For example,

```csharp
using System;

public class Account {
  private double balance = 0.0;
  private String name = "";

  Account(double amount, String person) : this (person){
    balance = amount;
    Console.WriteLine("(double amount, String person) constructor");
  }

  Account (String person) : this() {
```

```
    name = person;
    Console.WriteLine("(String person) constructor");
  }
  Account () {
    Console.WriteLine("Default constructor");
  }

  public static void Main() {
    Account acc = new Account(120.00, "John Hunt");
  }
```

The effect of compiling and running this code is:

```
C:\c#>Account
Default constructor
(String person) constructor
(double amount, String person) constructor
```

In this example, the three constructors each allow different amounts of information to be provided. However, the actual initialization of each instance variable only occurs in a single place each time. Thus any changes to the way in which the initialization process is performed for that instance variable are localized to a single constructor.

An annoying feature of C# is that subclasses of Account do *not* inherit these constructors and must define their own (see below), which can then call the superclass constructors.

13.6 Calling Superclass Constructors

As noted above, subclasses do not inherit their parent class's constructors. Instead they get to call their parent class's constructors. That is, you are always guaranteed that the initialization process for each class back up the inheritance hierarchy will be executed when you create an instance of a subclass. This is important, as superclass methods may rely on the initialization process having been completed for them to operate correctly. In fact, this is so important that a superclass constructor will *always* be called by a subclass constructor. If you do not provide such an explicit call automatically C# will call the superclass's default (zero parameter) constructor for you. For example, consider the following application. This defines three classes: Person, its direct subclass Employee and the class Manager, which is in turn a subclass of Employee. The class manager has two constructors – a default constructor and a single parameter constructor. Nowhere is there any indication of any explicit calls to the parent class constructors. Each constructor in all the classes prints out a message.

```
using System;
class Person
{
  public Person()
```

```
    {
      Console.WriteLine("In default Person constructor");
    }
  }

  class Employee : Person
  {
    public Employee()
    {
      Console.WriteLine("In default Employee constructor");
    }
  }

  class Manager : Employee
  {
    public Manager()
    {
      Console.WriteLine("In default Manager constructor");
    }

    public Manager(String name)
    {
      Console.WriteLine("In (String name) Manager constructor");
    }
  }

  class Tester
  {
    public static void Main() {
      Manager m1 = new Manager();
      Console.WriteLine("-------------------------");
      Manager m2 = new Manager("Denise");
    }
  }
```

The result of compiling and executing this code is:

```
C:\c#>Tester
In default Person constructor
In default Employee constructor
In default Manager constructor
-------------------------
In default Person constructor
In default Employee constructor
In (String name) Manager constructor
```

Note that it did not matter which manager constructor was called: all the constructors in the parent classes were called (in fact, an additional constructor in the Object class was also called). Also note that the constructor that is highest in the inheritance hierarchy executes first.

You can of course control which constructor is called in the parent class if you need to. This is done by specifying base rather than this in the method specification. For example:

```csharp
using System;

class Person
{
  public Person()
  {
    Console.WriteLine("In default Person constructor");
  }
}

class Employee : Person
{

  public Employee(String name)
  {
    Console.WriteLine("In (String name) Employee constructor");
  }
}

class Manager : Employee
{

  public Manager(String name, int age) : base(name)
  {
    Console.WriteLine("In (String name, int age) Manager constructor");
  }
}

class Tester
{
  public static void Main() {
    Console.WriteLine("------------------------");
    Manager m2 = new Manager("Phoebe", 21);
  }
}
```

The result of compiling and executing this code is:

```
C:\c#>Tester
------------------------
In default Person constructor
In (String name) Employee constructor
In (String name, int age) Manager constructor
```

Note that this time the one parameter constructor in Employee was called, but that the default constructor in Person was still executed.

Note that if you do not define any constructors then C# provides a default constructor for you. However, if you define one or more constructors then C# does not provide the default constructor.

13.7 The Main Method

The Main method should not be used to define the application program. This tends to happen when people move from C to C#, since in C the main function is exactly where the main functionality is placed. It is, therefore, unfortunate that the name Main is used for this method. The Main method should only ever do a very few things:

- Create an instance of the class within which it is defined. It should never create an instance of another class. If it does then you are not thinking in an object-oriented manner.
- Send the newly created instance a message so that it initializes itself.
- Send the newly created instance a message that triggers off the application's behaviour.

The PetrolCar and DieselCar classes are good examples of this. Both classes create a new instance (of the class) and send it the message startUp. Nothing else happens in the Main method; all the work is done in the instance methods.

There is one situation in which you may break this rule. That is where the class you are defining is not intended to be the root class of the application. This class would not normally possess a Main method and, if you define one, it can be ignored when the class is used within a larger application. This is done by specifying to the C# compiler which class contains the Main method.

Therefore, you can use the Main method to provide a test harness for the class. If you do not delete this Main method, then it is available to those who modify or update the class at a later date. It can also act as a simple regression test.

Chapter 14

Encapsulation and Polymorphism

14.1 Introduction

This chapter discusses the encapsulation and polymorphic features of C#. It illustrates how the encapsulation facilities can allow quite fine-grained control over the visibility of elements of your programs. The concept of packages is also discussed, along with some concrete examples. The polymorphic nature of C# concludes the chapter.

14.2 Encapsulation

In C#, you have a great deal of control over how much encapsulation is imposed on a class and an object. You achieve it by applying modifiers to classes, instance and class variables and methods.

14.2.1 Class Modifiers

You can change the visibility of a class by using a modifier keyword before the class keyword in the class definition, for example:

```
public class Person {...}
```

A public class is visible everywhere. A class that is local to a particular file has no modifier. It can be defined within a file containing other classes.

A third option for classes is internal. A class with internal access is one that is accessible by all classes in the same assembly. Classes defined in other assemblies would not be able to access an internal class.

Examples of the three options for defining classes are:

```
public class Person ....
internal class Student
class Subject
```

14.2.2 Variable Modifiers

The amount of encapsulation imposed by a class is at the discretion of the programmer. You can allow complete access to everything within the class, or you can impose various levels of restrictions. In particular, you can control how much access another class has to the instance and class variables of a class. You do this by using a modifier keyword before the type of the variable, for example:

```
public static int MAX_VALUE = 100;
protected String name = "John Hunt";
private int count = 0;
```

Table 14.1 lists the modifiers and their meanings. Generally it is a good idea to impose as much encapsulation as possible. Thus everything should be hidden unless it has to be visible to other classes, in which case you should allow the minimum amount of visibility.

Table 14.1 The effect of a variable or method modifier.

public	Visible everywhere (the class must also be public)
no modifier	Visible in current file
protected	Visible in current class and in subclasses in other packages
private	Visible only to current class
internal	Accessible from classes in the same assembly
internal protected	Accessible by classes in the same assembly and subclasses anywhere

Notice that protected is weaker than using no modifier! You should use no modifier in preference to protected.

14.2.3 Method Modifiers

You can also limit the access of other classes to methods. You do this by using a modifier keyword before the return type of the method. The modifiers are the same as for variables:

```
public void SetName(String name) {...}
private static int CountInstances() {...}
protected Object FindKey() {...}
internal double GetRate() {...}
```

14.3 Namespaces

Namespaces are used to organize groups of related classes into a hierarchical structure that can be referenced in other programs.

Namespaces are encapsulated units that can possess classes, interfaces and sub-packages. Namespaces are extremely useful and in a normal development environment are essential:

- They allow you to associate related classes and interfaces.
- They resolve naming problems that would otherwise cause confusion.
- They allow some privacy for classes, methods and variables that should not be visible outside the package. You can provide a level of encapsulation such that only those elements that are intended to be public can be accessed from outside the package.

The .NET runtime environment for C# provides a number of namespaces, such as System, System.Text, System.Drawing and System.Windows.Forms. The System namespace holds the core classes provided by the Runtime Environment. These include the class Array, the GC (Garbage Collector class), the Math class, the Object class (root of all other classes in C#) and the String class. In general, you use these namespaces as the basis of your programs.

14.3.1 Declaring a Namespace

A namespace is defined using the namespace keyword at the start of the namespace. Unlike some languages (such as Java) a single file can contain multiple namespaces. The namespace statement is of the form:

```
namespace <name-of-namespace>
{
  ... contents of namespace ...
}
```

For example, if we decided to place the Person class within a namespace People we could write:

```
using System;
namespace People
{
  public class Person {
    public String name;

    public static void Main() {
      Person p = new Person();
      p.name = "John";
      Console.WriteLine("Person: " + p.name);
    }
  }
}
```

This code defines a new namespace, People, that contains a single class, Person. The class Person in turn defines a single public instance variable name (this is bad style in general but OK for this example). The Main method then creates an instance of the class Person, sets the name to "John" and prints it out. You have now defined your first package.

Namespaces should be unique to ensure that there are no name conflicts. One naming convention is that a namespace name is made up of a number of components separated by a full stop. The first part of these components corresponds to the domain name of your organization (for example Com.Jaydeetee). Typically this is followed by a name that is meaningful to the users of that namespace. Thus I might wish to create a namespace with the name Com.Jaydeetee.People.

Such a naming convention is referred to as "nested namespaces" in C# and can be defined in one of two ways. The first approach is to create one namespace and then to create another inside that. For example, to create the namespace Com.Jaydeetee.People we could write:

```csharp
using System;

namespace Com
{
  namespace Jaydeetee
  {
    namespace People
    {
      public class Person {
        public String name;

          public static void Main() {
            Person p = new Person();
            p.name = "John";
            Console.WriteLine("Person: " + p.name);
          }
      }
    }
  }
}
```

Note that the namespace statements are nested one inside the other. Also note that one namespace can have more than one nested namespace; thus this is also feasible:

```csharp
using System;

namespace Com
{
  namespace Jaydeetee
  {
    namespace People
    {
      ...
    }
    namespace Dogs {
      public class Dog {

      }
    }
```

```
    }
}
```

In this case the namespace Com.Jaydeetee possesses two namespaces: People and Dogs.

Obviously, in many situations you might not want to do this and there is a lot of additional space taken up with the nested namespace statements. There is therefore a shorthand form for this that allows you to define the outer and inner namespaces in one go. This form is:

```
namespace <level1namespace>.<level2namespace>...<levelnnamespace>
{
    ... content of namespace...
}
```

For example:

```
using System;

namespace Com.Jaydeetee.People
{
    ... content of namespace ...
}
```

14.3.2 Assemblies

Before we go any further with namespaces we need to consider assemblies. Assemblies are the way in which C# code is often packaged for distribution or release. When C# code is compiled it is actual processed into the Intermediate Language (IL). This code can be placed in an assembly for access by other programs written using the .NET framework (whether they are written in C# or not). The assembly is comprised of one or more files that contain all the IL, a manifest of the contents of the assembly, the assemblies this assembly depends on and other files.

To create an assembly we can use one of the compiler command line options. If we specify /t (or /target) followed by a ":library" then the compiler will emit a .dll file (named after the first file being compiled by default). For example, if we issue the following command:

```
csc /t:library People.cs
```

we will obtain a file called People.dll that can be used when compiling other classes not in the People namespace.

In general there is correlation between the name of a namespace and the name of an assembly. For example, the System.Net namespace is in System.Net.dll.

14.3.3 Using Namespaces

Once you have defined a namespace and placed it in an assembly you are in a position to release it to other developers who can then use the class in your namespace. To make a namespace available to the current code you need to do a couple of things. First you need to make the assembly available within the current file. This can be done via the `using` statement. For example, we have been doing this for the `System` namespace in every program we have written so far:

```
using System;
```

In fact, the `using` keyword is really a shorthand form that allows the contents of the assembly to be referenced with the assembly name. That is, we do not need to include the `System` package to use the `System.Console` class; we could write:

```
System.Console.WriteLine("John Hunt");
```

This would be tedious if we had to use the `Console` class many times or had many classes from a package. Thus we write:

```
using System;
...
Console.WriteLine("Hello John");
```

However, the two versions are exactly equivalent.

In some cases you do not have a choice. For example, if two namespaces defined a class `Person` and you needed to use both namespaces, if you wrote:

```
Person p = new Person()
```

to which version of `Person` would you be referring? The compiler would not know. In such a case you might still need to write:

```
Com.Jaydeetee.People.Person p = new Com.Jaydeetee.People.Person();
```

However, C# alleviates this problem to some extent by allowing an alias to be provided for a class. For example, we could define:

```
using JDTPerson = Com.Jaydeetee.People.Person
```

Then you can use the alias instead of the fully qualified class name, for example:

```
JDTPerson p = new JDTPerson();
```

14.3.4 Compiling Using Assemblies

Let us assume that we have already created a `People.dll` assembly containing the `Com.Jaydeetee.People` namespace. We can now use this namespace in other programs (such as the one below).

```
using System;
using Com.Jaydeetee.People;

class Test
{
  public static void Main() {
    Person p = new Person();
    p.name = "John";
    Console.WriteLine("Person: " + p.name);
  }
}
```

However, in order to successfully compile this class we need to tell the C# compiler where to find the People assembly. This can be done by giving the compiler another command line option. This option (/reference or /r for short) allows the developer to specify assemblies that should be used to compile the current file (or files). For example, to use the People.dll assembly to compile the above Test program we could issue the following command:

```
C:\c#>csc /r:People.dll Test.cs
```

The result of compiling this would be a file Test.exe that can be executed as normal (that is, you do not need to specify the assembly when running the executable). Thus the effect of running the program would be:

```
C:\c#>Test
Person: John
```

14.4 Polymorphism

Polymorphism is the ability to send the same message to completely different objects, all of which respond to that message in their own way. C#'s polymorphic abilities are derived from its use of dynamic (or late) binding. In addition, the same method name can be used with different parameters to allow apparently the same method to be declared a number of times within the same class.

14.4.1 Dynamic or Late Binding

Dynamic or late binding refers to the way in which C# decides which method should be run. Instead of determining the method at compile-time (as a procedural language might), it can determine virtual methods at run-time. That is, if a method that could be overridden in a subclass (that is, it is marked as virtual) then the compiler can leave determining exactly which version of the method will execute at run-time until run-time. That is, the run-time environment can look to see what class of object has received the message and then decide which method to run. Obviously this has performance implications and it is why methods that can be overridden must be marked as such when the class is defined. This allows C# to determine which methods must be left for late (run-time) binding and which can be determined at compile-time. Note that Java has the opposite approach, which provides for greater flexibility but at a performance cost.

As an example of using polymorphism, consider the following classes:

```
using System;
public class Vehicle {
  public virtual void Drive() {
    Console.WriteLine("Drive a vehicle");
  }
}

public class Car : Vehicle {
  public override void Drive() {
    Console.WriteLine("Drive a car");
  }
}
```

We can use these two classes within a test harness, as follows:

```
public class Example {
  public static void Main() {
    Vehicle v = new Vehicle();
    Car c = new Car();
    v.Drive();
    c.Drive();
    v = c;
    v.Drive();
  }
}
```

When this application is executed, the version of Drive defined in the class Car is called twice, whereas the version in the superclass Vehicle is called only once:

```
C:\c#>Example
Drive a vehicle
Drive a car
Drive a car
```

The variable v was declared to be of type Vehicle. When it was assigned the instance of Car and it received the message Drive, it responded with the Car version of Drive, which was chosen at run-time (based on the object held by v).

14.4.2 Method Selection/Overloading

When the C# system selects a method in response to a message, it does so using three things:

- the class of the receiving object
- the name of the method
- the type (and order) of the parameters

The third element means that you can define two methods in the same class, with the same name, but with different parameters (note that you need to be a little careful with automatic conversion of types). Also note that no mention has been made of the return type of the method – it is not used to distinguish between methods and therefore you cannot have two methods whose signatures are identical except for the return type – this will generate a compiler error. Finally, a method also cannot differ only in whether it is using out or ref parameters.

This ability to have more than one method with the same name in a class is referred to as method overloading.

The system works out which method you want to call at run-time by examining the parameters. For example, consider the class Lorry in the following listing:

```csharp
using System;

public class Vehicle {

  public virtual void Drive() {
    Console.WriteLine("Drive a vehicle");
  }
}

public class Lorry : Vehicle {

  public void Load (int i) {
    Console.WriteLine("Loading integers " + i);
  }

  public void Load (String s) {
    Console.WriteLine("Loading strings " + s);
  }
}

public class LorryExample {

  public static void Main () {
    Lorry l = new Lorry();
    l.Load(10);
    l.Load("John");
  }
}
```

This class, Lorry, has two methods called Load, both of which take a single parameter. However, the parameters are of different types. This means that the C# system can distinguish between the two methods, and thus no conflict arises. Thus the Main method in the LorryExample class has no problem with the two calls to the method Load one with an integer and one with a String. The result therefore of compiling and executing this example is:

```
C:\c#>LorryExample
Loading integers 10
Loading strings John
```

You can also use this approach to provide class constructors.

14.4.3 Method Hiding

There is a certain subtlety to the way in which C# resolves which method to call when methods are overloaded through the inheritance hierarchy. The example we saw above with the Lorry had both the Load methods defined in the class Vehicle. Thus there was no issue relating to where C# should look for the methods. However, in the following example there is also a method Load in the class Vehicle that takes a short:

```
using System;

public class Vehicle {

  public virtual void Load(short s) {
    Console.WriteLine("Loading shorts " + s);
  }
}

public class Lorry : Vehicle {

  public void Load (int i) {
    Console.WriteLine("Loading integers " + i);
  }

  public void Load (String s) {
    Console.WriteLine("Loading strings " + s);
  }
}

public class LorryExample {

  public static void Main () {
    Lorry l = new Lorry();
    l.Load(10);
    l.Load("John");
    short s = 5;
    l.Load(s);
```

```
        ((Vehicle)l).Load(s);
    }
}
```

Now if you look at the Main method presented above you might reasonably expect that the result will be:

```
Loading integers 10
Loading strings John
Loading shorts 5        // Wrong!
Loading shorts 5
```

After all, the variable s is of type short and thus the two statements:

```
l.Load(s);
((Vehicle)l).Load(s);
```

should be equivalent. But they aren't, and the result presented above is wrong!

When C# tries to resolve which methods to call it searches back up the inheritance hierarchy. At each level it tries to find if there is a possible match (without reference to any levels above at this point). A short can be converted to an int, so there is a potential match at the Lorry level. C# therefore stops searching for a closer match and executes the version it finds at that level.

To force C# to look at the version of Load written in the class Vehicle we must first cast the variable l to Vehicle which will force C# to consider the Vehicle class (which is what is done in the final statement of the Main method).

Thus the actual output of the ExampleLorry program is:

```
C:\c#>LorryExample
Loading integers 10
Loading strings John
Loading integers 5
Loading shorts 5
```

14.4.4 Variable-Length Parameter Lists

The final aspect of polymorphism that we shall consider is the use of variable length parameter lists. That is, it is sometimes useful to allow a method to take a variable number of parameters. That way, if some parameters are optional they do not need to be provided.

Variable length parameter lists are supported in C# via the keyword params. This keyword changes the way that the compiler looks up methods. When the compiler finds a call to a method with a variable set of parameters it first checks to see if there is an exact match (overloading). If not, then it places each of the optional parameters into an array that is accessible within the method. For example:

```
using System;

public class Car {

  public void Drive() {
    Console.WriteLine("Drive a car");
  }

  public void Drive(String town) {
    Console.WriteLine("Drive to {0}", town);
  }

  public void Drive(String town, params String [] args) {
    Console.Write("Drive to {0} via ", town);
    for (int i=0; i<args.Length; i++) {
      Console.Write("{0} " , args[i]);
    }
    Console.WriteLine("");
  }
}

public class Example {

  public static void Main() {

    Car c = new Car();
    c.Drive();
    c.Drive("Bath");
    c.Drive("Bath", "London", "Reading", "Swindon");
  }
}
```

The above class has three versions of the method Drive; one that takes no parameters, one that takes one parameter and one that takes a variable number of parameters. In the Main method we then call the zero parameter method, the one parameter method and the method Drive with four parameters. The result of compiling and executing this program are:

```
C:\c#>Car
Drive a car
Drive to Bath
Drive to Bath via London Reading Swindon
```

As described earlier the end result is that the call to Drive with four parameters is converted into a call to Drive with two parameters, the second of which is an array of Strings. Note that any type that is appropriate could be used for the type of the parameter array.

Interestingly, this also means that we could call `Drive` by passing in a string and array of strings. The result would be that the version of `Drive` that supports variable length parameter lists would be called directly.

In general it is usually good style in these cases to overload methods such as `Drive` with one-, two- and three-parameter versions plus the variable length version.

Chapter 15

Nested Classes

15.1 Introduction

A nested class is a class that is defined within the scope of another class (referred to as the outer class). This is often useful if one class is to act as a dedicated helper of another class.

15.2 What Are Nested Classes?

Nested classes are classes that exist inside other, top-level, classes. They possess very specific properties that include being:

- defined within the scope of an existing class
- able to access the outer class's static variables
- able to be an interface specification
- able to have default, private, protected or public visibility
- able to be abstract

For example, in the following class Employee, two nested classes are defined that are used to represent an address and a wage. Thus the structure of the class is as illustrated in Figure 15.1.

The source code for the class, and its two nested classes, is presented below:

```
using System;

public class Employee {
    int age = 0;
    public String name = "Bob";
    static double rate = 12.45;
    Address address;
    Wage wage;
```

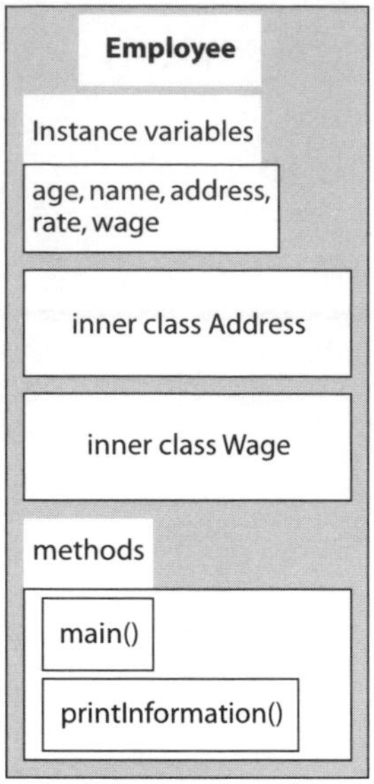

Figure 15.1 The structure of the Employee class.

```
public Employee (String aName, int number,
      String aStreet, String aCity,
      double ratePerHour, int hours) {
  name = aName;
  rate = ratePerHour;
  address = new Address(number, aStreet, aCity);
  wage = new Wage(hours);
}

// Nested class -------------------------------------
public class Address {
  int number = 0;
  String street = "";
  String city = "";
  public Address (int num, String aStreet, String aCity) {
    number = num;
    street = aStreet;
    city = aCity;
  }
  public void PrintDetails() {
    Console.WriteLine(number + " " + street + " , " + city);
  }
}
```

```
// Nested class -------------------------------------
public class Wage {
  int hoursWorked = 0;
  public Wage (int hours) {
    hoursWorked = hours;
  }
  public void PrintDetails() {
    Console.WriteLine("Pay packet = " +
    hoursWorked * GetRate());
  }
}

//----------------------------------------------------------
public static void Main () {
 Employee e = new Employee("John", 37, "High Street",
    "Bath", 2.45, 36);
  e.PrintInformation();
}

public void PrintInformation() {
  Console.WriteLine("\nFor Employee: " + name);
  address.PrintDetails();
  wage.PrintDetails();
}

public static double GetRate() {
  return rate;
}
}
```

The result of executing this application is:

```
C:\c#>Employee
For Employee: John
37 High Street, Bath
Pay packet = 88.2
```

The rate variable referenced by the GetRate method refers to a static variable in the encapsulating class Employee. Thus, nested classes can access static (but only static) variables and methods from the enclosing class.

In many ways, the top-level class can act as an object package containing zero or more nested classes. This is particularly useful for component-oriented development.

15.3 How and When Should I Use Nested Classes?

15.3.1 As Helper Classes

Nested classes are often used as helper classes to perform some specific function (such as implementing a particular action), to implement some generic features (such as an interface to be used throughout the outer class but nowhere else) or to provide a particular view on to some data (by providing an iterator or enumerator etc.). In general they are not used as a "cheap" way of packing a whole set of classes together and only need to reference the top-level class. However, it is worth noting that this is a programming idiom that could be used.

15.3.2 As Event Handlers

A very common use of a nested class is with a GUI. The nested class can be used to handle a user event and determine what action an application should take next.

15.3.3 As a Way of Overcoming Single Inheritance

Nested classes can be very useful as a way of overcoming single inheritance in C#. Let us say, for example, that you have two classes and you want to make an object that can exploit both superclass behaviours and extend them. One way of doing this is to have the outer class extend the most appropriate superclass and the nested class extend the other class. As the outer class can create and work with the nested class they can combine their behaviours to exploit both parent classes. Of course you could do this with two separate classes; however, by using a nested class nothing outside of the outer class need even know that a second class is being involved at all!

15.3.4 Laying Out a C# Class With Nested Classes

You should try to follow these guidelines when laying out a C# class which contains named nested classes:

- Try to avoid mixing variables, methods and nested classes when laying out the class – this will only lead to confusion. Instead group variable declarations together, methods together and nested classes together. You don't need to worry about which comes first, as the C# compiler is a multiple pass compiler which will sort out forward references.
- Don't use the outer class as a cheap global "database". One temptation is to treat the outer class as a global blackboard onto which you can write global data (thus providing a limited scope global database). This is not good programming style and may jeopardize future development.

15.3.5 Nested Class Guidelines

This section provides some guidelines on the definition and implementation of nested classes:

- Make a nested class private by default. That way you will stop the outer class merely being a "cheap" package. If you have to make the nested classes non-private then at least you must make this decision explicitly.
- Use nested classes for separate but related objects.
- Use nested classes as helper classes which support a particular functionality or abstraction.
- Be careful how you document nested classes.

Chapter 16

Arrays in C#

16.1 Introduction

In this chapter we consider how arrays are created, manipulated and accessed in C#.

16.2 Arrays

Arrays in C# are objects, like most other data types. Like arrays in any other language, they hold elements of data in an order specified by an index. They are zero-based arrays, as in C, which means that an array with 10 elements is indexed from 0 to 9.

To create a new array, you must specify the type of array object and the number of elements in the array. The number of elements is specified by an integer between square brackets. As an array is an instance, it is created in the usual way using the new operation:

```
new String[10];
```

This creates an array capable of holding 10 string objects. We can assign such an array instance to a variable by specifying that the variable holds/references an array. You do this by indicating the type of the array to be held by the variable along with the array indicator:

```
String [] names;
```

Notice that we do not specify the number of array locations that are held by the array variable. This is because arrays are reference types; that is, the variable will hold a reference (or pointer) to the array, and thus the size of the array does not affect the size of the address held by the variable.

Also note that this format differs from that used in C, where you might write String args []. In some languages (such as Java) you can use either format; however, C# is tidier and forces you to use the <type> [] identifier approach. This is also the most semantically meaningful, as you are creating a variable of a specific type (and that type is for example String Array)!

We can now create an array and assign it to our variable:

```
String [] names = new String [4];
```

However, notice that what we have done is to create a String array that can hold four strings. At present we have not created any String objects, and thus this array currently holds four null values.

Note that if we created an array of ints then that array would directly hold ints, but that those ints would all have the value 0. For example:

```
int [] ia = new int[4];
```

There is a short-cut way to create and initialize an array. This can be done at the point that the array is declared using {..} and then the values for the array in a comma-separated list within the brackets. For example:

```
String [] names = {"John", "Denise", "Phoebe", "Adam"};
int [] ia = {1, 2, 5, 7, 9, 2, 3};
Person pa = { new Person("John"), new Person("Denise") };
```

The first example creates an array of four elements containing the strings "John", "Denise", "Phoebe" and "Adam". We can change any of these fields by specifying the appropriate index and replacing the existing value with a new string:

```
names [3] = "Isobel";
```

The above statement replaces the string "Adam" with the string "Isobel". Merely being able to put values into an array would be of little use; we can access the array locations in a similar manner:

```
Console.WriteLine("The name in position 2 is {0}", names[1]);
```

The above statement results in the following string being printed:

```
The name in position 2 is Denise
```

As arrays are objects we can also obtain information from them. For example, to find out how many elements are in the array we can use the instance variable Length:

```
names.Length
```

Arrays are fixed in length when they are created, whereas ArrayLists (see the next chapter) can change their length. To obtain the size of an array, you can access the property Length.

Arrays can be passed into and out of methods very simply by specifying the type of the array, the name of the variable to receive the array and the array indicator.

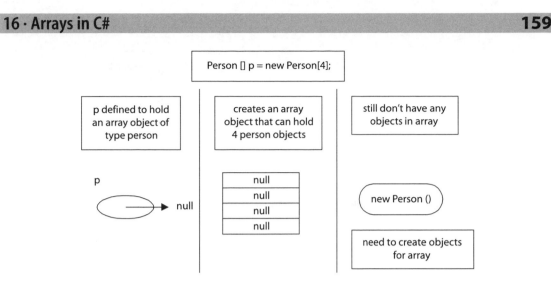

Figure 16.1 Creating an array of objects.

16.2.1 Arrays of Objects

The above examples have focused on arrays of strings; however, you can also create arrays of any type of object, but this process is a little more complicated (it is actually the exactly the same for strings, but some of what is happening is hidden from you). For example, assuming we have a class Person, then we can create an array of Persons:

```
Person [] p = new Person[4];
```

It is important to realize what this gives you. It provides a variable p which can hold a reference to an array object of Persons. At present this array is empty and *does not* hold references to any instances of Person. Note that this indicates that the array is actually an array of references to the instances "held" in the array as opposed to an array of those instances. This is illustrated in the first part of Figure 16.1. To actually make it hold instances of Person we must add each Person instance to the appropriate array location. For example:

```
p[0] = new Person();
p[1] = new Person();
p[2] = new Person();
p[3] = new Person();
```

This is illustrated in the last part of Figure 16.1 and in Figure 16.2. Thus the creation of an array of objects is a three-stage process:

1. Create a variable which can reference an array of the appropriate type of object.
2. Create the array object.
3. Fill the array object with instances of the appropriate type.

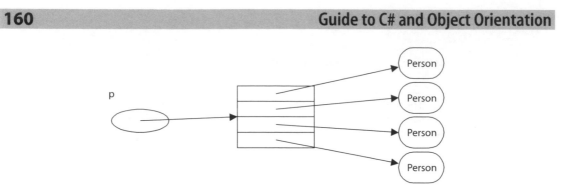

Figure 16.2 The complete array structure.

16.2.2 Basic Type Arrays

It should be noted that an array of basic types is exactly that. It is not an array of references to the basic types. Thus an array of basic types is simpler and the generation of such an array produces an array containing the specified value or the default (zero) values, for example:

```
int totals [] = {0, 2, 5, 1, 7};
```

16.2.3 Multi-Dimensional Arrays

As in most high-level languages, multi-dimensional arrays can be defined in C#. This can be done by specifying more than one dimension when creating the array. To do this you specify two or more dimensions within the [] used to specify the size of the array when instantiating it (e.g. new int [3, 3]). The variable to hold such an array must then be declared to be of type[,]; for example (int [,]). You can also use the shorthand form to initialize the contents of the array. For example:

```
using System;

public class Test {

  public static void Main() {
    int [,] a = new int[3, 3];
    int [,] d = { {1, 1}, {3, 2}, {4, 5} };
  }
}
```

Both the statements in the Main method create a multidimensional array object. The first creates a square 3 × 3 array, while the second initializes a 3 × 2 array.

To access elements of a two-dimensional array you need to specify both indices: for example pa[1, 2]. This can be used both to set a value in an array and to access a value in an array. For example:

```
using System;

public class Test {

  public static void Main() {
    int [,] a = new int[3, 3];
    int [,] d = { {1, 1}, {3, 2}, {4, 5} };

    a[0, 0] = 12;
    Console.WriteLine(a[0, 0]);
  }
}
```

When compiled and run this of course prints out the value 12.

16.2.4 Jagged/Ragged Arrays

In C# it is also possible to have jagged or ragged arrays. Ragged arrays are non-square arrays. These are actually arrays made up of arrays (that is, they are an array of arrays). In this situation it is possible to have ragged arrays, as the second dimension is made up of separate array objects. For example, the following code defines a ragged two-dimensional array in which the first row has four elements and the second has five.

```
using System;

public class Test2 {

  public static void Main() {
    String [] [] f = new String[2][];
    f[0] = new String[4];
    f[1] = new String[5];
  }
}
```

However, it is instructive to consider what this actually means. It states that a string array f can hold references to other string arrays that in turn can hold actual string objects. Thus to create these arrays and objects for the Person class we would:

1. Define the variable p as holding a reference to an array of arrays:

   ```
   Person [][] p;
   ```

2. Create the multi-dimensional array:

   ```
   p = new Person[2][];
   ```

Note that we have to specify the first dimension as it is necessary to allocate enough space for the required references. We do not have to specify the second dimension as these can be specified in the subsequent array object creation messages.

3. Create the sub-arrays:

```
p[0] = new Person[2];
p[1] = new person[2];
```

4. We are now ready to add instances to the two-dimensional array, for example:

```
p[0][0] = new person("John");
```

As you can see from this last example, ragged multi-dimensional arrays are accessed in exactly the same way as single dimensional arrays with one indices following another (note each is within its own set of square brackets – []).That is, you can access this two ragged dimensional array by specifying a particular position within the array using the same format:

```
Console.WriteLine(matrix[2][2]);
```

16.2.5 Array Conversions

In C# it is possible to convert one array into another as long as certain conditions are met. Conversions are allowed between arrays based on the number of dimensions and the types of the elements (it must be possible to convert between the two).

An implicit conversion is allowed in the following cases:

1. The dimensions of the two arrays are the same.
2. It is possible to cast the type of the first array to the type of the second array (e.g. Person to Object).
3. Both arrays hold reference types (e.g. objects).

An explicit conversion has the same requirements as for implicit conversions. The only difference is that the programmer must perform the conversions manually.

16.2.6 System.Array

The Array class in the System namespace provides methods for creating, manipulating, searching and sorting arrays. It is also the root class for all the array classes created for each type in the system. It provides static methods for operations such as sorting searching and reverse the contents of an array.

Array Sorting

The Array class provides a Sort method that can be used to sort the contents of an array. This is an overloaded method that can either use the natural ordering of the contents of the array or use an object that implements the IComparator interface to determine the order. For example:

```
using System;

public class Test4 {

  public static void Main() {
    String [] s = {"John", "Denise", "Phoebe", "Adam"};
    Array.Sort(s);
    foreach (String item in s)
    {
      Console.WriteLine(item);
    }
  }
}
```

The result of running this program is a sorted array of strings:

```
C:\c#>Test3
Adam
Denise
John
Phoebe
```

Searching

It is also possible to search the contents of an array using the Array class method BinarySearch. As with the Sort method this is an overloaded method that can use the natural comparison of the objects to compare as well as an object that implements the IComparator interface to perform the comparison. For example:

```
using System;

public class Test3 {

  public static void Main() {
    String [] s = {"John", "Denise", "Phoebe", "Adam"};
    int pos = Array.BinarySearch(s, "Phoebe");
    Console.WriteLine(pos);
  }
}
```

The result of this program is the value 2 (remember that C# arrays are zero-based).

Array Reversal

Calling Array.Reverse() on an array can reverse the order of all the elements in an array. For example:

```
using System;

public class Test4 {

  public static void Main() {
    String [] s = {"John", "Denise", "Phoebe", "Adam"};
    Array.Reverse(s);
    foreach (String item in s)
    {
      Console.WriteLine(item);
    }
  }
}
```

The result of running this program is that the strings in the array are reversed in order:

```
C:\c#>Test4
Adam
Phoebe
Denise
John
```

16.2.7 The Main Method

At this point you are ready to review the parameter passed into the second form of the Main method. As a reminder, it has the following format:

```
public static void Main (String [] args) {
  ...
}
```

From this you can see that the parameter passed into the Main method is an array of strings. This array holds any command line arguments passed into the program.

We now have enough information to write a simple program which parses the main method command line arguments:

```
public class ParseInput {
  public static void Main (String [] args) {
    if (args.Length == 0) {
      Console.WriteLine("No arguments");
    }
    else {
      for (int i = 0; i < args.length; i++) {
        Console.WriteLine("Argument number" + i + " is " + args[i]);
      }
    }
  }
}
```

This is a very simple program but it provides the basics for a command line parser. Do not worry if you do not understand the syntax of the whole program; we cover if statements and for loops later in the book.

16.2.8 Arrays and Methods

Arrays in C# are passed into methods by value (Figure 16.3) . However, as they only hold a reference to the objects they contain, if those objects are modified internally, the array outside the method is also modified. This can be the cause of extreme frustration when trying to debug programs. Arrays can also be returned from methods:

```
modifiers static-specifier type [] methodName (...)
public String [] ReturnNames () {
  ...
}
```

As an example of an array-based application, consider the following class, ArrayDemo, which calculates the average of an array of numbers. This array is created in the main method and is passed into the processArray method as a parameter. Within this method, the values of the array are added together and the total is divided by the number of elements in the array (i.e. its length):

```
using System;

public class ArrayDemo {
  public static void Main () {
    ArrayDemo d = new ArrayDemo();
    int [] anArray = {1, 4, 7, 9};
    d.ProcessArray(anArray);
  }
  public void ProcessArray (int [] myArray) {
    int total = 0, average = 0;
      for (int i = 0; i < (myArray.Length); ++i){
        total = total + myArray[i];
      }
    average = total / myArray.Length;
    Console.WriteLine("The average was {0}", average);
```

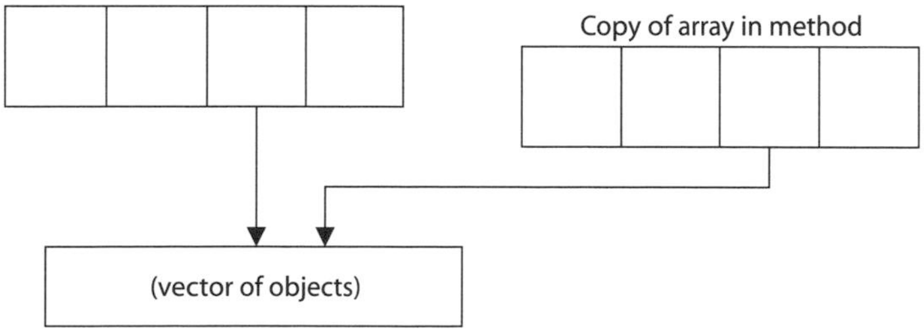

Figure 16.3 Passing an array into a method.

```
    }
}
```

The result of running this program is:

5

Chapter 17

The Collections API

17.1 Introduction

C# possesses the System.Collections namespace. This namespace contains classes that can be used to hold collections of objects or to build custom collections of objects. A collection is a single object representing a group of objects (such as a list or dictionary). That is, they are a *collection* of other objects. Collections may also be referred to as containers (as they contain other objects). These collection classes are often used as the basis for data structures and abstract data types. In general, a collection should be used wherever some significant behaviour is associated with the data in the collection (arrays can be used elsewhere). For example, a SortedList may need to support the idea of adding and removing elements from the list, but also maintaining some sort order etc.

The collection classes are called by names such as ArrayList, BitArray, Hashtable and SortedList, as well as Stack and Queue etc. Some of the collection classes, for example, ArrayList, provide functionality similar to existing data structure classes such as Arrays, but are more flexible to use (at a small performance cost). The collection classes can only hold objects; thus if you wish to hold the basic types within them, they will need to be boxed.

17.2 Data Structure Classes

Figure 17.1 illustrates the relationships between the root class, Object, the data structure classes and the interfaces IList, IDictionary and ICollection which they implement. The boxes indicate classes and the ovals indicate an interface. Class names in italics indicate abstract classes. The solid lines indicate inheritance, while the dashed lines indicate implementation (of an interface).

The root class, Object, is defined in the namespace System. The other classes are all defined in the System.Collections package. DictionaryBase and CollectionBase are abstract classes, which cannot be used to create instances. The other six classes are all concrete classes, which can create instances.

167

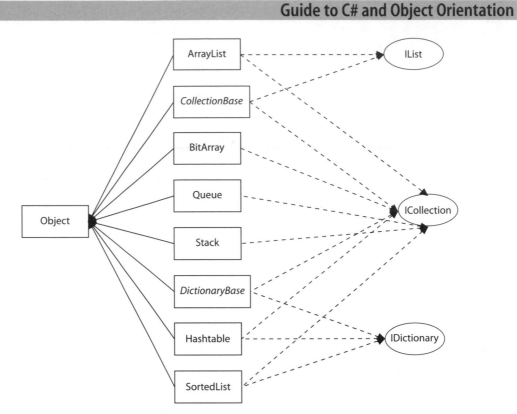

Figure 17.1 The data structure classes.

17.3 What Is in the Collections API?

The collection classes and interfaces in C# are collectively referred to as the Collections framework. Collections are the C# mechanism for building data structures of various sorts; it is therefore important to become familiar with the collection framework and its functionality.

Interface ICollection is the root of all collections in the API. Figure 17.2 summarizes the collection API in C#. Some of the classes illustrated are abstract classes on which others build. In fact, the collection class hierarchy is a classic example of the use of interfaces and abstract classes and how they can be used to group together functionality as well as indicate what is expected of subclasses. Now is a good time to stop and examine the Collections API itself.

The Collections API can be divided up in the following manner:

Figure 17.2 The interfaces defined in the Collections API.

- *Collection interfaces* There are four collection interfaces which represent the core types of collections supported by the Collections API. These interfaces are ICollection, IDictionary, IList and IEnumerable. We will look in more detail at these interfaces later.
- *Abstract implementations* These provide the abstract root classes for the collection hierarchy. They specify the behaviour which must be implemented by subclasses which provide the features of a Collection, a Dictionary etc.
- *Concrete implementations* These are general-purpose implementations of the core collection interfaces.
- *Synchronization* It is possible to synchronize a collection by wrapping it in a synchronization wrapper. For example:

```
ArrayList list = ArrayList.Synchronized(new ArrayList());
```

Where appropriate the collection class provides a synchronizing wrapper via a static method.
- *Array sorting and searching* Static methods on the Array class provide for sorting and searching.

The basic operations that are performed by the collection data structures include adding and removing elements, determining the size of the collection, querying the presence or absence of elements and iterating over the elements.

17.4 Collection Interfaces

The interfaces that comprise the collection hierarchy are designed to allow manipulation of collections in an implementation-independent fashion. This should allow for interoperability among unrelated APIs and applications that take collections as input or return them as output. This should reduce the effort required to design, implement, maintain and understand such APIs and applications. The collection framework should also help in the production of reusable software. The interfaces which form the basis of the Collections framework are presented in Table 17.1.

If you wish to define your own collection classes, then implementing one of these interfaces could be your starting point. The details of these interfaces are presented below.

Table 17.1 The interfaces in the Collections framework.

Interface	Description
ICollection	Defines size, enumerators and synchronization methods for all collections
IComparer	Exposes a method that compares two objects
IDictionary	Represents a collection of associated keys and values
IDictionaryEnumerator	Enumerates the elements of a dictionary
IEnumerable	Exposes the enumerator, which supports a simple iteration over a collection
IEnumerator	Supports a simple iteration over a collection
IHashCodeProvider	Supplies a hash code for an object, using a custom hash function
IList	Represents a collection of objects that can be individually indexed

17.5   The core interfaces

At the heart of the collections framework are the interfaces that define the core concepts (and group the collections classes into different areas). The core interfaces in the Collections framework are:

- `ICollection`
- `IList`
- `IDictionary`

`IDictionary` and `IList` are more specialized interfaces that are based on the `ICollection` interface. These are each considered in more detail below.

17.5.1   `ICollection`

The `ICollection` interface is the interface that acts as the root of (almost) all collection classes. It defines the methods that all collections must implement.

The interface defines only one method and a few properties (see Tables 17.2 and 17.3). As `ICollection` is a direct sub-interface of the `IEnumerator` interface, it also specifies the `GetEnumerator` method from that interface. This allows developers a great deal of freedom in how to structure a collection.

Table 17.2 Public instance properties of `ICollection`.

Count	When implemented by a class, gets the number of elements contained in the `ICollection`
IsSynchronized	When implemented by a class, gets a value indicating whether access to the `ICollection` is synchronized (thread-safe)
SyncRoot	When implemented by a class, gets an object that can be used to synchronize access to the `ICollection`

Table 17.3 Public instance methods of `ICollection`.

CopyTo	When implemented by a class, copies the elements of the `ICollection` to an `Array`, starting at a particular `Array` index

Any object can be stored into any collection (however, implementations of a particular collection may limit the type of object they hold). This means that a collection can be a very flexible way of holding other objects. Typically, collections are used as data structures; however, they can also be used as temporary holding places for groups of calculations, results, classes etc.

There are a number of terms associated with collections that are in general use (including within C#) that are worth being familiar with, including:

- Collections that do not support any modification operations (such as Add, Remove or Clear) are referred to as unmodifiable. Collections that are not unmodifiable are referred to modifiable.

- Collections that additionally guarantee that no change in the Collection will ever be observable via "query" operations (such as Size or Contains) are referred to as immutable. Collections that are not immutable are referred to as mutable.
- Lists that guarantee that their size will remain constant even though the elements may change are referred to as fixed-size. Lists that are not fixed-size are referred to as variable-size.

Some implementations may restrict what elements (or, in the case of Maps, keys and values) may be stored. Possible restrictions include requiring elements to:

- be of a particular type
- be comparable to other elements in the collection
- be non-null
- obey some arbitrary predicate

If a programmer attempts to add an element that violates an implementation's restrictions, then that collection should generate a exception.

A common design principle associated with Collections is that all general-purpose Collection implementation classes should provide two "standard" constructors: a void (no arguments) constructor, which creates an empty Collection, and a constructor with a single argument of type ICollection, which creates a new Collection with the same elements as its argument. In effect, the latter constructor allows the user to copy any Collection, producing an equivalent Collection of the desired implementation type.

17.5.2 IList

A list is an ordered collection of elements. That is, a list has a very specific sequence to the elements it contains. That order is determined by the order in which objects are added to the ordered collection/List instance. An implementation of the IList interface can hold any type of object. Implementations of the IList interface can be used in situations where the order in which the objects were added to the instance must be preserved. In general, IList implementations will allow duplicate objects (although any particular implementation may reject duplicates and thus throw a runtime exception). They may allow null objects, although again any particular implementation may decide to reject null values.

There is a range of order-related properties and methods which allow objects to be added and accessed with reference to the order in the List instance. For example, it is possible to access an object at a particular location, to find the position of an object or the last position of an object using the Item property and methods such as IndexOf(Object), IndexOf(Object, int) and Insert(Object). Note that, like arrays, Lists are zero-based, thus the first location in a List is position zero. In addition this interface inherits all the properties and methods defined in the ICollections interface.

To process Lists it would certainly be possible to iterate over the elements of the List using a standard for loop and the Item property. However, the time taken to access a particular object is linear with respect to its position in the list. It is therefore more efficient to use one of the Enumerator access methods provided by a List (see below). The methods defined in this interface (in addition to those inherited from Collection) are presented in Tables 17.4 and 17.5.

Table 17.4 Public instance properties of IList.

IsFixedSize	When implemented by a class, gets a value indicating whether the IList has a fixed size
IsReadOnly	When implemented by a class, gets a value indicating whether the IList is read-only
Item	When implemented by a class, gets or sets the element at the specified index. In C#, this property is the indexer for the IList class

Table 17.5 Public instance methods of IList.

Add	When implemented by a class, adds an item to the IList
Clear	When implemented by a class, removes all items from the IList
Contains	When implemented by a class, determines whether the IList contains a specific value
IndexOf	When implemented by a class, determines the index of a specific item in the IList
Insert	When implemented by a class, inserts an item to the IList at the specified position
Remove	When implemented by a class, removes the first occurrence of a specific object from the IList
RemoveAt	When implemented by a class, removes the IList item at the specified index

17.5.3 The IDictionary interface

An IDictionary object is an object that represents a set of associations between a key and a value. It is an abstract subclass of Object. It can be used as the basis of many other dictionary like classes (such as ListDictionary and ResultPropertyCollection) as well as the basis of a developers own dictionary like implementations. The elements in an IDictionary are unordered, but each has a definite name or *key*. Thus an object that implements the IDictionary interface can be regarded as an unordered collection of object values with external keys. Tables 17.6 and 17.7 list the properties and methods of the Idictionary interface.

IDictionary implementations fall into three categories: read-only, fixed-size and variable-size. A read-only IDictionary cannot be modified. A fixed-size IDictionary does not allow

Table 17.6 Public instance properties of IDictionary.

IsFixedSize	When implemented by a class, gets a value indicating whether the IDictionary has a fixed size
IsReadOnly	When implemented by a class, gets a value indicating whether the IDictionary is read-only
Item	When implemented by a class, gets or sets the element with the specified key. In C#, this property is the indexer for the IDictionary class
Keys	When implemented by a class, gets an ICollection containing the keys of the IDictionary
Values	When implemented by a class, gets an ICollection containing the values in the IDictionary

Table 17.7 Public instance methods of `IDictionary`.

Add	When implemented by a class, adds an entry with the provided key and value to the `IDictionary`
Clear	When implemented by a class, removes all entries from the `IDictionary`
Contains	When implemented by a class, determines whether the `IDictionary` contains an entry with the specified key
GetEnumerator	When implemented by a class, returns an `IDictionaryEnumerator` for the `IDictionary`
Remove	When implemented by a class, removes the entry with the specified key from the `IDictionary`

the addition or removal of elements, but it allows the modification of existing elements. A variable-size `IDictionary` allows the addition, removal and modification of elements.

17.6 Comparisons

In order to sort a collection, the objects within the collection either need to be `IComparable` or they need to be able to be compared using an `IComparer`. `IComparable` and `IComparer` are two interfaces which can be implemented so that collections of classes can be sorted.

- `public interface IComparable`. This interface defines the `CompareTo(Object)`. This method should allow one object to be compared to another. The result of this comparison is referred to as the natural ordering of the objects. The interface assumes that concrete implementations of this interface will implement the `int CompareTo(Object o)` method such that the method return negative if the receiver is less than the object passed to the method, zero if they are equal and positive if the receiver is greater. Note that this interface is defined in the `System` namespace.
- `public interface IComparer`. This interface defines a comparison function, which imposes a total ordering on some collection of `Objects`. Comparators can be passed to a sort method (such as `Array.Sort`) to allow precise control over the sort order. The `IComparer` interface specifies one method: the `int Compare(Object x, Object y);` method. This method assumes that the result returned is negative if first object is less than the second, zero if they are equal and a positive number if the first is greater than the second. The default implementation of this interface is the `Comparer` class.

17.7 Abstract Implementations

A set of abstract classes are provided which implement the Collections API interfaces. These classes are `CollectionBase`, `ReadOnlyCollectionBase` and `DictionaryBase`. They provide basic implementations for many of the methods specified in their associated interfaces (note the naming convention). We shall consider each of these classes below.

17.7.1 CollectionBase

The CollectionBase class provides a skeleton implementation of a Collection. This implementation represents what is often referred to as a bag or multiset. Abstractly, a Bag can be considered to be any collection of objects, which can be of any class; these objects are the elements of the Bag. It is a general placeholder for collections of objects. There is no order assumed. It is the most general form of collection available in C#. A CollectionBase type of collection is always modifiable. To create an un-modifiable collection see ReadOnlyCollectionBase.

If you are confused by this description of a bag, think of it as a shopping bag. At a supermarket, you pick objects up from the shelves and place them in your shopping bag. For example, you pick up a pint of milk, a box of cornflakes, a packet of biscuits, three bags of potato crisps, and a few bananas (see Figure 17.3).

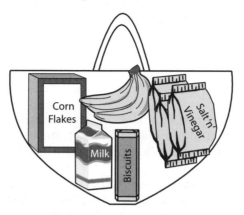

Figure 17.3 A shopping bag.

Each of the objects in the bag is a different type of thing, with different characteristics etc. There is no particular order to them: they will have moved about in the bag while you were shopping and while you brought them home. When you reach into the bag at home to remove the objects, the order in which they come out will not be predictable. If you think of a bag collection in these terms then you will not be far off the mark.

The CollectionBase class is provided to make it easier for implementers to create a strongly typed custom collection. Implementers should simply extend this base class instead of creating their own.

When subclassing the CollectionBase it is important to be aware of the On* methods. These are overridden (where appropriate) by subclasses to give a subclass some control over the inherited behaviour. The methods are:

- OnClear Performs additional custom processes when clearing the contents of the CollectionBase instance.
- OnClearComplete Performs additional custom processes after clearing the contents of the CollectionBase instance.
- OnInsert Performs additional custom processes before inserting a new element into the CollectionBase instance.

- `OnInsertComplete` Performs additional custom processes after inserting a new element into the `CollectionBase` instance.
- `OnRemove` Performs additional custom processes when removing an element from the `CollectionBase` instance.
- `OnRemoveComplete` Performs additional custom processes after removing an element from the `CollectionBase` instance.
- `OnSet` Performs additional custom processes before setting a value in the `CollectionBase` instance.
- `OnSetComplete` Performs additional custom processes after setting a value in the `CollectionBase` instance.
- `OnValidate` Performs additional custom processes when validating a value.

17.7.2 `ReadOnlyCollectionBase`

The abstract `ReadOnlyCollectionBase` can be used as the root of all non-mutable collections. This base class is provided to make it easier for implementers to create a strongly typed read-only custom collection. Implementers should simply extend this base class instead of creating their own. Members of this base class are protected and are intended to be used through a derived class only.

17.7.3 `DictionaryBase`

This abstract class provides a basic implementation for the `IDictionary` interface. This base class is provided to make it easier for implementers to create a strongly typed custom collection. Implementers should simply extend this base class instead of creating their own. Members of this base class are protected and are intended to be used through a derived class only.

17.8 Concrete Implementations

As stated earlier in this chapter, these classes are general-purpose implementations of the core collection interfaces. The classes are summarized in Table 17.8. All the classes are unsynchronized, as this greatly improves their performance. They can be synchronized by using a synchonizing

Table 17.8 Concrete collection classes.

`ArrayList`	Implements the IList interface using an array whose size is dynamically increased as required
`BitArray`	Manages a compact array of bit values, which are represented as Booleans, where true indicates that the bit is on (1) and false indicates the bit is off (0)
`Hashtable`	Represents a collection of associated keys and values that are organized based on the hash code of the key
`Queue`	Represents a first-in, first-out collection of objects
`SortedList`	Represents a collection of associated keys and values that are sorted by the keys and are accessible by key and by index
`Stack`	Represents a simple last-in-first-out collection of type Object

wrapper which can be obtained using the appropriate `Collection` class static method (for example `ArrayList.Synchronized(new ArrayList());`).

As the concrete collection classes implement the appropriate associated interfaces we will not list the complete set of methods for each class. Instead we will only look at the new classes and consider the inheritance relationships between the classes and what constructors they provide. In some cases an example of using that class is also provided.

17.8.1 `ArrayList`

An `ArrayList` is a resizeable list collection. Essentially this is an unsynchronized list of objects. It has an initial capacity (the `Capacity` property) and a current size (the `Count` property). The `Item` property allows access to a specific element in an `ArrayList`. There are also methods for adding and insert elements, for removing them and for testing for the presence of elements.

The `ArrayList` class provides the following constructors:

- `ArrayList()` constructs an array list with a capacity of 10.
- `ArrayList(ICollection)` constructs an `ArrayList` containing the elements of the specified `ICollection`.
- `ArrayList(int)` constructs an empty `ArrayList` with the specified initial capacity.

As an example, consider the following `ArrayListTest` class that uses an `ArrayList`. This class creates a simple list and adds four strings to it (one of which is a duplicate):

```
using System;
using System.Collections;

public class ArrayListTest {
  public static void Main() {
    ArrayList list = new ArrayList(10);
    Console.WriteLine(list.Capacity);
    list.Add("John");
    list.Add("Denise");
    list.Add("Phoebe");
    list.Add("John");

    foreach (String str in list) {
      Console.WriteLine("Item {0} ", str);
    }
  }
}
```

The results obtained from running this example are illustrated below:

```
C:\csharp\chapter17>ArrayListTest
10
Item John
```

```
Item Denise
Item Phoebe
Item John
```

Note that ArrayList allows duplicates.

17.8.2 BitArray

A BitArray is a class that holds collections of binary values (represented for example as true and false). It provides facilities for manipulating the binary values (via methods such as Not, Or and Xor). An example of creating a BitArray is presented below:

```csharp
using System;
using System.Collections;

public class BitArrayTest {

  public static void Main() {

    // Create and initialize several BitArrays.
    bool [] values = {true, false, true, false, false};
    BitArray bitArray = new BitArray( values );
    // Display the properties and values of the BitArrays.
    Console.WriteLine( "bitArray" );
    Console.WriteLine( "\tCount: {0}", bitArray.Count );
    Console.WriteLine( "\tLength: {0}", bitArray.Length );
    Console.WriteLine( "\tValues:" );
    IEnumerator enumerator = bitArray.GetEnumerator();
    while ( enumerator.MoveNext() ) {
      Console.Write( "\t{0}", enumerator.Current );
    }
    Console.WriteLine();
  }
}
```

The result of compiling and running this class is:

```
C:\csharp\chapter17>BitArrayTest
bitArray
    Count: 5
    Length: 5
    Values:
    True  False  True  False  False
```

17.8.3 The Hashtable class

This is a concrete class that implements the IDictionary interface. It implements a simple hash table, such as that found in some other languages (e.g. Java and Common LISP) or in libraries available for other languages (e.g. C). The great advantage of C# is that everyone has the same type of Hashtable. In Pascal or C, almost everyone has to invent their own or purchase a library to get the same functionality. This, of course, leads to problems of consistency between implementations.

You create an instance of a hash table using the Hashtable constructor with the parameters specified in Table 17.9.

Table 17.9 The Hashtable constructor parameters.

no parameters	Creates a new empty hash table with a default initial capacity and default load factor
int initialCapacity	Creates a new empty hash table of size initialCapacity and default load factor
int initialCapacity float loadFactor	Creates a new hash table of size initialCapacity and the specified load factor

The load factor is the point at which the hash table should grow and be rehashed. The load factor should be a real number between 0.0 and 1.0. When the number of entries is greater than the product of the load factor and the current capacity, the size of the hash table is increased and then it is rehashed. The new size of the hash table is twice the original size plus 1.

Here is a simple Hashtable example you might like to type in and try out:

```
using System;
using System.Collections;

public class HashtableTest {
  public static void Main () {
    Example e = new Example();
    e.example();
  }
}

class Example {
  public void example () {
    Hashtable x = new Hashtable();
    x.Add("jjh", "John");
    x.Add("pdh", "Phoebe");
    x.Add("dec", "Denise");
    x.Add("ajh", "Adam");
    Console.WriteLine("The value at dec is {0}", x["dec"]);
    Console.WriteLine("The value at jjh is {0}", x["jjh"]);
    Console.WriteLine("The whole contents of the hashtable is:");
    IDictionaryEnumerator e = x.GetEnumerator();
    Console.WriteLine( "\tKey\t.\tValue" );
```

```
    Console.WriteLine( "\t---\t.\t-----" );
    while ( e.MoveNext() ) {
      Console.WriteLine( "\t{0}\t:\t{1}", e.Key, e.Value );
    }
    Console.WriteLine();
  }
}
```

The result of compiling and executing this program is:

```
C:\csharp\chapter17>HashtableTest
The value at dec is Denise
The value at jjh is John
```

The whole contents of the hashtable are:

```
Key  .  Value
---  .  -----
pdh  :  Phoebe
ajh  :  Adam
dec  :  Denise
jjh  :  John
```

In addition to the methods defined in the IDictionary interface, Hashtable also provides the instance protocols shown in Tables 17.10 and 17.11. The Hashtable class assumes that the key objects in the table implement the hashCode and the Equals methods. In addition, for efficiency, the size of the hash table should be a prime number larger than the actual size required. For example, if the table is intended to hold 100 keys, then it should be created with a default size of 151.

Notice that, by default, all hash tables return an object (i.e. an instance of the class Object). It is therefore necessary to cast the returned object into the correct class. For example, if the values in a hash table are strings then it is necessary to execute the following code:

```
result = (String)aHashtable[aKey];
```

Table 17.10 Public instance properties of Hashtable.

Count	Gets the number of key-and-value pairs contained in the Hashtable
IsFixedSize	Gets a value indicating whether the Hashtable has a fixed size
IsReadOnly	Gets a value indicating whether the Hashtable is read-only
IsSynchronized	Gets a value indicating whether access to the Hashtable is synchronized (thread-safe)
Item	Gets or sets the value associated with the specified key. In C#, this property is the indexer for the Hashtable class
Keys	Gets an ICollection containing the keys in the Hashtable
SyncRoot	Gets an object that can be used to synchronize access to the Hashtable
Values	Gets an ICollection containing the values in the Hashtable

Table 17.11 Public instance methods of Hashtable.

Add	Adds an entry with the specified key and value into the Hashtable
Clear	Removes all entries from the Hashtable
Clone	Creates a shallow copy of the Hashtable
Contains	Determines whether the Hashtable contains a specific key
ContainsKey	Determines whether the Hashtable contains a specific key
ContainsValue	Determines whether the Hashtable contains a specific value
CopyTo	Copies the Hashtable entries to a one-dimensional Array instance at the specified index
Equals	Overloaded. Determines whether two Object instances are equal
GetEnumerator	Returns an enumerator that can iterate through the Hashtable
GetHashCode	Serves as a hash function for a particular type, suitable for use in hashing algorithms and data structures like a hash table
GetObjectData	Implements the ISerializable interface and returns the data needed to serialize the Hashtable
GetType	Gets the Type of the current instance
OnDeserialization	Implements the ISerializable interface and raises the deserialization event when the deserialization is complete
Remove	Removes the entry with the specified key from the Hashtable
ToString	Returns a String that represents the current Object

17.8.4 SortedList Collection Class

A SortedList internally maintains two arrays to store the entries to the list; that is, one array for the keys and another array for the associated values. An entry is a key-and-value pair. The capacity of a SortedList is the number of entries that the list can hold. As elements are added to a SortedList, the capacity is automatically increased as required through reallocation. The capacity can be decreased by calling TrimToSize or by setting the Capacity property explicitly.

The keys of a SortedList can be sorted either according to a specific IComparer implementation specified when the SortedList is instantiated or according to the IComparable implementation provided by the keys themselves. In either case, a SortedList does not allow duplicate keys.

Operations on a SortedList tend to be slower than operations on a Hashtable because of the sorting. However, the SortedList offers more flexibility by allowing access to the values either through the associated keys or through the indexes. A key cannot be a null reference, but a value can be a null value. Indexes in this collection are zero-based.

An example of the SortedList class in uses is presented below:

```
using System;
using System.Collections;

public class SortedListTest {

  public static void Main() {
```

```
      // Create and initialize a new SortedList.
      SortedList sortedList = new SortedList();
      sortedList.Add("John", "PhD");
      sortedList.Add("Denise", "PhD");
      sortedList.Add("Adam", "C.Eng");
      sortedList.Add("Phoebe", "MBA");

      // Display the properties and values of the SortedList.
      Console.WriteLine( "Count: {0}", sortedList.Count );
      Console.WriteLine( "Capacity: {0}", sortedList.Capacity );
      Console.WriteLine( "Keys and Values:" );

      IDictionaryEnumerator e = sortedList.GetEnumerator();
      Console.WriteLine( "\tKey\t.\tValue" );
      Console.WriteLine( "\t---\t.\t-----" );
      while ( e.MoveNext() ) {
        Console.WriteLine( "\t{0}\t:\t{1}", e.Key, e.Value );
      }
      Console.WriteLine();
   }
}
```

The result of compiling and running this example is presented below:

```
C:\csharp\chapter16>SortedListTest
Count:  4
Capacity: 16
Keys and Values:
  Key     . Value
  ---     . -----
  Adam    : C.Eng
  Denise  : PhD
  John    : PhD
  Phoebe  : MBA
```

Note that the SortedList has sorted the entries in the list into key order (i.e. Adam is first and Phoebe is last).

17.8.5 The Queue Class

A Queue is a first in, first out (FIFO) type of collection. That is, elements can be added to a queue and removed from the queue in the same order. The primary methods on a Queue are the Enqueue method for adding an object to the queue, Dequeue for removing an object from the queue, and Peek (for examining the object at the front of the queue). For example:

```csharp
using System;
using System.Collections;

public class QueueTest {

  public static void Main() {

    // Create and initialize a new Queue.
    Queue queue = new Queue();
    queue.Enqueue("John");
    queue.Enqueue("Denise");
    queue.Enqueue("Phoebe");
    queue.Enqueue("Adam");

    // Display the properties and values of the Queue.
    Console.WriteLine( "Count: {0}", queue.Count );
    Console.WriteLine( "Values: " );

    Console.WriteLine( "{0}", queue.Dequeue() );
    Console.WriteLine( "{0}", queue.Dequeue() );
    Console.WriteLine( "{0}", queue.Dequeue() );
    Console.WriteLine( "{0}", queue.Dequeue() );
  }
}
```

The result of compiling and running this class is:

```
C:\csharp\chapter16>QueueTest
Count:  4
Values:
John
Denise
Phoebe
Adam
```

17.8.6 The Stack Class

The class Stack, provides a basic stack object with the required last in, first out behaviour (LIFO). It provides three constructors that can take zero parameters, an ICollection (on which the stack will be based) and an int for its initial size. The stack can also grow as required. The main methods on a Stack are Push (to add objects to a stack) and Pop (to remove objects from a stack). The following program illustrates the use of the Stack class:

```csharp
using System;
using System.Collections;
```

```
public class StackTest {

   public static void Main() {

      // Create and initialize a new Queue.
      Stack stack = new Stack();
      stack.Push("John");
      stack.Push("Denise");
      stack.Push("Phoebe");
      stack.Push("Adam");

      // Display the properties and values of the Queue.
      Console.WriteLine( "Count: {0}", stack.Count );
      Console.WriteLine( "Values: " );

      Console.WriteLine( "{0}", stack.Pop() );
      Console.WriteLine( "{0}", stack.Pop() );
      Console.WriteLine( "{0}", stack.Pop() );
      Console.WriteLine( "{0}", stack.Pop() );
   }
}
```

The result of compiling and running this class is:

```
C:\csharp\chapter16>StackTest
Count:  4
Values:
Adam
Phoebe
Denise
John
```

17.9 The System.Collections.Specialized namespace

This namespace provides some additional collection classes. These are listed in Table 17.12. These are specific versions of the general collection classes that are is some way specialized. For example, the ListDictionary class is an efficient dictionary class for small sets of key–value pairs.

17.10 Enumeration

Any object that is an instance of a class that implements the IEnumerable interface produces a list of the elements it contains. You can access the list elements one at a time. The classes Hashtable, BitArray and SortedList (from the above examples) all illustrate the use of enumerators. You can

Table 17.12 Specialized collections.

Class	Description
CollectionsUtil	Provides some general utilities, such as creating case-insensitive sorted lists
ListDictionary	This is a simple implementation of IDictionary using a singly linked list. This will be smaller and faster than a Hashtable if the number of elements is 10 or less. This should not be used if performance is important for large numbers of elements
StringCollection	Represents a collection of strings
StringDictionary	Implements a Hashtable with the key strongly typed to be a string rather than an object

access the elements contained in instances of any class that implements the IEnumerable interface iteratively. This is an extremely useful feature, as any programmer who has used Java, Lisp, Smalltalk or POP11 knows.

The IEnumerable interface defines a single method, GetEnumerator(), that the implementing class must provide. The GetEnumerator() method obtains an enumerator for an object's contents. An Enumerator is a class that implements the IEnumerator interface. The details of this interface are presented in Tables 17.13 and 17.14.

Table 17.13 IEnumerator properties.

Current	Gets the current element in the collection

Table 17.14 IEnumerator instance methods.

MoveNext	Advances the enumerator to the next element of the collection
Reset	Sets the enumerator to its initial position, which is before the first element in the collection

The enumerator obtained from an enumerable collection can then be used to access the elements in the collection in turn. The MoveNext() method determines whether any further elements remain in the enumeration and moves the enumerator forward to the next element in the enumeration. The Current property, then returns the current element from the list.

You can use such an enumeration to apply the same message to all elements of a ArrayList (or collection). For example, to apply the printself message to all elements of a ArrayList, we could write:

```
IEnumerator e = list.GetEnumerator() ;
while (e.MoveNext()) {
  temp = e.Current();
  temp.printself();
}
```

17.11 Iteration over Dictionaries

Dictionaries are slightly different from lists. This is because they contain key–value pairs (essentially two lists of objects). When you enumerate over the elements of a dictionary you obtain references to both the key and the value. For example, in the Hashtable example we wrote:

```
IDictionaryEnumerator e = x.GetEnumerator();
while ( e.MoveNext() ) {
    Console.WriteLine( "\t{0}\t:\t{1}", e.Key, e.Value );
}
```

Notice that in the above example what was returned from the hash table was an IDictionaryEnumerator (implementing) class. This variation on an enumerator has properties Key and Value rather than just the current value of the list-based enumerator.

17.12 Summary

It is likely that, just as in Smalltalk and Java, these classes will become the most used classes in C#. The various Collections API interfaces and classes will form the basis of the data structures you build and will be the cornerstone of most of your implementations. For those of you coming from a Lisp-style language these concepts won't have seemed too strange. However, those of you coming from languages such as C, Pascal or Ada may well have found the idea of a collection and a set quite bizarre. Stick with them, try them out, implement some simple programs using them and you will soon find that they are easy to use and extremely useful. You will very quickly come to wonder why every language doesn't have the same facilities!

Chapter 18

An Object-Oriented Organizer

18.1 Introduction

This chapter presents a detailed example application constructed using the data structure classes. The application is intended as an electronic personal organizer. It contains an address book, a diary (or appointments section) and a section for notes. The remainder of this chapter describes one way of implementing such an organizer. At the end of the chapter, there is a programming exercise.

18.2 The Organizer Class

This application involves more than one class and has a more complex architecture than anything you have seen so far (see Figure 18.1). It also illustrates another important concept in object orientation, that of an object within an object. These are often referred to as *part-of* hierarchies, i.e. one object is *part-of* another. This should not be confused with the class hierarchy, which is a *kind-of* hierarchy.

An instance of the Organizer class contains three other objects. These objects are held in the instance variables addressBook, appointments and notes. The instances within

Figure 18.1 The structure of an Organizer object.

addressBook and appointments are Hashtable objects, while the notes instance variable holds an ArrayList object.

18.3 The Class Definition

The purpose of the Organizer class is to provide some of the facilities of a personal organizer. The class definition is illustrated below. We shall build this definition up throughout the chapter:

```
using System;

using System.Collections;

public class Organizer {
  // Instance variable definitions
  private Hashtable addressBook = new Hashtable();
  private Hashtable appointments = new Hashtable();
  private ArrayList notes = new ArrayList();
  ...
  // all methods go here
  ...
}
```

We have defined the class and its instance variables. Notice that we have made the instance variables private. This ensures that objects outside the Organizer class cannot access the variables directly; they must access the information via specified interfaces. Also notice that we have imported the System.Collections namespace, as we are using both the Hashtable and ArrayList classes. In addition, we have initialized the instance variables so that they hold the appropriate objects.

18.4 The Updating Protocol

Now we define the methods for the *updating* protocol. That is, we define all the methods associated with adding new information to the organizer.

The addNote method adds a new note to the notes instance variable. It is an extremely simple method that requires no additional explanation:

```
public void AddNote(String aNote) {
  notes.Add(aNote);
}
```

The AddAddress method adds a new address to the addressBook. It first checks to see if the name provided is already in the address book. If it is, an error message is generated; otherwise the name and address are added to the book. Notice that we use another instance method addressFor (part of the accessing protocol) to determine whether the addressee is already present; if not, it returns the result null (you can use the null value instead of any object, in this case a string). The AddAddress method is illustrated below:

```
public void AddAddress(String name, String location) {
  String alreadyThere;
  alreadyThere = AddressFor(name);
  if (alreadyThere == null)
  {
    addressBook.Add(name, location);
    Console.WriteLine("Added " + name +
        " to the address book");
  }
  else
  {
    Console.WriteLine("An entry for " + name +
        " is already present");
  }
}
```

The method for adding a new appointment is essentially the same as the AddAddress method:

```
public void NewAppointment(String anAppointment, String aDate) {
  String alreadyThere;
  alreadyThere = AppointmentFor(aDate);
  if (alreadyThere == null) {
    appointments.Add(aDate, anAppointment);
    Console.WriteLine("Added " + anAppointment +
        " for " + aDate);
  }
  else
  {
    Console.WriteLine("An entry for " + aDate + " is already present");
  }
}
```

18.5 The Accessing Protocol

Next, we define the methods associated with obtaining information from the organizer. That is, we define all the methods used to access information within the instance variables.

The AddressFor method retrieves an address from the address book. Although the return type of the method is String, it can also return a null value. Also, notice that we must cast the result obtained from the hash table addressBook to a String:

```csharp
public String AddressFor(String name) {
  String address;
  address = (String) addressBook[name];
  if (address == null)
    Console.WriteLine("No address for " + name);
  return address;
}
```

The `AddressFor` method retrieves an appointment from the appointments instance variable. It is essentially the same as the `AddressFor` method:

```csharp
public String AppointmentFor(String aDate) {
  String appointment;
  appointment = (String) appointments[aDate];
  if (appointment == null)
    Console.WriteLine("No appointment for " + aDate);
  return appointment;
}
```

Finally, the `PrintNotes` method displays all the notes which have been made in the organizer:

```csharp
public void PrintNotes() {
  Console.WriteLine("\n\t Notes");
  Console.WriteLine("\t-------\n");
  foreach (String item in notes) {
    Console.WriteLine(item);
  }
}
```

The above method uses special characters, known as escape characters, which help to control the printed text. The characters \t and \n indicate a tab and a line feed, respectively.

18.6 The `Main` Method

Once you have defined all the methods, you are ready to use your organizer. The `Organizer` class is not intended as an application in its own right. Instead it is intended to be used with other classes as part of a larger application. To mimic this behaviour we have created a `Test` class that holds the `Main` method. The main method in `Test` is used to exercise the `Organizer` class to illustrate typical behaviour:

```csharp
public class Test {
  public static void Main() {
    Organizer organizer = new Organizer();
    Console.WriteLine("Adding test information\n");
```

```
organizer.AddAddress("John", "Room 47");
organizer.AddAddress("Denise", "Room 42");
organizer.NewAppointment("Meeting with Denise", "10/10/01");
organizer.AddNote("I must do all my work");
Console.WriteLine("\nNow performing tests\n");
Console.WriteLine("Johns address is " + organizer.AddressFor("John"));
Console.WriteLine("Appointments for 10/10/01 are "
    + organizer.AppointmentFor("10/10/01"));
organizer.PrintNotes();
}
}
```

This method shows how the organizer can be used. It creates a new organizer and adds some entries to it (see Figure 18.2).

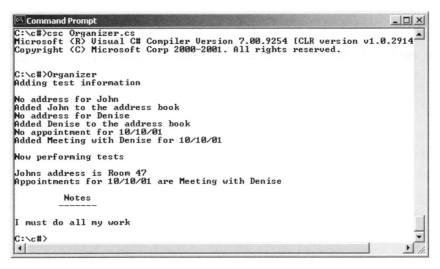

Figure 18.2 Running the organizer as an application.

Try your organizer out in a similar way. Extend its functionality. For example, provide a way of deleting an address or replacing it with a new one.

18.7 The Full Listing

The complete listing for the Organizer class is presented below:

```
using System;
using System.Collections;

public class Organizer {
```

```
// Instance variable definitions
private Hashtable addressBook = new Hashtable();
private Hashtable appointments = new Hashtable();
private ArrayList notes = new ArrayList();

public void AddNote(String aNote) {
  notes.Add(aNote);
}

public void PrintNotes() {
  Console.WriteLine("\n\t Notes");
  Console.WriteLine("\t-------\n");
  foreach (String item in notes) {
    Console.WriteLine(item);
  }
}

public void AddAddress(String name, String location) {
  String alreadyThere;
  alreadyThere = AddressFor(name);
  if (alreadyThere == null)
  {
    addressBook.Add(name, location);
    Console.WriteLine("Added " + name +
        " to the address book");
  }
  else
  {
    Console.WriteLine("An entry for " + name + " is already present");
  }
}

public String AddressFor(String name) {
  String address;
  address = (String) addressBook[name];
  if (address == null)
    Console.WriteLine("No address for " + name);
  return address;
}

public void NewAppointment(String anAppointment, String aDate) {
  String alreadyThere;
  alreadyThere = AppointmentFor(aDate);
  if (alreadyThere == null) {
    appointments.Add(aDate, anAppointment);
    Console.WriteLine("Added " + anAppointment + " for " + aDate);
```

```
      }
      else
      {
        Console.WriteLine("An entry for " + aDate + " is already present");
      }
    }

    public String AppointmentFor(String aDate) {
      String appointment;
      appointment = (String) appointments[aDate];
      if (appointment == null)
        Console.WriteLine("No appointment for " + aDate);
      return appointment;
    }
  }

  public class Test {
    public static void Main() {
      Organizer organizer = new Organizer();
        Console.WriteLine("Adding test information\n");
        organizer.AddAddress("John", "Room 47");
        organizer.AddAddress("Denise", "Room 42");
        organizer.NewAppointment("Meeting with Denise", "10/10/01");
        organizer.AddNote("I must do all my work");
        Console.WriteLine("\nNow performing tests\n");
        Console.WriteLine("Johns address is " + organizer.AddressFor("John"));
        Console.WriteLine("Appointments for 10/10/01 are "
            + organizer.AppointmentFor("10/10/01"));
      organizer.PrintNotes();
    }
  }
```

18.8 Exercise – the Financial Manager Project

As an exercise, try implementing a Financial Manager application. This application should allow the user to:

1. Add a deposit to a current account for a specified amount.
2. Make a payment (withdrawal) from a current account for a specified amount.
3. Get the current balance of a current account.
4. Print a statement of all payments and deposits made, in the order in which they happened, to the transcript.

Create a subclass of Object (for example, FinancialManager) to hold the current balance and handle deposits and withdrawals. You should be able to specify the user's name and initial balance to the constructor. Use an ArrayList class to hold the statement. Create a test class with a main method that resembles the following code:

```csharp
public class Test {
  public static void Main () {
    FinancialManager fm = new FinancialManager("John", 0.0);
    fm.Deposit(25.00);
    fm.Withdraw(12.00);
    fm.Deposit(10.00);
    fm.Deposit(5.00);
    fm.Withdraw(8.00);
    Console.WriteLine("The current balance is {0}",
            fm.balance());
    fm.Statement();
  }
}
```

The sample output from this Test class might look like:

```
The current balance is 20.0
Statement:
Deposit   0.0
Deposit   25.0
Withdraw  12.0
Deposit   10.0
Deposit   5.0
Withdraw  8.0
```

Part 4

Further C#

Chapter 19

Control and Iteration

19.1 Introduction

This chapter introduces control and iteration in C#. In C#, as in many other languages, the mainstay of the control and iteration processes are the `if` and `switch` statements and the `for` and `while` loops.

19.2 Control Structures

19.2.1 The `if` Statement

The basic format of an `if` statement in C# is the same as that in C. A test is performed and, depending on the result of the test, a statement is executed. A set of statements to be executed can be grouped together in curly brackets: {}. For example, we can write:

```
if (a == 5)
    Console.WriteLine ("true")
else
    Console.WriteLine ("false");
```

or we can write:

```
if (a == 5) {
    Console.Write("a = 5");
    Console.WriteLine("The answer is therefore true");
}
else {
    Console.Write("a != 5");
    Console.WriteLine("The answer is therefore false");
}
```

Of course, the if statement need not include the optional else construct:

```
if (a == 5) {
  Console.Write("a = 5");
  Console.WriteLine("The answer is therefore true");
}
```

You must have a Boolean (type bool) in a condition expression, so you cannot make the same equality mistake as in C. The following code always generates a compile-time error:

```
if (a = 1) {
  ...
}
```

Unfortunately, assigning a bool to a boolean variable results in a bool (all expressions return a result) and thus the following code is legal, but does not result in the intended behaviour (the string "Hello" is always printed on the console):

```
public class Test {
  public static void Main () {
    boolean a = false;
    if (a = true)
      Console.WriteLine("Hello");
  }
}
```

You can construct nested if statements, as in other languages:

```
if (count < 100)
  if (index < 10)
    {...}
  else
    {...}
else
  {...}
```

However, it is easy to get confused. C# does not provide an explicit if-then-elseif-else type of structure. In some languages, including C#, you can write:

```
if (n < 10)
  print ("less than 10");
else if (n < 100)
  print ("greater than 10 but less than 100");
else if (n < 1000)
  print ("greater than 100 but less then 1000");
else
  print ("greater than 1000");
```

This code is intended to be read as laid out above. However, if we write it in C#, it should be laid out as below:

```
if (n < 10)
  print ("less than 10");
else if (n < 100)
    print ("greater than 10 but less than 100");
  else if (n < 1000)
      print ("> than 100 but < 1000");
    else
        print ("> than 1000");
```

This code clearly has a very different meaning (although it may have the same effect). This can lead to the infamous "dangling else" problem. Another solution is the switch statement. However, as you will see, the switch statement has significant limitations.

19.2.2 The Conditional Operator

C# has inherited the conditional operator from C. This has both good and bad points. It is good because it is a very concise and efficient way of performing a test and carrying out one of two operations. It is bad because its terse nature is not clear to non-C programmers. However, it is a part of the language and all C# programmers must understand it.

The C# conditional operator has three operands which are separated by two symbols in the following format:

```
boolean expression ? true expression : false expression
```

The boolean expression determines whether the true or false expression is evaluated. For example, the following expression prints the maximum of two numbers:

```
Console.WriteLine(m >= n ? m : n);
```

The conditional operator, unlike an if statement, returns a value. It can therefore be used in an assignment statement. For example, we can assign the larger of two numbers to a third variable:

```
x = (m >= n) ? m : n;
```

Notice that this is becoming less readable (unless you are an experienced C programmer, in which case you would argue that it is obvious!).

19.2.3 The switch Statement

The conditional operator is not the only control statement that C# inherits from C; it also inherits the (flawed) C switch statement. This is a multi-way selection statement (similar to the case or select statement of some other programming languages). The structure of the switch statement is basically:

```
switch (expression) {
  case label1 :
    ...
    break;
  case label2 :
    ...
    break;
  ...
  default: ...
}
```

The expression returns an integer value and the case labels represent the possible values produced by the expression. Each case label is followed by one or more statements that are executed until a break, goto or return statement is encountered. A switch statement may include a default statement that is executed if none of the case labels matches the integer in the expression.

The switch statement has two major flaws. The first flaw is the need to "break" out of each case block. This is a major problem that has led to many software bugs. For example, in December 1989 the long-distance telephone service in the USA was disrupted by a software problem in the AT&T electronic switching systems. The problem was allegedly traced to the misuse of a break statement in a C program. The inclusion of such a feature has serious implications for the construction of high integrity software. To alleviate this problem (at least to some extent) C# requires that there is either a break at the end of every case block (i.e. a case statement with code in) or a goto another case label in the switch statement. For example:

```
using System;

public class Test {

  public static void Main () {
    int i = 10;
    switch (i) {
    case 1 :
    case 5 :
      Console.WriteLine("1 and 5");
      break;
    case 10 :
      Console.WriteLine("10");
      goto case 20;
    case 20 :
      Console.WriteLine("20");
      break;
    default:
      Console.WriteLine("Default");
      break;
    }
  }
}
```

The result of compiling and running this program is:

```
C:\c#>Test
10
20
```

This is an improvement on the switch statements found in language such as C, C++ and Java.

The second major flaw is the inability of the switch statement to deal with anything other than integer comparisons (i.e. types such as short, int, long) and strings. Note that this means you cannot use double or any type of object in such a comparison. However, you can write:

```
using System;

public class StringTest {

  public static void Main () {
    String name = "John";
      switch (name) {
      case "John" :
        Console.WriteLine("Hello John");
        break;
      case "Denise" :
        Console.WriteLine("Hello Denise");
        break;
      case "Adam" :
        Console.WriteLine("Hello Adam");
        break;
      default:
        Console.WriteLine("Hello Phoebe");
        break;
    }
  }
}
```

The result of compiling and running this code is:

```
C:\c#>StringTest
Hello John
```

19.3 Iteration

Iteration in C# is accomplished using the for, while and do-while statements. Just like their counterparts in other languages, these statements repeat a sequence of instructions a given number of times.

19.3.1 for Loops

A for loop in C# is very similar to a for loop in C. It is used to step a variable through a series of values until a given test is false. Many languages have a very simple for loop, for example:

```
for i = 1 to 10 do
   ...
endfor;
```

In this construct, you do not need to specify the end condition, nor how the variable i is incremented; in C#, you must specify both:

```
for (initial-expression; test; increment-expression)
   statement
```

This has the disadvantage of making the for construct more complicated, but it does offer a great deal of control. One point to note with this for loop is that the boolean test expression indicates the condition that must hold while the loop is repeated. That is, it is a *while true* loop, rather than an *until true* loop. An example for loop is presented below:

```
for (int n = 1; n <= 10; n = n + 1)
   Console.WriteLine(n);
```

This loop assigns n the initial value 1. While n <= 10, it executes the WriteLine method and increments the value of n. We can repeat more than one statement if we enclose them in curly brackets: { }. Note that n is what would be described as a loop variable and only has scope within the loop. This is because we declared it within the initial-expression part of the for loop. If we wanted the scope of the variable to be greater than the loop we could have defined it outside the loop, for example:

```
using System;

class LoopTest {

   public static void Main() {
      int i;
      for (i = 1; i <= 4; i ++) {
         Console.WriteLine(i);
      }
      Console.WriteLine("The final value of i = " + i);
   }
}
```

Thus the variable i is still available after the loop has completed. The result of running this program is (note the final value of i):

```
C:\c#>LoopTest
1
2
3
4
The final value of i = 5
```

As in C, you can use a comma-delimited list to initialize and increment (decrement) several variables in a for loop. The expressions separated by commas are evaluated from left to right:

```
using System;

class LoopTest2 {

  public static void Main() {
    for (int i = 0, j = 10; i < 10; i++, j--) {
      Console.WriteLine (i + " : " + j);
    }
  }
}
```

The result of executing this program is:

```
C:\c#>LoopTest2
0 : 10
1 : 9
2 : 8
3 : 7
4 : 6
5 : 5
6 : 4
7 : 3
8 : 2
9 : 1
```

19.3.2 while Loops

The while loop exists in almost all programming languages. In most cases, it has a basic form such as:

```
while (test expression)
  statement
```

This is also true for C#. The while expression controls the execution of one or more statements. If more than one statement is to be executed then the statements must be enclosed in curly brackets {}:

```
n = 1;
while (n <= 10) {
  Console.WriteLine(n);
  n++;
}
```

The above loop tests to see if the value of n is less than or equal to 10, and then prints the current value of n before incrementing it by one. This is repeated until the test expression returns false (i.e. $n > 11$).

You must assign n an initial value before the condition expression. If you do not provide an initial value for n, it defaults to null and the comparison with a numeric value raises an exception.

19.3.3 do Loops

In some cases, we want to execute the body of statements at least once; you can accomplish this with the do loop construct:

```
do
  statement
while (test expression);
```

This loop is guaranteed to execute at least once, as the test is only performed after the statement has been evaluated. As with the while loop, the do loop repeats until the condition is false. You can repeat more than one statement by bracketing a series of statements into a block using curly brackets {}:

```
n = 10;
do {
  Console.WriteLine(n);
  n--;
} while (n > 0);
```

The above do loop prints the numbers from 10 down to 1 and terminates when $n = 0$.

19.3.4 foreach

In many cases, what is needed during a loop is the ability to get each element in an array or a collection in turn and then perform some operation on them. This can certainly be done with the standard for loop; however, C# provides a more elegant way of doing exactly this: the foreach statement. For example, we could write the following using a for loop:

```
using System;
using System.Collections;

public class PeopleTest1 {
```

```
public static void Main() {
  ArrayList list = new ArrayList();
  list.Add("John");
  list.Add("Denise");
  list.Add("Phoebe");
  list.Add("Adam");
  for (int i=0; i<list.Count; i++) {
    String p = (String)list[i];
    Console.WriteLine(p);
  }
}
}
```

Notice that we need to check the number of elements in the list using the Count property and to convert the element obtained from the list to that of type String (by default the type will be marked as Object). The result of running this program is:

```
C:\c#>PeopleTest1
John
Denise
Phoebe
Adam
```

However, using the foreach statement we could have written:

```
using System;
using System.Collections;

public class PeopleTest2 {

  public static void Main() {
    ArrayList list = new ArrayList();
    list.Add("John");
    list.Add("Denise");
    list.Add("Phoebe");
    list.Add("Adam");
    foreach (String p in list) {
      Console.WriteLine(p);
    }
  }
}
```

Notice that I no longer need to check for how many items are in the list; nor do I need to perform any explicit type casting (it is done for me). The end result of the two programs is identical. foreach can also be used with arrays. However, the second example is more elegant!

19.3.5 break and continue

There are two statements that can be used to refine the behaviour of the iteration constructs for, while and do. These statements are break and continue. The effect of break is to break out of a loop, while the effect of continue is to jump to the next iteration of the loop. For example, in the following code when the loop variable i has the value 4 the continue statement is executed. This will cause the current iteration of the loop to be terminated immediately and the next to start:

```csharp
using System;
class LoopTest3 {
  public static void Main() {
    for (int i = 1; i <= 5; i ++) {
      if (i == 4) {
        continue;
      }
      Console.WriteLine(i);
    }
  }
}
```

The effect of this is that the number 4 will not be printed:

```
C:\c#>LoopTest3
1
2
3
5
```

If we changed the continue to a break then the loop would terminate at that point in time. Thus the output would be:

```
C:\c#>LoopTest3
1
2
3
```

19.3.6 The goto Statement

C# also includes a goto statement. This can be used to jump the execution of the code to a labelled line elsewhere in the program. For example:

```csharp
using System;

class LoopTest4 {

  public static void Main() {
```

```
    for (int j=0; j< 5; j++) {
      for (int i = 1; i <= 5; i ++) {
        if (i == 4) {
          goto outer;
        }
        Console.WriteLine(j + " " + i);
      }
    }
    outer : Console.WriteLine("The end");
  }
}
```

The result of running this program is that when the loop variable i has the value 4, then the goto statement will jump the thread of execution out of the nested loops to the line labelled outer. The result of running this program is therefore:

```
C:\c#>LoopTest4
0 1
0 2
0 3
The end
```

However, the goto statement has been identified as being of considerable harm if not used carefully. Therefore C# prohibits some of the most dangerous aspects of goto statements. A goto cannot be used to jump into a statement block for example. In fact, the only places where their use is recommended is to jump out of nested loops (as above) or within the switch statement.

19.3.7 An Example of Loops

As a concrete example of the for and while loops, consider the following class. It possesses a method which prints numbers from 0 to 1 less than the MaxValue static variable:

```
using System;

public class Counter {
  // A static variable
  public static int MaxValue = 10;

  public static void Main () {
    Counter c = new Counter();
    c.count();
  }

  public void count() {
    int i;
    Console.WriteLine("----- For -------");
```

```
    for (i = 0; i < MaxValue; ++i) {
      Console.Write(" " + i);
    }
    Console.WriteLine(" ");
    Console.WriteLine("----- While -------");
    i = 0;
    while (i < MaxValue) {
      Console.Write(" " + i);
      ++i;
    }
    Console.WriteLine(" ");
    Console.WriteLine("-------------------");
  }
}
```

The result of running this application should be:

```
C:\c#>Counter
----- For -------
0 1 2 3 4 5 6 7 8 9
----- While -------
0 1 2 3 4 5 6 7 8 9
-------------------
```

19.4 Recursion

Recursion is a very powerful programming idiom found in many languages. C# is no exception. The following class illustrates how to use recursion to generate the factorial of a number:

```
using System;

public class Factorial {

  public static void Main () {
    Factorial f = new Factorial();
    Console.WriteLine(f.factorial(5));
  }

  public int factorial (int aNumber) {
    Console.WriteLine(aNumber);
    if (aNumber == 1)return 1;
    else return aNumber + factorial(--aNumber);
  }
}
```

The result of running this application is illustrated in Figure 19.1.

Figure 19.1 Running the factorial application.

19.5 Summary

You have now learned the basics of the language, including conditional and iteration statements. You are now ready to consider a much larger application in C#.

Chapter 20

Attributes and Versioning

20.1 Introduction

In this chapter we consider C# attributes and the use of versioning within classes and inheritance.

20.2 Attributes

20.2.1 What Are Attributes?

Attributes are nothing more than simple annotations that are placed on elements of source code (such as classes, class and instance variables, and methods). These annotations can be used by development tools, browsers, the run-time environment, debuggers etc. to aid them in their tasks. Attributes can also be used to convey important information to designers and developers. As such, attributes are simple lightweight devices for passing information.

The actual information stored in the attribute is held with metadata about the element being annotated. This allows it to be retrieved at run-time as well as by other tools. The process that allows this information to be obtained is called reflection.

20.2.2 Using Attributes

To use an attribute, all that you need do is to place the attribute in square brackets before the element to be annotated. For example, there is an attribute to indicate whether a class should be serializable or not (essentially whether an object can be saved to a file or not). To mark a class as serializable we would use the serializable attribute on the whole class thus:

```
[Serializable]
public class Family
{
  ... content of class ...
}
```

20.2.3 Conditional Attributes

C# provides a special type of attribute called a conditional attribute that can be used to control what methods are called. For example it can be used to turn on certain methods for debugging purposes. For example:

```
[Conditional("DEBUG")]
```

20.2.4 User-Defined Attributes

Within a particular development project you might wish to define your own attributes. These could be used by project-specific tools or to ensure consistency with project-specific guidelines etc. To do this an attribute class can be defined.

An attribute class is a class that defines the name of the attribute, how the attribute is instantiated and any information that should be stored with the attribute. An attribute class must extend the class System.Attribute and by convention should be named <name>Attribute.

For example, consider the following attribute class. This class is intended to define an attribute that can be used to link a C# class to the Rose model containing the design of that class. This could for example, allow a browser tool to take the user straight to the design model of the implemented C# class:

```csharp
using System;

public class DesignLinkAttribute : System.Attribute
{
  private String url;
  public DesignLinkAttribute(String url)
  {
    this.url = url;
  }
  public String URL
  {
    get
    {
      return url;
    }
    set
    {
      url = value;
    }
  }
}
```

To use this new attribute we would need to use the attribute notation (square brackets). Inside the square brackets we would need to put the attribute name and any parameters to be passed to it. In this case the attribute name is DesignLink (note that the Attribute part has been dropped) and the parameter is the location of the Rose model. For example:

```
[DesignLink("c:/rose/easel.dml")]
class Easel
{
}
```

One problem with the attribute we have defined is that it could be used anywhere. However, we may only want it to be applied to classes and possibly interfaces. To limit its use we should assign an attribute to the attribute class definition! This is the AttributeUsage attribute (defined by the class AttributeUsageAttribute in the System namespace). This attribute can be used to limit the attribute being defined to one or more elements of a C# program. It takes as a parameter AttributeTarget values (defined by the enumeration AttributeTargets in the System namespace). For example to limit our attribute to be applicable only to classes we could write:

```
[AttributeUsage(AttributeTargets.Class)]
```

In fact the options provided by the AttributeTargets enumeration are:

All	Attribute can be applied to any element
Assembly	Attribute can be applied to an assembly
Class	Attribute can be applied to a class.
Constructor	Attribute can be applied to a constructor
Delegate	Attribute can be applied to a delegate
Enum	Attribute can be applied to an enumeration
Event	Attribute can be applied to an event
Field	Attribute can be applied to a field
Interface	Attribute can be applied to an interface
Method	Attribute can be applied to a method
Module	Attribute can be applied to a module
Parameter	Attribute can be applied to a parameter
Property	Attribute can be applied to a property
ReturnValue	Attribute can be applied to a Return value
Struct	Attribute can be applied to a value type

Thus if we wanted to restrict our attribute to interfaces we could also write:

```
[AttributeUsage(AttributeTargets.Interface)]
```

If we wish to allow our attribute to be used with classes, interfaces and structs we could *or* the attribute target values thus:

```
[AttributeUsage(AttributeTargets.Class | AttributeTargets.Interface |
AttributeTargets.Struct)]
```

Note that, just like with normal classes, multiple constructors could be defined to allow the attribute to be created with different amounts of information.

20.2.5 Attribute Parameters

Unlike ordinary classes, there are significant restrictions on the types that you can use with attributes. Attribute parameters can only be of the following types:

- `String`
- `bool`, `byte`, `char`, `double`, `float`, `short`, `int`, `long`
- `Object`
- `System.Type`
- An enumeration that has public accessibility (not nested inside a non-public element)
- A one-dimensional array of one of the above

20.3 Versioning

As classes evolve over time, compatibility between classes can become an issue. In general, it is a good idea to take care when modifying classes that are heavily used or have subclasses, as any changes (at least to their "protocol") can have major impacts elsewhere within a project.

Having said that, software can last a long time. During this time requirements, constraints and designs can change. For example, a C# framework developed last year for handling information on books, articles etc. for a publishing house might well not be sufficient for the company's needs next year. One problem with such frameworks is that ideally you want to take into account all possible uses and extensions of that framework. However, today we might not know what those uses and extensions are. Indeed, we might not even be the ones who are using the frameworks, classes and interfaces.

In many cases this is not a problem. However, one of the features of a framework in particular is that some details may be left abstract or may be virtual. The expectation is that some detail of the class or virtual method will be supplied by the using class at a later date.

This is of course standard practice, and quite normal. Over time we might decide that we need additional methods in our framework. However, we may have no knowledge of how the framework has been used or indeed what classes and methods have been provided by subclasses of classes in our framework.

If, when we extend our framework (for example create version 2.0 of our framework), we happen to define a method in our framework which is already defined in a subclass of our framework, then when users recompile the code they will get a message stating that they have tried to override a non-virtual method. They will then get a compiler error. They will therefore need to change the name of their method. Thus they would avoid their code replacing the code in the framework and causing the framework to fail – although for the users of the framework it might be annoying, as they would have to find every reference to this method in their code and change it to the new name!

What happens if the method they have defined was specified as virtual (i.e. a subclass could override it) and the method defined in the framework was also virtual? For example, the framework class Book now defines a virtual method Publish():

```
using System;
public class Book {
  public virtual void Publish() {}
}
```

Prior to the inclusion of this method in the class Book, the class TextBook (a direct subclass of Book) already had a virtual method Publish():

```
public class TextBook : Book
{
  public virtual void Publish() {}
}
```

If we try to compile TextBook we would now obtain a compiler error:

```
Book.cs(9,24): warning CS0114: 'TextBook.Publish()' hides inherited member
  'Book.Publish()'. To make the current member override that
  implementation, add the override keyword. Otherwise add the new keyword
Book.cs(4,24): (Location of symbol related to previous warning)
```

Notice something strange in this compiler error. It correctly noted that we should use the keyword override to show that we are intending to override the method Publish() in the class TextBook. However, it also gave us the option of using the keyword new! What does this mean? We can use the keyword new to indicate to the compiler that we do not wish to consider the method Publish() an override for the method in the parent class; rather, that it is the intended behaviour. For example:

```
using System;

public class Book {
  public virtual void Publish() {
    Console.WriteLine("Book.Publish()");
  }
}

public class TextBook : Book
{
  public new virtual void Publish() {
    Console.WriteLine("TextBook.Publish()");
  }
}
```

```
public class test {
  public static void Main() {
    Book b = new TextBook();
    b.Publish();
    TextBook tb = new TextBook();
    tb.Publish();
    ((Book)tb).Publish();
  }
}
```

In this example, rather than state that the method Publish() in the class TextBook overrides the parent class method we use the keyword new. The result of running this program is:

```
C:\c#>Book
Book.Publish()
TextBook.Publish()
Book.Publish()
```

Consequently, where the Runtime thinks that we meant to use the Book class it gives us the Book class version (i.e. in the rest of the framework that knows nothing about the textbook). However, wherever we refer directly to TextBook (the users' code) we get the TextBook version of the method.

Notice the difference in behaviour compared with overriding the method Publish. For example:

```
using System;

public class Book {
  public virtual void Publish() {
    Console.WriteLine("Book.Publish()");
  }
}

public class TextBook : Book
{
  public override void Publish() {
    Console.WriteLine("TextBook.Publish()");
  }
}

public class test {
  public static void Main() {
    Book b = new TextBook();
    b.Publish();
    TextBook tb = new TextBook();
    tb.Publish();
    ((Book)tb).Publish();
```

```
    }
}
```

If we modify the TextBook class (as above) to state that the Publish() method is an override and re-run the Main method we get:

```
C:\c#>Book
TextBook.Publish()
TextBook.Publish()
TextBook.Publish()
```

In this case it is clear that in all situations we use the replacement for the method Publish()!

Chapter 21

Delegates

21.1 Introduction

Delegates specify a contract between a caller and an implementor of some functionality. They can be used to provide a callback mechanism in C# and are used extensively in event handling.

21.2 Delegates

A delegate is exactly that: it is something to which an object "delegates" the responsibility for some functionality. For example, in human terms a manager might delegate the responsibility for booking a flight to their secretary or PA. The manager does not know (or indeed often care) how the secretary performs the booking process, as long as the result is that a flight is booked. The manager initiates the whole process, and tells the secretary when the journey is and where it is to, but from that point on the secretary takes over. Taking the analogy further, if the secretary is from an agency the manager may not even know the secretary, except as a provider of this service.

21.3 Delegates in C#

Delegates are exactly like the secretary – they perform some service for another object. To ensure that the delegate and the user class can work together, a delegate specification must be provided. This is like an interface in that it defines the return type of the delegate, the parameters that the delegate must take and the name of the delegate.

Delegates differ from interfaces in a number of ways:

- They are defined via the keyword delegate.
- They are defined within the "user" class.
- They are created at run-time (whereas interfaces are created at compile-time).

- Instances must be created at run-time that implement the delegate.
- Implementors of delegates are wrapped inside a delegate object. The wrapper acts as the glue that links the "user" object with the delegate implementor.

21.4 Defining a Delegate

To declare a delegate we use the following syntax:

```
<access-modifier> delegate <return-type> <name-of-delegate(<parameters>);
```

This syntax is used within the body of a class to define a delegate for that class.

For example, let us assume that we wish to create a class whose objects can hold collections of objects sorted in different ways (we will ignore the collections framework for the moment). We could do this by defining a class **Set** that uses a delegate that specifies how the elements in the set should be compared. This will allow us to plug in different comparison delegates that can alter the way that the set is sorted.

For example:

```csharp
using System;

public class Person {
  public int age;
  public String name;

  public Person(String name, int age) {
    this.age = age;
    this.name = name;
  }

  public override String ToString() {
    return name + ": " + age;
  }
}

public class Set
{
  Object [] data = new Object[4]; // Keeping it simple
  int position = 0;

  public delegate int SortTest(Object obj1, Object obj2);

  public void Add(Object obj)
  {
    if (position < data.Length) {
```

```
          data[position] = obj;
          position++;
        } else {
        Console.WriteLine("Out of space");
        }
    }

    public void Sort(SortTest test)
    {
      for (int i=0; i<data.Length; i++) {
        for (int j=i+1; j<data.Length; j++) {
          int code = test(data[i], data[j]);
          if (code == 1) {
            Object temp = data[i];
            data[i] = data[j];
            data[j] = temp;
          }
        }
      }
    }

    public void Print()
    {
      for (int i=0; i<data.Length; i++)
      {
        Console.Write("{0} ,", data[i]);
      }
      Console.WriteLine("");
    }
}

public class Tester
{
  public static int SortTest(Object obj1, Object obj2)
  {
    int result = 0;
    Person p1 = (Person)obj1;
    Person p2 = (Person)obj2;
    result = String.Compare(p1.name, p2.name);
    return result;
  }
}

public class Sort {
  public static void Main() {
    Set s = new Set();
```

```
    s.Add(new Person("John", 37));
    s.Add(new Person("Denise", 34));
    s.Add(new Person("Phoebe", 4));
    s.Add(new Person("Adam", 2));
    s.Print();
    s.Sort(new Set.SortTest(Tester.SortTest));
    s.Print();
  }
}
```

The result of executing this program is:

```
C:\csharp>Sort
John: 37 ,Denise: 34 ,Phoebe: 4 ,Adam: 2 ,
Adam: 2 ,Denise: 34 ,John: 37 ,Phoebe: 4 ,
```

In this case the delegate SortTest defined in the class set is implemented by the class Tester. To do this, the class Tester uses a static (or class-side) method that matches the specification of the delegate.

Notice that there is nothing in the class Tester that explicitly states that it will provide an implementation for a delegate (let alone the delegate in the class set).

Also note that in the Main method test harness the Tester class and its static method must be wrapped inside the delegate object. This is done by creating a new instance of the delegate containing a reference to the implementor method. Note that this reference to the implementor method specifies the class implementing the method followed by the method without any parameters. At this point it is not a call to the Tester.SortTest is merely a reference to it for future use. (Those with a C++ background could draw analogies with function pointers at this stage.)

21.5 Static and Instance Methods

In the previous example, the implementor of the delegate was a static method on the class Tester. However, the implementor of a delegate could be a static method or an instance method. In the above example a static method was used so that we did not have to create an instance of the class Tester just to use the method SortTest. However, in many cases we wish to use instance methods available via objects that are used elsewhere in an application. The following example modifies the earlier program to use an instance method as the implementor of a delegate.

```
using System;

public class Person {
  public int age;
  public String name;
```

```
    public Person(String name, int age) {
      this.age = age;
      this.name = name;
    }

    public override String ToString() {
      return name + ": " + age;
    }
}
public class Set
{
  Object [] data = new Object[4];  // Keeping it simple
  int position = 0;

  public delegate int SortTest(Object obj1, Object obj2);

  public void Add(Object obj)
  {
    if (position < data.Length) {
      data[position] = obj;
      position++;
    } else {
      Console.WriteLine("Out of space");
    }
  }

  public void Sort(SortTest test)
  {
    for (int i=0; i<data.Length; i++) {
      for (int j=i+1; j<data.Length; j++) {
        int code = test(data[i], data[j]);
        if (code == 1) {
        Object temp = data[i];
        data[i] = data[j];
        data[j] = temp;
        }
      }
    }
  }

  public void Print()
  {
    for (int i=0; i<data.Length; i++)
    {
      Console.Write("{0} ,", data[i]);
    }
```

```
      Console.WriteLine("");
    }
  }

  public class Tester
  {
    public int SortTest(Object obj1, Object obj2)
    {
      int result = 0;
      Person p1 = (Person)obj1;
      Person p2 = (Person)obj2;
      result = String.Compare(p1.name, p2.name);
      return result;
    }
  }

  public class Sort2 {
    public static void Main() {
      Set s = new Set();
      s.Add(new Person("John", 37));
      s.Add(new Person("Denise", 34));
      s.Add(new Person("Phoebe", 4));
      s.Add(new Person("Adam", 2));
      s.Print();
      Tester t = new Tester();
      s.Sort(new Set.SortTest(t.SortTest));
      s.Print();
    }
  }
```

The effect of executing this program is exactly the same as the previous example:

```
C:\csharp>Sort2
John: 37 ,Denise: 34 ,Phoebe: 4 ,Adam: 2 ,
Adam: 2 ,Denise: 34 ,John: 37 ,Phoebe: 4 ,
```

21.6 Multicasting

Although the examples presented above use a one-to-one mapping between a delegate and a method, there is no reason why a delegate should not reference more than one method. When a delegate references more than one implementor this is referred to as multicasting. If a delegate has more than one implementor then each implementor is called in turn synchronously. The call order is based on the order in which they were added. The only exception to this is if one of the methods in the "invocation list" throws an exception.

To add more than one implementor to a delegate the += operator has been overloaded. For example:

```
n += new MultiTest.Notify (t1.notify)
```

In turn, the -= has been overloaded to remove an implementor. For example:

```
n -= new MultiTest.Notify (t1.Notify);
```

The following program provides a complete example:

```
using System;

public class MultiTest
{
  public delegate void Notify(String message);

  public static void Main() {
    Tester1 t1 = new Tester1();
    Tester2 t2 = new Tester2();
    Notify n = new MultiTest.Notify(t2.Notify);
    n += new MultiTest.Notify(t2.Notify);
    n("Hello");
  }
}

public class Tester1
{
  public void Notify(String message)
  {
    Console.WriteLine("Tester1 {0} " , message);
  }
}

public class Tester2
{
  public void Notify(String message)
  {
    Console.WriteLine("Tester 2 {0}", message);
  }
}
```

The effect of executing this program is:

```
C:\csharp>Multi
Tester 2 Hello
Tester 2 Hello
```

Notice that we could have written the following:

```
new MultiTest.Notify (t1.Notify)
```

as

```
new Notify (t1.Notify)
```

as we are in the same class as the one that defines the delegate.

21.7 Delegates as Static Properties

One issue with all the examples that have gone before is that whenever anything uses the delegate they have to write the appropriate code to create a wrapper that will hold the delegate implementation. If one class requires a delegate, a second class implements the delegate and a third class will bring them together. This means that the programmer of the third class needs to do this. We could hide this level of detail from the third class by providing the delegate on demand as a property. For example, we could have written the Tester class as:

```
public class Tester
{
  public int SortTest(Object obj1, Object obj2)
  {
    int result = 0;
    Person p1 = (Person)obj1;
    Person p2 = (Person)obj2;
    result = String.Compare(p1.name, p2.name);
    return result;
  }

  public Set.SortTest SortTester {
    get {
      return (new Set.SortTest(this.SortTest));
    }
  }
}
```

Then in the Main method we could have written:

```
s.Sort(Tester.SortTester);
```

which hides a great deal of the detail and provides a simpler interface for the user of the Tester class.

21.8 Usage

The most common usage of delegation is with the C# implementation of event handling.

21.9 Summary

Delegates provide a very convenient way of dynamically plugging in functionality to an object. The delegate framework provides a very clean interface for such fine-grained component-based plug and play behaviour. "Fine-grained" is the key here. If a whole object needs to be plugged into another object then interfaces are sufficient; however, if we need only one or two functions then delegates are appropriate.

Chapter 22

Exception Handling

22.1 Introduction

This chapter considers exception handling and how it is implemented in C#. You are introduced to the object model of exception handling, to the throwing and catching of exceptions, and how to define new exceptions and exception-specific constructs.

22.2 What Is an Exception?

In C#, almost everything is an object, including exceptions. All exceptions must extend the class Exception or one of its subclasses, which allows an exception to be thrown or raised. Figure 22.1 presents part of the Exception class hierarchy.

The Exception class has two categories of subclasses: ApplicationException and SystemException. ApplicationExceptions are thrown by a user program, not by the .NET Runtime. If you are designing an application that needs to create its own exceptions, derive from the ApplicationException class. Thus ApplicationException should be the root of any user-defined exceptions (we will look at how to do this later).

SystemException is thrown by the common language runtime when errors occur that are nonfatal and recoverable by user programs. These errors result from a failed run-time check (such as an array out-of-bound error), and can occur during the execution of any method. That is, SystemExceptions represent problems that can be resolved by your own programs.

Another important category of exception is the IOException hierarchy. The IOException is the root of all exceptions generated by input–output operations (such as reading from files). Subclasses of IOException include DirectoryNotFoundException, FileNotFoundException and FileLoadException. IOException is itself a direct subclass of Exception.

Note that all the exceptions we have seen so far have ended with the word Exception. This is a common convention and is followed throughout C#. If you define your own exceptions you should also follow this convention.

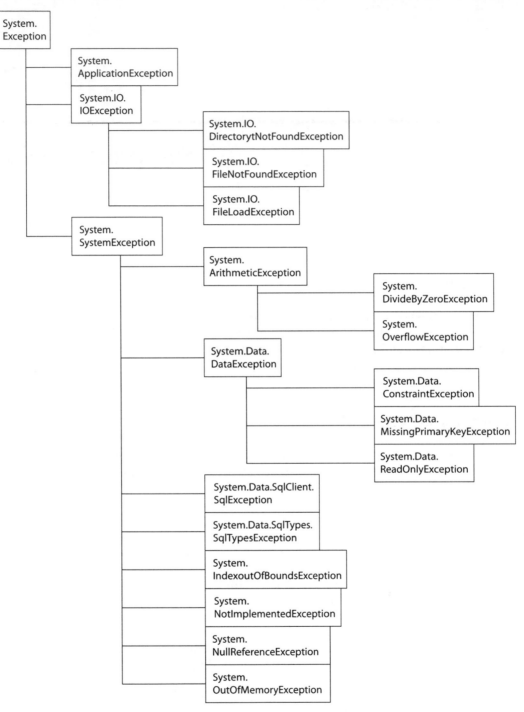

Figure 22.1 Part of the Exception class hierarchy.

An exception can be thrown explicitly by your code or implicitly by the operations you perform. In either case, an exception is an object. If you want to throw the exception explicitly yourself then you will first need to create a new instance of the appropriate exception class, and you must instantiate it before you do anything with it. You do this by sending the throw message to an instance of the appropriate exception. For example, to raise a `DivideByZeroException` for a divide by zero error, we write:

```
throw new DivideByZeroException("Division By Zero");
```

The exception is caught by the first handler (`try` block) that is defined on the `DivideByZeroException` (or one of its parent classes).

22.3 What Is Exception Handling?

An exception moves the flow of control from one place to another. In most situations, this is because a problem occurs which cannot be handled locally, but can be handled in another part of the system. The problem is usually some sort of error (such as dividing by zero), although it can be any problem (for example, identifying that the postcode specified with an address does not match). The purpose of an exception, therefore, is to handle an error condition when it happens at run-time. Table 22.1 lists the terms used in exception handling.

Table 22.1 Terms used in exception handling.

Exception	An error that is generated at run-time
Raising an exception	Generating a new exception
Throwing an exception	Triggering a generated exception
Handling an exception	Processing code that deals with the error
Handler	The code that deals with the error (referred to as the `catch` block)
Signal	A particular type of exception (such as *out of bounds* or *divide by zero*)

It is worth considering why you should wish to handle an exception; after all, the system does not allow an error to go unnoticed. For example, if we try to divide by zero, then the system generates an error. This may mean that the user has entered an incorrect value, and we do not want users to be presented with a dialog suggesting that they enter the system debugger. We can use exceptions to force the user to correct the mistake and rerun the calculation.

Different types of error produce different types of exception. For example, if the error is caused by dividing an integer by zero, then the exception is a *divide by zero* exception. The type of exception is identified by objects called signals that possess exception handlers. Each handler can deal with exceptions associated with its class of signal (and its subclasses).

An exception is initiated when it is thrown. The system searches back up the execution stack until it finds a handler that can deal with the exception (i.e. it searches for a `try` block of the appropriate type). The associated handler then processes the exception. This may involve

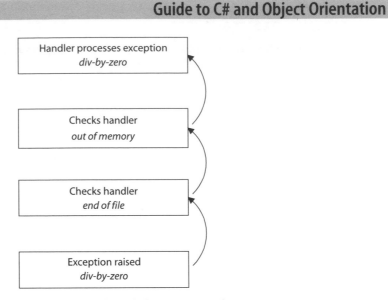

Figure 22.2 Searching through the execution stack.

performing some remedial action or terminating the current execution in a controlled manner. In some cases, it may be possible to restart executing the code.

As a handler can only deal with an exception of a specified class (or subclass), an exception may pass through a number of other blocks before it finds one that can process it.

Figure 22.2 illustrates a situation in which a *divide by zero* exception is raised. This exception is passed up the execution stack, where it encounters an exception handler defined for an *End of File* exception. This handler cannot handle the *divide by zero* exception, so it is passed further up the execution stack. It then encounters a handler for an *out of memory* exception. Again, it cannot deal with a *divide by zero* exception and the exception is passed further up the execution stack until it finds a handler defined for the *divide by zero* exception. This handler then processes the exception.

In C#, exceptions are objects and you create and throw an exception by sending messages.

22.4 Throwing an Exception

To create and throw an exception you need to determine which exception class is appropriate (for example, is DivideByZero appropriate or should you use its direct superclass ArithmeticException?). You then need to make an instance of this class. Unlike other objects you should only create an instance of an exception where you actually need it. This is because when the instance is created a record of the current call stack is made. This is useful for debugging problem situations. Thus it needs to reflect the actual situation in which the exception was raised.

Once you have raised an exception (instantiated an exception) you can then throw the exception. The exception will then be handled by a try–catch block somewhere or will reach the default exception handler, which will present the exception back to the command line.

For example, consider the following code:

```
using System;

public class ExceptionTest1 {
  public static void Main(String [] args) {
    int i, j;
    if (args.Length == 2) {
      i = Convert.ToInt32(args[0]);
      j = Convert.ToInt32(args[1]);

    if (j==0) {
      throw new DivideByZeroException("j is zero");
    }

    Console.WriteLine(i / j);
    }
  }
}
```

This class takes input from the command line and checks to see whether the divisor is zero or not. If it is, then it throws an exception. If it is not, then a division is performed and the (integer) result is printed to the standard output.

If an exception is thrown by the statement

```
throw new DivideByZeroException("j is zero")
```

then the exception dialog shown in Figure 22.3 is presented to the user.

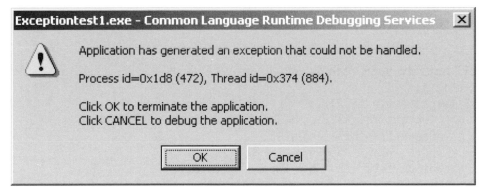

Figure 22.3

If Cancel is selected then a window with further details is presented to the user (including the exception message).

22.5 Catching an Exception

You can catch an exception by implementing the try–catch–finally construct. This construct is broken into three parts:

- try block
  The try block indicates the code that is to be monitored for the exceptions listed in the catch expressions.
- catch expressions
  You can use an optional catch expression to indicate what to do when certain classes of exception occur (e.g. resolve the problem or generate a warning message). More than one catch expression can be included. This allows different exceptions to be handled in different ways.
- finally block
  The optional finally block runs after the try block exits (whether or not this is due to an exception being raised). You can use it to clean up any resources, close files etc.

This construct may at first seem confusing. However, once you have worked with it for a while you will find it less daunting. Typically, you use the same incantation of the construct; concentrate on the details of the code within the try block and do not worry about the exception handling mechanism.

The following example uses the construct to handle the DivideByZero exception that can be raised by the expression (a / b). The try block incorporates the file call to the DoDivision method, and the code in the catch block states what should happen if an DivideByZeroException is raised. In this case, it prints a message. The message in the finally block is always printed.

```csharp
using System;

public class ExceptionTest2 {

  public int DoDivision(int a, int b) {
    return a / b;
  }

  public static void Main(String [] args) {
    int i, j;
    if (args.Length == 2) {
      i = Convert.ToInt32(args[0]);
      j = Convert.ToInt32(args[1]);

      ExceptionTest2 et2 = new ExceptionTest2();

      int result =0;
      try
      {
        result = et2.DoDivision(i, j);
      }
```

```
      catch (DivideByZeroException exp)
      {
        Console.WriteLine("Message: {0} ", exp.Message);
        Console.WriteLine("Stack Trace: {0} ", exp.StackTrace);
      }
      finally
      {
        Console.WriteLine("Finally...");
      }
      Console.WriteLine(result);
    }
  }
}
```

The Main method extracts the values to be used for the division process from the command line. These come in as strings to the Main method and are converted to integers. They are then passed to the DoDivision method inside the try block. If this method raises an DivideByZeroException, the message associated with the exception as well as the exception's stack trace is printed. Once the try block is processed, the finally block prints out "Finally...". The result of compiling and executing this code is:

```
C:\c#>Exceptiontest2 1 0
Message: Attempted to divide by zero.
Stack Trace:  at ExceptionTest2.Main(String[] args)
Finally...
0
```

We can extend this example further by providing more than one catch block. For example:

```
using System;

public class ExceptionTest3 {

  public int DoDivision(int a, int b) {
    if (a > 10) {
      throw new ArithmeticException("Greater than 10");
    }
    return a / b;
  }

  public static void Main(String [] args) {
    int i, j;
    if (args.Length == 2) {
      i = Convert.ToInt32(args[0]);
      j = Convert.ToInt32(args[1]);
```

```
        ExceptionTest3 et3 = new ExceptionTest3();

        int result =0;
        try
        {
          result = et3.DoDivision(i, j);
        }
        catch (DivideByZeroException exp)
        {
          Console.WriteLine("Message: {0} ", exp.Message);
          Console.WriteLine("Stack Trace: {0} ",
              exp.StackTrace);
        }
        catch (ArithmeticException exp) {
          Console.WriteLine("Exception Message: {0} ", exp.Message);
        }
        finally
        {
          Console.WriteLine("Finally...");
        }
        Console.WriteLine(result);
      }
    }
  }
```

This version now has two catch blocks; one for the DivideByZeroException and one for the ArithmeticException (that is thrown when the first value provided on the command line is greater than 10).

The results of compiling and executing this program are presented below:

```
C:\c#>ExceptionTest3 1 0
Message: Attempted to divide by zero.
Stack Trace: at ExceptionTest3.DoDivision(Int32 a, Int32 b)
  at ExceptionTest3.Main(String[] args)
Finally...

0
C:\c#>ExceptionTest3 11 2
Exception Message: Greater than 10
Finally...
0

C:\c#>ExceptionTest3 10 2
Finally...
5
```

Notice that the DivideByZeroException is placed before the ArithmeticException. This is for a very good reason. What the catch block actually says is catch all exceptions of this type or any subtype. Thus the ArithmeticException will catch all ArithmeticExceptions and all exceptions that are instances of subclasses of ArithmeticException. One of those subclasses is DivideByZeroException. Thus we need to place the DivideByZeroException first to make sure that we catch that one first. Note that the C# compiler will check this for you if you are not sure.

You can also nest try–catch blocks. That is, you can place one try–catch block inside a try block, a catch block or the optional finally block as necessary. For example:

```
try
{
  try
  {
    result = et3.DoDivision(i, j);
  }
  catch (ArithmeticException exp)
  {
    Console.WriteLine("Message: {0} ", exp.Message);
  }
}
catch (DivideByZeroException exp)
{
  Console.WriteLine("Message: {0} ", exp.Message);
  Console.WriteLine("Stack Trace: {0} ", exp.StackTrace);
}
```

22.6 Defining an Exception

You can define your own exceptions, which can give you more control over what happens in particular circumstances. To define an exception, you create a subclass of the ApplicationException class or one of its subclasses. For example, to define a DuplicateException, we can extend the ApplicationException class and generate an appropriate message:

```
public class DuplicateException : ApplicationException
{
  public Object offender;
  public DuplicateException (Object anObject) :
      base("DuplicateException with " + anObject)
  {
    offender = anObject;
  }
}
```

This class explicitly handles duplicate exceptions. The following code is an example of how we might use DivideByZeroException:

```
public class Example
{
  private String [] data;
  public static void Main (String [] args)
  {
    Example temp = new Example(args);
    try {
      temp.test();
      Console.WriteLine("Strings all unique");
    }
    catch (DuplicateException exception) {
      Console.WriteLine("Oops: {0}",
          exception.Message);
    }
  }
  public Example(String [] args)
  {
    data = args;
  }
  public void test()
  {
    for (int i=0; i<data.Length; i++) {
      for (int j=i+1; j<data.Length; j++) {
        if (data[i] == data[j]) {
        throw new DuplicateException(data[i]);
        }
      }
    }
  }
}
```

In this example, we check to see whether a string exists in the array of strings more than once. If it does, we create a new instance of the DuplicateException class and throw it. The test method delegates responsibility for this exception to the calling method (in this case, the Main method). The Main method catches the exception and prints a message.

The result of compiling and executing this code is:

```
C:\c#>Example John Denise Phoebe Adam
Strings all unique
C:\c#>Example John Denise John Phoebe Adam
Oops: DuplicateException with John
```

22.6.1 Nesting Exceptions

There are times when the code that your code calls throws an exception and what you want to do is to catch that exception, perform some sort of housekeeping operation and then pass the exception on. You can do this directly using the throws clause or you can wrap the exception you have received up in another exception. This is useful if, for example, you are receiving a system exception of some form, but you want to present it to your calling code as some form of application exception (to make comprehension of the problem easier). This technique is referred to as nesting exceptions.

To nest an exception you need to create a new exception that contains the existing exception. If you look at the constructors for the Exception classes you will notice that not only are they overloaded, but that the overloaded constructors often take another exception as one of the parameters. For example the Arithmetic exception has a constructor defined as taking a string and an exception. Thus we can write:

```
try
{
   ... code that throws the DivideByZeroException ...
}
catch (DivideByZeroException e)
{
   throw new ArithmeticException("Big problem", e);
}
```

Any calling code that catches the arithmetic exception now has access to the message ("Big problem") and to the original divide by zero exception. The original exception is available via the InnerException property.

Part 5

Graphical User Interfaces

Chapter 23

Graphical User Interfaces

23.1 Introduction

In this chapter we will look at the creation of graphical user interfaces. Such interfaces typically present sophisticated combinations of graphical components such as buttons, text fields, menus, toolbars, tables and trees. We will not attempt to cover all the graphical components available. Rather, we will discuss the basic concepts on which these other components build.

It is worth noting at this point that many developers will initially think of using the window drawing tools in IDEs such as Visual Studio .NET to create their graphical applications. Indeed, this is a very good idea if those tools provide what you need. However, in many cases they do not. For example, if the display presented to the user as part of the GUI is dependent on what the user is doing, what options have been selected etc., then you may need to create your display dynamically at run-time. In such situations you may very well need an understanding of the underlying structures and behaviours used to create the GUIs. In many cases it is also useful to have such an understanding even if you always intend to use a tool such as Visual Studio .NET for GUI creation, as what those tools do will be clearer to you.

23.2 Windows Forms Overview

The System.Windows.Forms namespace contains a set of classes, interfaces, structs and enumerated types that allow the creation of sophisticated Graphical User Interface (GUI) based applications. For anyone who has been used to frameworks such as the Microsoft Foundation Class Library (MFC) you will find that what is on offer is similar to what you have been used to, but much richer in functionality. For example, to create a window you now need to extend the Form class. This class provides all the functionality required to create that window. At the simplest level all that is required is that you register the object created from your class with the Application class. To build up sophisticated displays you instantiate other classes and add them to the Form class you have created etc.

In terms of terminology there are two types of class in the System.Windows.Forms namespace. One type is referred to as a **control**, and these are the graphical components used within a window (such as buttons, text fields and labels). The other type, termed a **container**, is something that can hold other types of control. These include the Form itself (it contains all the other elements within it), Panel, GroupBox etc. In fact, as almost everything in the System.Windows.Forms namespace extends from the Control class, this means that a container can contain any type of control (including other containers). Part of the class hierarchy for the classes in the System.Windows.Forms namespace is presented in Figure 23.1. This diagram illustrates the classes that will be used in this chapter and the next two chapters. There are many other classes in the namespace and you should become familiar with them. The classes in italics are abstract classes. The remainder of the classes are all concrete classes.

The one very special class in the System.Windows.Forms namespace is the Form class. Although this is a type of control it is a special control in that it is the top-level control/ container. The Form is a special type of container that represents the overall window.

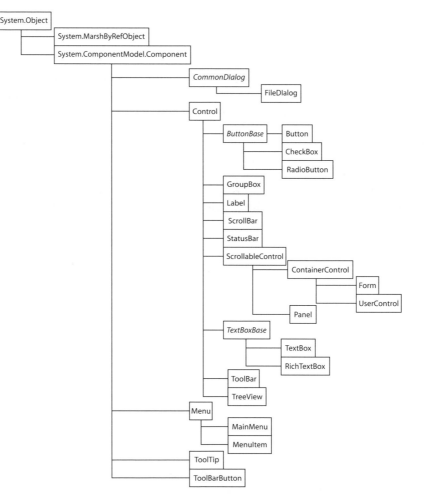

Figure 23.1 Part of the class hierarchy for graphical controls.

As all the GUI components in the System.Windows.Forms namespace are classes, it is possible to create your own graphical components by subclassing an existing class. For example, if I wish to make my own type of Button, I could do so by subclassing this to create MyButton.

23.3 The Control Class

The Control class is the root of almost all the GUI classes in the System.Windows.Forms namespace (see Figure 23.1). Thus the facilities defined in this class are available for all GUI components whether they are controls or containers.

Table 23.1 Public static properties of the Control class.

DefaultBackColor	Gets the default background colour of the control
DefaultFont	Gets the default font of the control
DefaultForeColor	Gets the default foreground colour of the control
ModifierKeys	Gets a value indicating the current state of the SHIFT, CTRL, and ALT modifier keys
MouseButtons	Gets a value indicating the state of the left, right, and middle mouse buttons
MousePosition	Gets the position of the mouse in screen coordinates

Tables 23.1–23.3 summarize the properties and methods available on the Control class. In fact, the Control class also provides behaviour that supports data binding, context menus, drag and drop, and cut and paste type functionality, as well as anchoring and docking (described later in this chapter).

Table 23.2 Public instance properties of the Control class.

Bounds	Gets or sets the bounding rectangle for the control
Cursor	Gets or sets the cursor that is displayed when the user moves the mouse pointer over this control
Controls	Gets or sets the collection of controls contained within the control
Dock	Gets or sets which edge of the parent container a control is docked to
Enabled	Gets or sets a value indicating whether the control is enabled
Focused	Gets a value indicating whether the control has input focus
Font	Gets or sets the current font for the control
ForeColor	Gets or sets the foreground colour of the control
Height	Gets or sets the height of the control
Location	Gets or sets the coordinates of the upper-left corner of the control relative to the upper-left corner of its container
Name	Gets or sets the name of the control
Parent	Gets or sets the parent container of this control
Visible	Gets or sets a value indicating whether the control is visible
Width	Gets or sets the width of the control

Table 23.3 Public instance methods of the `Control` class.

FindForm	Retrieves the form that this control is on. The control's parent may not be the same as the form
Focus	Sets focus to the control
Hide	Hides the control
Refresh	Forces the control to invalidate its client area and immediately repaint itself and any child controls
SetBounds	Sets the bounds of the control
Show	Makes the control display by setting the visible property to true
ToString	Returns a String that represents the current Object
Update	Forces the control to paint any currently invalid areas

23.4 The Form Class

A window on the screen is represented by a `Form` within a C# application. It is a top-level container that holds all other types of container and control. Thus a `Form` is the object that handles displaying the borders of the window, the icon in a window, the text of the title of the window, the minimize, maximize and close buttons, and the top-level menu (as illustrated in Figure 23.2).

It is possible to modify the look of the *form* by setting the title text, the icon, the control box, the minimize box and the maximize box etc. You can also assign menus to your form (using the `MainMenu` class) as well as to designate a button object as the "Enter" or `AcceptButton` button and another as the "Escape" or `CancelButton` button. These are special buttons that can be used to provide default behaviour whenever the "Enter" or "Escape" keys are pressed.

The other thing a `Form` has is contents: that is, graphical components (either controls or containers) that are held within it. As all containers are also controls (by virtue of class inheritance), all the contents of a `Form` are held in a collection of controls know as the `Controls` property.

The following application illustrates the use of the `Form` class:

```
using System;
using System.Windows.Forms;

public class SimpleHelloWorld : Form {
  public static void Main() {
    Application.Run(new SimpleHelloWorld());
  }
  public SimpleHelloWorld() {
    this.Text = "Simple Hello World";
  }
}
```

This program creates a new instance of the `SimpleHelloWorld` class (a direct subclass of `Form`) that sets the title of the window (as defined by the `Text` property) to "Simple Hello World". This new instance is then run by the `Application` class. The `Application` class has static methods to start and stop applications and threads, and to process Windows messages. In this case we are using the Run method, which takes a Form as a parameter. This version of the Run method executes a standard application message loop on the current thread and makes the specified form visible.

The result of compiling and running this application is the window presented in Figure 23.2.

Figure 23.2 A simple graphical application.

Obviously this is a very simple example that merely creates an empty window (Form) and sets the title bar. However, it illustrates the basic concepts to be employed.

23.5 Building Up a GUI

The next step after creating a very basic window is to provide some content for that window. The following program adds a button to the display and sets the size of the overall window. Note that in this program I have defined a private method called InitializeComponent. This is to follow the convention used by the Visual Studio .NET tools. If you had created a GUI using such a tool you would find that it would create a private void InitializeComponent() method with the code in that method for creating the display. This does not mean that what I have written below could be viewed in the Form's drawing tool in Visual Studio, merely that I am following the same convention.

```
using System;
using System.Windows.Forms;

public class SimpleHelloWorld : Form {

  public static void Main() {
    Application.Run(new SimpleHelloWorld());
  }
  public SimpleHelloWorld() {
    InitializeComponent();
  }

  private void InitializeComponent() {
    // Set up the form
```

```
        this.Size = new System.Drawing.Size(400, 200);
        this.Text = "Hello World Window";
        // Create the button and locate it
        Button b = new Button();
        b.Text = "Hello World";
        b.Dock = DockStyle.Fill;
        this.Controls.Add (b);
    }
}
```

There are a couple of points to note about the InitializeComponent method. Firstly it sets both the Size property and the Text property of the main window. Secondly it creates a Button object, sets the text for the button to display, specifies where the button should be located and then adds it to the window. These last two steps deserve a little more explanation.

The button has a property, Dock, that specifies where the button should be located within the containing component (in this case the Form). Note that we could position the button explicitly to a particular location within the window. However, by using a dock position we can cause the button to fill up the available space. The use of docking will be discussed in more detail later, but for the moment note that System.Windows.Forms.DockStyle.Fill is used to specify that the button will fill up the centre of the containing Form.

Once the button is appropriately configured we can then add the button to the controls held by the Form. Notice that we do not add the button directly to the window; rather, we add it to the Controls property of the window via the Add method.

The result of compiling and running this program is illustrated in Figure 23.3. Notice that for the moment we will not worry about capturing the user's clicks on the button (see the next chapter for event handling in GUIs).

Figure 23.3 Adding a button to a simple GUI.

We could continue further down this road, adding additional features such as the initial position of the window, modifications to the style of border used, and images on the button. All these things are illustrated in the next listing of this program:

```
using System;
using System.Drawing;
using System.Windows.Forms;

public class SimpleHelloWorld : Form {

  public static void Main() {
    Application.Run(new SimpleHelloWorld());
  }
  public SimpleHelloWorld() {
    InitializeComponent();
  }

  private void InitializeComponent() {
    this.Size = new System.Drawing.Size(100, 100);
    this.Text = "Hello World Window";
    // Set the start position of the form to the centre of the screen.
    this.StartPosition = FormStartPosition.CenterScreen;
    // Set the border style of the form
    this.FormBorderStyle = FormBorderStyle.SizableToolWindow;

    Button b = new Button();
    b.Text = "Hello World";
    b.Dock = System.Windows.Forms.DockStyle.Fill;

    b.Image = Image.FromFile("exe.bmp");
    // Align the image and text on the button.
    b.ImageAlign = ContentAlignment.MiddleRight;
    b.TextAlign = ContentAlignment.MiddleLeft;

    ToolTip toolTip = new ToolTip();
    toolTip.SetToolTip(b, "My tool tip");

    this.Controls.Add (b);

  }
}
```

The result of compiling and executing this program is presented in Figure 23.4. Note that this button has both text and an icon. The text is positioned to the middle left of the button, while the image is positioned on the middle right of the button. Also notice that we have defined some tool tip text for the button (displayed in Figure 23.4).

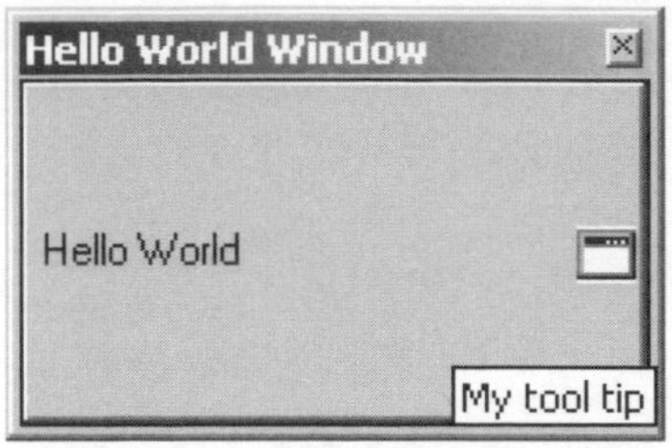

Figure 23.4 Adding additional features to the GUI (including tool tip text).

23.6 Using Panels Within Forms

Obviously the examples presented thus far are a little simplistic. Most GUIs will not comprise a single button, but will present some sort of display that needs to be made up of various graphical components ordered in an appropriate manner. To achieve this it is useful to build the GUI up in stages using components known as Panels that act as containers for other graphical components. Just as a Form is a type of control that can contain other graphical components (containers or controls), a panel is a type of container. One significant difference between a Panel and a Form is that a Panel cannot be a top-level container; that is, a Panel must be contained within something else (this something else may be another Panel – giving nested panels – or it may be a form).

Typically, you would use panels to subdivide or group a window (or form) by function or logical grouping or for other aesthetic reasons. For example, you may group all the input criteria together in some search tool and all results in a separate grouping (both groupings could be displayed in separate panels).

Note that there is also a GroupBox container control that is similar to a Panel. However, only a Panel can have scrollbars and only a GroupBox can have a caption. To display scroll bars in a Panel the AutoScroll property of the Panel needs to be set to true. It is also possible to set other properties on a Panel such as the background colour (BackColor – note the spelling of Color), the background image and the BorderStyle. The BorderStyle property determines if the panel is outlined with no visible border (None), a plain line (FixedSingle), or a shadowed line (Fixed3D). It is also possible to set the size of the panel and the position of a panel inside its container, as well as adding graphical controls to the container. Figure 23.5 illustrates all of these ideas. This GUI application has a toolbar across the top, an exit button across the bottom and a panel in the middle of the display. The middle panel contains two sub-panels (we therefore have nested panels, which is quite normal). Each nested panel contains a label and a text field. The top panel has a background colour of Red while the lower nested panel has a background colour of Blue. The outer panel also has a 3D shaded border style.

The program that generated the GUI application in Figure 23.5 is presented below. Note that we need to set the location and the size of the panel in order for our form-like display to work. If we had not set the size, for example, a default size would have been used that would have been too deep but not wide enough! Note that we also had to set the size and position of the label and the text box within the nested panels to gain the desired effect – this is why many people use a GUI drawing tool such as Visual Studio .NET.

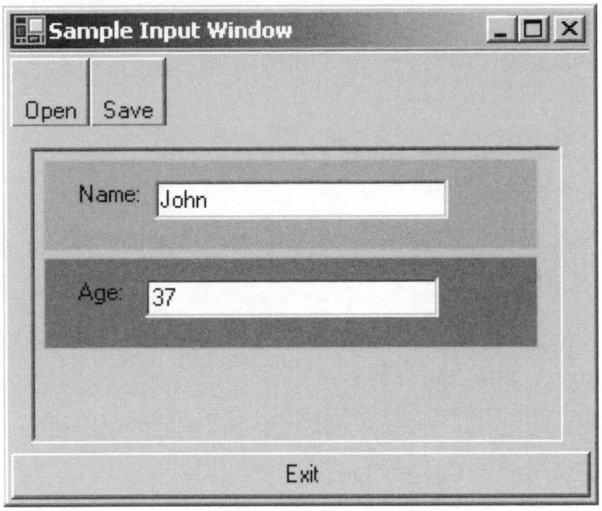

Figure 23.5 A multi-panel display.

```
using System;
using System.Drawing;
using System.Windows.Forms;

public class SampleForm : Form {

  public static void Main() {
    Application.Run(new SampleForm());
  }
  public SampleForm() {
    InitializeComponent();
  }

  private void InitializeComponent() {
    this.Size = new Size(300, 250);
    this.Text = "Sample Input Window";

    // Set up a toolbar
    ToolBarButton tbb1 = new ToolBarButton();
    ToolBarButton tbb2 = new ToolBarButton();
    ToolBar toolBar = new ToolBar();

    // Set the Text properties.
    tbb1.Text = "Open";
    tbb2.Text = "Save";
```

```csharp
// Add the ToolBarButtons to the ToolBar.
toolBar.Buttons.Add(tbb1);
toolBar.Buttons.Add(tbb2);

// Add the ToolBar to the Form.
this.Controls.Add(toolBar);

// Set up an inner panel
Panel panel1 = new Panel();

// Set up the name panel
Panel namePanel = new Panel();
namePanel.Location = new Point(5,5);
namePanel.Size = new Size(250, 45);
namePanel.BackColor = Color.Red;
TextBox name = new TextBox();
Label label1 = new Label();

// Initialize the Label and TextBox controls.
label1.Location = new Point(15,10);
label1.Text = "Name:";
label1.Size = new Size(40, 20);
name.Location = new Point(55,10);
name.Text = "";
name.Size = new Size(150, 20);

// Add the Label and TextBox to the Panel.
namePanel.Controls.Add(label1);
namePanel.Controls.Add(name);

// Add the name panel to the inner panel
panel1.Controls.Add(namePanel);

// Set up the age panel
Panel agePanel = new Panel();
agePanel.Size = new Size(250, 45);
agePanel.Location = new Point(5,55);
agePanel.BackColor = Color.Blue;
TextBox age = new TextBox();
Label label2 = new Label();

// Initialize the Label and TextBox controls.
label2.Location = new Point(15,10);
label2.Text = "Age:";
label2.Size = new Size(30, 20);
age.Location = new Point(50, 10);
```

```
        age.Text = "";
        age.Size = new Size(150, 20);
        // Add the Label and TextBox to the Panel.
        agePanel.Controls.Add(label2);
        agePanel.Controls.Add(age);
        // Add the name panel to the inner panel
        panel1.Controls.Add(agePanel);

        // Initialize the Panel control.
        panel1.Location = new Point(10,50);
        panel1.Size = new Size(270, 150);
        // Set the Borderstyle for
        // the Panel to three-dimensional.
        panel1.BorderStyle = System.Windows.Forms.BorderStyle.Fixed3D;

        // Add the Panel control to the form.
        this.Controls.Add(panel1);

        // Set up a button
        Button b = new Button();
        b.Text = "Exit";
        b.Dock = System.Windows.Forms.DockStyle.Bottom;

        this.Controls.Add (b);

    }
}
```

23.7 Docking

It is possible to dock graphical components (containers and controls) to a position relative to their container. For example, it is possible "dock" the left side of a control to the left side of its container. Similarly, it is possible to dock the top, bottom and right-hand side of a control to its container's equivalent positions. The remaining docking position is "fill". This docking position is equivalent to docking the centre of the control to the centre of the container and resizing the container to fill up any available space. These are illustrated in Figure 23.6.

The use of docking is very useful, as it takes away concerns regarding explicit positioning of components. In addition, the docked edge of the control is resized to match that of its container control. This is shown in Figure 23.7.

The various different dock style options are defined in the System.Windows.Forms.DockStyle enumerated type. This includes the option None for do not dock. Note that if Left or Right is selected, the left and right edges of the control are resized to the same size as the containing control's edge. Likewise, if Top or Bottom is selected, the top and bottom edges of the control are resized to the same size as the containing control's edge.

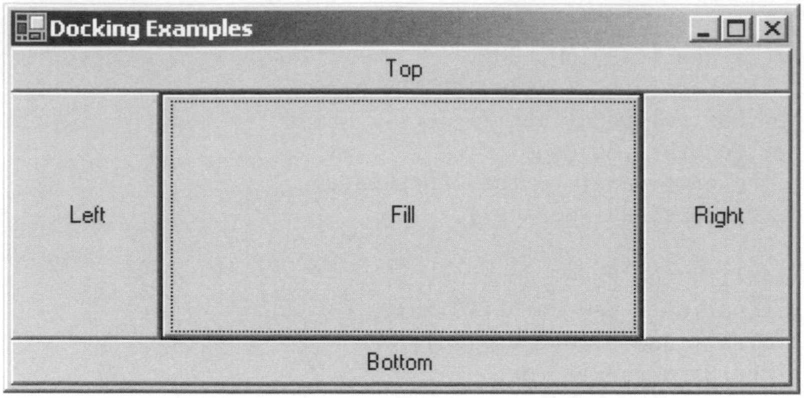

Figure 23.6 Using docking in a GUI application.

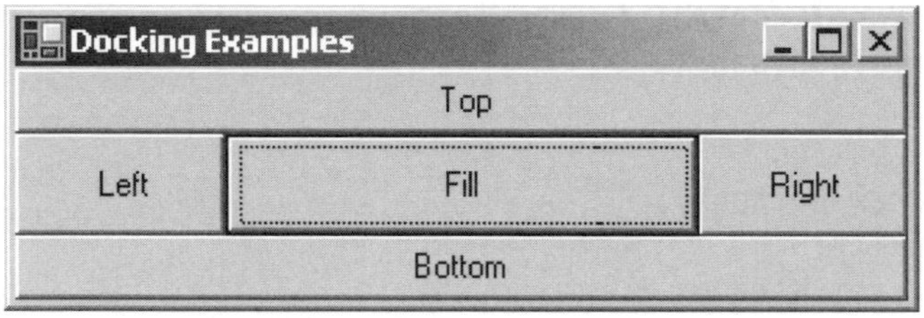

Figure 23.7 The effect of resizing with docked components.

The program that generated the "Docking Examples" window is presented below. This program essentially creates five button objects and sets the DockStyle to one of the five locations on a form. Each button has been given the text associated with the dock style used to locate it.

```csharp
using System;
using System.Windows.Forms;

public class DockTester : Form {

    public static void Main() {
        Application.Run(new DockTester());
    }

    public DockTester() {
        InitializeComponent();
    }

    private void InitializeComponent() {
        this.Size = new System.Drawing.Size(400, 200);
        this.Text = "Docking Examples";
```

```
      CreateButtons();
   }

   private void CreateButtons() {
      Button b = new Button();
      b.Text = "Fill";
      b.Dock = System.Windows.Forms.DockStyle.Fill;
      this.Controls.Add (b);

      b = new Button();
      b.Text = "Left";
      b.Dock = System.Windows.Forms.DockStyle.Left;
      this.Controls.Add (b);

      b = new Button();
      b.Text = "Right";
      b.Dock = System.Windows.Forms.DockStyle.Right;
      this.Controls.Add (b);

      b = new Button();
      b.Text = "Bottom";
      b.Dock = System.Windows.Forms.DockStyle.Bottom;
      this.Controls.Add (b);

      b = new Button();
      b.Text = "Top";
      b.Dock = System.Windows.Forms.DockStyle.Top;
      this.Controls.Add (b);
   }
}
```

23.8 Anchoring

One thing to note about the use of docking is that the component is docked right against the edge of the container – no gap is left. In many cases this might be exactly what you want. However, if you require a gap between the side of the container and the inner control you can use an Anchor.

An anchor sets up a relationship between the inner control and the container that is maintained if the container is resized. Essentially, the inner control is anchored off the edge of the container rather than docked against it (consider the analogy with ships and harbours).

When a container is resized the inner control is not (by default) resized, but its position remains constant with regard to its position relative to an edge of the container. A control can be anchored to any combination of control edges. If the control is anchored to opposite edges of its container (for example, to the top and bottom), it resizes when the container resizes. If the anchor property of a control is set to None then when a container resizes (for example 20 pixels) the control will move half of that (for example 10 pixels).

The enumerated type AnchorStyle defines all the available options for setting the anchor property of a component.

Chapter 24

Event Handling

24.1 Introduction

In this chapter we will look at how event handling is implemented in C# and in particular how user inputs (such as button clicks) that generate events can be handled in our C# programs.

24.2 Event Handling in General

Event handling is associated with dealing with a situation in which something has happened and the software developer needs to be notified of that situation. Sometimes the code written to deal with these situations is referred to as a callback and sometimes as an event handler; in either case, the same basic principles apply. That is, the developer must implement (in C#) a method that matches some specification that allows it to be called when the "event" occurs. This event could be some threshold being reached in some sensor, it could be a message being received from some broadcast mechanism or it could be some user interaction with a GUI. In general, this event handling method will be called when the event occurs and will be passed some data to allow it to determine the sender of the event and any event-specific data. The event handler can then determine what action the application should take.

Figure 24.1 attempts to illustrate the interactions that take place when handling GUI events in a little more detail. The figure illustrates the three main steps with respect to a Button, these are:

1. The user clicks on the button.
2. The button creates an EventArgs object. This is an object that contains any additional data that should be provided to the event handler. This step is referred to as raising an event in C# terminology.
3. The button then calls an appropriate handler method (on an object somewhere) passing in a reference to itself (as the sender of the event) and the event args.
4. The handler method can then perform whatever operations it needs to.

In the next section we will look at how this event handling model is implemented in C#.

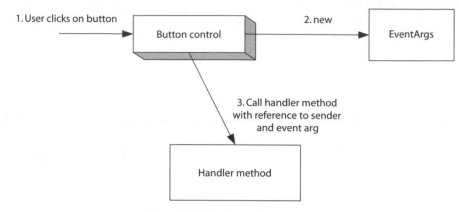

Figure 24.1 Event handling concepts.

24.3 Event Handling in C#

In C#, delegates (discussed in Chapter 21) are used to support the implementation of the event handling mechanism. That is, to provide an event handler you must implement a delegate. A delegate is a specification for a method that will be implemented by a client of the class defining the delegate. That is, it states what the signature of the method must be (in terms of return type and parameters). The delegate can then be referenced in the code of the class defining the delegate. At run-time an actual method must be provided for that delegate (the delegate implementation) and will be the method actually called.

Thus when creating an event handler the first thing to know is what the signature of the delegate is that you must implement. For example, the convention for graphical components is that the delegates have a return type of void and take two parameters of type Object and EventArgs. Thus if I wished to write an event handler for a graphical component I could write:

```
// EventArgs defined in System namespace
private void Handler(object sender, EventArgs e) {
  Console.WriteLine(e.ToString());
  Console.WriteLine("Hello World");
}
```

This defines a method with the same return type and parameters called Handler.

The next thing I need to do is to link the implementation of the delegate with the delegate specification. This is done by creating a new instance of the delegate type EventHandler. This is a standard delegate for GUI components. Next we must link our Handler method to it. For example:

```
new EventHandler(Handler);
```

This new delegate must be added to the list of event handlers registered with (for example) a button. This is done by adding the delegate to the buttons click event.

An event on a component looks very much like a property. However, events allow only limited access to the event. For example, it is not possible to assign an object directly to an event, it is only possible to add or remove objects using the += and -= operators. For example:

```
EventHandler h = new EventHandler(Handler);
button.Click += h;
...
button.Click -=h;
```

The above code snippet creates an event handler delegate linked to the method Handler. It then adds this delegate to the click event on the button. Later it then removes the delegate from the button.Click event. In between these two operations the method Handler would be called each time the user clicked on the button. For a complete example of creating an event handler for a button see the listing at the end of this chapter.

24.4 The Inner Workings

The previous section provides a programmer's view of using the event handling model in C#. In this section we will briefly look at some of the concepts used to implement the event and the delegate.

The event itself is defined on a class using the keyword event. An event is defined by a delegate type (such as EventHandler). Also, all the plumbing required for adding, removing and raising an event and sending it to each of the listeners interested in the event is provided by the C# runtime. Thus to define a new class that uses the EventHandler delegate we could write:

```
public class MyButton {
  public event EventHandler Click;
  protected void OnCLick() {
    if (Click != null)
      Click(this, null);
  }
}
```

The rest will be provided by the C# environment.

There are a number of conventions associated with event handling that are useful to know and will simplify your task as a developer. These are listed below:

- All event handlers should be named such that they end in "EventHandler", for example MouseEventHandler.
- The return type of all event handlers should be void.
- All event handlers should have two parameters named sender and e. The sender parameter represents the object that raised the event and calls the delegate. The sender parameter is always of type object, even if it is possible to employ a more specific type. The state associated with the event is encapsulated in an instance of an event class named e. Use an appropriate and specific event class for its type.

Actually this is a requirement of the .NET Framework, but not of the C# language itself. Thus if you want to interoperate with other .NET Framework languages you must follow this convention.

- All event classes extend System.EventArgs. For example:

```
public class MouseEvent : EventArgs {
}
```

- All event class names should end in "EventArgs"; for example:

```
public class MouseEventArgs : EventArgs {
  private int x;
  private int y;
  public MouseEventArgs(int x, int y)
    { this.x = x; this.y = y; }
  public int X { get { return x; } }
  public int Y { get { return y; } }
}
```

24.5 An Example

To illustrate how you might implement a graphical application that will handle user inputs, consider the following program. This program creates a Form containing a single button. Whether the user clicks on this button the event arguments and a string are printed out. Although this is very simple, it does illustrate the basic idea.

```
using System;
using System.Windows.Forms;
using System.Drawing;
public class BasicWindowForm : Form {
  protected Button button;

  public BasicWindowForm(){
    Init();
  }

  private void Init(){
    this.Size = new Size(100, 100);
    this.Text = "Basic Window Form";
    CreateButtons();
  }

  private void CreateButtons(){
```

```
   button = new Button();
   button.Text = "Hello World!";
   button.Dock = DockStyle.Fill;
   this.Controls.Add (button);

   //Wire up event handler for button
   // Event Handler class defined in the System namespace
   button.Click += new EventHandler(Handler);
}
// EventArgs defined in System namespace
private void Handler(object sender, EventArgs e) {
  Console.WriteLine(e.ToString());
  Console.WriteLine("Hello World");
}

public static void Main(){
  Application.Run(new BasicWindowForm());
}
}
```

The result of compiling and running this application is illustrated in Figure 24.2. When the user clicks on the button in the window, the following is printed out into the command window:

```
C:\csharp\chapter24>BasicWindow
System.EventArgs
Hello World
```

Figure 24.2 Running the GUI application.

Note that we could have added more than one event handler to the button. Also note that the event handler could have handled input from more than one graphical component. For example, we might use the same event handler delegate for both a menu and a button performing the same operation.

Chapter 25

The JDEdit Application

25.1 Introduction

In this chapter we will examine the implementation of a complete graphical application that uses the classes and structures explored in the last two chapters.

25.2 JDEdit

The JDEdit application is a simple text editor that handles RTF (Rich Text Format) files. The application itself is illustrated in Figure 25.1. It is a minimal word processing application in that no search, replace or find functionality has been provided. Nor indeed is it possible within the tool to change

Figure 25.1 The JDEdit text processor.

font, create headings etc. (although files created with applications such as Word can do this and such features can be rendered within the application). This may make it sound very basic – which it is – but I do not want to obscure the basic structure of the application with unnecessary functionality.

The main functionality of the application is:

- Load an RTF file
- Illustrate the file being edited by including the filename on the title bar
- Save an RTF file
- Exit the application
- Allowing rendering of RTF files
- Allow new text to be input
- Provide a menu bar and text area
- Check to see whether a save is required on exit
- Visually indicate to the user that a file needs saving (by appending a "*" to the file name)

This involves creating a graphical application based on the Form class, providing that application with a menu bar and text area and implementing event handlers and appropriate supporting logic.

In the remainder of this chapter we will look at each element of the application. As the concepts that these elements use have already been discussed this discussion will be quite brief.

25.3 The Structure of JDEdit

The structure of the JDEdit application is illustrated in Figure 25.2. In this diagram the one class implemented specifically for this application is the JDEdit class. All the other classes are provided by the C# environment.

The main structure of the application illustrates that the JDEdit class extends the Form class. It then contains a reference to an instance of the RichTextBox class (a type of text area that understands RTF). It also contains a reference to the MainMenu and a file dialog for saving

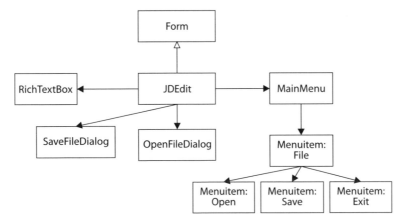

Figure 25.2 The structure of the JDEdit application.

and opening files. In turn, the MainMenu object holds references to the menu structure of the main menu.

The main JDEdit class defines the static and instance variables that make up the application, the Main method for the application and the constructor. It also contains the methods that set up the display, define the event handles and provide support functions (such as opening and saving a file).

The main JDEdit class directly extends the Form class. It provides two read-only static constants (one for supported filters and one for the title of the application). It also provides four instance variables. These variables hold a reference to the RichTextBox, the file dialogs and a Boolean flag used to determine whether a save is required for not. It also provides the Main method that runs the application. The part of the class that handles these functions is presented below, along with the constructor:

```
using System;
using System.Windows.Forms;
using System.ComponentModel;
using System.Drawing;
using System.IO;

public class JDEdit : Form {

  // Static variables
  private readonly static String filters =
    "Rich Text Format (*.rtf)|*.rtf|All Files (*.*)|*.*";
  private readonly static String title = "JDEdit";

  // Instance variables
  private RichTextBox textArea;
  private SaveFileDialog sfd;
  private OpenFileDialog ofd;
  private bool saveRequired;

  public JDEdit(){
    InitializeComponent();
  }
...

  // Starts the main application
  public static void Main(){
    Application.Run(new JDEdit());
  }
}
```

Notice that the constructor calls the InitializeComponent() method. We could have done all the initialization of the components in the Main method. However, to maintain consistency with the Visual Studio .NET conventions, we have placed all the initialization in a separate method (called InitializeComponent()).

The InitializeComponent method sets up the text area, the main menu, the window title, the size of the application, the open and save file dialogs etc. This method is presented below:

```
private void InitializeComponent(){
  this.textArea = new RichTextBox();
  this.Size = new Size (400, 300);
  this.Text = title;
  this.Menu = new MainMenu();

  ofd = new OpenFileDialog();
  ofd.Filter = filters;
  sfd = new SaveFileDialog();
  sfd.Filter = filters;

  SetupMenus();
  SetupTextArea();
}
```

The first line of this method creates an instance of a RichTextBox and stores that in the textArea instance variable. The RichTextBox component/control, defined in the System.Windows.Forms namespace, is used for displaying, entering, and manipulating text with formatting. The RichTextBox control inherits a great deal from its parent class TextBox, but adds the ability to display fonts, colours and links; to load text and embedded images from a file; to undo and redo editing operations; and to find specified characters. The RichTextBox control is used in the JDEdit application to provide text display features similar to word processing applications such as Microsoft Word. Like the TextBox control, the RichTextBox control can display scrollbars; but unlike the TextBox control, it displays both horizontal and vertical scrollbars by default.

Depending upon how sophisticated we wished to make the JDEdit application, we could exploit the default behaviour of the RichTextBox to supporting searching as well as many other functions, for example:

```
textArea.Find("Text", RichTextBoxFinds.MatchCase);
```

One we have set up the text area we then specify the size and title of the JDEdit application window (both inherited from Form). Following from this we create and store a MainMenu object for the window and then set up the FileDialog objects. The method concludes by calling the two setup methods. These methods set up the text area and the menu on the MainMenu.

25.4 The Menu Bar and Menus

To create a menu bar with drop-down menus on it, you must add MenuItems to the menu bar. In the case of the JDEdit application we have one drop-down menu "File". This menu contains three sub-menu items (Open, Save and Exit), plus a separator. This is illustrated in Figure 25.3.

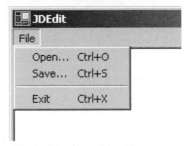

Figure 25.3 The File menu on the JDEdit application.

The setup method for the menu is presented below:

```
private void SetupMenus() {
  //Add File Menu
  MenuItem miFile = this.Menu.MenuItems.Add("File");
  miFile.MenuItems.Add(
    new MenuItem("Open...",
        new EventHandler(this.FileOpen_Clicked), Shortcut.CtrlO));
  miFile.MenuItems.Add(
    new MenuItem("Save...",
        new EventHandler(this.FileSave_Clicked), Shortcut.CtrlS));
  miFile.MenuItems.Add("-");  // Gives us a separator
  miFile.MenuItems.Add(
    new MenuItem("Exit",
        new EventHandler(this.FileExit_Clicked), Shortcut.CtrlX));
}
```

This menu creates a File.Menu item by adding a string to the MenuItems property of the MainMenu object. This has the effect of returning a MenuItem object. This menu item can be used to add individual options to the main File menu. Again this is done via the Add method being called on the MenuItems property. In the case of these File menu items, we also specify an EventHandler and a shortcut key. The shortcut key indicates which key is used to act as the menu activation (for example Control-O causes the Open menu item to be activated as though the user selected it from the File menu).

The event handlers for the menu items are defined within the JDEdit application itself; thus references to the this object and the methods that will act as the delegate implementation are provided. These methods are listed below:

```
//File->Exit Menu item handler
private void FileExit_Clicked(object sender, EventArgs e) {
  Close();
}

//File->Open Menu item handler
private void FileOpen_Clicked(object sender, EventArgs e) {
```

```
    Open();
}

//File->Open Menu item handler
private void FileSave_Clicked(object sender, EventArgs e) {
    Save();
}
```

As you can see from the above, each of the event handlers calls back to an appropriate method in the main application. This simplifies the operation of the application in cases where Open(), Save() or Close() need to be called from other areas.

The Open method uses the OpenFileDialog to allow the user to select the file to load. Once the text changed handler is de-registered from the text area the specified file is then loaded into the text area (using the RichTextBox method LoadFile). Note that the saveRequired flag and the application title are set as appropriate. The Open method is presented below:

```
private void Open() {
    if (ofd.ShowDialog() == DialogResult.OK) {
        String filename = ofd.FileName;
        Console.WriteLine("Open: {0}", filename);
        textArea.TextChanged -= new EventHandler(this.TextArea_TextChanged);
        textArea.LoadFile(filename);
        textArea.TextChanged += new EventHandler(this.TextArea_TextChanged);
        saveRequired = false;
        this.Text = title + ": " + filename;
    }
}
```

The Save method uses the SaveFileDialog object to allow the user to specify the filename to use when saving the file. It then uses the SaveFile method on the RichTextBox class to save the contents of the text area to a file. It then resets the saveRequired and application title appropriately. The Save method is presented below.

```
private void Save() {
    DialogResult dr = sfd.ShowDialog();
    if (dr == DialogResult.OK) {
        String filename = sfd.FileName;
        Console.WriteLine("Saving to: {0}", filename);
        textArea.SaveFile(filename, RichTextBoxStreamType.RichText);
        saveRequired = false;
        this.Text = title + " : " + filename;
    }
}
```

The Close() method used by the FileExit_Clicked method is inherited from the Form class by the JDEdit class and thus does not need to be implemented here.

25.5 The RichTextBox Setup

The RichTextBox object is configured via the SetupTextArea method presented below:

```
private void SetupTextArea() {
  textArea.Text = "";
  textArea.Dock = DockStyle.Fill;
  textArea.WordWrap = false;
  textArea.AcceptsTab = true;
  textArea.TextChanged += new EventHandler(this.TextArea_TextChanged);
  this.Controls.Add(textArea);
}
```

The RichTextBox is instantiated in the InitializeComponents method (although it could have been instantiated here instead). This method then initializes the text in the RichTextBox to the null string. It then indicates that it should fill the centre of the container it is added to (in this case the JDEdit application window). The WordWrap property is then set to false. This property indicates whether a multiline text box control automatically wraps words to the beginning of the next line when necessary. Next the AcceptsTab property is set to true (false is the default). If this property is false, then tab moves the focus on to the next field, whereas setting the property to true allows tabs to be entered into the text area. Finally, before adding the text area to the controls of the JDEdit Form an event handler is created to deal with the TextChanged event. This event is used to notify the JDEdit application when a user types into the RichTextBox. This allows the saveRequired flag to be set to true. The TextChanged event handler is illustrated below:

```
// Handles notification of changes in text area
private void TextArea_TextChanged(object sender, EventArgs e) {
  if (!saveRequired) {
    saveRequired = true;
    this.Text = this.Text + "*";
  }
}
```

Note that when a file is being loaded into the JDEdit application we must remove this event handler and re-register it after the file is loaded. Otherwise we will be notified of the change in the text area due to the file loading.

25.6 Monitoring the Application Closure

There are various On* methods defined on a Form that can be used for monitoring various activities. Some of the very many On* protected methods are:

- OnActivated: Raises the Activated event
- OnClosed: Raises the Closed event
- OnClosing: Raises the Closing event
- OnCursorChanged: Raises the CursorChanged event
- OnDeactivate: Raises the Deactivate event
- OnDragDrop: Raises the DragDrop event
- OnDragEnter: Raises the DragEnter event
- OnDragLeave: Raises the DragLeave event
- OnDragOver: Raises the DragOver event
- OnMouseDown: Raises the MouseDown event
- OnMouseEnter: Raises the MouseEnter event
- OnMouseHover: Raises the MouseHover event
- OnMouseLeave: Raises the MouseLeave event
- OnMouseMove: Raises the MouseMove event
- OnMouseUp: Raises the MouseUp event
- OnMouseWheel: Raises the MouseWheel event
- OnMove: Raises the Move event
- OnResize: Raises the Resize event

In our case we want to deal with the situation where the window is being asked to close down. This will allow our application to determine whether a dialog should be displayed to allow the user to save the current working file if it has been modified since the last save or load. The implementation of the OnClosing method is presented below:

```csharp
protected override void OnClosing(CancelEventArgs e) {
  base.OnClosing(e); // Call parent class method
  if (saveRequired) {
    DialogResult dr = MessageBox.Show(this,
        "Do you want to save the current changes?",
        "Save Changes?",
        MessageBoxButtons.YesNoCancel,
        MessageBoxIcon.Question);
    switch (dr) {
      case DialogResult.Yes:
        Save();
        break;
      case DialogResult.No:
        break;
      case DialogResult.Cancel:
        e.Cancel = true;
        break;
    }
  }
}
```

When the window starts to close this method is automatically called.

25.7 The Full Listing

This section provides the complete listing for this very simple application.

```csharp
using System;
using System.Windows.Forms;
using System.ComponentModel;
using System.Drawing;
using System.IO;

public class JDEdit : Form {

  // Static variables
  private readonly static String filters =
    "Rich Text Format (*.rtf)|*.rtf|All Files (*.*)|*.*";
  private readonly static String title = "JDEdit";

  // Instance variables
  private RichTextBox textArea;
  private SaveFileDialog sfd;
  private OpenFileDialog ofd;
  private bool saveRequired;

  public JDEdit(){
    InitializeComponent();
  }

  private void InitializeComponent(){
    this.textArea = new RichTextBox();
    this.Size = new Size (400, 300);
    this.Text = title;

    this.Menu = new MainMenu();

    ofd = new OpenFileDialog();
    ofd.Filter = filters;

    sfd = new SaveFileDialog();
    sfd.Filter = filters;

    SetupMenus();
    SetupTextArea();
  }

  private void SetupTextArea() {
```

```csharp
    textArea.Text = "";
    textArea.Dock = DockStyle.Fill;
    textArea.WordWrap = false;
    textArea.AcceptsTab = true;
    textArea.TextChanged +=
        new EventHandler(this.TextArea_TextChanged);
    this.Controls.Add(textArea);
}

private void SetupMenus() {
    //Add File Menu
    MenuItem miFile = this.Menu.MenuItems.Add("File");
    miFile.MenuItems.Add(new MenuItem("Open...",
        new EventHandler(this.FileOpen_Clicked), Shortcut.CtrlO));
    miFile.MenuItems.Add(new MenuItem("Save...",
        new EventHandler(this.FileSave_Clicked), Shortcut.CtrlS));
    miFile.MenuItems.Add("-");  // Gives us a separator
    miFile.MenuItems.Add(new MenuItem("Exit",
        new EventHandler(this.FileExit_Clicked), Shortcut.CtrlX));
}

private void Open() {
    if (ofd.ShowDialog() == DialogResult.OK) {
        String filename = ofd.FileName;
        Console.WriteLine("Open: {0}", filename);
        textArea.TextChanged -= new EventHandler(this.TextArea_TextChanged);
        textArea.LoadFile(filename);
        textArea.TextChanged += new EventHandler(this.TextArea_TextChanged);
        saveRequired = false;
        this.Text = title + ": " + filename;
    }
}

private void Save() {
    DialogResult dr = sfd.ShowDialog();
    if (dr == DialogResult.OK) {
        String filename = sfd.FileName;
        Console.WriteLine("Saving to: {0}", filename);
        textArea.SaveFile(filename, RichTextBoxStreamType.RichText);
        saveRequired = false;
        this.Text = title + " : " + filename;
    }
}

// Handles notification of changes in text area
private void TextArea_TextChanged(object sender, EventArgs e) {
```

```csharp
  if (!saveRequired) {
    saveRequired = true;
    this.Text = this.Text + "*";
  }
}

//File->Exit Menu item handler
private void FileExit_Clicked(object sender, EventArgs e) {
  Close();
}
//File->Open Menu item handler
private void FileOpen_Clicked(object sender, EventArgs e) {
  Open();
}

//File->Open Menu item handler
private void FileSave_Clicked(object sender, EventArgs e) {
  Save();
}

// Specifies what should happen when a close is requested
protected override void OnClosing(CancelEventArgs e) {
  base.OnClosing(e); // Call parent class method
  if (saveRequired) {
    DialogResult dr = MessageBox.Show(this,
      "Do you want to save the current changes?",
      "Save Changes?",
      MessageBoxButtons.YesNoCancel, MessageBoxIcon.Question);
    switch (dr) {
      case DialogResult.Yes:
        Save();
        break;
      case DialogResult.No:
        break;
      case DialogResult.Cancel:
        e.Cancel = true;
        break;
    }
  }
}

// Starts the main application
public static void Main(){
  Application.Run(new JDEdit());
}
}
```

Part 6

C# Development

Chapter 26

Streams and Files

26.1 Introduction

This chapter deals with files and file IO. It first introduces the File and FileInfo classes (and the DirectoryInfo class). The chapter then discusses the second most used class hierarchy in C#: the Stream classes. The Stream classes are used (among other things) for accessing files. The stream classes can be found in the System.IO namespace.

Notice that the Stream classes and hierarchies are quite large and complex. You should therefore not worry if you are unable to grasp the facilities provided by all the classes (or indeed how they relate to each other). This chapter does not attempt to provide a complete description of the classes; rather, it tries to offer a taste of what streams can do and why they are provided. You should refer to the C# online reference material for further details.

26.2 Files

When I first came to C# I had anticipated that accessing information in a file would involve a class called something like File. I quickly found such a file in the System.IO namespace. However, this file did not provide access to the contents of a file. Instead it provided information on a file (via static methods). In fact, the File class provides static methods for the creation, copying, deletion, moving and opening of files. The File class can also be used with streams to access the contents of a file, but it does not itself provide access to those contents. As an example of what you can use the File class for, consider the following example program:

```
using System;
using System.IO;

public class FileTest {
  public static void Main(String[] args) {
    String filename = "";
```

```
    // Obtain the file to write from the command line
    if (args.Length < 1) {
      PrintUsage();
      return;
    } else {
      filename = args[0];
    }
    if (File.Exists(filename)) {
      Console.WriteLine("{0} exists!", filename);
      Console.WriteLine("\tCreation time: {0}",
          File.GetCreationTime(filename));
      Console.WriteLine("\tLast Access time: {0}",
          File.GetLastAccessTime(filename));
      Console.WriteLine("\tLast Write time: {0}",
          File.GetLastWriteTime(filename));
      Console.WriteLine("\tFile Attributes: {0}",
          File.GetAttributes(filename));
      File.Copy(filename, filename + ".bak");
    }
  }

  private static void PrintUsage() {
    Console.WriteLine("Usage: FileTest <filename>");
  }
}
```

The result of compiling and executing this program is:

```
C:\csharp\chapter26>FileTest test.txt
test.txt exists!
  Creation time: 19/10/2001 15:54:01
  Last Access time: 19/10/2001 16:05:00
  Last Write time: 18/10/2001 17:14:47
  File Attributes: ReadOnly, NotContentIndexed
```

Also note that the file test.txt.bak was created:

```
18/10/2001  17:20         4 test.txt.bak
```

26.3 FileInfo

In the System.IO namespace there is also a class called FileInfo. This class has a set of *instance* methods that match the *static* methods of the File class. FileInfo can be used in a similar manner to file (that is to obtain information about a file, to move it, copy it, delete it etc.). It can also help in accessing the contents of the file, although it again does not directly provide access the contents of the file. For example:

```csharp
using System;
using System.IO;
public class FileInfoTest {

  public static void Main(String[] args) {
    String filename = "";
    // Obtain the file to write from the command line
    if (args.Length < 1) {
      PrintUsage();
      return;
    } else {
      filename = args[0];
    }
    FileInfo file = new FileInfo(filename);
    if (file.Exists) {
      Console.WriteLine("{0} exists!", file.ToString());
      Console.WriteLine("\tCreation time: {0}",
        file.CreationTime);
      Console.WriteLine("\tLast Access time: {0}",
        file.LastAccessTime);
      Console.WriteLine("\tLast Write time: {0}",
        file.LastWriteTime);
      Console.WriteLine("\tFile Attributes: {0}",
        file.Attributes);
      Console.WriteLine("\tFile extension: {0}",
        file.Extension);

      file.CopyTo(filename + ".old");
    }
  }

  private static void PrintUsage() {
    Console.WriteLine("Usage: FileInfoTest <filename>");
  }
}
```

Note that the static get methods on the File class have been replaced by properties on the instance of FileInfo. Also note that there are a few additional properties and methods available on a FileInfo object than for the static class File. The result of compiling and executing this program is presented below:

```
C:\csharp\chapter26>FileInfoTest test.txt
test.txt exists!
```

```
Creation time: 19/10/2001 15:54:01
Last Access time: 19/10/2001 16:11:42
Last Write time: 18/10/2001 17:20:32
File Attributes: ReadOnly, NotContentIndexed
File extension: .txt
```

Once again the file obtained from the filename passed into this program is copied. This time to a file with a ".old" extension:

```
18/10/2001 17:20           4 test.txt.old
```

An interesting question to ask is why C# provides both the File class and the FileInfo class. Partly this is because if you merely wish to test for the existence of a file it is undesirable to have to create an instance of an object (which may be thrown away immediately) just to do this. Also, the tests in the File class perform security checks (e.g. on access rights) every time the methods are run, whereas they are not repeated if they are run more than once on the same object in FileInfo.

26.4 Directory and DirectoryInfo

The Directory and DirectoryInfo classes are mirrors of their File versions, but at the directory level rather than the file level. For example, both provide methods for creating, moving and enumerating through directories and subdirectories. The Directory class provides static methods for this while the DirectoryInfo class provides instance properties and methods to do this. For example, the following very simple program lists the contents of the current directory:

```
using System;
using System.IO;
public class DirectoryTest {

  public static void Main() {
    String [] contents = Directory.GetFiles(".");
    foreach(String file in contents) {
      Console.WriteLine(file);
    }
  }
}
```

The result of this program is that the files in the current directory are printed to the console, thus:

```
C:\csharp\chapter26>DirectoryTest
.\DirectoryTest.cs
.\DirectoryTest.exe
.\FileInfoTest.cs
.\FileInfoTest.exe
```

```
.\test.txt
.\test.txt.bak
.\test.txt.old
```

26.5 Streams

26.5.1 What Is a Stream?

Streams are objects that serve as sources or sinks of data. At first this concept can seem a bit strange. The easiest way to think of a stream is as a conduit of data flowing from or into a "pool". Some streams read data straight from the "pool" and some streams read data from other streams. These streams then do some "useful" processing of the data and are referred to as "filter" streams. Figure 26.1 illustrates this idea. In this figure the initial stream reads data from the data source; the FileStream then handles taking the data from the source and providing it in a meaningful way to a filter stream. In this case the FilterStream is a BinaryReader that can convert the low-level bytes provided by the FileStream into ints, floats, longs etc. That is, it filters the input to create more meaningful data types (Figure 26.1).

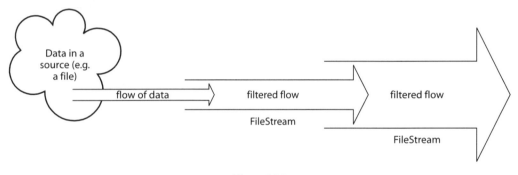

Figure 26.1

There are a number of types of stream in the C# system, and each has a wide range of uses. Figure 26.2 illustrates part of the structure of the Stream class hierarchy.

The abstract Stream, TextWriter and TextReader classes are the root classes of the stream hierarchies. Below them are stream classes for reading, writing, accessing external files and strings, etc. In addition there are BinaryReader and BinaryWriter classes that are used to read and write basic types to streams.

A stream may be input-only (TextReader) or output only (TextWriter); it may be specialized for handling files (FileStream); it may be an internal stream (which acts as a source or sink for data internal to the system for example MemoryStream and StringReader and StringWriter) or an external stream (which is the source or sink for data external to the system). A string is a typical example of an internal source or sink; a file is a typical example of an external source or sink.

Typically, a stream is connected to an external device or a collection of data. If a stream is connected to an external device (for example a file), then it acts as an interface to that device. It

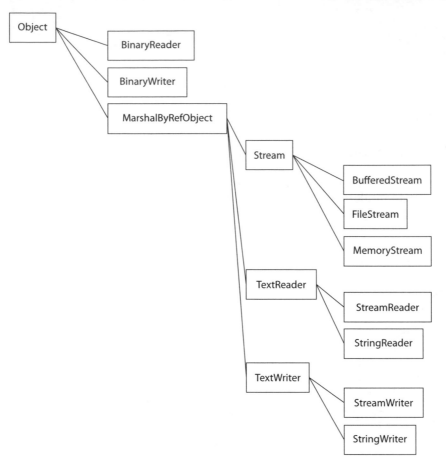

Figure 26.2 The structure of part of the Stream class hierarchies.

allows messages to be sent to and received from the external device object, enabling it to accomplish various activities, including input and output. If a stream is connected to a collection (such as a string) it acts as a way to process the contents of the collection. In both cases, the stream views the source (or sink) of the data as being able to provide (or receive) a data item on request.

TextReaders and TextWriters are of particular interest as they simplify the task of writing programs that are not dependent on a specific character encoding. They make it easier to write a program that works with ASCII, Unicode etc., which is important if you are developing systems which might be used in different parts of the world, using different encodings to represent features of different languages. By default, C# uses Unicode (an international standard character encoding) internally, but text readers and writers can convert to standard ASCII for files.

26.5.2 Using the IO Classes

Streams are often combined to provide the required functionality. This section looks at reading and writing basic types such as int, reading strings via readers and writing them via writers.

Reading and Writing Basic Types

To read and write basic types we need to convert the basic bytes read by the actual data source reading streams into ints, floats, doubles, shorts, longs, bools etc. To do this we need to use a BinaryReader wrapped around appropriate lower level streams. This is illustrated in Figure 26.3. In this diagram a low-level data-reading FileStream reads data from a file. This data is passed to a BinaryReader in order to convert it to the appropriate type.

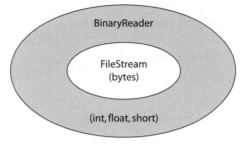

Figure 26.3 Reading basic types.

The actual source code that implements this structure is presented below:

```
using System;
using System.IO;

public class FileReader {

  public static void Main(String[] args) {
    String filename = "";
    int data;
    // Obtain the file to write from the command line
    if (args.Length < 1) {
      PrintUsage();
      return;
    } else {
      filename = args[0];
    }

    // Create the reader for data.
    FileStream fs =
         new FileStream(filename, FileMode.Open, FileAccess.Read);
    BinaryReader r = new BinaryReader(fs);
    // Read data from Test.data.
    data = r.ReadInt32();
    r.Close();
    Console.WriteLine("Data read in is {0}", data);
  }
```

```csharp
    private static void PrintUsage() {
      Console.WriteLine("FileRead <filename>");
    }
  }
```

Notice that when we open the `FileStream` which connects us to the underlying data file, not only must we specify the file to connect to, but also the mode (as defined by `FileMode.Open`) and the type of file access (`FileAccess.Read`).

The result of executing this program on an existing file is:

```
C:\csharp\chapter26>FileReader test.txt
Data read in is 32
```

To write basic data types out to a file you use a similar approach. Essentially, instead of a `BinaryReader` type class you use a `BinaryWriter` type class. Thus to write the data to the file `test.txt` you would write:

```csharp
using System;
using System.IO;

public class FileWriter {

  public static void Main(String[] args) {
    String filename = "";
    int data;
    // Obtain the file to write from the command line
    if (args.Length < 2) {
      PrintUsage();
      return;
    } else {
      filename = args[0];
      data = 32;
    }
    if (File.Exists(filename)) {
      Console.WriteLine("{0} already exists!", filename);
    }

    FileStream fs = new FileStream(filename, FileMode.Create);
    // Create the writer for data.
    BinaryWriter w = new BinaryWriter(fs);
    // Write data to Test.data.
    w.Write(data);
    w.Close();
    fs.Close();
  }
```

```
    private static void PrintUsage() {
      Console.WriteLine("FileWriter <filename> int");
    }
  }
```

If we wished to guarantee that this program will only work if there is not already a file of the specified name then we could specify `FileMode.CreateNew` to the `FileStream` constructor.

The result of compiling and running this program is that a new file is created with the specified contents.

Reading and Writing Strings

Reading and writing strings is, as has been stated, complicated by the need to translate between the ASCII character set and the Unicode character set used within C#. However, the `TextReader` and `TextWriter` subclasses provide facilities for this, and thus you should always use these classes when reading and writing strings.

As with reading basic data types, you need to have a low-level byte-reading stream to allow you to obtain data from the data source (for example a file). An example of such a stream is of course the `FileStream`. This can be wrapped inside a `StreamReader` (a subclass of `TextReader`) that will convert the bytes into Unicode characters within `String` objects. This is illustrated in Figure 26.4.

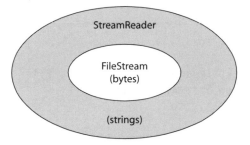

Figure 26.4 Reading basic types.

In the case of reading strings from files, the operation is thought to be common enough that a shortcut has been provided for the `FileStream` and `StreamReader` constructs via the `File` and `FileInfo` classes. This is done from the `OpenText` method. Thus we can write:

```
FileStream fs = new FileStream(filename, FileMode.Open, FileAccess.Read);
StreamReader sr = new StreamReader(fs);
```

or

```
StreamReader sr = File.OpenText(filename);
```

In either case we can then write:

```
String data = r.ReadLine();
sr.close();
```

So why have we told you about both approaches? The answer is that a File (or FileInfo) based approach only works when reading text from files. However, there are other sources of text, such as sockets.

As a complete example of reading strings from a file consider the following program:

```
using System;
using System.IO;

public class FileRead {

  public static void Main(String[] args) {
    String filename = "";
    String data;
    // Obtain the file to write from the command line
    if (args.Length < 1) {
      PrintUsage();
      return;
    } else {
      filename = args[0];
    }

    // Create the reader for data.
    FileStream fs =
        new FileStream(filename, FileMode.Open, FileAccess.Read);
    StreamReader r = new StreamReader(fs);
    // Read data from Test.data.
    data = r.ReadLine();
    r.Close();
    Console.WriteLine("Data read in is {0}", data);
  }

  private static void PrintUsage() {
    Console.WriteLine("Usage:TextFileReader <filename>");
  }
}
```

Writing strings to files can be accomplished using Writer classes. For example, to create a TextWriter we can write:

```
FileStream fs = new FileStream(filename, FileMode.Create);
// Create the writer for data.
StreamWriter sw = new StreamWriter(fs);
```

or

```
StreamWriter sw = File.CreateText(filename);
```

In either case we can then write:

```
sw.Write(data);
sw.Close();
```

As an example of a complete text reading program see below:

```
using System;
using System.IO;

public class TextFileWriter {

  public static void Main(String[] args) {
    String filename = "";
    String data;
    // Obtain the file to write from the command line
    if (args.Length < 2) {
      PrintUsage();
      return;
    } else {
      filename = args[0];
      data = args[1];
    }
    if (File.Exists(filename)) {
      Console.WriteLine("{0} already exists!", filename);
    }

    FileStream fs = new FileStream(filename, FileMode.Create);
    // Create the writer for data.
    StreamWriter w = new StreamWriter(fs);
    // Write data to Test.data.
    w.Write(data);
    w.Close();
    fs.Close();
  }

  private static void PrintUsage() {
    Console.WriteLine("TextFileWriter <filename> <String>");
  }
}
```

26.6 Summary

In this chapter, you have encountered streams and their use in file input and output. Many simple C# applications do not access files. However, if you need to store information or share it between applications, then you need to interact with the host file system. You have now seen the basic facilities available, and should spend some time exploring the stream and file facilities available in C#.

Chapter 27

Serialization

27.1 Introduction

If you save object information without serialization, then you can only save the ASCII version of the data held by the object. You need to reconstruct the data into objects when you read the text file, which means that you have to indicate that certain data is associated with certain objects and that certain objects are related. This is very time-consuming and error-prone. It is also very unlikely that the ASCII data written out by someone else is in the right format for your system.

Serialization allows you to store objects directly to a file in a compact and encoded form. You do not need to convert the objects or reconstruct them when you load them back in. In addition, everyone else who uses serialization can read and write your files. This is useful not only for portability but also for sharing objects.

The name "serialization" comes from situations that can arise when saving more than one related object to a file. For example, in Figure 27.1 four objects are related by references and are held by another object Family (within a vector).

If, when we want to save the whole family to file, we merely save each object independently, we also have to save copies of the objects that they reference. In the above example, we would end up with multiple copies of Phoebe. If we can determine whether an object has already been saved to disk, then we can record a reference to the previously saved object, so that the original

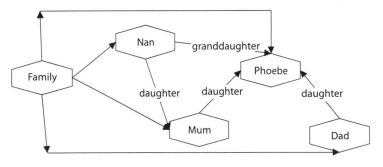

Figure 27.1 Related objects.

289

structure can be restored at a later date. This reference is referred to as a serial number (hence the name serialization).

Each object is stored to disk with its own serial number. If an object has been stored, then a reference to its serial number is included with any object that references it. For example, if Phoebe has serial number 1 then, when Mum, Dad or Nan are saved, they merely record that they reference the object with serial number 1.

In C# there are actually two different ways in which you can serialize an object. One is to binary format (which is typically smaller in size and faster to perform) and the other is to an XML format (which is almost human-readable). There are four namespaces that provide the classes, interfaces, structs and enumerations used within serialization. These are System.Runtime.Serialization, System.Runtime.Serialization.Formatters, System.Runtime.Serialization.Formatters. Binary (for binary serialization) and System.Runtime.Serialization.Formatters.Soap (for XML-based serialization). These are briefly outlined below:

- System.Runtime.Serialization contains classes that can be used for serializing and deserializing objects. Serialization is the process of converting an object or a graph of objects into a linear sequence of bytes for either storage or transmission to another location. Deserialization is the process of taking in stored information and recreating objects from it.
- System.Runtime.Serialization.Formatters provides common enumerations, interfaces and classes that are used by serialization formatters.
- System.Runtime.Serialization.Formatters.Binary contains the BinaryFormatter class, which can be used to serialize and deserialize objects in binary format.
- System.Runtime.Serialization.Formatters.Soap Contains the SoapFormatter class, which can be used to serialize and deserialize objects in the SOAP format.

27.2 Binary Serialization

27.2.1 Saving Objects

For an object to be serializable, its class must be marked as such by the attribute Serializable. To save an object to file in binary format, you use the BinaryFormatter class. However, a BinaryFormatter must use a stream, such as FileStream, to write data into a file:

```
using System;
using System.IO;
using System.Runtime.Serialization;
using System.Runtime.Serialization.Formatters.Binary;
using System.Collections;

[Serializable]
public class Person {
  private String name;
  private int age;
  public Person(String n, int a) {
```

```
      name = n;
      age = a;
    }
}

[Serializable]
public class Family : ArrayList {
}

public class TestWrite {
  public static void Main() {
    Person p1 = new Person("John", 37);
    Person p2 = new Person("Denise", 34);
    Person p3 = new Person("Phoebe", 4);
    Person p4 = new Person("Adam", 2);
    Family f = new Family();
    f.Add(p1);
    f.Add(p2);
    f.Add(p3);
    f.Add(p4);
    FileStream fs = File.Create("Family.bin");
    BinaryFormatter bf = new BinaryFormatter();
    bf.Serialize(fs, f);
    fs.Close();
  }
}
```

The above code results in all the objects held by family being saved to the file Family.bin using serialization. The file created is 328 bytes in size on a Windows 2000 machine.

Hopefully the above example illustrates that, although you may find the concepts confusing, serialization is easy to work with.

27.2.2 Reading Objects

To read objects that have been serialized to file back into an application, you need to use the BinaryFormatter class again. Again it needs to use a FileStream, but this time the method Deserialize will be used (instead of the Serialize method). As the Deserialize method returns objects of type Object, the deserialized object must be cast back to the Family class. This is illustrated in the following example:

```
using System;
using System.IO;
using System.Runtime.Serialization;
using System.Runtime.Serialization.Formatters.Binary;
using System.Collections;
```

```
[Serializable]
public class Person {
  private String name;
  private int age;
  public Person(String n, int a) {
    name = n;
    age = a;
  }
  public override String ToString() {
    return name + " , " + age;
  }
}

[Serializable]
public class Family : ArrayList {
}

public class TestRead {
  public static void Main() {
    FileStream fs = File.OpenRead("Family.bin");
    BinaryFormatter bf = new BinaryFormatter();
    Object obj = bf.Deserialize(fs);
    Console.WriteLine(obj);
    fs.Close();
  }
}
```

Notice that you must cast the object retrieved by the readObject method into the appropriate class (just as with ArrayLists and hash tables).

27.3 XML Serialization

27.3.1 Saving Objects

To save an object to file in XML format, you use the SoapFormatter class. However, a SoapFormatter must use a stream, such as FileStream, to write data into a file:

```
using System;
using System.IO;
using System.Runtime.Serialization;
using System.Runtime.Serialization.Formatters.Soap;
using System.Collections;
```

```
[Serializable]
public class Person {
  private String name;
  private int age;
  public Person(String n, int a) {
    name = n;
    age = a;
  }
}

[Serializable]
public class Family : ArrayList {
}

public class TestXmlWrite {
  public static void Main() {
    Person p1 = new Person("John", 37);
    Person p2 = new Person("Denise", 34);
    Person p3 = new Person("Phoebe", 4);
    Person p4 = new Person("Adam", 2);
    Family f = new Family();
    f.Add(p1);
    f.Add(p2);
    f.Add(p3);
    f.Add(p4);
    FileStream fs = File.Create("Family.xml");
    SoapFormatter bf = new SoapFormatter();
    bf.Serialize(fs, f);
    fs.Close();
  }
}
```

The above code results in all the objects held by family being saved to the file Family.xml using XML-based serialization. The file created is 1123 bytes in size on a Windows 2000 machine and the program takes considerably longer to run than the binary version.

The XML file generated is presented below:

```
<SOAP-ENV:Envelope xmlns:xsi="http://www.w3.org/2001/XMLSchema-instance"
xmlns:xsd="http://www.w3.org/2001/XMLSchema" xmlns:SOAP-ENC="http://
schemas.xmlsoap.org/soap/encoding/" xmlns:SOAP-ENV="http://
schemas.xmlsoap.org/soap/envelope/" SOAP-ENV:encodingStyle="http://
schemas.xmlsoap.org/soap/encoding/" xmlns:a1="http://schemas.microsoft.com/
clr/assem/TestXmlWrite">
<SOAP-ENV:Body>
<a1:Family id="ref-1">
<ArrayList_x002B__items href="#ref-3"/>
```

```
<ArrayList_x002B__size>4</ArrayList_x002B__size>
<ArrayList_x002B__version>4</ArrayList_x002B__version>
</a1:Family>
<SOAP-ENC:Array id="ref-3" SOAP-ENC:arrayType="xsd:ur-type[16]">
<item href="#ref-4"/>
<item href="#ref-5"/>
<item href="#ref-6"/>
<item href="#ref-7"/>
</SOAP-ENC:Array>
<a1:Person id="ref-4">
<name id="ref-8">John</name>
<age>37</age>
</a1:Person>
<a1:Person id="ref-5">
<name id="ref-9">Denise</name>
<age>34</age>
</a1:Person>
<a1:Person id="ref-6">
<name id="ref-10">Phoebe</name>
<age>4</age>
</a1:Person>
<a1:Person id="ref-7">
<name id="ref-11">Adam</name>
<age>2</age>
</a1:Person>
</SOAP-ENV:Body>
</SOAP-ENV:Envelope>
```

SOAP (Simple Object Access Protocol) is a Microsoft standard for the interchange of information between object systems based on XML tagging. If you wish to create your own encoding then you should use the XmlSerializer class.

27.3.2 Reading Objects

To read objects that have been serialized to an XML file back into an application, you need to use you use the SoapFormatter class again. Again it needs to use a FileStream, but this time the method Deserialize will be used instead of the Serialize method.

```
using System;
using System.IO;
using System.Runtime.Serialization;
using System.Runtime.Serialization.Formatters.Soap;
using System.Collections;

[Serializable]
public class Person {
```

```
    private String name;
    private int age;
    public Person(String n, int a) {
      name = n;
      age = a;
    }
    public override String ToString() {
      return name + " , " + age;
    }
  }

[Serializable]
public class Family : ArrayList {
}

public class TestXMlRead {
  public static void Main() {
    FileStream fs = File.OpenRead("Family.xml");
    SoapFormatter sf = new SoapFormatter();
    Object obj = sf.Deserialize(fs);
    Console.WriteLine(obj);
  }
}
```

27.4 Controlling Serialization

It is also possible to indicate that a particular instance variable should not be serialized using the NonSerialized attribute. This indicates to the serialization system that the instance variable should be ignored. This is useful for information that is not "persistent" and should not be saved along with the object or for data that cannot be serialized (for example instances of the class Thread cannot be serialized). To do this you can define an instance variable thus:

```
[NonSerialized]
private int count;
```

27.5 Custom Serialization

In some situations, you may need to implement your own version of how serialization should save the information in an object. For example, you may not need to save the information held in all the instance variables, but only one or two variables from a set of 20. This would minimize the size of the serialized objects on disk. A user-defined class can implement the ISerializable interface. This interface defines one method GetObjectData. This method is defined as:

```
void GetObjectData(
  SerializationInfo info,
  StreamingContext context
);
```

In addition, any class implementing this interface must also provide a constructor that takes a SerializationInfo object and a StreamContext parameter:

```
<class-name>(SerializationInfo info, StreamContext content)
{...}
```

The GetObjectData method must write info, the information required to restore the object, to the SerializationInfoobject. In turn, the constructor is expected to read that information back into an object, setting instance variables as appropriate from the info parameter. In either case, you should use the Add or Get methods defined on the SerializationInfo class to handle the instance variable data.

If you are confused by what the method and the constructor do, then think of it this way: "These methods define what information is saved to the file or restored from the file, for a particular class of object".

If you try to save an object that is not serializable, then an exception is thrown. This exception identifies the class of the non-serializable object.

Notice that the way in which you define how an object can be saved to a file or restored from a file is classic object orientation. That is, the object itself defines how it should be saved to a file. The parameter to GetObjectData is the info object that will be used to write data to the file, but the info object does not decide what is written.

27.6 Summary

In this chapter you have encountered how serialization within C# works, how objects can be written in both binary and XML format to files, and how they can be retrieved again.

Chapter 28

Sockets in C#

28.1 Introduction

A "Socket" is an end point in a communication link between separate processes. In C#, sockets are objects which provide a way of exchanging information between two processes in a straightforward and platform-independent manner (see the classes in the `System.Net` and `System.Net.Sockets` namespaces).

28.2 Socket to Socket Communication

When two separate processes wish to communicate they can do so via sockets. Each process has a socket which is connected to the other's socket. One process can then write information out to the socket, while the second process can read information back in from its socket. To achieve this, the streams model, already used for file access, is exploited. Associated with each socket are two streams, one for input and one for output. Thus to pass information from one process to another, you write that information out to the output stream of one socket and read it from the input stream of another socket (assuming the two sockets are connected). This is illustrated in Figure 28.1. This has the great advantage that once the network connection has been made, passing information between processes is not significantly different from reading and writing information with any other stream.

28.3 Setting up a Connection

To set up the connection, one process must be running a program that is waiting for a connection while the other must try to reach the first. The first is referred to as a server socket, while the second just as a socket. Typically the server socket will accept a connection, the result of which is a new socket to handle the interchange with the client. The server could do this in a separate thread, allowing the server to return immediately to service other client requests.

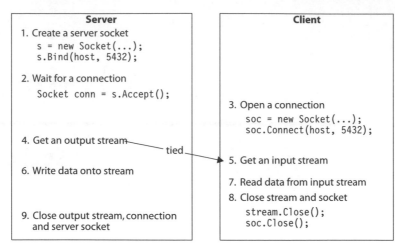

Figure 28.1 Socket to socket communication.

For the second process to connect to the first (the server socket) it must know what machine the first is running on and which port it is connected to. A port number is a logical point of communication on a computer. Port numbers in the TCP/IP system are 16 bit numbers in the range 0–65536 (a description of TCP/IP is beyond the scope of this book; see Parker (1994) for further information). Generally, port numbers below 1024 are reserved for pre-defined services (which means that you should avoid using them unless you wish to communicate with one of those services, such as telnet, SMTP mail or ftp).

For example, in Figure 28.1 the server socket connects to port 5432. In turn, the client socket connects to the machine on which the server is executing and then to port number 5432 on that machine. Nothing happens until the server socket accepts the connection. At that point the sockets are connected and the socket streams are bound to each other.

28.4 An Example Client–Server Application

28.4.1 The System Structure

Figure 28.2 illustrates the basic structure of the system we are trying to build. There will be a server object running on one machine and a client object running on another. The client will connect up to the server using sockets in order to obtain information.

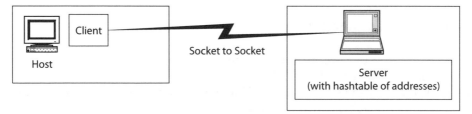

Figure 28.2 The simple client–server application.

The actual application being implemented is an address book. The addresses of employees of a company are held in a Hashtable. This hash table is set up in the Server's constructor, but could equally be held in a database etc.

28.4.2 Implementing the Server Application

We shall describe the server application first. This is the C# application program that will service requests from clients for information. To do this it must provide a socket that will listen for client requests for connections. Listing 28.1 presents the annotated source code for the Server class. Note that the earlier diagram simplified the way in which a socket is bound to a port on a machine (or that a connection is bound to a port on a specific machine).

Listing 28.1 The Server Application.

```csharp
using System;
using System.IO;
using System.Net;
using System.Net.Sockets;
using System.Collections;

public class Server {
  // Instance variable to hold names and addresses
  private Hashtable addressTable;

  // Main method to start the erver application
  public static void Main () {
    Server s = new Server();
    s.Start();
  }

  public Server() {
    Console.WriteLine("Initializing Server data");
    // Set up names and addresses
    addressTable = new Hashtable(10);
    addressTable.Add("John", "C45");
    addressTable.Add("Denise", "C44");
    addressTable.Add("Phoebe", "B52");
    addressTable.Add("Isobel", "E23");
  }

  public void Start() {

    Socket serverSocket = null;
    Socket socket = null;
    NetworkStream stream = null;
    StreamWriter writer = null;
```

```csharp
StreamReader reader = null;

Console.WriteLine("Starting server");
try{
  // Register service on port 1234
  serverSocket = new Socket(AddressFamily.InterNetwork,
      SocketType.Stream,
      ProtocolType.Tcp);
  serverSocket.Bind(new IPEndPoint(IPAddress.Parse("127.0.0.1"),1234));

  Console.WriteLine("Server bound to console");
  serverSocket.Listen(0);
  // Wait for a connection from a client
  while (true) {
    // Wait here and listen for a connection
    Console.WriteLine("Waiting for client connection ...");
    // Accepting a connection provides a socket to handle
    // client-server communications
    socket = serverSocket.Accept();
    Console.WriteLine("Connection accepted");
    stream = new NetworkStream(socket);
    reader = new StreamReader(stream);
    writer = new StreamWriter(stream);

    Console.WriteLine("Reading client data");
    String queryString = reader.ReadLine();
    Console.WriteLine("Client data is : {0} ", queryString);

    // Now obtain information from addressTable
    // need to cast the result ot a string as Object is returned
    // by default.
    String result = (String)addressTable[queryString];

    Console.WriteLine("Result is {0} ", result);

    // Return information to client
    // Get a communications stream from the socket
    Console.WriteLine("Sending data to client");
    writer.Write(result);
    writer.Flush();
    Console.WriteLine("Data sent, closing connection");

    reader.Close();
    reader = null;
    writer.Close();
    writer = null;
```

```
            socket.Close();
            socket = null;
        }
    } catch(SocketException e){
        Console.WriteLine("Error Initializing Socket: "+ e.ToString());
    } catch (IOException exp) {
        Console.WriteLine("Error in Socket Communication: "+ exp.ToString());
    }
  }
}
```

Essentially the Server in Listing 28.1 sets up the addressTable to contain a Hashtable of the names and addresses available. It then waits for a client to connect to it. This is done by creating a Socket (in this case on port 1234). It then enters a loop where it continually waits for connections, processes requests and waits for the next connection. When the connection is made, it uses the input stream of its socket to obtain the information provided by the client. Note that although this is a socket to socket communication, as streams are used the way to pass a String is exactly the same as writing that String out to a file. It then queries the addressTable and returns the result. Having done all this it closes its connection to the socket. It is now ready for the next query. As you can see from this, the program is actually very straightforward. This is thanks primarily to the C# Socket and Stream classes that hide a great deal of the implementation details often associated with socket communications.

The server can be started in one Windows command window and set to wait for incoming connections. For example, the result of the server after processing two requests from two clients is that it waits for a third, for example:

```
C:\csharp\chapter28>Server
Initializing Server data
Starting server
Server bound to console
Waiting for client connection ...
Connection accepted
Reading client data
Client data is : John
Result is C45
Sending data to client
Data sent, closing connection
Waiting for client connection ...
Connection accepted
Reading client data
Client data is :
Result is
Sending data to client
Data sent, closing connection
Waiting for client connection ...
```

28.4.3 Implementing the Client Application

The client application is essentially a very simple program that creates a link to the server application. To do this it creates a socket that connects to the server's host machine, and in our case this socket is connected to port 1234. It then uses a stream writer to pass a string to the server. Having done that, it waits for the server to provide a response. The response is the result of querying the database for the address associated with the supplied name. This is then printed out with an appropriate message.

The annotated source code for the Client program is presented in Listing 28.2.

Listing 28.2 The Client program.

```
using System;
using System.IO;
using System.Net;
using System.Net.Sockets;

public class Client {

  public static void Main (String [] args) {
    String query = null;
    if (args.Length == 0) {
      Console.WriteLine("Usage: Client <name>");
    } else {
      query = args[0];
    }

    try {
      // First get a socket connection to the Server object
      Console.WriteLine("Requesting connection to server");
      Socket socket = new Socket(AddressFamily.InterNetwork,
              SocketType.Stream,
              ProtocolType.Tcp);
      // Connect to host using IPEndPoint
      socket.Connect(new IPEndPoint(IPAddress.Parse("127.0.0.1"),1234));
      Console.WriteLine("Connection successful");

      NetworkStream stream = new NetworkStream(socket);
      StreamReader reader = new StreamReader(stream);
      StreamWriter writer = new StreamWriter(stream);

      Console.WriteLine("Writing data to the server");
      writer.Write(query + "\n");
      writer.Flush();

      Console.WriteLine("Waiting for server response");
```

```
        // New get the response
        String result = reader.ReadLine();
        Console.WriteLine("Server response obtained");

        // Once we get the result - print it out
        if (result == null) {
        Console.WriteLine("No address is held for " + query);
        } else {
        Console.WriteLine("Address for {0} is {1} ", query, result);
        }

        Console.WriteLine("Closing connection to server");
        reader.Close();
        writer.Close();
        socket.Close();
      } catch (Exception e) {
        Console.WriteLine("Error during socket communications: " +
                          e.ToString());
      }
    }
  }
}
```

An example of using the client to query the server is presented below. Remember that the client should be started in a separate command window:

```
C:\csharp\chapter28>Client John
Requesting connection to server
Connection successful
Writing data to the server
Waiting for server response
Server response obtained
Address for John is C45
Closing connection to server
C:\csharp\chapter28>Client
Usage: Client <name>
Requesting connection to server
Connection successful
Writing data to the server
Waiting for server response
Server response obtained
No address is held for
Closing connection to server
```

Chapter 29

Data Access

29.1 Introduction

Almost every commercial system I have been involved with, at some point, must integrate with a database system. In general this has been a relational database system such as SQL Server, Oracle or Sybase. It is therefore necessary for any object-oriented language which is to be used for commercial development to provide an interface to such databases. However, each database vendor often provides its own proprietary (and different) API. In many cases they are little more than variations on a theme; however, they tend to be incompatible. This means that if you were to write a program that was designed to interface with one database system, it is unlikely that it would automatically work with another.

   In this chapter we consider in detail the data access-oriented classes in C#. We will look at how the OLE DB class operates and use a simple Microsoft Access database to illustrate this. We will then look at the SQL specification classes, the ODBC classes and the use of ADO. of course you could easily produce a whole book on the subject of data access in C#; as this is just one chapter in this book we will only be able to scratch the surface, but at least it will be able to point you in the right direction if you need to read data from a database.

29.2 OLE DB

OLE DB is an API for accessing data that is based on the use of COM (that is, OLE DB is essentially a set of COM interfaces). OLE DB is particularly powerful as it supports the concept of accessing data from any source of data that has an OLE DB data provider. Thus you can use OLE DB to access data from databases, spreadsheets, files etc. Each OLE DB provider exposes data from a particular type of data source (for example SQL Server databases, Microsoft Access databases, or Microsoft Excel spreadsheets). This means that what you need to know in order to access any OLE DB-compliant database, spreadsheet or file is minimal.

In the rest of this chapter we will look at how to access a simple database using OLE DB. We shall use Microsoft Access, as this is a commonly available database management system (DBMS) on Windows machines (and although it is limited as a DBMS *per se*, it is enough for these examples).

To work with OLE DB, you need to follow these steps:

1. Decide on the provider (in our case Microsoft Access is being used).
2. Create a connection object.
3. Open the connection object.
4. Create a command object for the SQL statement.
5. Execute the command.
6. Retrieve any data returned, if indeed you were selecting data.
7. Close the connection.

These steps will be examined in more detail below.

29.3 Registering a Provider

When using the OLE DB API a data provider must be specified. This is the part of the OLE DB that handles the actual connection to the source of the data (such as Microsoft Access, Oracle or SQL Server). This is done when a connection is made. Part of the command string to the connection specifies which driver will implement the data provider. The following types of driver are compatible with OLE DB:

- `sqloleddb`: Microsoft OLE DB Provider for SQL Server
- `msdaora`: Microsoft OLE DB Provider for Oracle
- `Microsoft.Jet.OLEDB.4.0`: OLE DB Provider for Microsoft Jet (i.e. Microsoft Access)

Depending on which driver you choose, different parameters may be required following the provider element of the connection specification string. For example, if you are connecting to Oracle you might be required to provider the user and password as well as the host machine and port to connect to. If you are using Microsoft Access you might only be required to provide the name of the MDB file containing the Access database.

As we are going to be using Microsoft Access we shall be using the `Microsoft.Jet.OLEDB.4.0` provider. This will require a data source (i.e. the Access MDB file). Thus our string specifying the driver and additional parameters for the connection will be:

```
"Provider=Microsoft.Jet.OLEDB.4.0;Data Source=CONTACTS.MDB"
```

where the database is held in the `CONTACTS.MDB` file, which in this case is in the same directory as our application.

29.4 Opening a Connection

Listing 29.1 presents sample code that uses the OLE DB classes to connect to a Microsoft Access database (we shall look at each element of this class in turn before providing a complete listing of the class). We must first make the OLE DB API available. This is done by importing the System.Data.OleDB namespace. Next, the application sets up the string to be used to specify how to connect to the data source (this string was discussed in the previous section). We then create an instance variable for the connection. The constructor for the class then calls the private Init() method. This method is where the OleDBConnection object is actually created. It is instantiated using strConnect, which specifies the provider etc. However, no attempt is made to actually connect to the data source until the Open() method is called. As this could give rise to an exception, the call to Open() must be wrapped inside a try-catch block. This try-catch block handles the OleDBException class. At present, this listing does not show any access to the database, it merely shows the opening and subsequent closing of the connection. The closing of the connection is handled by the CloseConnection method. A connection is closed by calling Close() on it. Again it may throw the OleDBException, and thus it must be wrapped in a try-catch block.

Listing 29.1 Connecting to OLE DB.

```
using System;
using System.Data;

// Access OLE specific classes
using System.Data.OleDb;

public class OleDBTest {
  private string strConnect="Provider=Microsoft.Jet.OLEDB.4.0;Data Source="+
      "CONTACTS.MDB";
  private OleDbConnection connection = null;
  ...
  public OleDBTest() {
    Init();
  }

  private void Init() {
    connection = new OleDbConnection(strConnect);
    try {
      connection.Open();
    } catch (OleDbException e) {
      Console.WriteLine(e.Message);
    }
  }
  ...

  private void CloseConnection() {
    if (connection.State.ToString()!="Closed") {
      try {
```

```
        connection.Close();
    } catch (OleDbException) {
        Console.WriteLine("Cannot close connection!");
    }
  }
}
```

29.5 Creating a Table

So far we have examined how to connect to a database. However, we have not considered how the database tables are created. Obviously the tables might not be created by a C# application; for example they could be generated by a legacy system. However, in many situations it is necessary for the tables in the database to be updated (if not created) by a C# program. Listing 29.2 presents two methods that first create and then populate the tables in our Access database.

Listing 29.2 Setting up the tables.

```
public void Create() {
  Console.WriteLine("Creating People table");
  String strCommand = "CREATE TABLE People "+
          "(id char(3), name char(10), address char(15))";
  OleDbCommand cmd=new OleDbCommand(strCommand,connection);
  cmd.ExecuteNonQuery();
  Console.WriteLine("Table created");
}
...

public void Insert() {
  Console.WriteLine("Adding 2 People");

  // Build a SQL Insert statement string for all the input-form
  // field values.
  String strCommand = "INSERT INTO People " +
          "(id, name, address) VALUES ('1', 'John', 'C45')";
  OleDbCommand cmd=new OleDbCommand(strCommand,connection);
  int count = cmd.ExecuteNonQuery();

  strCommand = "INSERT INTO People "+
          "(id, name, address) VALUES ('2', 'Denise', 'A56')";
  cmd=new OleDbCommand(strCommand,connection);
  count += cmd.ExecuteNonQuery();

  Console.WriteLine("{0} rows of data added", count);
}
```

Note that in the above examples we used the ExecuteNonQuery() method on both command objects. This is because this is the method to use with SQL statements that do not return data (other than an int to indicate the number of additions to the database).

29.6 Obtaining Data From a Database

Having made a connection with a database we are now in a position to obtain information from it. Listing 29.3 builds on the application in listing 29.1 by querying the database for some information. This is done by obtaining an OleDbCommand object from the Connection object. This object is provided with the SQL to execute and the connection to use. This is done as a string within which the actual SQL statements are specified. In this case the SQL statement is:

```
SELECT *
FROM People
```

This is pure SQL. The SELECT statement allows data to be obtained from the tables in the database. In this case the SQL states that all the fields (columns) of the table People should be retrieved. To actually read information from the database the ExecuteReader method is called on the OleDbCommand. This produces a reader object (of type OleDBDataReader) that provides access to the results of the select statement.

Listing 29.3 Querying the tables.

```
public void Select() {

    string strCommand="SELECT * FROM People;";
        OleDbCommand cmd=new OleDbCommand(strCommand,connection);
    OleDbDataReader reader=cmd.ExecuteReader();
    while (reader.Read())
    {
      Console.Write(reader["id"].ToString());
      Console.Write("\t");
      Console.Write(reader["name"].ToString());
      Console.Write("\t");
      Console.Write(reader["address"].ToString());
      Console.WriteLine();
    }
    reader.Close();
}
```

A reader in some ways resembles a table of data within which each row contains the data that matched the SQL statement. Within the row, the columns contain the fields specified by the SQL. A reader maintains a cursor pointing to its current row of data. Initially the cursor is positioned before the first row. The Read() method moves the cursor to the next row and returns a Boolean value to indicate whether there is any data to read. Thus when the last read is made and there is no more data left the method will return false.

The information held in the reader can be accessed in two ways. First, it can be accessed by specifying the name of the column to be retrieved (for example reader["id"] will access information retrieved from the column named id). The second way is to specify the column position to one of the Get methods: for example, reader.GetString(2) indicates that we wish to get the string in column 2. There are a range of Get methods, including GetString, GetInt16, GetInt32, GetFloat and GetDouble.

In fact, the reader maintains the connection to the data source while it is in use and accesses information as and when requested from the data source. If you wish to use an in-memory cache of data retrieved from a database, then you should use a DataSet. This is an object that can be "filled" by a data adapter with data. For example:

```
OleDbConnection con = new OleDbConnection(strConnect);
OleDbCommand cmd = new OleDbCommand(strConnect,con);
OleDbDataAdapter da = new OleDbDataAdapter(cmd);
con.Open();
// Create the dataset and add the Categories table to it:
DataSet ds = new DataSet();
ds.Tables.Add("People");
da.Fill(ds,"People");
con.Close();
```

In the above code, note that we can close the connection immediately after filling the DataSet. This is because we have now cached all the data retrieved in the DataSet. As all the data has been cached it is easy to find out how many rows there are in the People table inside the DataSet (note that DataSets can hold more than one table). This is done as follows:

```
Console.WriteLine("{0} rows in People table",
    ds.Tables["People"].Rows.Count);
```

To access information in the DataSet we must obtain the DataTable that actually contains our data and then access information in that; for example:

```
DataTable dt = ds.Tables["People"];
foreach(DataRow row in dt.Rows){
  foreach(DataColumn col in dt.Columns){
    Console.WriteLine(row[col]);
  }
}
```

29.6.1 Full Listing

The complete listing is presented below. The program has three options: 'C' to create a table; 'I' to insert data; and 'S' to select data.

```csharp
using System;

// Access OLE specific classes
using System.Data.OleDb;

public class OleDBTest {
  private string strConnect="Provider=Microsoft.Jet.OLEDB.4.0;Data Source="+
            "CONTACTS.MDB";
    private OleDbConnection connection = null;

  public static void Main(String [] args) {
    OleDBTest db = new OleDBTest();
    if (args.Length != 1) {
      PrintUsage();
    } else if (args[0] == "c") {
      db.Create();
    } else if (args[0] == "i") {
      db.Insert();
    } else if (args[0] == "s") {
      db.Select();
    } else {
      PrintUsage();
    }
    db.CloseConnection();
  }

  public OleDBTest() {
    Init();
  }

  private void Init() {
    connection = new OleDbConnection(strConnect);
    try
    {
      connection.Open();
    }
    catch (OleDbException e)
    {
      Console.WriteLine(e.Message);
    }
  }

  public void Create() {
    Console.WriteLine("Creating People table");
    String strCommand = "CREATE TABLE People (id char(3), name char(10),
        address char(15))";
```

```csharp
      OleDbCommand cmd=new OleDbCommand(strCommand,connection);
      cmd.ExecuteNonQuery();
      Console.WriteLine("Table created");
  }

  public void Select() {
  string strCommand="SELECT * FROM People;";
    OleDbCommand cmd=new OleDbCommand(strCommand,connection);
  OleDbDataReader reader=cmd.ExecuteReader();
  while (reader.Read())
  {
    Console.Write(reader["id"].ToString());
    Console.Write("\t");
    Console.Write(reader["name"].ToString());
    Console.Write("\t");
    Console.Write(reader["address"].ToString());
    Console.WriteLine();
  }
  reader.Close();
}

  public void Insert() {
    Console.WriteLine("Adding 2 People");

    // Build a SQL Insert statement string for all the input-form
    // field values.
    String strCommand = "insert into People (id, name, address)
            values ('1', 'John', 'C45')";
    OleDbCommand cmd=new OleDbCommand(strCommand,connection);
    int count = cmd.ExecuteNonQuery();

    strCommand = "insert into People (id, name, address)
            values ('2', 'Denise', 'A56')";
    cmd=new OleDbCommand(strCommand,connection);
    count += cmd.ExecuteNonQuery();

    Console.WriteLine("{0} rows of data added", count);
  }

  private void CloseConnection() {
  if (connection.State.ToString()!="Closed") {
    try {
      connection.Close();
    } catch (OleDbException) {
      Console.WriteLine("Cannot close connection!");
    }
```

```
      }
    }

    private static void PrintUsage() {
      Console.WriteLine("Usage: OleDBTest <c>, <i> or <s>");
    }
  }
```

The result of running and compiling this program is that we can create and populate the Access database illustrated in Figure 29.1. The result of running with the select option is:

```
C:\csharp\chapter29>OleDBTest s
1    John        C45
2    Denise      A56
34   Tim         B52
```

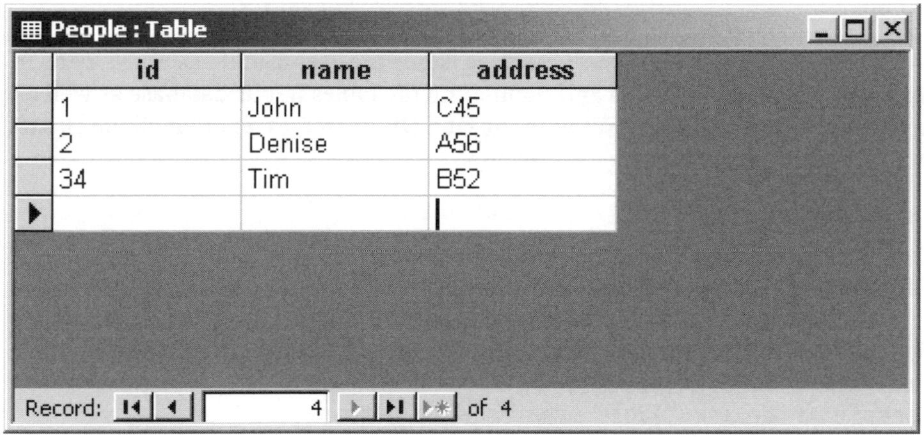

Figure 29.1 The People table in Access.

29.7 Accessing SQL Server

Although you can access SQL Server databases from the OLE DB classes, C# also provides a number of classes specific to its own enterprise level database system in the System.Data.SqlClient namespace. These classes follow a very similar pattern to those used for the OLE DB API. For example, using the SQL Server specific classes we could write:

```
private void Init() {
  connection = new SqlConnection(strConnect);
  try
  {
    connection.Open();
```

```
    }
    catch (SqlException e)
    {
      Console.WriteLine(e.Message);
      throw e;
    }
}
```

which is essentially the same structure as with the OLE DB classes, except that we are now using the SqlConnection class (rather than the OleDbConnection class). The string passed to this class is different, however, as it is now SQL Server-specific. The definition of the connection string might now look like:

```
private string strConnect="server=localhost;" +
                          "uid=jjh;pwd=;" +
                          "database=contacts";
```

This indicates the server hosting the SQL Server system, the user id and password to log in with and the database to connect to. Creating and populating the tables in our database as well as selecting from the database tables is the same as with the OLE DB classes, except that all the classes used are from the SqlClient namespace, for example:

```
public void Create() {
  Console.WriteLine("Creating People table");
  String strCommand = "CREATE TABLE People (id char(3),
          name char(10), address char(15))";
  SqlCommand cmd= new SqlCommand(strCommand, connection);
  cmd.ExecuteNonQuery();
  Console.WriteLine("Table created with return code");
}
public void Insert() {
Console.WriteLine("Adding 2 People");

  // Build a SQL Insert statement string for all the input-form
  // field values.
  String strCommand = "insert into People (id, name, address)
          values ('1', 'John', 'C45')";
  SqlCommand cmd=new SqlCommand(strCommand,connection);
  int count = cmd.ExecuteNonQuery();

  strCommand = "insert into People (id, name, address)
          values ('2', 'Denise', 'A56')";
  cmd=new SqlCommand(strCommand,connection);
  count += cmd.ExecuteNonQuery();

  Console.WriteLine("{0} rows of data added", count);
```

```
}
public void Select() {

string strCommand="SELECT * FROM People;";
  SqlCommand cmd=new SqlCommand(strCommand,connection);
SqlDataReader reader=cmd.ExecuteReader();
while (reader.Read())
{
  Console.Write(reader["id"].ToString());
  Console.Write("\t");
  Console.Write(reader["name"].ToString());
  Console.Write("\t");
  Console.Write(reader["address"].ToString());
  Console.WriteLine();
}
reader.Close();
}
```

Again we can also use a DataSet if we wish to cache the data.

29.8 ODBC

One of the philosophies of reuse is that we do not want to have to keep reimplementing the wheel. This means we do not want to have to rewrite our C# code just because it is using a different database. ODBC was originally a Microsoft initiative to provide a common interface to ODBC-compliant databases. It has now grown to be wider than just Microsoft: for example, a number of databases more normally associated with Unix-based systems or IBM mainframes now offer an ODBC interface. As such, ODBC provides a very effective way to access information from a wide variety of database systems. ODBC is feasible as most vendors implement most (if not all) of the standard SQL, thus allowing a common denominator. SQL stands for Structured Query Language and is used for obtaining information from relational databases. SQL is a large topic in its own right and is beyond the scope of this book. Reference is therefore made to appropriate books at the end of the chapter.

One potential problem with such an approach is that although the developer's interface is the same, different implementations of an application would be needed to link to different databases. In the C# interface this is overcome in ODBC by allowing different providers to be specified that provide different back-end drivers. Developers are now insulated from the details of the various relational database systems that they may be using and have a greater chance of producing portable code.

29.8.1 What Is ODBC?

Essentially, ODBC is a basic SQL interface to a database system that assumes only "standard" SQL features. Thus specialist facilities provided by different database vendors cannot be accessed. ODBC is able to connect to any database by using different data providers. These act as the interfaces

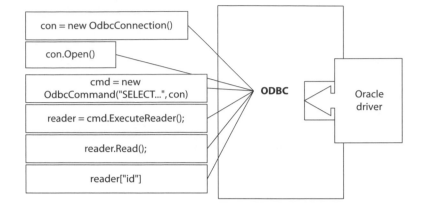

Figure 29.2 The structure of the ODBC and the C# interface.

between the ODBC and databases such as Oracle, Sybase, Microsoft Access and SQL Server, and shareware systems such as MiniSQL. The idea is that the front end presented to the developer is the same whatever the database system, while the appropriate back end is loaded as required by the provider and any database specific details are handled by the provider. The ODBC then passes the programmer's SQL to the database via the back end. For example, specifying the Oracle provider is done via the msdaora provider, while the SQL Server provider is indicated via the sqlolddb type. This is illustrated in Figure 29.2, which illustrates some of the most commonly used methods provided by the ODBC, along with the ODBC driver (note that any number could have been provided). Such a setup would allow a C# program to connect to an Oracle database through the ODBC driver. There are an increasing number of database drivers becoming available for ODBC. At present, databases such as Oracle, Sybase and Ingres all have their own drivers. This allows features of those databases to be exploited. However, even databases that are not directly supported can be accessed via the ODBC driver, thus making a huge range of databases available to the C# developer.

There is a very definite series of steps that must be performed by any ODBC program. These involve loading an appropriate driver, connecting to a database, executing SQL statements and closing the connection made. These are discussed in more detail later in this chapter.

29.8.2 Using ODBC

To use the ODBC classes you will need to make sure that you have the System.Data.Odbc.dll assembly and that you compile with this. Once you have this assembly you will find that the pattern to use when accessing data via ODBC is the same as that used with OLE DB and SQL Server: you create a connection, you open it, you obtain a command and then execute that command. For example:

```
private void Init() {
  connection = new OdbcConnection(strConnect);
  try
  {
```

```
      connection.Open();
    }
    catch (OdbcException e)
    {
      Console.WriteLine(e.Message);
      throw e;
    }
}

public void Create() {
  Console.WriteLine("Creating People table");
  String strCommand = "CREATE TABLE People (id char(3), name char(10),
address char(15))";
  OdbcCommand cmd=new OdbcCommand(strCommand,connection);
  cmd.ExecuteNonQuery();
  Console.WriteLine("Table created with return code");
}

public void Select() {
  string strCommand="SELECT * FROM People;";
    OdbcCommand cmd=new OdbcCommand(strCommand,connection);
    OdbcDataReader reader=cmd.ExecuteReader();
  while (reader.Read())
  {
    Console.Write(reader["id"].ToString());
    Console.Write("\t");
    Console.Write(reader["name"].ToString());
    Console.Write("\t");
    Console.Write(reader["address"].ToString());
    Console.WriteLine();
  }
  reader.Close();
}

public void Insert() {
    Console.WriteLine("Adding 2 People");

  // Build a SQL Insert statement string for all the input-form
  // field values.
  String strCommand = "insert into People (id, name, address)
            values ('1', 'John', 'C45')";
  OdbcCommand cmd=new OdbcCommand(strCommand,connection);
  int count = cmd.ExecuteNonQuery();

  strCommand = "insert into People (id, name, address)
            values ('2', 'Denise', 'A56')";
```

```
    cmd=new OdbcCommand(strCommand,connection);
    count += cmd.ExecuteNonQuery();

    Console.WriteLine("{0} rows of data added", count);
}

private void CloseConnection()
    {
      if (connection.State.ToString()!="Closed")
      {
      try
      {
        connection.Close();
      }
      catch (OdbcException)
      {
        Console.WriteLine("Cannot close connection!");
      }
    }
}
```

29.9 Exploiting ADO.NET

ADO.NET is a development of the ADO (ActiveX Data Objects) framework from Microsoft that provides tight integration with the .NET Framework. It allows a common interface for accessing data from multiple sources in different formats in *n*-tier Web-enabled applications. It is particularly well tuned for working with SQL Server, OLE DB and XML. In fact, you have already seen something of ADO.NET because the DataSet class presented earlier is a key element in the whole of the ADO .NET framework. So what is so special about the ADO .NET framework?

The basic concept behind ADO .NET is one of "disconnected" data access. Traditional application models have generally assumed that a connection-based approach will be used to data access; that is, a permanent connection can be maintained for a user to a database. This would allow data to be read, manipulated, updated and deleted interactively with a database via that permanent connection. However, applications increasingly rely on multi-tier architectures in which a permanent connection to an underlying database cannot be guaranteed. They therefore need a "disconnected" model. In this model the data is retrieved from a database into a "dataset". Note that the data providers used with ADO .NET are completely extensible: you can write your own data providers to access legacy systems, proprietary data sources etc.

The ADO.NET components have been designed to factor data access from data manipulation. That is, one part of the ADO .NET framework will provide data access, while a second allows data manipulation. The data access part has been discussed in some detail earlier in this chapter as it is provided by the SQL client and OLE DB classes. The second aspect of the ADO .NET framework is the dataset. A dataset holds one or more tables. These tables can be searched, processed, updated, written back to the underlying database, etc. This means that the in-memory structures can mimic the behaviour of the permanent backing store structures, but without the need for a permanent database connection. In this model a connection to a database is only required when populating the dataset or when writing changes back to the database.

To use the ADO features you will need to important the System.Data namespace, as it is this namespace that provides the ADO .NET classes (such as DataSet and DataTable).

29.10 Further Reading

See Microsoft (1997) for a description of ODBC and Stephens (1997) for further information about SQL.

Chapter 30

Remoting in .NET

30.1 Introduction

In an earlier chapter we looked at how different C# programs running in different processes could communicate via sockets. This approach is relatively straightforward to use and exploits the widely adopted sockets communication model. However, C# offers another way of enabling programs to communicate – .NET Remoting. Indeed, Remoting is surprisingly simple to use and may well be preferable to sockets for .NET communication. This is because the resulting software is simpler and easier to maintain than using sockets. For example, a distributed software system resembles a software system executing within a single virtual machine except for the addition of one line to a client and two lines associated with a server!

30.2 Remoting

Remoting in the .NET framework is one of the facilities provided in C# for implementing distributed systems (others include sockets and interfaces to COM etc.). Remoting is similar in concept to Remote Procedure Calls (RPC) for procedural languages. Essentially, an object can invoke a method on another object in a separate process (potentially on a different machine and even a different operating system).

The Remoting Framework provides a number of services, such as activation and lifetime control, as well as communication channels responsible for transporting messages to and from remote applications. Formatters are used to encode and decode the messages before they are sent along a channel. Applications can use binary encoding where performance is critical or XML encoding where interoperability with other remoting frameworks is essential.

Remoting is surprisingly straightforward, merely requiring the developer to:

- select the type of communications channel to be used
- subclass an appropriate server class (for example `MarshalByRefObject`)
- write a setup program that will register the server as a service

- implement a client to use the remote object
- register the client with the remoting framework

We will look at each of these steps in a little more detail. It is important to note that a great deal of the hard work involved in designing, implementing and installing distributed applications is hidden from you when you use the Remoting Framework. For example, the details of how a call to a remote method are transmitted to that object processed and the results returned are hidden. The protocol used is never made explicit to the program you write.

30.2.1 Selecting the Type of Channel

A channel is the means of communication that can take a stream of data and pass that data from a source to a sink (and in many cases back again). The two default channels provided with C# are the TcpChannel (which uses the common TCP/IP communications protocol) and the HttpChannel, (which communicates via the HTTP protocol). A particular remote object can support multiple channels (to allow clients that need specific channel support to work with the same server). In turn clients need to indicate which channels they wish to use. Both of these can be done in an XML-based configuration file or programmatically in the server and client.

30.2.2 Subclassing a Server Class

Once you have determined the channel (which could be left until you decide to deploy the application), you can start to define the server class. To do this you need to:

- subclass a remote server (e.g. System.MarshalByRefObject)
- provide implementations for the methods to be available remotely
- define a constructor for the server (if you wish to configure the server in some way)
- set up and install the server (via a server process)

These steps sound complex, but are in reality straightforward. For example, Listing 30.1 illustrates the source code for the helloServer remote object class. As you can see, it extends the MarshalByRefObject class that allows it to operate as a remote object. It also defines a single method GetString(String), which takes a string and returns a string in response. It further defines an instance variable, count, to show how many times the method GetString has been called on an instance of the HelloServer class. That, at this point, is all there is to the HelloServer remote object!

Listing 30.1 The HelloServer class.

```
using System;
namespace Hello {

  public class HelloServer : MarshalByRefObject {

    private int count = 1;
```

```
    public String GetString(String name) {
      Console.WriteLine("Receiving remote request number {0}", count);
      count++;
      String message = "Hello " + name + ", from remote server";
      Console.WriteLine("Replying with {0}", message);
      return message;
    }
  }
}
```

Next we must define the program that will register our remote object with the remoting system. This program is presented in Listing 30.2.

Listing 30.2 The ServerSetup application.

```
using System;
using System.Threading;
using System.Runtime.Remoting;
using System.Runtime.Remoting.Channels;
using System.Runtime.Remoting.Channels.Http;

public class ServerSetup
{

  public static void Main(string[] args)
  {
    if (args.Length == 0) {
      Console.WriteLine("Usage: ServerSetup <server config file>");
      return;
    }

    Console.WriteLine("Configure remote object");

    String filename = args[0];
    Console.WriteLine("Loading configuration file: {0}", filename);
    // Now go and actually register the remote object
    RemotingConfiguration.Configure(filename);

    Console.WriteLine("ServerSetup is ready to process remote messages.");
    // Cause the server application not to terminate
    AutoResetEvent ready = new AutoResetEvent(false);
    ready.WaitOne();

  }
}
```

The `ServerSetup` program now uses a configuration file to register the remote object. This is done using the `RemoteConfiguration` class and the method `Configure` (which takes a filename). The format of this configuration file is presented in Listing 30.3.

Listing 30.3 `ServerSetup.exe.config`.

```
<configuration>
<system.runtime.remoting>
  <application name="RemoteHelloWorld">
    <service>
    <wellknown mode="Singleton"
          type="Hello.HelloServer, Hello"
          objectUri="HelloServer.soap" />
    </service>
    <channels>
    <channel port="1234"
          type="System.Runtime.Remoting.Channels.Http.HttpChannel,
          System.Runtime.Remoting" />
    </channels>
  </application>
</system.runtime.remoting>
</configuration>
```

The configuration file uses XML to define how the server will be registered, how it will communicate with clients and what it will be called etc. This configuration file is called `ServerSetup.exe.config`; although you can call this file whatever you want, a convention is that it should be named after the executable it is associated with (with a `.config` extension). This is because if you wish to use Internet Information Services (IIS) it will expect this convention. Also, although you can use any filename for your remoting configuration file, application security settings are only enforced if they are contained in a file that has the name of the form `<application>.<extension>.config`.

The configuration file specifies a remote application called `RemoteHelloWorld`. A remote application is essentially a logical grouping of remote services.

The main elements of the configuration file in Listing 30.3 are the service tag and the channels tag. The service tag indicates what service is being provided, while the channels tag indicates how the server will communicate with clients.

The service tag from the `ServerSetup.exe.config` is presented below:

```
<service>
<wellknown mode="Singleton"
          type="Hello.HelloServer, Hello"
          objectUri="HelloServer.soap" />
</service>
```

A well-known object is a server-activated object. The service tag contains a well-known tag. This states that the remote object is an instance of `Hello.HelloServer` and that it can be obtained from the assembly Hello.dll (the two parameters for the type attribute). The name of the remote object is HelloServer.soap and it will operate in Singleton mode. This means that one instance of the class will be created to service all client requests (the other option is SingleCall, which will create a new instance for each client).

The channels tag from the above example is:

```
<channels>
<channel port="1234"
         type="System.Runtime.Remoting.Channels.Http.HttpChannel,
         System.Runtime.Remoting" />
</channels>
```

This states that the server will communicate off port number 1234 and that it will use HttpChannel as the basis of its communication.

Note that the ServerSetup program must not terminate. If it does then the server process will terminate and the remote object will not be available to service requests from clients. To ensure that we do not terminate (and that we do not waste expensive resources in the setup program), we merely wait on a thread-based event. This causes the main thread to go into a waiting state where it will not be scheduled for execution. This topic is covered in more detail in the next chapter; for the moment merely accept that the following statements are an efficient way to stall the setup program:

```
AutoResetEvent ready = new AutoResetEvent(false);
ready.WaitOne();
```

We are now in a position to compile the HelloServer class and the ServerSetup program. To do this use the following commands (assuming that both files are in the same directory):

```
echo compiling HelloServer
csc /t:library /out:Hello.dll HelloServer.cs
echo Compiling server setup
csc /r:System.Runtime.Remoting.dll ServerSetup.cs
```

Notice that we have specified the library option to the C# compiler when compiling the HelloServer.cs file as this will create an assembly (in this case an assembly called Hello.dll).

30.2.3 The HelloClient

As we now have a server object that can be registered with the Remoting framework, we can now create a client object. In our case we want to create a class that will obtain a string from the command line and print out the result returned from the HelloServer object. Listing 30.4 presents the HelloClient class definition.

Listing 30.4 The HelloClient class.

```
using System;
using System.Runtime.Remoting;
```

```csharp
using Hello;

public class HelloClient
{
  public static void Main(String[] args)
  {
    Console.WriteLine("Starting Remoting Client");
    if (args.Length == 0) {
    Console.WriteLine("Usage: HelloClient <name>");
    return;
    }
    String name = args[0];
    String configFilename = "HelloClient.exe.config";

    Console.WriteLine("Configuring Remoting from {0}", configFilename);
    RemotingConfiguration.Configure(configFilename);

    Console.WriteLine("Obtaining Local Proxy for HelloServer");
    HelloServer hs = new HelloServer();

    Console.WriteLine("Calling hs.GetString({0})", name);
    String greeting = hs.GetString(name);

    Console.WriteLine("Result returned\n\t {0}", greeting);
  }
}
```

The HelloClient is an extremely simple class. It obtains the first command line parameter and uses that as the string to pass to the HelloServer. It then uses an XML-based configuration file (in this case HelloClient.exe.config) to specify the remote object that it wishes to connect to. It obtains a reference to the HelloServer from the remoting framework (it will be presented with a local proxy). This is determined through the configuration file (although it could have been specified programmatically if required).

The HelloClient.exe.config file looks like this:

```xml
<configuration>
  <system.runtime.remoting>
    <application name="HelloClient">

      <client url="http://localhost:1234/RemoteHelloWorld">
        <wellknown type="Hello.HelloServer, Hello"
            url="http://localhost:1234/RemoteHelloWorld/HelloServer.soap" />
      </client>

      <channels>
```

```
        <channel type="System.Runtime.Remoting.Channels.Http.HttpChannel,
                System.Runtime.Remoting" />
    </channels>

    </application>
  </system.runtime.remoting>
</configuration>
```

Note that the `client url` attribute must specify the machine that the remote object is running on, the port to connect to and the remote application name to connect to (in this case `RemoteHelloWorld`). The `wellknown` tag (which specifies the remote object) then allows the client to specify that type of object expected, where to find the metadata relating to the object's API (via `Hello.dll`) and the URL to use to find a reference to that remote object. This URL specifies the machine, the port, the remote application and the name of the remote object (in this case `HelloServer.soap`). The channel tag then specifies the channel for communication (which must match that used with the server setup).

We are now in a position to compile the `HelloClient` class. This can be done using the following command:

```
csc /r:Hello.dll /out:HelloClient.exe HelloClient.cs
```

This indicates that when compiling the `HelloClient.cs` file the `Hello.dll` assembly should be used. It also specifies that the resultant executable should be called `HelloClient.exe` (which is the default).

30.2.4 Running the Application

We are now in a position where we can start to run the application. To do this we must first start up the server via the `ServerSetup`. We will do this in one command window. Once this is done we will then start up the client in a separate command window. The result of doing this is presented in Figure 30.1.

In Figure 30.1, the top left command window is running the `SetupServer` program (and thus the `HelloServer` remote object), while the bottom right window has run the `HelloClient` program three times with different parameters). Note that the counter used with the `HelloServer` output is incrementing – try changing the mode to `SingleCall` and see the effect (the count appears always to remain at 1, as a new server object is created for each client).

30.2.5 What Is Happening?

At this point it is worth considering what is going on here. How is it that the client program appears to be able to call a method on an object in another process, yet other than the call to `RemotingConfiguration.Configure(configFilename)` there is nothing to indicate that the `HelloServer` object is remote?

What is actually happening is that the act of configuring the remoting system for the `HelloServer` class ensures that if we try to create a local reference to it what actually happens

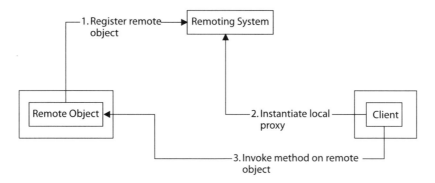

Figure 30.1 Running the Remoting example.

is that a local proxy is constructed. This local proxy acts as a bridge between the client code and the Remoting system to deal with requests and the return of results etc. Thus the interaction between server object, client and remoting system is essentially that presented in Figures 30.2 and Figure 30.3. Figure 30.2 illustrates the overall steps and Figure 30.3 the end result.

Figure 30.2 How the registry manages RMI references.

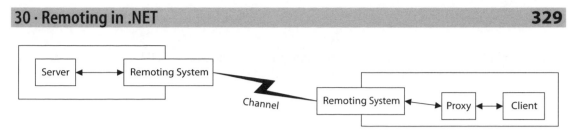

Figure 30.3 Using the remoting system.

Essentially, the remoting system creates a proxy object that represents the class and returns to the client object a reference to the proxy. When a client calls a method, the remoting infrastructure fields the call, checks the type information, and sends the call over the channel to the server process. A listening channel picks up the request and forwards it to the server remoting system, which locates (or creates, if necessary) and calls the requested object. The process is then reversed, as the server remoting system bundles the response into a message that the server channel sends to the client channel. Finally, the client remoting system returns the result of the call to the client object through the proxy.

30.3 Remoting Details

30.3.1 Remote Objects and Channels

Remote objects can be registered either programmatically or by specifying the remote objects in configuration files. Registering remote objects in configuration files allows administrators of applications that expose or consume remote objects to change the location of the objects without recompiling the application.

To publish remote objects so that they can be accessed remotely, they must be specified within the <service> section within the <application> tag. This is a child of the <system.runtime.remoting> tag.

30.3.2 Server-Side Registration

Remoting provides two different activation models: well-known or client-activated. Objects are normally registered in the Web.config file when they are hosted through Internet Information Services (IIS), or in the <application.config> file (such as ServerSetup.exe.config) when the objects are hosted directly.

30.3.3 Default Lifetime

You can specify a default lifetime for all client-activated objects at the application level.

```
<configuration>
  <system.runtime.remoting>
    <application>
```

```
            <lifetime leaseTime = "10M" sponsorshipTimeOut = "2M"
                    renewOnCallTime = "2M" LeaseManagePollTime = "10s"/>
        </application>
      </system.runtime.remoting>
</configuration>
```

- leaseTime is the default lease time for the application. Valid time units are D for days, M for minutes, S for seconds and MS for milliseconds.
- sponsorshipTimeOut is the time that the lease manager waits for the sponsor to respond when notified that a lease has expired. If the sponsor does not respond in the specified time, the remote object is garbage collected.
- RenewOnCallTime is the amount of time that the lease time is extended between function calls on the object.
- LeaseManagerPollTime is the amount of time the lease manager sleeps after checking for expired leases.

30.3.4 Well-Known Objects

When publishing well-known or server-activated objects, you must indicate whether the object is a single-call or singleton object, the type of the object, and the endpoint where the object can be accessed.

```
<configuration>
  <system.runtime.remoting>
    <application>
      <service>
      <wellknown mode = "singlecall" type = "myType,myAssembly"
              objectUri = "myType.soap"/>
      </service>
    </application>
  </system.runtime.remoting>
</configuration>
```

- The mode attribute indicates whether the object is a singleton or singlecall object.
- The type attribute is the type and assembly of the object (type,assembly).
- The objectUri attribute is the endpoint of the object's Uniform Resource Identifier (URI). This is the last part of the URL the client points to when using the object. When an object is hosted in IIS, the objectUri extension must be .soap or .rem, so that the request will be routed to the .NET remoting HTTP handler.

30.3.5 Client-Activated Objects

Use the <activated tag to expose client-activated objects that your application provides.

```
<configuration>
  <system.runtime.remoting>
    <application>
      <service>
      <activated type = "myClientActivatedType,myAssembly">
      </activated>
      </service>
    </application>
  </system.runtime.remoting>
</configuration>
```

The type attribute in the `<activated>` tag is the type and assembly of the object, as it is in the `<wellknown>` tag.

It is also worth noting the different between passing an object to a remote method as a pass-by-value parameter or a pass-by-reference parameter. When a client calls a remote method, if the parameters passed to the method are `Serializable` a copy of these parameters will be sent to the server. In turn, if the result returned is serializable then a copy will be sent back to the client. If either are themselves remote objects then a reference to the remote object will be passed as appropriate.

30.3.6 Programmatic Configuration

Although we have looked at configuring remoting applications using files it is also possible to configure a remote application programmatically. For example, we could write:

```
ChannelServices.RegisterChannel(new HttpChannel());
WellKnownServiceTypeEntry WKSTE = new
WellKnownServiceTypeEntry(typeof(ServiceClass),"HttpService",
WellKnownObjectMode.SingleCall);
RemotingConfiguration.ApplicationName = "HttpService";
RemotingConfiguration.RegisterWellKnownServiceType(WKSTE);
```

Chapter 31

Concurrency

31.1 Introduction

This chapter presents and explains a short example of how concurrency can be accomplished within C#.

31.2 Concurrent Processes

The concepts behind object-oriented programming lend themselves particularly well to the concepts associated with concurrency. For example, a system can be described as a set of discrete objects communicating with one another when necessary. In C#, only one object may execute at any moment. However, conceptually at least, there is no reason why this restriction should be enforced. The basic concepts behind object orientation still hold, even if each object executes within a separate independent process.

Traditionally, a message send is treated like a procedural call, in which the calling object's execution is blocked until a response is returned. However, we can extend this model quite simply to view each object as a concurrently executable program module, with activity starting when the object is created and continuing even when a message is sent to another object (unless the response is required for further processing). In this model, there may be very many (concurrent) objects executing at the same time. Of course, this introduces issues associated with resource allocation etc., but no more so than in any concurrent system.

One implication of the concurrent object model is that objects are larger than in the traditional single execution thread approach, because of the overhead of having each object as a process. A process scheduler for handling these processes and resource allocation mechanisms mean that it is not feasible or useful to have integers, characters etc. as separate processes.

C# provides a number of different features that allow a developer to exploit concurrency. The simplest is starting a completely new process (known as a thread) to run some part of an application in. A developer can build on this by adding the ability to wait for a thread to finish before continuing (joining threads), to have one thread notify another that it can proceed, to call methods asynchronously and to wait on a set of threads (before continuing execution). We will look at each of these in this chapter.

31.3 Threads

A C# process is a preemptive lightweight process termed a *thread*. Every thread (process) has an associated priority which can be used to allow one thread to pre-empt another. Threads of equal priority can be time-sliced: that is, C# can effectively share the processor time among processes of the same priority. Threads with a higher priority are executed before threads with a lower priority. A thread with a higher priority may interrupt a thread with a lower priority. By default, a process inherits the same priority as the process that spawned it.

The class Thread in the System.Threading namespace provides for the creation and control of a thread. It can also be used to sets a threads priority, and gets its status.

A thread is a "lightweight" process because it does not possess its own address space and it is not treated as a separate entity by the host operating system. Instead, it exists within a single machine process using the same address space.

It is useful to get a clear idea of the difference between a thread (running within a single machine process) and a multi-process system.

31.3.1 Thread States

The thread that is currently executing is termed the active thread. A thread can also be suspended (i.e. waiting to use the processor) or stopped (waiting for some resource). Figure 31.1 illustrates the thread states and the messages or actions that cause the state to change. The thread states are defined by the enumeration ThreadState in the System.Threading namespace.

Notice that a thread is considered to be alive unless the method to be run within the thread terminates after which it can be considered dead.

A live thread can be running, sleeping (waiting for a Wait, Sleep or Join event), interrupted, suspended etc. The runnable state indicates that the thread can be executed by the processor, but it is not currently executing. This is because an equal or higher priority process is already executing and the thread must wait until the processor becomes free. Thus the diagram shows that the scheduler can move a thread between the running and runnable state (in fact, C# does not distinguish between these two states). This could happen many times as the thread executes for a while and is then removed from the processor by the scheduler and added to the waiting queue before being returned to the processor again at a later date.

The members of the ThreadState enumeration are presented in Table 31.1.

31.3.2 Creating a Thread

A thread is created by instantiating a new instance of a Thread class (remember that in C# most things are objects, and threads that represent concurrent processes are no exception). To indicate to the thread what it should execute, a delegate is defined. This delegate specifies the method to call when the Thread begins execution following a call to the Start method.

Table 31.1 The members of the ThreadState enumeration.

Member Name	Description
Aborted	The thread has aborted
AbortRequested	The thread is being requested to abort
Background	The thread is being executed as a background thread
Running	The thread is being executed
Stopped	The thread has stopped. This is for internal use only
StopRequested	The thread is being requested to stop. This is for internal use only
Suspended	The thread has been suspended
SuspendRequested	The thread is being requested to suspend
Unstarted	The thread has not been started
WaitSleepJoin	The thread is blocked on a call to Wait, Sleep, or Join

The method to run in the thread is defined by a delegate:

```
public delegate void ThreadStart();
```

The method to run within the thread must have the same signature as the delegate (that is, it must return void and take no parameters).

Thus to create a new thread we could write:

```
Thread t = new Thread(new ThreadStart(p.DoSomething));
```

Note that the class Thread is a sealed class (a class you cannot inherit from). Thus to start a new thread with a specific functionality we must first define a class that will provide an implementation for the delegate. In the above example the DoSomething method. That is, a developer defines a class that specifies the operations or actions that the new thread (of execution) performs. Thus, a thread is an independent object running (at least conceptually) on the processor.

As a thread is an object, it can be treated just like any other object: it can be sent messages, it has instance properties and it can provide methods. Thus, the multi-threaded aspects of C# all conform to the object-oriented model. This greatly simplifies the creation of multi-threaded systems as well as the maintainability and clarity of the resulting software.

Once a new instance of a thread is created, it must be started. Before it is started it cannot run, although it exists (see Figure 31.1).

31.4 The Thread Class

The Thread class in the System.Threading namespace defines all the facilities required to create a class that can execute within its own lightweight process.

Tables 31.2–31.5 summarize the most common Thread methods.

There are a number of properties and methods that obtain information about the status of the process:

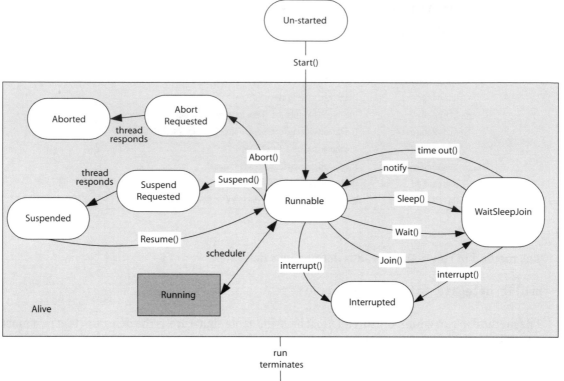

Figure 31.1 Thread states.

Table 31.2 Public static (shared) properties of the Thread class.

CurrentThread	Gets a reference to the currently running thread

Table 31.3 public static methods of the Thread class.

Sleep	Overloaded; suspends the current thread for a specified time

Table 31.4 Public instance properties of the Thread class.

IsAlive	Gets a value indicating whether the thread has been started and is not dead
IsBackground	Gets or sets a value indicating whether or not this thread is a background thread
Name	Gets or sets the name of the thread
Priority	Gets or sets the priority of a thread
ThreadState	Gets the state of this thread

Table 31.5 Public instance methods of the Thread class.

Abort	Overloaded; Raises a ThreadAbortException in the thread, which usually results in the thread's death
Equals	Overloaded; Determines whether two Object instances are equal
Interrupt	Interrupts a thread that is in the WaitSleepJoin thread state
Join	Overloaded; waits for a thread
Resume	Resumes a thread that has been suspended
Start	Begins execution at the ThreadStart that was supplied at construction
Suspend	Either suspends the thread, or if the thread is already suspended, has no effect
ToString	Returns a String that represents the current Object

- IsAlive This property tests to see whether the thread has started execution and has not yet terminated.
- IsBackground This property tests to see whether the thread is executing in the background.

There are properties and methods associated with a thread's priority, including:

- Priority Allows the priority of the thread to be obtained or updated.

The legal priorities for a thread are defined by the ThreadPriority enumeration in the System.Threading namespace. Table 31.6 lists the members (and their meanings) in this enumeration.

Every thread has a unique name. If you do not provide one, then a name is automatically generated by the system:

- Name A property that provides access to the thread name.

It is also possible to put a thread to sleep for a number of milliseconds using the Sleep method. For example:

```
Thread.Sleep(1000);
```

This specifies that the current thread should sleep for 1000 milliseconds.

Table 31.6 Members of the ThreadPriority enumeration.

Member name	Description
AboveNormal	The higher priority
BelowNormal	The lower priority
Highest	The highest priority
Lowest	The lowest priority
Normal	The average priority

31.4.1 Implementing a Thread

To create a class that can be executed as a separate thread, you must define a method that will provide an implementation for the ThreadStart delegate

To create such a class, you must follow these steps:

1. Define a class.
2. Define the delegate implementation. For example:

```csharp
using System;
using System.Threading;

class HelloThread {
  private String msg;
  public HelloThread(String msg) {
    this.msg = msg;
  }
  public void DoRun() {
    while (true) {
      Console.Write(msg);
    }
  }
}
```

In this example the DoRun method will provide an implementation for the delegate in the Thread class

3. Create an instance of the class.
4. Create an instance of the Thread class using the Thread(ThreadStart start) constructor. This requires that the delegate wrapper is created with a reference to the DoRun method:

```csharp
HelloThread h1 = new HelloThread("A");
Thread t1 = new Thread(new ThreadStart(h1.DoRun));
```

5. Send the Start message to the thread instance. This schedules the new thread and causes the start method to execute.

```csharp
t1.Start();
```

The following complete program defines a class whose instances will run in separate threads. This class, HelloWorld, prints out a string to the console repeatedly while it is awake. The program also defines a test harness Main method that will create three instances of the HelloWorld class, create three threads for these three instances and then start the execution of those threads. It will also loop forever, sleep for 1000 milliseconds, waking up and printing a new line message and then sleeping again. The effect of this program should be that the other three threads share the processor while the main thread is asleep (printing out their own strings while they are awake). When the main thread wakes it it will break the line of A, B and C etc.

```
using System;
using System.Threading;

class HelloThread {
  private String msg;
  public HelloThread(String msg) {
    this.msg = msg;
  }
  public void DoRun() {
    while (true) {
      Console.Write(msg);
    }
  }
}

public class ThreadTest {
  public static void Main() {
    HelloThread h1 = new HelloThread("A");
    HelloThread h2 = new HelloThread("B");
    HelloThread h3 = new HelloThread("C");

    Thread t1 = new Thread(new ThreadStart(h1.DoRun));
    t1.Start();
    Thread t2 = new Thread(new ThreadStart(h2.DoRun));
    t2.Start();
    Thread t3 = new Thread(new ThreadStart(h3.DoRun));
    t3.Start();

    while (true) {
    Thread.Sleep(100);
    Console.WriteLine(
        "\n---------------> Wake up call <---------------------");
    }
  }
}
```

The effect of compiling and executing this program is illustrated in Figure 31.2. As you can see from this screen dump, each HelloWorld thread gets a chance to run, before being swapped with the next one. Thus we see a line of As, then Bs and then Cs repeated. At some point the main thread gets to execute again and cuts in with its "Wake up call" print and then sleeps again, and so on. Thus this example illustrates the effect of a multi-threaded program.

31.4.2 Asynchronous Method Calls

The previous example of a multi-threaded program essentially starts off new methods in separate processes and then continues in the current process. This is similar to an asynchronous method call.

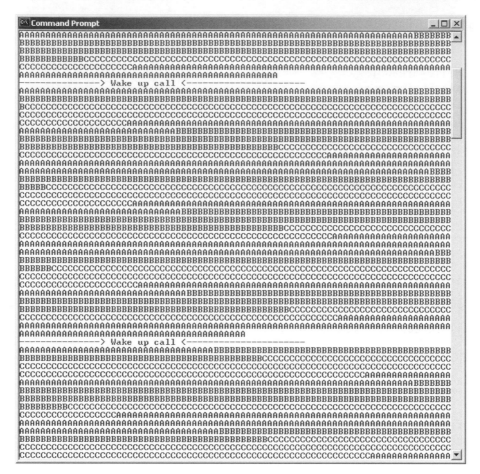

Figure 31.2

C# provides a convenient way to handle this: it allows methods to be invoked in a separate thread. These two facilities are provides by the compiler to make asynchronous methods calls easier. The two methods are BeginInvoke (which starts a method in a separate thread) and EndInvoke that can be used to wait for an invoked method to complete. For example:

```csharp
using System;
using System.Threading;

public class Caller
{
  delegate void Printer(String s);

  public void MyRun(String s)
  {
```

```
      Printer p = new Printer(Console.WriteLine);
      IAsyncResult iar = p.BeginInvoke(s, null, null);
      // p.EndInvoke(iar);
      Console.WriteLine("Go to Sleep");
      Thread.Sleep(1000);
      Console.WriteLine("End");
   }
}

class Tester
{
  public static void Main()
  {
    Caller c = new Caller();
    c.MyRun("John");
  }

}
```

The effect of compiling and executing this program is that the string "Go to Sleep" is printed out immediately followed by the string "John" (note the order here). Then some 1000 milliseconds later the string "End" is printed:

```
C:\csharp>Caller
Go to Sleep
John
End
```

The behaviour of this program can be altered by uncommenting the EndInvoke method call. This will cause the Main method to wait until the invoked method completes.

31.4.3 Joining Threads

In some cases it is necessary to wait until one thread has completed execution before another continues. However, it may still be useful for both threads to be running at the same time for at least a period of time. For example, a user who is inputting information into a screen in a GUI application may not be able to move to the next screen until all the data has been retrieved from the server. However, we may be able to start that retrieval process now and only wait in the event that the retrieval process has not completed when the user has entered all the data on the current screen. This can be done using a Join.

A Join causes one thread to wait for another thread to complete before it continues. In the following example, one thread will execute the Print method in the Printable class while the main method will print out the message "Joining Thread". At this point the main thread will wait for the thread executing Printable. In turn the Printable thread will be sleeping for 1000 milliseconds (mimicking a call to a server or a search through a database etc.).

```csharp
using System;
using System.Threading;

public class Printable {
  private String s;

  public Printable(String s) {
    this.s = s;
  }
  public void Print() {
    Thread.Sleep(1000);
    Console.WriteLine(s);
  }
}

public class Tester
{
  public static void Main()
  {
    Printable p = new Printable("Hello John");
    Thread t1 = new Thread(new ThreadStart(p.Print));
    Console.WriteLine("Starting thread");
    t1.Start();
    Console.WriteLine("Joining Thread");
    t1.Join();
    Console.WriteLine("Joined Thread Completed");
  }
}
```

The effect of compiling and executing this program is that the first two strings are printed out immediately. There is then a pause before the remainder of the output is generated:

```
C:\csharp>Printable
Starting thread
Joining Thread
... pauses here ...
Hello John
Joined Thread Completed
```

In some cases it is necessary to wait for more than one thread to complete before continuing. This can be done using Waits. A Wait is a bit like an event handler; that is, a thread will wait for an event to occur before continuing. The abstract class WaitHandle provides some static methods that allow a thread to wait for a set of threads to complete (e.g. WaitAll). The WaitHandle subclass AutoResetEvent acts as an event that can release one thread when the Set method is called on it.

For example, in the following program the Printable class presented above is modified to have a property done that returns an AutoResetEvent object. This event can then be used with a WaitHandle method to monitor the status of the thread containing the Printable object. Note that the Print method of the Printable class now calls the method Set once the Print method has completed its behaviour. Thus once the Printable object has "printed" it notifies the AutoResetEvent that anything waiting could be released.

The Main method in this example collects all the AutoResetEvent objects from each of the Printable objects and places then in an array of WaitHandles. This is then used as a parameter to the WaitAll method. This method causes the Main method to wait until *all* the AutoResetEvent objects are notified that they have been Set.

```
using System;
using System.Threading;

public class Printable {
  private String s;
  private AutoResetEvent done;

  public Printable(String s) {
    this.s = s;
    done = new AutoResetEvent(false);
  }

  public void Print() {
    Thread.Sleep(1000);
    Console.WriteLine(s);
    done.Set();
  }

  public AutoResetEvent Done {
    get {
      return done;
    }
  }
}

public class Tester
{
  public static void Main()
  {
    Printable p1 = new Printable("A");
    Thread t1 = new Thread(new ThreadStart(p1.Print));
    Printable p2 = new Printable("B");
    Thread t2 = new Thread(new ThreadStart(p2.Print));
    Printable p3 = new Printable("C");
    Thread t3 = new Thread(new ThreadStart(p3.Print));
    Console.WriteLine("Waits list");
    WaitHandle[] waits = new WaitHandle[3];
```

```
      waits[0] = p1.Done;
      waits[1] = p2.Done;
      waits[2] = p3.Done;
      Console.WriteLine("Starting threads");
      t1.Start();
      t2.Start();
      t3.Start();
      WaitHandle.WaitAll(waits, 10000, false);
      Console.WriteLine("Threads Completed");
    }
}
```

The effect of compiling and executing this program is that the output pauses after printing "Starting Threads". The letters A, B and C are printed before the final output "Threads Completed" is printed. Note that this string is printed after all the other threads have notified their AutoResetEvent that they have completed their behaviour.

```
C:\csharp>Printable2
Waits list
Starting threads
... pauses here ...
A
B
C
Threads Completed
```

31.4.4 Synchronization

In a multi-threaded program issues of data integrity can occur. For example, consider what happens if two threads both possess a reference to a single object (say some sort of queue). This single object can be accessed by code running in two separate threads (let's call them t1 and t2). Let us assume a situation where thread t1 is adding data to the queue and thread t2 is consuming data from the queue.

Let us briefly consider one possible implementation for the Queue class (we will not use the Queue class defined in the System.Collections namespace for this exercise).

```
public class Queue {
  private ArrayList contents = new ArrayList(10);

  public void Add(Object obj) {
    contents.Add(obj);
  }

  public Object Get() {
    Object obj = contents[0];
    contents.RemoveAt(0);
```

```
    return obj;
  }

  public bool IsEmpty() {
    int result = contents.Count;
    if (result == 0) {
      return true;
    } else {
      return false;
    }
  }
}
```

This implementation of a Queue contains an instance of the class ArrayList and the methods Add, Get and IsEmpty. This allows thread t1 to add information and thread t2 to retrieve information. This is illustrated in Figure 31.3.

As C# is a time-slicing system (that is, it tries to share a single processor among the competing threads), it tries to enable both thread t1 and t2 to appear to execute together. This is illustrated in Figure 31.3 by the chequered bars. Each bar is active when it is white. Thus as time progresses down the diagram threads t1 and t2 both get a chance to execute.

However, note that the method Get is made up of three separate statements. The first identifies the object to remove from the queue, the second removes it and the third returns it. What

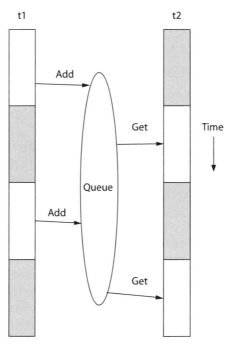

Figure 31.3 Interacting threads.

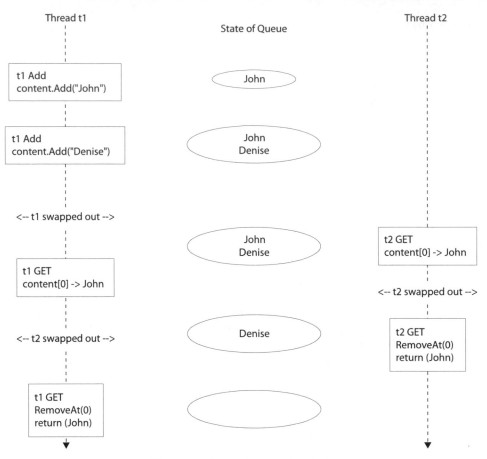

Figure 31.4 The need for synchronization.

happens if the scheduler swaps thread t2 out in the middle of this method? Let us examine this scenario in a bit more detail.

In Figure 31.4 the two threads t1 and t2 are interacting with the Queue object. Thread t1 is adding and getting data from the queue while thread t2 is getting data from the queue. However the scheduler is swapping t1 and t2 off and on to the processor. The result is that each thread does a bit of its work, is then suspended and is then resumed.

In the scenario presented in Figure 31.4 t1 adds two strings to the queue. It is then swapped out. t2 now executes and starts to run the Get method far enough to have obtained a reference to the first string in the queue. However, it is now swapped out. t1 begins to execute again. This time it starts to run the Get method on the queue. This also gets hold of a reference to the first string in the queue. It is itself then swapped out. Thread t2 then gets to complete the Get method, which causes it to remove the first element in the queue (the string "John"). It then returns the string "John" as the result of the method Get – which is correct. At some point in the future thread t1 gets to execute again. It then also removes the first element in the queue (the string "Denise") and returns the string "John" as the result of the Get method – which is wrong. Owing to the interaction of these two threads we have lost the reference to the string

"Denise". The reason for this problem is that the method Get should have been treated as autonomous (at least from the perspective of the queue object). That is, no other method that modified the state of the queue should have been allowed to be executed (methods on the queue class that relate to other queue objects obviously don't count).

Monitors can be used to overcome this problem. Think of a monitor as a bit like a key hanging outside an office. The office is currently locked and you need the key to gain entry to the office. However, you must take the key with you when you enter the office. This means that no one else can enter the office while you have the key. They must line up outside the office door waiting for the key to be returned. When you complete your task in the office you leave the office and re-lock the door. You then hang the key up on a hook outside the office. This allows the person at the front of the queue waiting to enter the office to obtain the key and enter. Thus only one person is inside the office at a time. In C# terms, only one method that is "monitored" can be executing on one object at a time.

As with most things in C#, monitors are implemented by classes. We could thus rewrite the above Queue class as:

```csharp
public class Queue {
  private ArrayList contents = new ArrayList(10);

  public void Add(Object obj) {
    Monitor.Enter(this);
    contents.Add(obj);
    Monitor.Exit(this);
  }

  public Object Get() {
    Monitor.Enter(this);
    Object obj = contents[0];
    contents.RemoveAt(0);
    Monitor.Exit(this);
    return obj;
  }

  public bool IsEmpty() {
    int result = contents.Count;
    if (result == 0) {
      return true;
    } else {
      return false;
    }
  }
}
```

Thus monitors provide a simple means of synchronization between multiple threads. Essentially, once a block of code is within a monitored section of code, associated methods cannot run at the same time on the same object (note the use of this).

However, strictly speaking this is not the end of the story. What happens if the Get method for some reason throws an exception after it has notified the Monitor class that it has entered a monitored block? The answer is that the Exit notification never occurs and no other monitored block of code will be able to execute. We should therefore really place the monitored code in a try-catch block with a finally statement that notifies the monitor of the exit. For example, we could write:

```
Object obj= null;
try {
  Monitor.Enter(this);
  obj = contents[0];
  contents.RemoveAt(0);
}
finally
  {
  Monitor.Exit(this);
  }
return obj;
```

However, this is a little long-winded and easy to forget. C# therefore provides a shortcut that is exactly equivalent to the above. This is the **lock** statement, for example:

```
Object obj= null;
lock(this)
{
  obj= contents[0];
  contents.RemoveAt(0);
}
return obj;
```

In some situations you may wish to make the whole of a method monitored. This can be done by using an attribute:

```
[MethodImpl(MethodImplOptions.Synchronized)]
```

31.5 A Producer/Consumer Example

The above synchronization examples still miss one aspect of a producer/consumer relationship with our Queue class – notification of process. That is, if thread t2 gets to the point of wanting to read some data from the queue, but there is no data currently in the queue (the IsEmpty method returns true), what should it do? One option is that it sleep for a while, wake up, test the queue again and then go back to sleep if there is no data. This is not very efficient. Even less efficient is for it to keep looping until some data does become available. Another option is for it to wait until the queue notifies it that there is some data available. This can be done by handling a wait via an AutoResetEvent event.

The idea here is that each queue object should have its own AutoResetEvent object. When a thread needs to wait for some data to be made available, that thread should obtain a reference to the AutoResetEvent and wait on it. The queue should then set the event (allowing the waiting thread to be released) once some data is provided.

We can modify our Queue class to do this by adding a done property of type AutoResetEvent. We must also make sure that the Add method now calls the Set method on the event freeing any waiting threads (note that if nothing is waiting the call to Set has no effect – hence the need for IsEmpty). The modified version of the Queue class is presented below:

```
using System;
using System.Threading;
using System.Collections;

public class Queue {
  private ArrayList contents = new ArrayList(10);
  private AutoResetEvent ready = new AutoResetEvent(false);

  public AutoResetEvent ReadyEvent {
    get {
      return ready;
    }
  }

  private void SetReadyEvent() {
    ready.Set();
  }

  public void Add(Object obj) {
    lock(this) {
      contents.Add(obj);
      SetReadyEvent();
    }
  }

  public Object Get() {
    Object obj = null;
    lock(this){
      obj = contents[0];
      contents.RemoveAt(0);
    }
    return obj;
  }

  public bool IsEmpty() {
    int result = contents.Count;
    if (result == 0) {
```

```
      return true;
    } else {
      return false;
    }
  }
}
```

This is not quite the end of the story, as we now need to consider producer and consumer classes.

The producer class merely needs to add data to the Queue (in our case, strings). Note that the producer adds a string and then sleeps for 1000 milliseconds to mimic some sort of processing operation.

```
public class Producer {
  private Queue q;

  public Producer(Queue q) {
    this.q = q;
  }

  public void Run() {
    int count = 0;
    while (true) {
      try{
        Console.WriteLine("PT=> Providing data to queue");
        q.Add(count + "");
        count++;
        Thread.Sleep(2000);
      } catch (Exception e) {
        Console.WriteLine(e.StackTrace);
      }
    }
  }
}
```

The consumer class must, however, check to see whether there is any data in the queue. If there is not it must wait for some data to become available. It does this by obtaining the property ReadyEvent and calling the method WaitOne on it; that is, wait for one Set method to allow the current thread to become unblocked. This is illustrated below:

```
public class Consumer {
  private Queue q;

  public Consumer(Queue q) {
    this.q = q;
  }
```

```
      public void Run() {
        while (true) {
          try {
            Console.WriteLine("CT=> Get some data");
            if (q.IsEmpty()) {
              Console.WriteLine("CT=> must wait for data to arrive");
              q.ReadyEvent.WaitOne();
            }
            Console.WriteLine("CT=> " + q.Get());
          } catch (Exception e) {
            Console.WriteLine(e.StackTrace);
          }
        }
      }
    }
```

To bring this example together the following test harness executes the consumer and producer in separate threads both linked to a common queue:

```
  public class Test {
    public static void Main() {
      Queue q = new Queue();
      Console.WriteLine("Created Queue");
      Consumer ct = new Consumer(q);
      Thread consumerThread = new Thread(new ThreadStart(ct.Run));
      consumerThread.Start();
      Console.WriteLine("Started consumer thread");
      Console.WriteLine("Now wait to produce producer thread");
      try {
        Thread.Sleep(1000);
      } catch (Exception e) {
        Console.WriteLine(e.StackTrace);
      }
      Console.WriteLine("Starting producer thread");
      Producer pt = new Producer(q);
      Thread producerThread = new Thread(new ThreadStart(pt.Run));
      producerThread.Start();
      Console.WriteLine("Producer thread started");
    }
  }
```

The result of compiling and executing this program is that the Consumer Thread (CT in the output) must repeatedly wait for the Producer Thread (PT) to supply the necessary data. The output thus pauses while the PT sleeps. The output is thus:

```
C:\csharp\chapter31>ProducerConsumer
Created Queue
Started consumer thread
Now wait to produce producer thread
CT=> Get some data
CT=> must wait for data to arrive
... output pauses here ...
Starting producer thread
Producer thread started
PT=> Providing data to queue
CT=> 0
CT=> Get some data
CT=> must wait for data to arrive
... output pauses here ...
PT=> Providing data to queue
CT=> 1
CT=> Get some data
CT=> must wait for data to arrive
... output pauses here ...
PT=> Providing data to queue
CT=> 2
CT=> Get some data
CT=> must wait for data to arrive
...
```

Chapter 32

Using C# in ASP.NET

32.1 Introduction

First there was ASP (Active Server Page); then there was ASP.NET. Both can serve up data on HTTP requests dynamically using HTML and executable code embedded in the pages. The ASP.NET approach is a development of the original ASP approach that can exploit the .NET framework directly and C# in particular.

ASP (and from now on we will take ASP to indicate ASP.NET unless otherwise stated) is a Microsoft technology for creating Web pages that will dynamically generate some or all of their content. ASPs live on the Web server and are processed by the Web server to generate the actual page sent back to a Web client. This means that the Web clients never get to see the (in our case) C# code embedded in the ASP, just the results of executing that code.

An ASP file is essentially an HTML file that uses a `.aspx` extension and provides some additional ASP tags.

32.2 What Is an ASP?

The main aim of the ASP framework is the separation of presentation from application logic. That is, it aims to allow non-C# developers to design the ASPs using:

- HTML markup
- XML-like tags known as ASP tags

These ASP tags can then access server-side C# code or can embed C# code directly into the ASP. Thus the separation of concern is achieve by allowing C# developers to focus on standard C# classes and Web designers to concentrate on HTML, DHTML and the ASP tags.

It is useful to consider what happens to a ASP when a client requests an ASP. The ASP.NET page generally produces HTML code in response to an HTTP request. The page itself is "compiled" dynamically and loaded into the Web server. This is done by parsing each ASP.NET

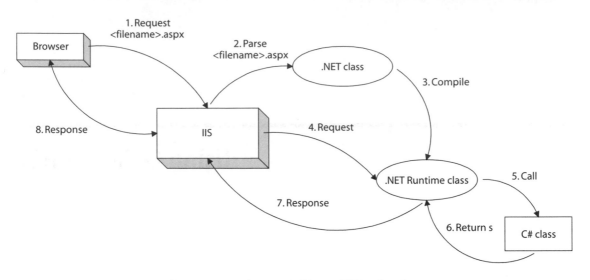

Figure 32.1 Translating an ASP into a .NET Runtime class.

page to check the syntax and generate a .NET class. This .NET run-time class is compiled and then invoked on the Web server. ASP.NET caches the compiled object, so subsequent requests do not go through the compile step and thus execute much faster.

Figure 32.1 illustrates the steps that occur the first time a user requests an ASP. These steps are described in more detail below:

1. Request `<filename>.aspx`. The first step is that the client browser must request the ASP file from the ASP-enabled Web server (in this case IIS).
2. The IIS server parses the `.aspx` file and a .NET class is generated.
3. The generated class is compiled and loaded into the IIS.
4. The Web server passes the request to the implementation of the ASP.
5. This "class" can then call out to other code as required. For example, it can call out to other C# classes.
6. Any information provided by the called code can be appended to the HTML from the ASP as required.
7. The HTML generated is returned to the Web server
8. The Web server returns the HTML page to the client browser
9. The client browser renders the response without ever seeing any server-side code.

32.3 A Very Simple ASP

To illustrate the ideas discussed above we will look at a very simple ASP. The ASP we will define is the ASP version of "Hello World". We will create an ASP that presents Hello followed by a string supplied from a C# class called BasicHello in a package Hello. The ASP, saved in a file called hello.aspx, is presented in Listing 32.1.

Listing 32.1 A very simple hello.aspx file.

```
<%@ Page Language="C#" Description="ASP.NET Component Test" %>
<%@ Import Namespace="Hello"%>
<html>
<script language="C#" runat=server>
void Page_Load(Object sender, EventArgs EvArgs) {
  String out = "";

  // Create the output.
  out = "<h1>BasicHelloWorld</h1>";
  out = out + "This is a simple test";
  out = out + "<p><hr><p>";
  out = out + "Hello ";
  Hello.BasicHello bh = new BasicHello();
  out = out + bh.GetName();
  out = out + "<br>";

  StringOut.InnerHtml = Out;
}
</script>
<body>
  <span id="Message" runat=server/>
</body>
</html>
```

We will work through this simple ASP.

- The first line specifies C# as a language, but it could just as easily have used Visual Basic or even JScript.
- In the second line the <%...%> is used to indicate script code, and in this case specifies the namespace Hello to import. Note that the assembly containing this namespace must be in the /bin directory of the application's starting point.
- Line 4 in the above listing tells the server to execute the code on the server rather than sending the code text back to the client as part of the HTML stream.
- After the script specification comes the Page_Load method. Web Forms provides special recognition of the commonly used Page_Load method (along with Page_Init, Page_DataBind, Page_PreRender, PageDispose and Page_Error). This method is automatically connected to event handlers for the standard page events.
- Inside this method is standard C# code with the generation of a string to contain the output.
- The final statement of this method adds the string to the HTML to be sent to the client

To use this ASP we will also need to implementation of the BasicHello class in the Hello namespace. This is a standard C# class and is presented in Listing 32.2.

Listing 32.2 The simple BasicHello class.

```
namespace Hello
  public class BasicHello {
    public String GetName() {
      return "John";
    }
  }
}
```

As this is only an example, Listing 32.2 is very basic. The string returned by the class is hard coded to be "John". However, this string could be provided by some other C# code, have been read from a database or accessed from some legacy code etc.

The BasicHello class must be compiled and added to an appropriate assembly. However, rather than run the class directly the assembly file must be installed in the appropriate place (the /bin directory of the application).

In the case of the .NET framework the Web server to be used will be the IIS (Internet Information Server). To install the ASP on IIS you must configure a virtual directory (using Internet Services Manager) that points to the directory where Hello.aspx is located. To create a virtual directory using the IIS snap-in, perform the following steps:

- Select the Web site or FTP site that you want to add a directory to.
- Click the Action button, point to New, and select Virtual Directory.
- Use the New Virtual Directory wizard to complete the task.

The end result of installing the ASP file and BasicHello class correctly on your IIS server is illustrated in Figure 32.2.

Although the example presented in Listing 32.1 is a very simple example, it does show an ASP that obtains some of its data from a C# class – this is the essence of all ASPs!

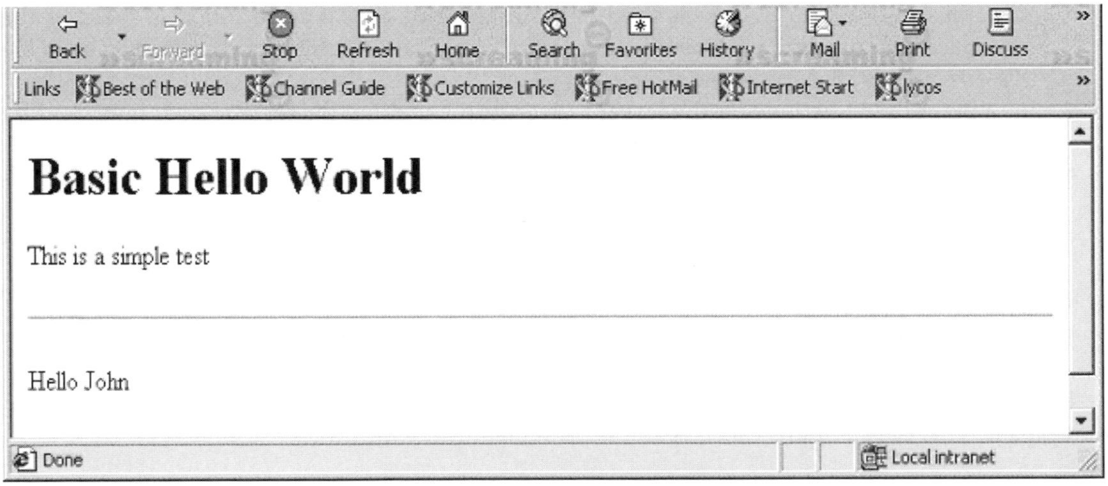

Figure 32.2 The result of running the simple ASP.

32.4 ASP.NET Tags

32.4.1 ASP Directives

ASP directives specify settings used by the page compilers when they processes ASP. NET Web Forms page (.aspx) files. When used, directives can be located anywhere in an .aspx file, though standard practice is to include them at the beginning of the file. Each directive can contain one or more attributes (paired with values) that are specific to that directive.

The ASP.NET framework supports a number of directives, including:

@ Page	Defines page-specific attributes used by the ASP.NET page parser and compiler. Can only be included in .aspx files
@ Import	Explicitly imports a namespace into a page
@ Implements	Declaratively indicates that a page implements a specified .NET Framework interface
@ Assembly	Declaratively links an assembly to the current page

32.4.2 Code Declaration Blocks

Defines member variables and methods compiled in the dynamically generated Page classes that represent the ASP.NET page. Code declaration blocks are defined using <script> tags that contain a runat attribute value set to "server". The <script> element can optionally use a language attribute to specify the language of its inner code. If none is specified, ASP.NET defaults to the language configured for the base page or user control (controlled using the @ Page directives). The format of a code declaration block is:

```
<script runat="server" language="codelanguage" Src="pathname">
  Code goes here...
</script>
```

32.4.3 Server-Side Object Tag Syntax

This is used to declare and instantiate C# classes inside ASP.NET pages. The syntax for a server-side object tag is:

```
<object id="id" runat=server class=".NET Framework Class Name">
```

where id is a unique name to use when referencing the object in subsequent code and class specifies the .NET Framework class to create. When parsed, this creates an instance of the named class referenced by its id that is available within the ASP. For example:

```
<html>
  <object id="ole" class="System.OleDBDataAdapter" runat="server"/>
  <script language="C#" runat=server>
    void Page_Load(Object sender, EventArgs EvArgs) {
```

```
        ole.Execute("DSN:money", "select * from stocks");
        ...
    }
  </script>
</html>
```

Chapter 33

Web-Based User Interfaces

33.1 Introduction

This chapter builds on the ASP.NET concepts presented in the previous chapter. In this chapter we will look at the creation of Web-based user interfaces. Such interfaces typically present combinations of graphical components such as buttons, text fields, drop-down selection boxes etc. Traditionally building such a Web page has involved writing HTML, DHTML, JScript etc. in order to cause forms, tables and other Web page components to produce the desired layouts. However, the use of ASP.NET and the System.Web.UI namespace makes the creation of such Web pages much more akin to the creation of a GUI application as described in Chapters 23, 24 and 25.

In this chapter we will consider the System.Web.UI namespace, the key classes Control and Page. We will also look at the System.Web.UI.HtmlControls namespace and the System.Web.UI.WebControls namespace.

33.2 Web Forms Overview

The System.Web.UI namespace contains a set of classes, interfaces, structs and enumerated types that allow the creation of sophisticated Web pages. These Web pages are referred to as Web Forms. The most important classes in this namespace are the Control class and the Page class (note the similarity of names to the System.Windows.Forms namespace where there is also a Control class). The Control class acts as the root of (almost) all Web-based controls. In turn, Page acts as the container for a set of controls within a Web page (in a similar manner to the Form acting as the top level container for a GUI application). To create a Web page the developer must extend the Page class and define what the content of that page should be.

The part of the class hierarchy for the Control class in the System.Web.UI namespace is illustrated in Figure 33.1. Note that the controls divide up into three subsections: one for high-level controls, such as Page, one for Web controls, such as button and label, and one for HtmlControls such as HtmlInputButton. These will each be discussed in more detail later in this chapter.

359

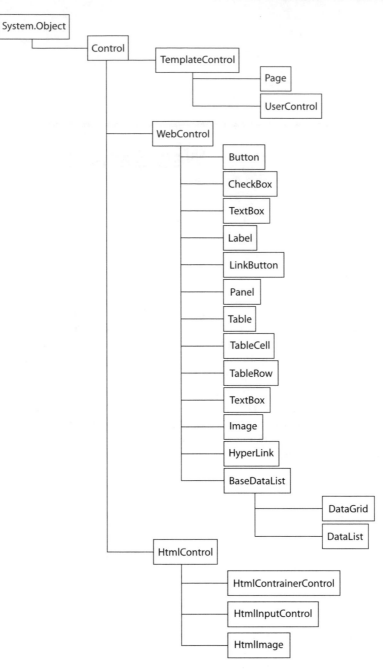

Figure 33.1 Part of the class hierarchy for Web controls.

Note that the HtmlControls are illustrated in Figure 33.2 on p. 364. As well as the Control and Page classes, another class of particular interest is the UserControl class. This class is similar to the Page class except that it does not include page-specific properties or methods. It is typically used as the parent class for developer-defined custom controls (rather than the more basic Control class).

33.3 The Control Class

The Control class is the root of almost all the Web forms classes (see Figure 33.1). Thus the facilities defined in this class are available for all Web components, such as buttons, text boxes and label images. Tables 33.1–33.3 summarize the properties and key methods of the System.Web.UI.Control class.

Table 33.1 Public instance properties of the System.Web.UI.Control class.

ClientID	Gets the server control identifier generated by ASP.NET
Controls	Gets a ControlCollection object that represents the child controls for a specified server control in the UI hierarchy
EnableViewState	Gets or sets a value indicating whether the server control maintains its view state, and the view state of any child controls it contains, when the current page request ends
ID	Gets or sets the programmatic identifier assigned to the server control
Page	Gets a reference to the Page instance that contains the server control
Parent	Gets a reference to the server control's parent control in the page UI hierarchy
Site	Gets information about the Web site to which the server control belongs
TemplateSourceDirectory	Gets the virtual directory of the Page or UserControl that contains the current server control
UniqueID	Gets the unique, hierarchically qualified identifier for the server control
Visible	Gets or sets a value that indicates whether a server control is rendered as UI on the page

Table 33.2 Public instance methods of the System.Web.UI.Control class.

DataBind	Binds a data source to the invoked server control and all of its child controls
Dispose	Enables a server control to perform final clean up before it is released from memory
HasControls	Determines whether the server control contains any child controls

Table 33.3 Protected instance methods of the System.Web.UI.Control class.

OnBubbleEvent	Determines whether the event for the server control is passed up the page's UI server control hierarchy
OnDataBinding	Raises the DataBinding event
OnInit	Raises the Init event
OnLoad	Raises the Load event
OnPreRender	Raises the PreRender event, which notifies the server control that

The above tables only summarize the methods available on the Control class. Note that the methods that are triggered if some event occurs (such as OnInit) are protected; that is, they are made available to the subclasses of Control rather than being used directly. Also note that a Control defines a Controls property that holds references to any contained controls.

33.4 The Page Class

The Page class performs a similar role to the Form class in the GUI-based framework. That is, it is a container for all the controls that make up that Web page. In fact, any Web page requested from a server hosting the .NET framework, whether it contains .NET code or only HTML text, is compiled as a Page object and cached in server memory.

The Page class is a subclass class of TemplateControl which is a direct subclass of Control (see Figure 33.1). This means that it inherits all the facilities provided by Control as well as providing specific behaviour required of a Web page within the ASP.NET framework. For example, as well as providing a Controls property, the Page class provides access to properties such as Application, Request, Response, Server and Session. It also provides access to a Cache property, an ErrorPage property and a (very useful) Trace property, as well as a Validators property (which has controls that are responsible for validating the page). These properties are described below.

The Application property gets the Application object for the current Web request. The Application object enables sharing of global information across multiple sessions and requests within an ASP.NET application. An ASP.NET application is the sum of all files, pages, handlers, modules and code within the scope of a virtual directory and its subdirectories on a single Web server.

The Cache property allows the page to cache objects such as database connections, dictionaries of values and array lists. This allows these objects to be reused without having to be recreated for the page.

The ErrorPage property allows the developer to specify that page to display when an error occurs.

The Request property returns the Request object provided by the HTTP Runtime, which allows you to access data from incoming HTTP requests. That is any information sent from a page being displayed via a Web browser. For example any information input into a form on a Web page and submitted back to the Web server.

The Request property returns the Request object that allows you to generate a response back to the Web client (i.e. a Web browser).

The Session property provides access to the current Session object provided by the ASP.NET framework. The Session object allows data to be saved for this user's session. Each user has their own session object.

The User property provides access to an object that allows the page to obtain information about the user requesting the page, such as the name of the current user etc.

The Validators property groups together controls that can validate themselves inside the page. Thus when a page is required to validate itself it can delegate this responsibility to the controls in the Validators property.

33.4.1 The `System.Web.UI.WebControls` Namespace

The controls in the `System.Web.UI.WebControls` namespace provide a rich set of Web page components, such as buttons, labels, lists, calenders and tables. These controls are objects that can be instantiated and used within a Web page (in a similar manner to the way in which GUI controls can be used within a `Form`). The controls are added to the page's control collection via the `Controls` property. The root of all the Web controls classes is the `WebControl` class, which is a direct subclass of `Control`. This class provides facilities such as tooltips, colour, fonts and border settings in a similar manner to those used with the GUI components.

As an example of the Web control classes consider the class `System.Web.UI.WebControls.Button`. This button class provides for a pushbutton on a Web page. This button can be either a submit button or a command button. The difference is that a submit button does not have a command name associated with it (as it merely "posts" data back to the server), whereas a command button does have a command name associated with it. This allows the button event handler to determine which (of several) buttons was clicked. This makes Web page programming more like GUI programming and thus provides a coherent model for user interface development.

Note that the event handler that you would write for the `Click` event follows the same conventions as those used with the GUI classes. That is, it must return `void`, and take the sender object and an event `args` parameter.

33.4.2 The `System.Web.UI.HtmlControls` Namespace

The `System.Web.UI.HtmlControls` namespace provides a set of controls that are similar to the `System.Web.UI.WebControls` but less feature rich. This may prompt the question "Why are there two namespaces with two sets of classes that perform very similar functions?". The answer is that the classes provided in the `System.Web.UI.HtmlControls` namespace may be easier to use if you are migrating older ASP applications. In addition, the objects used are available to client-side scripts, which may also be an important factor. Figure 33.2 illustrates part of the `System.Web.UI.HtmlControls` class hierarchy.

An interesting point to note is that the classes in this namespace map (almost) directly to HTML tags. Thus if you specify that one of these classes is to be used, then when the Web page is compiled (as described in the previous chapter) then the object is converted into the appropriate HTML that matches it. This is why the controls are referred to as `HtmlControls`.

33.5 Building up a Web Page

There are essentially two ways in which you can create a Web page (and they are not mutually exclusive). The first is to define an ASP that contains C# code as server-side scripts that are embedded within the ASP. The second is to use Web Forms to define a C# class that will provide the required behaviour. We will look at both approaches. It is worth noting at this point that in the .NET Framework both approaches end up being processed into a class that is loaded into the server to provide the required behaviour (see last chapter).

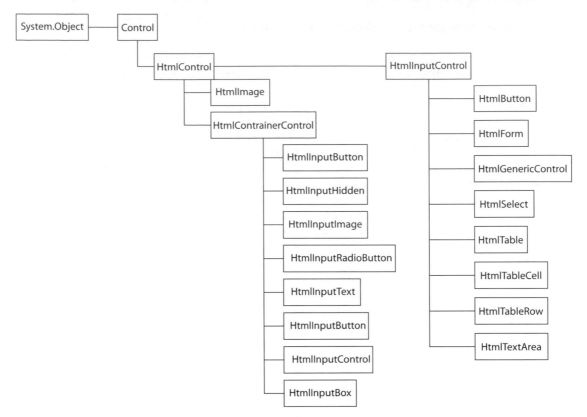

Figure 33.2 The HtmlControls class hierarchy.

33.5.1 Basic ASP

In Figure 33.3 we can see an ASP that defines a simple button that when clicked causes the Web page to be redisplayed with a message displayed below a horizontal line. How is this possible? The ASP file uses HTML controls to specify that certain aspects of the page should be run on the server. This is done via a code declaration block defined to run on the server and two data binding expressions that define a button and a text label.

A code declaration block defines code to be parsed and run for a Web page. The runat attribute of the block indicates whether the code is to be run on the client or server side. In the case of the ASP in Figure 33.3 the script specifies that the code should be run on the server. It also specifies that we are using the C# language. In general, the format of a code declaration block is:

```
<script language="code language" runat="server">
  ...
</script>
```

The HTML controls used within this Web page are related to the classes described earlier in this chapter. ,However they are implicitly specified and instantiated relative to the HTML encountered. For example, if we wrote:

```
<input id="b1" runat="server" type="button" value="Select" />
```

This would map to an HtmlInputButton with a reference id of "b1". Notice that again this example specifies that the code behind this button should run on the server. Thus when the user clicks on this button a request will be sent back to the server for the business logic behind the button to be executed.

The button can be linked to an event handler (just as GUI buttons could be linked to event handlers). There are two ways of doing this. One is via a declaration within the HTML tag itself, e.g.

```
onserverclick="ButtonHandler"
```

The other is via normal C# handler registration code, e.g.

```
b1.ServerClick += new EventHandler(ButtonHandler);
```

In the example presented in Figure 33.3 we have used two custom controls to link our label and button to the event handler. We will look at the label example first, as it is the simpler case.

Figure 33.3 A simple "Hello World" ASP.

A custom control is very similar to an HTML control except that it is not standard HTML. For example, in Figure 33.3 we wrote:

```
<asp:Label id="label1" runat="server"/>
```

This is a custom control that creates a new instance of the Label class and assigns it the id "label1". The runat attribute indicates that this is an object that will be managed on the server.

Note that the C# method defined in the script code declaration at the top of the file references the object held in the variable label1, for example:

```
void Button_Click(Object sender, EventArgs e) {
  label1.Text="Hello World!!";
}
```

This is a standard event handler as seen in Chapter 24. It will be run whenever the user clicks on the button (we will come to this in a moment). However, each time it is run it will set the text of the object referenced by the variable label1 to "Hello World!!". Thus the id in the custom control declaration becomes a variable available to our C# code.

The declaration of the button object is also handled via a custom control, for example:

```
<asp:Button id="b1"
  Text="Say Hello"
  OnClick="Button_Click"
  runat="server"/>
```

In this case this control declares a new button object, to be referenced via the id b1, with the text "Say Hello", that will run on the server. It also links the button to the Button_Click handler so that when the user clicks on the button, a call will be sent back to the server. The server will then run the Button_Click method and a new Web page will be generated as a result (with the modified label text incorporated).

33.5.2 Using a Page class

Using the Page class we can work with Web Forms. These are intended to offer a much simpler programming model than that available with the original ASP approach (and is similar in many ways to the servlets approach available in Java).

A Web Form consists of two components, the Web form itself and the code behind the form that provides its functionality. These two components together provide a much cleaner approach to Web development. In this approach the Web page and the C# code (or any .NET language) are separated out; thus the presentation (via the Web form) and the business logic (via the C# code) are independent. This has the potential for code reuse for the C# code as well as allowing C# developers to focus on C# development and Web designers to focus on the HTML-based Web page.

A Web Form has the extension .aspx and contains HTML as well as server-side directives to link it to the underlying C# code. The code that is "behind" the Web Form is located in a

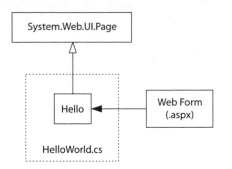

Figure 33.4 The relationship between the `.aspx` Web form and the C# code "behind" it.

separate class file (note that it is possible to place the two in the same file, but this is considered bad practice). This is illustrated in Figure 33.4.

An example of a simple `.aspx` file is presented below for a very simple "Hello World"-style Web application.

```
<%@ Page language="c#" codebehind="HelloWorld.cs" inherits="Hello" %>
<html>
  <head>
    <title>Hello World with a Web Form</title>
  </head>
  <body>
    <form runat=server>
      Text: <asp:Label id=username runat=server /> <br>
      <input type=submit />
    </form>
  </body>
</html>
```

The above page does a number of significant things:

1. It provides a page directive that specifies that the language to be used in the underlying code will be C#. This code (the "code behind" the Web Form) is defined in a file called `HelloWorld.cs` and the class that will be generated by the server based on this Web form will inherit from the `Hello` class (defined in the `HelloWorld.cs` file).
2. It then defines some HTML that is used to lay out the page (such as a title for the page).
3. It defines a form that links to the underlying C# code. This form displays a label following the `Text:` string that is generated by the "behind code".
4. Each time the submit button is clicked the underlying code will generate a new label to be displayed.

The "code behind", defined in the file `HelloWorld.cs` is presented below:

```
using System;
using System.Web.UI;
using System.Web.UI.WebControls;

public class Hello : Page {
  private Label username;
  private int count;

  // Constructor
  public Hello() {
    username = new Label();
  }

  public void Page_Init(Object sender, EventArgs e) {
    username.Text = "Hello " + count;
  }

  public void Page_Load(Object sender, EventArgs e) {
    count++;
    username.Text = "Hello" + count;
  }
}
```

The above listing defines a class called Hello. This is a standard C# class that extends the class System.Web.UI.Page. This is the Page class that acts as a container for all the controls used on the Web page. In this case there is only one control, a System.Web.UI.WebControls.Label object. This object has its text value set via the two page event handling methods.

A Page class supports a number of events including Init, Load, PreRender and Unload. To handle any of these events the developer must implement a Page_* method that takes a sender object and an EventArgs object. Thus if we implement the Page_Init(Object sender, EventArgs e) this method will be called when the Init event occurs.

In the above code we have implemented the Page_Init and Page_Load methods. These are explained below.

The Init event occurs once for each user of the page. It is akin to a constructor in that it is only called once when the object is first used (in this case on a per user basis). It is used to allow initialization code to be written for this page and happens before the controls on the page are created. Thus when the page is first loaded the method sets the username Label control to "Hello 0".

The Page_Load method is called after the Page_Init method as well as each time the user requests the page again (it may therefore be called multiple times). In our Page_Load method the instance variable count is incremented each time the method is called. It is then appended to the Hello string. Thus the first time it is called it changes the text in the username Label to "Hello 1". As this happens almost immediately after the init method we will find that the string displayed is "Hello 1". Each subsequent time that the page is called the count is incremented and the value changed. Note that this implies that the page object resides in memory while the client is still interacting with it. In fact, the server can cache the object out and recreate it rather than leave it in memory all the time. However, the perceived result is the same.

To use the Hello class with our Web Form we must compile the HelloWorld.cs file to an assembly (do not try to compile it as an executable as the compiler will complain that there is no Main method). To do this you can compile the HelloWorld.cs file using the following command line option:

```
csc /t:library HelloWorld.cs
```

This will create a HelloWorld.dll file. You must install this on your IIS installation in the /bin directory of your Web application's virtual directory. See IIS to see how to set up an application and its virtual directory (which is the root directory where your Web application resides). You will also need to install your .aspx file on IIS as appropriate.

The ASP.NET framework will then parse the Web Form and the C# file to create an object that will handle requests for this page. This object will reside on the server and will send only the resultant HTML back to the client. That is, the client will never see the C# code or the page directive linking the Web form with the code behind it.

Each time the user clicks on the submit button, a call is made back to the object resident on the server that processes that submission. The result is then that a new Web page is generated and sent back to the client.

Chapter 34

XML and C#

34.1 Introduction

By any standards XML is one of the hottest topics around at the moment. Almost everyone is talking about XML and the majority of modern programming languages now provide some way of accessing XML documents. C# is no exception, providing a number of ways of accessing the contents of an XML document. In this chapter we will look at the use of the DOM (Document Object Model) API defined by the World Wide Web Consortium (known as the W3C; see `http://www.w3c.org/`). This is a standard API that is specified in terms of interfaces that can be implemented in a particular language to provide a set of concrete classes for XML document creation, manipulation, searching and loading etc. This chapter begins with a brief overview of XML before covering C#'s implementation of the DOM API.

34.2 XML Introduced

34.2.1 What is XML?

XML is a data markup language. That is, it is used to mark up or describe data elements. Markup languages are not new. They have been around for some time (and indeed are still often invented – any time you create a new syntax for describing data, say in a file, then you are marking up that data). Older markup languages include SGML (Standard Generalized Markup Language), LaTeX and nroff. The latter two languages are used for describing text for processing by a formatting program to create something that can be viewed or printed. Even HTML is actually a form of markup (indeed, it stands for HyperText Markup Language).

So if markup languages are nothing new, why have XML? Firstly HTML, LaTeX etc. are not extensible and are designed for a very specific purpose. For example, HTML is designed for describing the contents of a Web page for display within a Web browser. SGML, on the other hand, is extensible but very heavyweight, requiring extensive proprietary systems to manage and process it. XML is a compromise between the two. XML (which actually stands for eXtensible Markup Language) builds on the strengths of SGML, but does not try to provide the

371

whole of the SGML model – only what is required most of the time. This follows the 80/20 rule: that is, 80% of the time only 20% of the functionality of, say, SGML is required.

As we have now seen, XML is designed for marking up data. However, XML itself is really very unsubstantial. It is necessary to define a vocabulary that creates the actual markup tags for the markup to have meaning. For example, we might create a definition for a set of tags to be used to "mark up" an invoice. The definition of the tags could be placed inside a DTD (a concept inherited from SGML) or the newer XMLSchema. In either case an XML file will be processed against the set of definitions to determine whether it is valid. That is, the XML file only contains tags defined in the definition and that the structure of the XML file matches that specified in the definition. One of XML's strong points is that it is possible to state that tag1 must be placed inside tag2 etc. In the case of XMLSchemas it is also possible to specify that a value must be a string, an integer, a positive value etc.

XML, however, is only about marking up data. It is not related to how that data is presented. This is in contrast, for example, to HTML. HTML is involved in both data markup and presentation. That is, HTML tells a browser how to present the data as well as the meaning of that data. In XML a separate file, for example an XSL file (XSL stands for XML Style Language) can be used to transform the XML into a presentation form. For example, it could convert an XML file into PDF format, Postscript format or indeed into HTML. This transformation aspect of XSL is referred to as XML Transformation or XSLT. An XSLT processor will apply an XSL specification to an XML document to convert the data in the XML file into the new format.

For any XML application we therefore need five things:

1. The definition of the XML tags to use
2. An XML document that marks up some data using the XML tags (for example in a file)
3. A parser that will compare the XML document with the definition
4. (Optionally) an XSL specification to describe how to translate an XML document into a viewable format
5. The application that will use the contents of the XML document

The above points are illustrated in Figure 34.1.

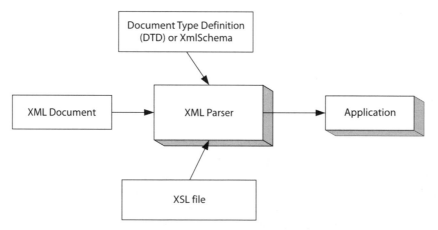

Figure 34.1 The components of an XML system.

34.2.2 What Do XML Documents Look Like?

Figure 34.2 illustrates a very simple sample XML document that defines a set of contacts and their addresses. The first line of this document is a processing instruction that specifies the version of XML that this file corresponds to. Following this is the root element of the XML document: this is the CONTACTS element, which the remaining tags are defined within.

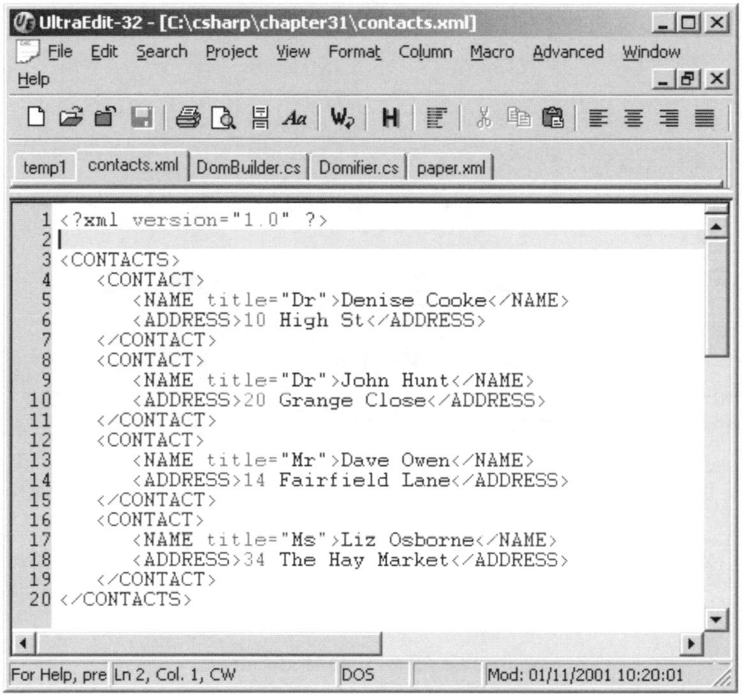

```
1  <?xml version="1.0" ?>
2
3  <CONTACTS>
4      <CONTACT>
5          <NAME title="Dr">Denise Cooke</NAME>
6          <ADDRESS>10 High St</ADDRESS>
7      </CONTACT>
8      <CONTACT>
9          <NAME title="Dr">John Hunt</NAME>
10         <ADDRESS>20 Grange Close</ADDRESS>
11     </CONTACT>
12     <CONTACT>
13         <NAME title="Mr">Dave Owen</NAME>
14         <ADDRESS>14 Fairfield Lane</ADDRESS>
15     </CONTACT>
16     <CONTACT>
17         <NAME title="Ms">Liz Osborne</NAME>
18         <ADDRESS>34 The Hay Market</ADDRESS>
19     </CONTACT>
20 </CONTACTS>
```

Figure 34.2 A simple XML document.

An important thing to remember about XML is that it is a hierarchical structure. This structure is illustrated in Figure 34.3. An XML document has a prolog that contains various information used by the XML processor (such as the version of XML being used) and a root element (that the rest of the XML document "hangs off"). The root element then holds the next level elements. In turn, these hold subsequent elements etc. (see also Figure 34.4).

Within any element there can be a CData element (essentially data that should be left as is). An XML document can also have entity references. Entity references are a bit like shorthand for other things. They have the form &<name>;, for example & is the entity reference for an ampersand (&). We could, for example, create an entity reference for a company name. Thus each time we wanted to reference a company name we would use the entity reference that would be expanded to the full name when the XML document is processed.

We should also deal with some standard terminology at this point. Firstly, the phrase "XML Document" is used to refer to the XML structure defined by the XML markup. This could be coming from a file, from a socket or via C# remoting. Any text marked up by the document is referred to as Parseable Character Data. The concepts presented so far are illustrated in Figure 34.4.

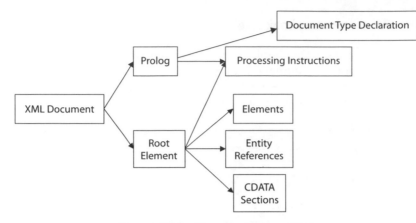

Figure 34.3 The hierarchical nature of XML.

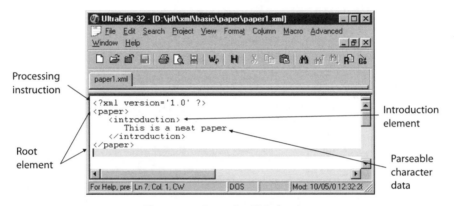

Figure 34.4 Parts of an XML document.

Another point to note is that each of the tag pairs in the file (e.g. CONTACTS in Figure 34.2) is referred to as an element. Each element must be well formed. That is, each element must follow the rules of XML. There must be a starting tag and a corresponding closing tag (indicated by the start tag preceded by a forward slash); for example <CONTACTS>...</CONTACTS>. An element below the CONTACTS elements is referred to as a child element. For example, <CONTACT> is a child element of <CONTACTS>. In turn <CONTACT is a parent element for <NAME>.

Elements can have attributes; for example, the <Name> tag in Figure 34.2 has an attribute title. This is a value (which must be in quotes – either double or single) that is linked directly with the element.

34.2.3 XML Vocabularies

XML vocabularies are XML specifications that define elements that can be shared amongst organizations. For example, the medical profession could create a vocabulary for describing diseases. This could then be used for passing information from doctors' surgeries to hospitals etc.

The actual set of vocabularies is growing all the time. Some of the early vocabularies (and thus the most developed) include:

- Mathematical Markup Language (MathML)
- Health Level 7
- Microsoft's BizTalk
- IBM's SpeechML
- Internet Open Trading Protocol (OTP)
- Open Financial Exchange Specification (OFE)
- Bioinformatic Sequence Markup Language (BSML)
- Development Markup Language (DML) for world development organizations – UNESCO

Some other vocabularies go beyond just the markup to include software systems that process those (see Figure 34.5). For example, Microsoft's Simple Object Access protocol (SOAP) is an XML vocabulary with extensive software support. Another example is SVG (Scalable Vector Graphics), which is an XML language for describing graphics that has a number of renderers available (the best being from Adobe).

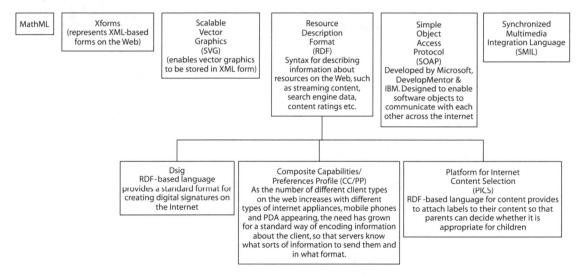

Figure 34.5 Established XML markup vocabularies.

There are also a set of related technologies that are still growing to support the definition, analysis, manipulation and processing of XML files. These are summarized in Figure 34.6.

34.2.4 Working With a DTD

So far we have glossed over the issue of defining the elements to be used within an XML application. As mentioned earlier, this can be done via either an XML Schema or a DTD (Document Type Definition). In the case of a DTD this can be an internal DTD (contained within the XML document itself) or an external DTD (contained in a separate file). Figure 34.7 illustrates an XML file with an internal

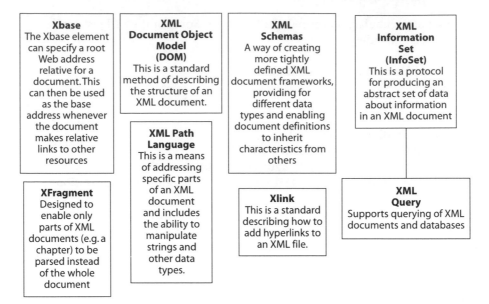

Figure 34.6 Related XML technologies.

DTD. When an XML file is compared with its definition (e.g. a DTD) and is found to match the rules described in that definition, it is termed valid.

To link an external DTD to an XML file we could use a Document Type Declaration that contained a SYSTEM entry followed by the location of the DTD (Figure 34.8). For example:

```
<!DOCTYPE paper SYSTEM "paper.dtd">
```

There are four kinds of declarations in an XML DTD. These are:

- element declarations
- attribute list declarations
- entity declarations
- notation declarations

Element declarations define the names of elements and the nature of their content. For example:

```
<!ELEMENT paper (abstract, introduction, section+, conclusion,
bibliography?)>
```

This defines an element called paper and its "content model". The content model defines what an element may contain. In this case it contains an abstract, an introduction, one or more sections, a conclusion and (optionally) a bibliography. These elements in turn must be defined elsewhere in the DTD. Notice that conclusion was said to be optional and that there would be one or more sections. Where was this defined? It was indicated by the occurrence indicators following the relevant entities (the + and the ? above). The occurrence indicators that can be used in a DTD are:

```
UltraEdit-32 - [C:\csharp\chapter31\paper.xml]                        _ □ ×
File   Edit   Search   Project   View   Format   Column   Macro   Advanced   Window   Help   _ ┌┐ ×

□ ☞ ☎ ◻ | ⎙ ◻ 冒 Aa | W₂ | H | ☰ | ✂ ▣ ▣ | ☰ ☰ ☰ ☰ | ⋔ ⋔ ⋔

temp1*│ contacts.xml │ DomBuilder.cs │ Domifier.cs │ paper.xml │

 1 <?xml version="1.0" ?>
 2
 3 <!DOCTYPE paper [
 4    <!ELEMENT paper (introduction, section+)>
 5    <!ATTLIST paper
 6                title CDATA #REQUIRED
 7                author CDATA #REQUIRED>
 8    <!ELEMENT introduction (#PCDATA)>
 9    <!ATTLIST introduction
10                heading CDATA #REQUIRED>
11    <!ELEMENT section (heading, body)>
12    <!ELEMENT heading (#PCDATA)>
13    <!ELEMENT body (#PCDATA)>
14 ]>
15
16 <!-- comment: XML document starts here -->
17
18 <paper title = "XML forever" author = "John Hunt">
19    <introduction heading ="The history">
20        The background to XML is interesting
21    </introduction>
22    <section>
23        <heading>The main event</heading>
24        <body>
25            So what is XML all about
26        </body>
27    </section>
28    <section>
29        <heading>The Conclusion</heading>
30        <body>
31            Where is XML heading
32        </body>
33    </section>
34 </paper>

For Help, pre Ln 2, Col. 1, CW        DOS          Mod: 01/11/2001 16:56:57    File Size: 895
```

Figure 34.7 An XML document with an internal DTD.

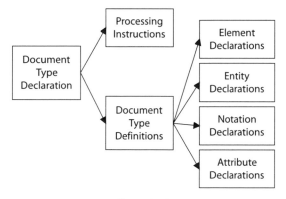

Figure 34.8

- ? zero or one occurrence
- * zero or more occurrences
- + one or more occurrence
- no symbol: one occurrence

At some point an element may wish to include some actual data (remember that XML is really about marking up data). Such data can be defined as parseable character data (indicated in a DTD by #PCDATA). For example:

```
<!ELEMENT author (#PCDATA | quote)*>
```

This states that author may contain 0 or more characters and a quote tag.

Finally, an element may also have attributes (as well as sub-elements or parseable characters). These attributes can be used to tell you more about the element. To define attributes for an element you need to identify:

- which elements may have attributes
- what attributes they may have
- what values the attributes may hold
- what default value each attribute has

An attribute in a declaration has three parts: a name, a type, and a default value. To define an attribute for an element an ATTLIST declaration is made. This contains all the attributes for that element, their type, whether they are required or not and any default values; for example:

```
<!ATTLIST paper
name  ID            #required
department CDATA    #implied
status ( accepted | submitted | inprogress ) 'inprogress'>
```

In the above example the paper element has three attributes. These are:

- name, which is an ID and is required
- department, which is a string (character data) and is not required
- status, which must be accepted, submitted or inprogress, and defaults to inprogress

34.3 The DOM API

There are two standard APIs for processing XML documents. These are the SAX (Simple API for XML parsing) and the DOM (Document Object Model). The SAX provides access to the data in an XML document as it is read in. In contrast, the DOM loads the whole XML document into memory in a hierarchical data structure (which is the document's object model). It is then possible to traverse the tree to access the information within it.

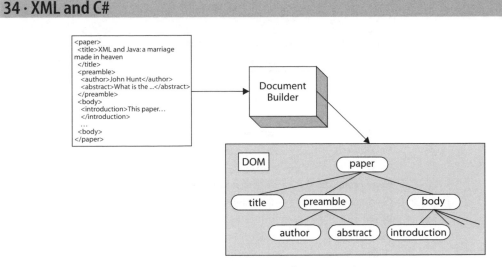

Figure 34.9 Creating a DOM from an XML document.

Why have two approaches? The SAX is excellent for situations where all you need to do is to access the data marked up by the XML document. However, if you need to manipulate that data, search it, restructure it or create new or modified XML documents, the DOM is much better.

There are in fact two standards for DOM: DOM Level 1 and DOM Level 2 Core. Together these define interfaces with methods and properties used to manipulate XML (see `http://www.w3c.org/DOM/`).

In this section we will concentrate on the DOM. The DOM takes an XML document and builds a tree-like structure that represents that XML document (as illustrated in Figure 34.9). It is now possible to get hold of any element in the tree (which is represented by a node object) and ask that element for its attributes, its child nodes, its value etc. This is done by a standard set of specifications. That is, the W3C specification for the DOM is actually a set of interfaces specifying what the various elements of the DOM API should do. Then in a particular language (for example C#) the interfaces are implemented to create concrete implementations. This means that moving from one DOM implementation to another should be straightforward.

As may be expected, C# comes with an implementation of the W3C DOM API. These interfaces and classes can be found in the `System.Xml` namespace. The mapping between the W3C specification interfaces and the C# implementation classes is presented in Table 34.1.

34.4 The DOM in C#

The C# (really the .NET) implementation of the DOM API supports all of DOM Level 1 and DOM Level 2 Core, but with a few minor naming changes. One aspect of the DOM which is not specified is how an XML document should be loaded. In C# the XML document is loaded into the DOM using an `XmlReader`. In turn, writing an XML document to a file (for example) can be done using an `XmlWriter`. To simplify this the save method is overloaded to take a filename and internally use an `XmlWriter` to write to it.

Table 34.1 Mappings between W3C nodes and C# classes.

W3C node type	C# class
Element	XmlElement
Attribute	XmlAttribute
Text	XmlText
CDATA Section	XmlCDataSection
Entity Reference	XmlEntityReference
Entity	XmlEntity
Processing Instruction	XmlProcessingInstruction
Comment	XmlComment
Document	XmlDocument
Document Type	XmlDocumentType
Document Fragment	XmlDocumentFragement
Notation	XmlNotation

The XmlDocument class represents the XML document itself. XmlDocument provides several overloaded Load methods for building a DOM tree from an input stream. Load takes a URI (Universal Resource Indicator) for a document, a TextReader, or an XmlReader reference. For example:

```
XmlDocument doc = new XmlDocument();
doc.Load("http://www.jaydeetee.com/data.xml");
```

The LoadXML method also provided by XmlDocument expects an XML string as opposed to a stream identifier.

Generating DOM documents programmatically relies on various create methods provided by the XmlDocument class. These create methods act as factories for different types of elements, attributes etc. For example:

```
XmlElement name = document.CreateElement("name");
  name.AppendChild(document.CreateTextNode("John"));
root.AppendChild(name);
```

With regard to saving an XMLDocument there are several overloaded Save methods that take URI, TextWriter and XmlWriter references or a string filename.

The following two sections present simple programs for creating an XML document using the DOM and reading an XML document using the DOM.

34.5 Creating an XML Document in C#

The following C# program, called DomBuilder, using the DOM API to create a (very) simple XML document. This document is then saved to file. The XML file created is illustrated in Internet Explorer 5.5 in Figure 34.9. Notice that the program takes the filename to which to save the XML as a command line parameter. Also notice that the XmlDocument object (held in the document instance variable) is used to create the elements contained within the XML document.

```csharp
using System;
using System.Xml;
using System.IO;
using System.Text;

public class DomBuilder {
  private XmlDocument document;
  private String filename;
  public static void Main (String [] args) {
    DomBuilder db = new DomBuilder(args[0]);
    db.Create();
    db.Save();
  }

  public DomBuilder(String file) {
    filename = file;
    document = new XmlDocument();
  }

  public void Create() {
    XmlElement root = document.CreateElement("employee");
    document.AppendChild (root);

    XmlElement name = document.CreateElement("name");
    name.AppendChild(document.CreateTextNode("John"));
    root.AppendChild(name);

    XmlElement dept = (XmlElement)document.CreateElement("dept");
    root.AppendChild(dept);
    dept.AppendChild(document.CreateTextNode("Support"));

    XmlElement manager = (XmlElement)document.CreateElement("manager");
    manager.AppendChild(document.CreateTextNode("Andy"));
    dept.AppendChild(manager);
  }

  public void Save() {
    try {
      document.Save(filename);
    } catch (IOException exp) {
      Console.WriteLine(exp.ToString());
    }
  }
}
```

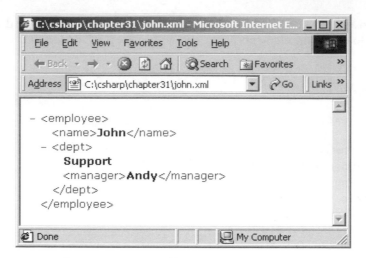

Figure 34.10 The XML file created by the DomBuilder.

The result of compiling this program and running it with the following statements is the XML file displayed in Figure 34.10:

```
Csc DomBuilder.cs
DomBuilder john.xml
```

34.6 Loading an XML Document in C#

This section presents a C# program that loads an XML file into a DOM and then traverses the DOM tree printing out the elements, their values, their attributes etc. Note that this program can either perform validation or not. Remember that an XML file must be well formed; however it is optional as to whether it is validated against a DTD. The Domifier program presented below can be run in either validating mode or standard mode. If it is run in validating mode it will check the XML file against the DTD. Figure 34.11 presents an XML file that contains an internal DTD (the Domifier program can work with external DTDs as well, but we are keeping things simple here). If the Domifier is run indicating that validation should be performed, then the internal DTD will be used to check the XML in the file.

To load an XML file into the XmlDocument the Domifier uses an XmlTextReader, which is a subclass of XmlReader. This type of XML reader does not perform any validation. To do validation it is necessary to wrap a validator around the basic XML reader; thus if validation is turned on a XmlValidatingReader is wrapped around the XML reader. As this is also a descendant of the XmlReader class this can also be passed to the Load method of the XmlDocument class. Thus the following code wraps a validating reader around the reader if validation is turned on and then passes the result to the Load method to actually perform the loading of the XML document.

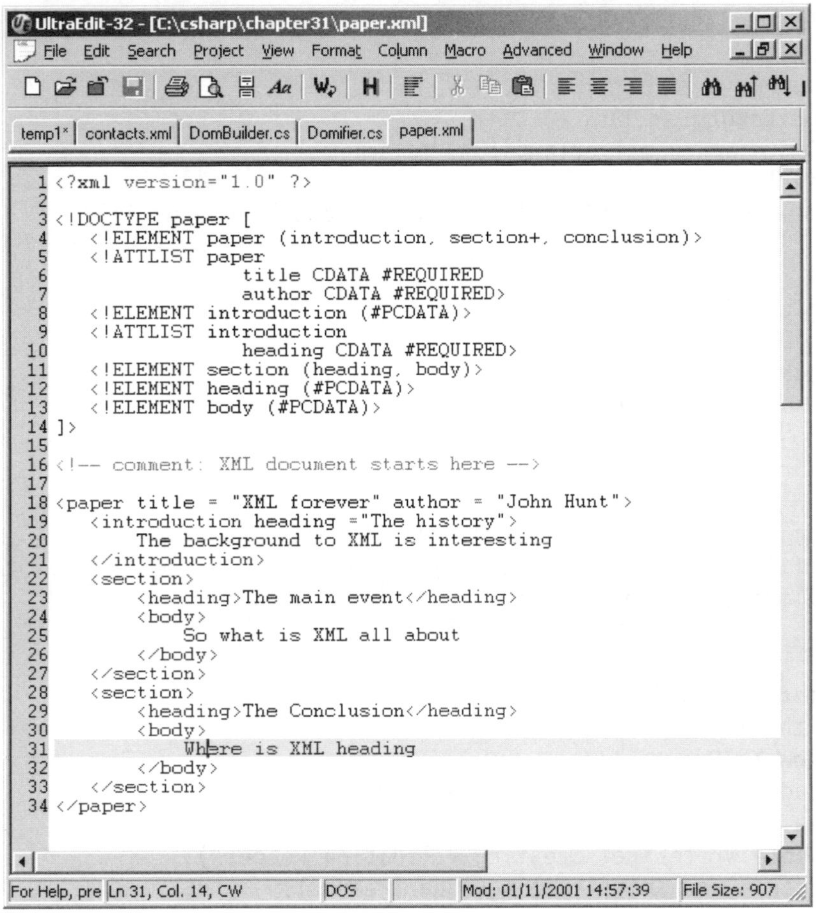

Figure 34.11 An XML file containing an internal DTD.

```csharp
using System;
using System.Xml;
using System.IO;
using System.Text;

public class Domifier {
  private String uri;
  private XmlDocument doc;
  private bool validating;

  public static void Main(String [] args) {
    Domifier dom = null;
    if (args.Length < 1) {
    Console.WriteLine (
```

```
            "Usage: Domifier xml-file <True/False>");
        return;
    }
    if (args.Length == 1) {
            dom = new Domifier(args[0], false);
        } else {
        dom = new Domifier(args[0], Convert.ToBoolean(args[1]));
        }
        try {
            dom.Load();
            dom.DisplayDOM();
        } catch (Exception exp) {
            Console.WriteLine(exp.ToString());
        }
    }
}

public Domifier(String file, bool validating) {
    uri = "file:" + new FileInfo(file).FullName;
    this.validating = validating;
}

public void Load() {
    //Load the XML file into an XmlDocument
    doc = new XmlDocument();
        XmlReader reader = new XmlTextReader(uri);;
        if (validating) {
            Console.WriteLine("Creating Validating Reader");
            reader = new XmlValidatingReader(reader);
        }
        doc.Load(reader);
    }

    public void DisplayDOM() {
        Println("Domifying " + uri);
        DisplayDOM(doc.DocumentElement, 0);
    }

    public void DisplayDOM(XmlNode node, int level) {
        indent(level);
        if (node.NodeType == XmlNodeType.Element) {
            Println(node.Name);
            XmlAttributeCollection attrColl = node.Attributes;
            for (int i=0; i < attrColl.Count; i++) {
                Indent(level + 1);
                Println("Attribute: " +
                    attrColl[i].Name +
```

```
          " : " +
          attrColl[i].Value);
      }
      XmlNodeList children = node.ChildNodes;
      level++;
      for (int i=0; i<children.Count; i++) {
        DisplayDOM(children.Item(i), level);
      }
    } else {
      Println(node.Name + ": " + node.Value);
    }
  }

  // Utility methods
  private void Println (String s) {
    Console.WriteLine(s);
  }

  public void Print(String s) {
    Console.Write(s);
  }

  public void Indent(int number) {
    StringBuilder sb = new StringBuilder(number);
    for (int i=0; i < number; i++) {
      sb.Append(" ");
    }
    sb.Append("+-");
    Print(sb.ToString());
  }
}
```

In the above listing the recursive DisplayDOM method actually does the work of traversing the DOM tree and displaying the results. It does this by checking to see the type of the node currently being visited. It then extracts either the name and value of the node, or if it is an element node (as opposed to a text node for example), it checks to see whether it has any attributes (and prints those if it does) and then checks to see whether the element has any children. If so, it calls itself recursively on each of the children. Note that an XML element that contains some text will be represented in the DOM as a node (of type element) with at least one child (of type text) that represents the text from the XML.

The effect of compiling and running this program is presented below:

```
C:\csharp\chapter34>Domifier paper.xml true
Creating Validating Reader
Domifying file:C:\csharp\chapter34\paper.xml
+-paper
  +-Attribute: title : XML forever
```

```
+-Attribute: author : John Hunt
+-introduction
  +-Attribute: heading : The history
  +-#text:
    The background to XML is interesting
+-section
  +-heading
    +-#text: The main event
  +-body
    +-#text:
      So what is XML all about
+-section
  +-heading
    +-#text: The Conclusion
  +-body
    +-#text:
    Where is XML heading?
```

Chapter 35

C# Style

35.1 Introduction

Good programming style in any language helps promote the readability, clarity and comprehensibility of your code. In many languages, there are established standards to which many people adhere (sometimes without realizing it). For example, the way in which a C or Pascal program is indented is a standard. However, style guidelines which have evolved for these procedural languages do not cover many of the issues which are important in C#. As languages that are not object-oriented do not have concepts of classes, instances and methods, they do not have standards for dealing with them.

Of course you should not forget all the pearls of wisdom and programming practices that you have learned using other languages. There are a number of acknowledged bad practices which are not specific to C#; for example, the use of goto-style constructs. In this chapter, we assume that you do not need an explanation of the basic concepts; instead, we try to concentrate on style issues specific to C#.

35.2 Code Layout

C# has inherited much of its language style from C, and many programmers have adopted a C style for program layout. Thus an if-then statement is laid out in the same way as in a C program. This offers two options:

```
if (size == 20) {
  total = total * size;
}
```

or

```
if (size == 20)
{
```

```
   total = total * size;
}
```

For more information on the style of C programming see Kernighan and Ritchie (1988).

35.3 Variables

35.3.1 Naming Variables

In C#, variable names such as t1, i, j, or temp should rarely be used. Variable names should be descriptive (semantic variables) or should indicate the type of object that the variable holds (typed variables). The approach that you choose depends on personal style and the situation in which the variables are used.

Semantic Variable Names

Instance and class variables tend to have semantic names. The semantic approach has the advantage that you need to assume less about what the variable is used for. Since subclasses can inherit instance and class variables, the point at which they are defined and the point at which they are used may be very distant. Thus any contextual meaning and commentary provided with their definition is lost. Examples of semantic variable names include:

```
score
currentWorkingMemory
TotalPopulationSize
```

Typed Variable Names

The typed approach is often adopted for parameter names, to indicate the class of object that is required by the method. For example:

```
Add(Object anObject)
Push(Object object)
```

Some methods use both the semantic and typed approaches:

```
Put(Object key, Object object)
```

Temporary Variables

Temporary variables, which are local to a method, often have a mixture of semantic and typed names. They may also have temp or tmp as part of their name to indicate their temporary nature. Larger methods often have semantic local variable names due to the additional complexity of such methods.

If you must use very short variable names (which are acceptable, for example, as counters in loops), stick to the traditional names. For example, using variables such as i, j and k for counters is a shorthand (inherited from Fortran) with which most people are familiar. Similarly, a temporary generic exception is often named e in C#; you can adopt the same convention.

Multiple Part Variable Names

If the variable name is made up of more than one word, the words should not be separated by "-" or "_", but by giving the first letter of all but the first word an initial capital:

```
theDateToday employeeRecord objectInList
```

This approach is often referred to as title case or Camel case (or modified title case for names starting with a lower-case letter – also known as Pascal case). Whether the first word in the variable is capitalized or not depends on the type of variable. Table 35.1 summarizes the conventions.

Table 35.1 Variable naming conventions.

Variable type	Convention
Class variable	Upper case
Class names	Initial capital
Temporary variables	Lower case
Instance variables	Lower case
Method parameters	Initial capital
Property	Initial capital

In the system-provided classes, the parts of a class variable name are separated by underscores:

```
Double.MAX_VALUE
StreamTokenizer.TT_EOF
```

You should follow this convention, but the C# system classes do not adhere rigidly to it. Some classes, such as File, use a title case approach and others, such as Color, ignore the convention completely:

```
File.pathSeparator
Color.red
```

35.3.2 Using Variables

- *Instance variables* should be used to hold local data or references to other objects. The other objects should be involved in some form of collaboration with the object (otherwise it does not need a reference to them).
- *Class variables* should be used as "constant" values which are referenced by all instances of a class. They should never be used as a form of global variable (such a use is frequently an indication that a solution has not been designed with the proper amount of care and attention). Occa-

sionally, a class may use its class variables to hold information about the instances, such as the number of instances created. However, this information should be private to the class.

Defining and Initializing Instance and Class Variables

You can declare class and instance variables anywhere within the body of a class. However, it is good style to declare them at the beginning. It is easier to follow the class structure if all the class variables (statically defined variables) are declared first, followed by the instance variables. If another programmer can find all such declarations in the same place, the code is easier to understand and maintain.

You should initialize variables when you declare them. If you cannot initialize them with the actual value to be used, then you should use a default value and set the actual value as soon as possible. For class variables you may do this within a static initialization block; for instance variables, you may do it within a constructor or an init method (depending on whether it is a standalone application or an applet).

One reason that you should initialize a variable is that it provides an indication to others of the information to be held by the variable. For example, stating that a variable can hold a string does not say very much. However, if you initialize the variable with the string "Mr Joe Bloggs", it says much more. The other reason that you should initialize a variable is that the C# compiler does not warn you about uninitialized class and instance variables (they are set to null). Your code may attempt to use a variable which has not been initialized, thus raising an exception.

Defining Temporary Variables

Temporary variables can be defined anywhere within a method body. However, it is good style to declare them at the start of the method as, once again, this is easier to read. It also implies that the programmer has given some thought to the variables that are required.

As a variable can be declared where and when it is used, it is common to find a variable declared within a loop. This means that it is declared every time the loop is executed:

```
for (i = 0; i < 10; ++i) {
  Integer count = new Integer(i);
}
```

This is very bad style, but it is an easy mistake to fall into if variables are declared anywhere.

Accessing Instance and Class Variables

In general it is always better to access instance and class variables via intermediate methods, referred to as *accessor* (or *getter* and *setter*) methods, rather than accessing or setting them directly. This is called variable-free programming, and it promotes the modularity of your methods. It insulates the methods against changes in the way the object (or class) holds instance (or class) information. This is a very important concept, as direct access to instance variables can limit the power of subclassing.

You can also protect variables from undesired changes. For example, you can put preconditions on an access method or return a copy of the contents of the variable so that it cannot be directly affected. To implement this, you should make judicious use of the C# visibility modifiers described earlier in the book.

35.4 Classes

35.4.1 Naming Classes

The naming of a class is extremely important. The class is the core element in any object-oriented program and its name has huge semantic meaning which can greatly affect the clarity of the program. Examples of C# system classes include:

```
HashTable
FileInputStream
SecurityManager
```

The above names are good examples of how a name can describe a class. The name of a class is used by most developers to indicate its purpose or intent. This is partly due to the fact that it is the class name which is used when searching for appropriate classes.

You should therefore use descriptive class names; classes with names such as MyClass or ProjectClass1 are of little use. However, class names should not be so specific that they make it appear that the class is unlikely to be of use except in one specific situation (unless, of course, this is the case). For example, in an application that records details about university lecturers, a class with a name such as ComputerScienceDepartmentLecturer is probably not appropriate, unless it really does relate only to lecturers in the Computer Science department. If this is the case, you need to ask yourself in what way computer science lecturers are different from other lecturers.

35.4.2 The Role of a Class

A subclass or class should accomplish one specific purpose; that is, it should capture only one idea. If more than one idea is encapsulated in a class, you should break the class down into its constituent parts. This guideline leads to small classes (in terms of methods, instance variables and code). Breaking a class down costs little but may produce major gains in reusability and flexibility.

A subclass should only be used to modify the behaviour of its parent class. This modification should be a refinement of the class and should therefore extend the behaviour of the class in some way. For example, a subclass may redefine one or more of the methods, add methods which use the inherited behaviour, or add class or instance variables. A subclass which does not do at least one of these is inappropriate.

35.4.3 Creating New Data Structure Classes

When working with data structures, there is always the question of whether to create a new data structure class to hold your data or whether to define a class which holds the data within one of its instance variables and then provide methods which access that variable.

For example, let us assume that we wish to define a new class, called `Account`, which holds information on deposits and withdrawals. We believe that we should use a hash table to hold the actual data, but should `Account` be a subclass of `HashTable` or of something else (for example, `Object`, with an instance variable holding an instance of `HashTable`)? Of course, it depends on what you are going to do with the `Account` class. If it provides a new data structure class (in some way), even if it is only for your application, then you should consider making it a subclass of `HashTable`. However, if you need to provide a functionally complex class which just happens to contain a hash table, then it is almost certainly better to make it a subclass of `Object`.

There is another point to consider: if `Account` is a subclass of `HashTable`, then any instance of `Account` responds to the whole of the `HashTable` protocol. You should ask yourself whether this is what you want, or whether a more limited protocol (one appropriate to an account object) is more suitable.

35.4.4 Class Comments

Every class, whether abstract or concrete, should have a class comment. This comment is the basic documentation for the class. It should, therefore, tell developers creating a subclass from the class, or users of the class, what they need to know. The comment may also contain:

- information about the author
- a history of modifications to the class
- the purpose, type and status of the class
- information about instance and class variables (including the class of object they hold and their use)
- information about collaborations between this class and others
- example usage
- copyright information
- class-specific information, such as the things that a subclass of an abstract class is expected to redefine

You should place the class comment just before the class. You can use the XML documentation from within C# to do this. An advantage of this is that the compiler will check that the XML documentation is correct (with respect to the parameters etc.).

In C# the XML tags must be preceded by a treble forward slash. The XML documentation then uses XML tags to mark up the comments. For example:

```
/// <summary>
/// The Person class holds the name and
/// age of an individual
/// </summary>
public class Person
{
  /// <summary> Constructor for Person </summary>
  /// <param name="name">Person name </param>
  /// <param name="age">Person age</param>
```

```
public Person(String name, int age)
{
  ...
```

You can use XML tags such as <summary>, <Remarks> and <code>, <example> and <see> to ensure that these items are highlighted. For methods, you can use <param>, <returns> and <exception> to document the return value, any parameter values and any exceptions raised.

Finally, you can also embed references to external files using <include>.

35.4.5 Using a Class or an Instance

In situations where only a single instance of a class is required, it is better style to define a class which is instantiated once than to provide the required behaviour in class-side methods.

Using a class instead of an instance is very poor style, breaks the rules of object orientation and may have implications for the future maintenance of the system.

35.5 Interfaces

An interface is a way of specifying the protocol that should be implemented by a set of objects that are members of different class hierarchies. You should use an interface in the following situations:

- as a specification mechanism, where one or more classes are intended to provide the same functionality
- where one or more (as yet undefined) user classes are anticipated and you must ensure that they provide the correct protocol
- where you must specify the type of a variable for a set of (as yet undefined) user classes

The above points assume that the classes come from different parts of the class hierarchy. If all classes have the same superclass, then you can use an abstract superclass instead of an interface.

35.6 Methods

35.6.1 Naming Methods

A method name should always start with a upper-case letter. If the method name is made up of more than one element then each element after the first, should start with a capital letter (title case):

```
account.Deposit(100);
account.PrintStatement();
```

The naming of methods is as important as the naming of classes. An appropriate method name not only makes the code easier to read, it also aids in reuse. You should select a method's name to illustrate the method's purpose. In addition, many programmers try to select a name that makes it possible to read an expression containing the method in a similar manner to reading a sentence.

In many situations, you define multiple methods with the same name but different parameters. This is possible because C# identifies a method by both its name and its parameter classes. Thus, different methods can be supplied to deal with different situations, resulting in less complex code and more flexibility. For example:

```
statement.Deposit(100);
statement.Deposit(date, 100);
statement.Deposit(100, date);
```

Methods which return `true` and `false` as the result of a test follow a common naming format throughout the C# system. These methods use a verb such as "is" or "equals" concatenated with whatever is being tested. In some cases, the method name expresses the test itself:

```
Equals(Object)
StartsWith(String)
IsAlive()
IsInterrupted()
```

In the first case, the method tests to see if the receiver is the same as the parameter. This method name is used in many different classes (for example, `String`).

In the second example, the method only tests part of the receiver, and its name reflects that. In the next two cases, some aspect of the receiver is tested. The third method tests whether a process is active, and the value being tested for is used as part of the method name.

35.6.2 Using Methods

In general, you should put a method as high up in the inheritance hierarchy as possible (as long as it makes sense to do so). The higher the method, the more visible it is to classes in other branches of the hierarchy, and the more method-level reuse you can achieve.

Think carefully about the purpose and placement of methods within a class. Just as a class should have a specific purpose, a method should also have a single purpose. If a method performs more than one function, then you should divide it into separate methods. In general terms, a method should be no longer than one A4 page.

Deciding how to break up the desired functionality into elements can be difficult in a procedural programming language. In C#, it is made more difficult by considerations of object encapsulation and reuse. However, you can bear the following questions in mind when determining whether your code is correctly placed within the methods:

- If the method does not refer to any aspect of the object (i.e. it does not use `super`, `this`, instance variables etc.), what does it do? Should it be there?
- How many objects does the method reference? A method should only send messages to a limited set of objects. This promotes maintainability, comprehensibility and modularity.
- Have you used accessor methods to access instance variables? Variable-free programming can greatly insulate the method from changes within the object.

- Is the behaviour encapsulated by the method intended for public or private (to the object) use? If it is a mixture of the two, then the method should be decomposed into two or more methods. The private code should be placed in a method that is defined to be private. This indicates to a developer (and enforces) that the method is not intended for external use.
- Does the method rely more on the behaviour of other objects than on its own object (that is, a series of messages is being sent to some object other than this)? If so, the method may be better placed in another object (or objects).

This last point is worth considering in slightly more detail. The series of messages in such a method may be better placed in a method in the class of the receiver object. This is because it really describes behaviour associated with that object. By placing it within the receiver object's class, all modifications to the behaviour of the receiver are encapsulated in that object. In addition, this behaviour may be useful to other objects; if you encode it within the receiver's class, other objects can gain access to that behaviour (rather than duplicating it in a number of places).

It is not easy to achieve good reuse of method-level code when code is poorly placed. Most messages should be sent to this. Structuring the code appropriately is probably one of the hardest things to do well in object-oriented programming; however, if you do it correctly it can pay very high dividends.

35.6.3 Class Methods and Instance Methods

The distinction between static (or class methods) and instance methods was discussed in more detail in Chapter 13. The main points are presented here as they are relevant to considerations of style in C#.

You should use the Main method to create instances and invoke the initial behaviour. You should use other class methods for the following purposes only:

- information about the class
- instance management and information
- documentation and examples
- testing facilities (regression-style)
- support for one of the above

Any other purposes should be performed by an instance method.

35.6.4 Constructors

You should only use a constructor to initialize an instance of a class in an appropriate manner. Do not place instance style functionality within the constructor. Instead, provide a separate method and call it from the constructor, so that you can reinitialize the object later if necessary.

35.6.5 Static Constructors

You should only use static constructors to initialize class variables that cannot be initialized by a simple initialization clause. It is easy to produce cyclic static initialization blocks and the result of such initialization is likely to be incorrect. Static constructors should immediately follow the class variable declarations and precede any method definitions (e.g. the Main method).

35.6.6 The Destructor Method

This method is executed when the garbage collector picks up an object. You should only use it to perform housekeeping operations that can be left until the object is destroyed. Do not place operations that should be performed as soon as all references to the object are removed (for example, closing a file) in the destructor method because you cannot guarantee exactly when the garbage collector will deal with the object.

35.6.7 Programming in Terms of Objects

It is all too easy, when you first start with C#, to write procedure-oriented code within methods. Indeed, many publicly available C# classes contain code which has clearly been written by a C or C++ programmer, rather than by someone writing in an object-oriented manner. In C#, you should try to think in terms of objects.

35.6.8 Positioning of Methods

Just as with variables, you should present class methods first, followed by instance methods. How you arrange the class methods is a matter of personal style – there is no real standard (as yet). However, you should at least follow these guidelines:

- Place the static initialization block immediately after the variable declarations.
- Group all constructors together.
- Place the Main method before general-purpose class methods.
- Group related class methods together.

Figure 35.1 shows a recommended order of methods.

35.7 Scoping

Scope modifiers can be applied to classes, to class and instance variables and to methods. In general, you should attempt to hide as much as possible from other objects; you should only make public items that must be public.

- When you decide that you must make a class public, limit access to it as much as possible.
- If a class or instance variable cannot be private, limit access to it. That is, use the default modifier in preference to protected (by default, the variable is only visible in the current package; protected means that it is visible in the package and in subclasses in other packages).
- If you do not want to allow something to be changed, make it sealed. You can make classes and methods final.

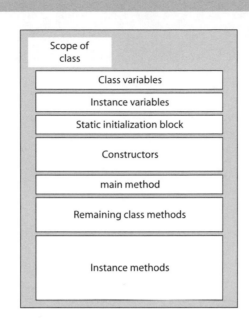

Figure 35.1 The layout of a class definition.

- Make a method private unless it is needed outside the class. If it is needed, limit access to it as much as possible.

If you are unclear about the modifiers and their meaning, refer to back to their definitions.

Chapter 36

C# Roundup

36.1 Introduction

Although throughout this book I have tried to cover all the important aspects of C#, there are a couple of subjects that do not fit neatly into any other section. This chapter therefore brings together a somewhat disparate group of topics in order that we provide complete coverage of the material necessary for those learning C#.

This chapter is structured in the following manner:

- Memory management in C#
- Converting classes
- The use of the `Main` method
- Compiler directives
- Assertions, debugging and tracing

36.2 Memory Management

36.2.1 Why Have Automatic Memory Management?

Any discussion of C# needs to consider how C# handles memory. One of the many advantages of C# over languages such as C++ is that it automatically manages memory allocation and reuse. It is not uncommon to hear C++ programmers complaining about spending many hours attempting to track down a particularly awkward bug only to find that it was a problem associated with memory allocation or pointer manipulation. Similarly, a regular problem for C++ developers is that of memory creep, which occurs when memory is allocated but is not freed up. The application either uses all available memory or runs out of space and produces a run-time error.

Most of the problems associated with memory allocation in languages such as C++ occur because programmers must not only concentrate on the (often complex) application logic but also on memory management. They must ensure that they allocate only the memory that is

399

required and deallocate it when it is no longer required. This may sound simple, but it is no mean feat in a large and complex application.

An interesting question to ask is "Why do programmers have to manage memory allocation?". There are few programmers today who would expect to have to manage the registers being used by their programs, although 20 or 30 years ago the situation was very different. One answer to the memory management question, often cited by those who like to manage their own memory, is that "It is more efficient; you have more control; and it is faster and leads to more compact code". Of course, if you wish to take these comments to their extreme, then we should all be programming in Assembler. This would enable us all to produce faster, more efficient and more compact code than that produced by Pascal, C++, C# or Java.

The point about high-level languages, however, is that they are more productive, introduce fewer errors, are more expressive and are efficient enough (given modern computers and compiler technology). The memory management issue is somewhat similar. If the system automatically handles the allocation and deallocation of memory, then the programmer can concentrate on the application logic. This makes the programmer more productive, removes problems due to poor memory management and, when implemented efficiently, can still provide acceptable performance.

36.2.2 Memory Management in C#

C# provides automatic memory management. Essentially, it allocates a portion of memory as and when required. When memory is short, it looks for areas that are no longer referenced. These areas of memory are then freed up (deallocated) so that they can be reallocated. This process is often referred to as "garbage collection".

The CLR Runtime uses an approach known as *mark and sweep* to identify objects which can be freed up. The garbage collection process searches from any root objects, i.e. objects from which the main method has been run, marking all the objects it finds. It then examines all the objects currently held in memory and deletes those objects that are not marked. It is at this point that an object's destructor method is executed.

A second process invoked with garbage collection is memory compaction. This involves moving all the allocated memory blocks together so that free memory is contiguous rather than fragmented.

36.2.3 When Is Garbage Collection Performed?

The garbage collection process runs in its own thread. That is, it runs at the same time as other processes within the Common Language Runtime (CLR). It is initiated when the ratio of free memory versus total memory passes a certain point.

You can also explicitly indicate to the .NET Runtime that you wish the garbage collector to run. This can be useful if you are about to start a process that requires a large amount of memory and you think that there may be unneeded objects in the system. You can do this as follows:

```
System.GC.Collect();
```

You can also force the suppression of the finalization process (the destructor methods). This is done as follows:

```
System.GC.SuppressFinalize();
```

36.3 Conversion of Classes

In some cases it may be desirable to provide a way of converting an object of one type to an object of another type. C# allows such conversations to be defined as static operator methods. These methods must either take a parameter of their encapsulating class or have a return type of their class. Conversion static methods can also be explicit or implicit. Implicit conversions are conversions that are always guaranteed to be safe and will never throw an exception. For example, casting from a short to an int will never cause a problem, as a short will always fit in an int. All implicit conversions can be triggered automatically by the C# runtime environment.

However, explicit conversions are those that might cause a problem (due to loss of information for example) and thus must be invoked explicitly – i.e. it is the programmer's responsibility to ensure that a problem will not occur. For example, if we cast a long to an int, the long value could be greater than the largest value that can be held in an int – thus we would have a loss of information.

As an example of writing a conversion method for a class, consider the class Person below. Note that it provides a static method with the following definition:

```
// Implicit Conversion Method
public static implicit operator Record(Person p) {
  return new Record(p.Name, p.Age);
}
```

As this method is implicit it should be used whenever the C# runtime finds an assignment between a Person object and a variable of type Record. When this situation is found this static operator method will be invoked. Note that the result of this method is that an instance of the Record class is returned. To create this instance the name and age of the person are extracted and provided to the constructor of the Record class.

To actually use this conversion method all we need to do is to take an instance of the class Person (referenced by the variable p, say) and assign it to a variable of type Record, for example:

```
Person p = new Person("John", 37);
Record r = p;
```

The result is that the information in the object referenced by the variable p has been transferred to the object held in the variable r. This is very neat and something missing in languages such as Java.

A complete listing of a worked conversion example presenting two classes is presented below. Note that the two classes Person and Record have no relationship to each other, other than the conversion static operator method!

```csharp
using System;

public class Person {
  private String name;
  private int age;

  public Person(String name, int age) {
    this.name = name;
    this.age = age;
  }

  public String Name {
    get {
      return name;
    }
  }

  public int Age {
    get {
      return age;
    }
  }

  public override String ToString() {
    return name + ": " + age;
  }

  // Implicit Conversion Method
  public static implicit operator Record(Person p) {
    return new Record(p.Name, p.Age);
  }
}

public class Record {
  private String identifier;
  private int value;
  public Record(String id, int value) {
    this.identifier = id;
    this.value = value;
  }

  public override String ToString() {
    return "Standard Record for " + identifier;
  }
}
```

```
public class TestConvert {
  public static void Main() {
    Person p = new Person("John", 37);
    Console.WriteLine(p);
    // Implicit conversion below
    Record r = p;
    Console.WriteLine(r);
  }
}
```

Conversions can also be defined between structs as well as classes.

36.4 The Main Method

You already know that the Main method is the entry point for an application. You also know that a Main method can either take no parameters or an array of strings representing the command line arguments. However, it should be noted that it is not possible to have both types of Main method in the same class! Thus for example we could write either version of the following class:

```
using System;

public class Test {
  public static void Main() {
    Console.WriteLine("No params");
  }
}
```

or with command line parameters (but not both):

```
using System;

public class Test {
  public static void Main(String [] args) {
    Console.WriteLine("{0} params", args.Length);
  }
}
```

However, it is also possible to make the Main method return a status. This is achieved by stating that the return type of the Main method is an int rather than a void. Thus we could write:

```
using System;

public class Test {
  public static int Main() {
```

```
        Console.WriteLine("No params");
        return 0;
    }
}
```

What about the situation where more than one class in the current compilation has a Main method? How should the compiler know which Main method is the entry point for the application? The one to be used to start the application can be indicated to the compiler via the command line option /main:<classname>. An interesting question is why might there be more than one Main method? It might be that additional Main methods may be present to provide test harnesses for subsystems or parts of the main application etc.

36.5 Compiler Directives

C# provides a limited set of compiler directives (note that we do not use the phrase "pre-processor directives", as strictly speaking in C# there is no pre-processor as there is no need for one). The compiler directives allow the developer some control over the result of the execution. For example, in the following program, the compiler directives determine which output line is compiled.

```
#define FULLOUTPUT

using System;

public class HellowWorld {
  public static void Main() {
    #if (FULLOUPUT)
    Console.WriteLine("Hello to the whole world");
    #else
    Console.WriteLine("Hello");
    #endif
  }
}
```

The following pre-processing directives are available:

- #define and #undef, which are used to define and undefine conditional symbols. These must come before any using statements in a C# file.
- #if, #elif (which means else if), #else and #endif, which are used to conditionally skip sections of source code.
- #line, which is used to control line numbers emitted for errors and warnings.
- #error and #warning, which are used to issue errors and warnings.
- #region and #endregion, which are used to explicitly mark sections of source code.

36.6 Assertions, Debugging and Tracing

36.6.1 Debugging and Tracing

It is useful when developing software systems to be able to introduce snippets of code that are useful for determining what is happening within the code. This is particularly useful when debugging software systems. In some cases these debugging statements are generally useful and rather than being removed completely from the code, it would be better to be able to switch them on and off. In C#, using the System.Diagnostics namespace, it is possible to apply the conditional attribute to a method. This conditional attribute takes a conditional string. If the string is defined when the code is compiled than the method is included in the source code. If not then any code that calls that method is modified to ignore that call. In this way source code can be included or not as required. For example, consider the following program:

```
using System;
using System.Diagnostics;

public class TestAssert {
  public static void Main() {
    Console.WriteLine("Before test");
    Test();
    Console.WriteLine("After test");
  }
  [Conditional("DEBUG")]
  public static void Test() {
    Console.WriteLine("Debugging");
  }
}
```

This program defines the Test method as being conditional on the string DEBUG being defined. If it isn't then the call to the function is ignored. Thus compiling this program as normal produces the following output:

```
C:\csharp\chapter36>TestDebug
Before test
After test
```

However, if we recompile using the /D command line option to the compiler with the string DEBUG we produce a different output, for example:

```
C:\csharp\chapter36>csc /D:DEBUG TestDebug.cs
Microsoft (R) Visual C# Compiler Version 7.00.9254 [CLR version v1.0.2914]
Copyright (C) Microsoft Corp 2000-2001. All rights reserved.
C:\csharp\chapter36>TestDebug
Before test
```

```
Debugging
After test
```

In this case the call to Test was not ignored and the debugging string was printed out.

An additional aspect of this is the use of the Debug class. This class can be used to output information on the behaviour of the system to a listener. The Debug class provides a number of write methods:

- Write(String): writes out the string
- WriteLine(String): writes out the string with a new line
- WriteIf(bool, String): only write out the string if the first parameter is true
- WriteLineIf(bool, String): only writes out the string and new line if the first parameter is true

As an example of using the Debug class, consider the TestDebug program modified to use the Debug class. This can be compiled as before with the same results.

```
using System;
using System.Diagnostics;
public class TestAssert {
  public static void Main() {
    Console.WriteLine("Before test");
    Test();
    Console.WriteLine("After test");
  }
  [Conditional("DEBUG")]
  public static void Test() {
    Debug.Listeners.Clear();
    Debug.Listeners.Add(new TextWriterTraceListener(Console.Out));
    Debug.WriteLine("Debugging");
  }
}
```

Tracing is similar to debugging, the main difference being that debugging is something that is used to identify a fault, whereas the tracing facilities in C# can be present for the lifetime of the application (for example in order to carry out auditing). Thus you should try to be careful with the use of tracing as it may affect the performance of the software system. Tracing is controlled by the TRACE attribute string being set (whereas debugging is conditional on the DEBUG attribute being set).

To further support debugging and tracing the BooleanSwitch and TraceSwitch classes can be used to turn on debugging or tracing conditionally. These classes can be controlled at runtime by an environment variable or by a registry entry.

For example, consider the following program (based on the TestDebug program presented earlier). This program has been modified such that the value of the BooleanSwitch is used to determine whether the debugging output is generated or not. Note that this code must still be compiled using the /D:DEBUG command line compiler option. If it is not, then the Test method is ignored and indeed both BooleanSwitch and TraceSwitch need either DEBUG or TRACE to be enabled to operate.

```
using System;
using System.Diagnostics;
public class TestSwitch {
  public static void Main() {
    Debug.Listeners.Clear();
    Debug.Listeners.Add(new TextWriterTraceListener(Console.Out));
    Console.WriteLine("Before test");
    Test();
    Console.WriteLine("After test");
  }

  [Conditional("DEBUG")]
  public static void Test() {
    BooleanSwitch debugFlag =
      new BooleanSwitch("DebugFlagEnvironmentVariable",
          "The debugging flag controlling debug output");
    Debug.WriteLineIf(debugFlag.Enabled, "Debugging");
  }
}
```

The BooleanSwitch object determines whether the string "Debugging" is printed by the Debug class via the WriteLineIf method. The BooleanSwitch object itself is instantiated by specifying the name of the environment variable that determines the state of the BooleanSwitch and a string providing a description of this BooleanSwitch.

If we compile and run this program the following is output:

```
C:\csharp\chapter36>csc /D:DEBUG TestSwitch.cs
Microsoft (R) Visual C# Compiler Version 7.00.9254 [CLR version v1.0.2914]
Copyright (C) Microsoft Corp 2000-2001. All rights reserved.

C:\csharp\chapter36>TestSwitch
Before test
After test
```

Note that no debugging information has been generated. This is because we have yet to set a value for the environment variable DebugFlagEnvironmentVariable. That is, when the BooleanSwitch constructor cannot find initial switch settings, the new switch is disabled (false) by default.

One way of setting DebugFlagEnvironmentVariable is to define a configuration file for the application. This can be done by creating a file with a .config extension. In this case our program is called TestSwitch.exe; thus, following the C# conventions, we will call our configuration file TestSwitch.exe.config. This file will then be automatically picked up by the C# Runtime and its contents processed.

The configuration file itself is defined in XML. The format of the XML file is illustrated below. Note that the <configuration> element contains a <system.diagnostics> element that contains a <switches> element that actually defines the values of the environment variables used by the two switch classes. In our case we define one variable called DebugFlagEnvironmentVariable and set it to 1. Zero indicates that the variable is turned off, any non-zero value is taken to mean that it is turned on.

```
<configuration>
  <system.diagnostics>
    <switches>
      <add name="DebugFlagEnvironmentVariable" value="1" />
    </switches>
  </system.diagnostics>
</configuration>
```

The result of defining this file and placing it in the same directory from which the TestSwitch application is run causes the output of the TestSwitch program to be modified to:

```
C:\csharp\chapter36>TestSwitch
Before test
Debugging
After test
```

Note that we did not need to recompile the TestSwitch program to change the behaviour of the program!

For tracing applications, the level value in the .config file has some more precise meanings. The TraceSwitch class understands four levels of information logging, listed in Table 36.1. These values are defined in the TraceLevel enumerated type.

Table 36.1 Tracing levels.

Level	Value
Off	0
Error	1
Warning	2
Info	3
Verbose	4

36.6.2 Assertions

Any software system, whether object-oriented or not, relies on the state of the system being "correct" at certain stages of its execution. To take a very simple example, when a numerical division operation is performed, the divisor must be non-zero. If this is not the case, the system may crash in an unpredictable and uncontrolled manner.

One way of indicating such requirements is to state that the system must be in some state either before or after an operation. Such a statement about the state of a software system is called an *assertion*.

Assertions often form the basis for software specification. In some systems, the assertions are embedded in the software as *annotations* or formal comments. However, it can be useful to make the assertions executable so that the correctness of the system is checked at run-time. In C# the Debug class includes a method Assert that directly supports the concept of assertions. The Assert method can be given a condition to test. If this condition is met nothing happens; if it fails, then an output is generated (by default this is done via a dialog box). For example, the following program defines a method Test that is marked as conditional on the string DEBUG. If this program is compiled with the /D option then the Assert method will be called when Test is called. As 1 is not equal to zero it will cause an output window to be generated:

```csharp
using System;
using System.Diagnostics;

public class TestAssert {
  public static void Main() {
    Test();
  }
  [Conditional("DEBUG")]
  public static void Test() {
    Debug.Assert(1 == 0, "Oops");
  }
}
```

The result of compiling this code and running it using the following statements is presented in Figure 36.1.

```
C:\csharp\chapter36>csc /D:DEBUG TestAssert.cs
Microsoft (R) Visual C# Compiler Version 7.00.9254 [CLR version v1.0.2914]
Copyright (C) Microsoft Corp 2000-2001. All rights reserved.

C:\csharp\chapter36>TestAssert
```

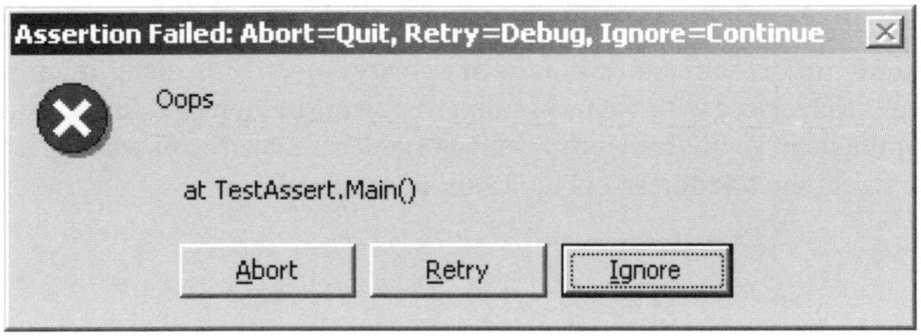

Figure 36.1 The output from an Assert method.

36.7 Using Pointers in C#

If you are from a C++ background you may be wondering whether C# has pointers or not. Indeed it does, and in fact any time you work with a reference type such as a class or struct you are using pointers. However, in general you do not have access to those pointers. This is considered a good thing, as more bugs have been introduced by the use of pointers and their manipulation than almost any other aspect of C and C++. Of course, many C++ die-hards will argue that you cannot do anything for real without direct access to pointers. A counter argument to that is that Java does not allow access to its pointers and has been used successfully for many applications. However, C# does provide limited access to pointers, via what is known as its unsafe context, to create unmanaged code.

One might well ask why, if Java succeeds without offering access to pointers directly, does C# permit this? The answer is that C# is allowed direct access to pointers for three very good and practical reasons:

1. You may need to access some structure generated with a pointer-aware language (such as C++).
2. Dealing with Advanced COM or Platform invocation situations.
3. To enhance performance.

Thus pointers are accessible for integrating other non-C# code and for performance reasons. The former is certainly justifiable; the latter should be approached with caution. The use of pointers in other situations is in general discouraged. It is worth noting that C# code written using pointers in an unsafe context cannot be verified to be safe, so it will be executed only when the code is fully trusted.

To use an unsafe contract in C# you must do two things. Firstly you must mark the code with the unsafe keyword and secondly you must compile the .cs file with a /unsafe directive to the compiler.

For example, the following code specifies that the contents of the method Process can use pointers:

```
public unsafe void Process() {...}
```

To declare a pointer we must specify the type of the pointer followed by a "*"; for example:

```
byte* ptrSrc = srcarray
```

This creates a pointer to the start address of the srcarray object. Note that this address can be fixed to overcome issues associated with the movement of objects in memory during garbage collection and memory compaction via the keyword fixed. For objects that are not types of arrays we can obtain the address using the & (address-of) operator. For example:

```
Person p = (&q);
```

The unsafe keyword can also be used during the declaration of a type such as a class or struct. For example:

```
public unsafe struct TreeNode {
  public Object obj;
  public TreeNode* left;
  public TreeNode* right;
}
```

In the above example left and right are pointers to the TreeNode objects that represent the left and right branches of this tree. Note that we do not need to use an unsafe context in C# to create a tree structure – we can just use structs or classes as normal.

As an example of a program that uses pointers, see Figure 36.2. This very simple program creates an array of ints. This array is then accessed via its address (int * Psrc). As an array is an object we must fix it in memory. Note that pSrc is a read-only value; thus we need a second pointer ptr so that we can access each element in the int array in turn. This is done within the for loop in which we obtain the address being used and the value at that address, and then increment the pointer.

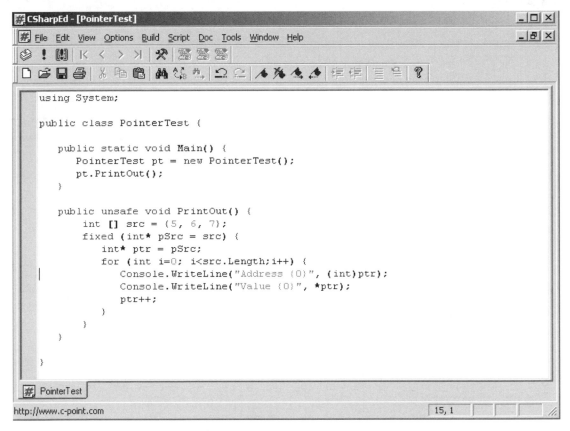

```
using System;

public class PointerTest {

    public static void Main() {
        PointerTest pt = new PointerTest();
        pt.PrintOut();
    }

    public unsafe void PrintOut() {
        int [] src = {5, 6, 7};
        fixed (int* pSrc = src) {
            int* ptr = pSrc;
            for (int i=0; i<src.Length;i++) {
                Console.WriteLine("Address {0}", (int)ptr);
                Console.WriteLine("Value {0}", *ptr);
                ptr++;
            }
        }
    }
}
```

Figure 36.2 A program using pointers.

The results of compiling and running this program are presented in Figure 36.3.

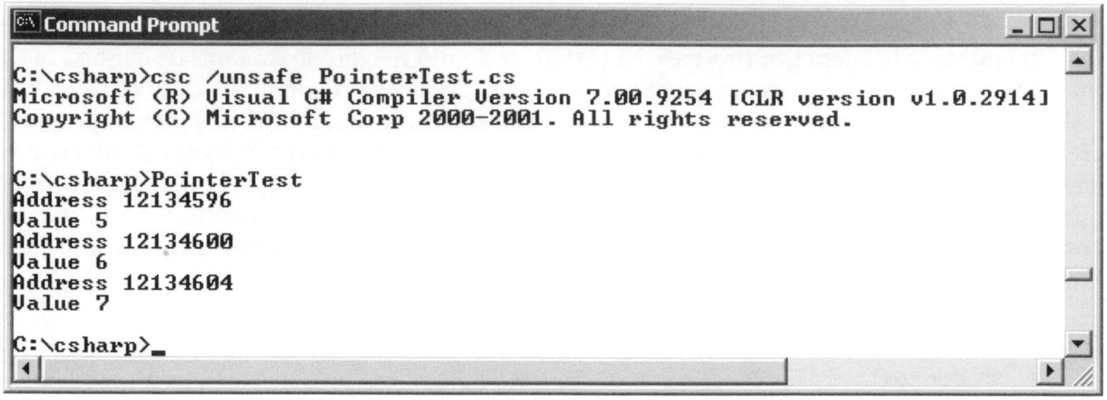

Figure 36.3 Running the simple pointer program..

Chapter 37

The .NET Environment

37.1 Introduction

Throughout this book we have talked about the .NET environment and how C# is one of the key elements of that environment. However, until now we have not gone into any detail about .Net. This is for two very good reasons. Firstly, while C# is an important element of .NET, C# can be used as a programming language without any reference to any other elements of .NET. Indeed, that is exactly the approach we have taken for most of this book. It should be noted that C# is an excellent object-oriented language within which to build applications, whether you are interested in .NET or not! The second reason is that at the time of writing the .NET framework is still evolving, and to some extent is more of a re-packaging of existing Microsoft services than a coherent environment. This will undoubtedly change, whereas the core of the C# language will not.

In this chapter we will look at the various elements that make up .NET and then look at the issues associated with interoperability between C# and the other languages that make up .NET.

37.2 .NET Overview

The .NET Framework is a coherent collection of tools, technologies and systems that have been designed to interoperate within a distributed environment based on the Internet. What does this mean? Essentially it means that Microsoft has gone back to the drawing board and looked at creating an environment that should make it easier (than using COM or DNA etc.) to create applications that may be one, two or n-tier and may or may not use the Internet for distributed communication. Into this mix it has added its existing server suite (such as SQL Server, Exchange and IIS). At present these are not .NET-specific servers (although that is likely in the future). .NET itself can be divided up into various aspects: the Framework, the servers, Web services and ultimately the smart client layer, such as new .NET-enabled devices, including cellphones and games machines. At present the first two are well established, the Web services are in beta testing (via .NET My Services)

413

and other aspects of .NET are still in development. We will therefore focus on the .NET Framework and the servers below.

37.3 The .NET Framework

The .NET Framework has two main components: the Common Language Runtime and the .NET Framework class library. On top of this are classes that provide for GUI applications and Web page generation, as well as other services that support SOAP and HTTP. This is illustrated in Figure 37.1.

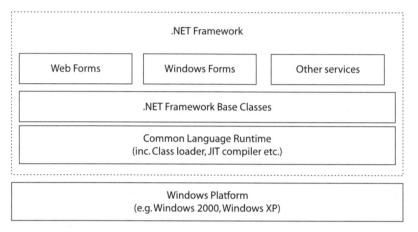

Figure 37.1 The structure of the .NET Framework.

We will consider the core Common Language Runtime and the .NET Framework classes in the remainder of this section.

37.3.1 Common Language Runtime

The Common Language Runtime (CLR) manages the execution of code compiled for the .NET framework. It is essentially a hardware abstraction layer that hides the actual processor from the program to be executed. In this respect it performs a similar role to the Smalltalk Virtual Machine and the Java Virtual Machine (JVM). That is, when your C# program runs it runs within the CLR. Exactly how it does this is up to the CLR. At present the CLR uses a JIT (Just-In-Time) Compiler to convert your program into something that can execute on the processor. Along the way it performs certain verification (of the code) and security checks.

However, it is important to realize that the CLR does not interpret the C# code. In fact the CLR "executes" MSIL (or Microsoft Intermediate Language). This is a processor-independent P-code that your C# program is "translated" into. In fact C++, VisualBasic, JScript and other languages can be "translated" into MSIL and executed within the CLR. Thus the process of compiling a C# program generates MSIL rather than directly executable code!

In fact, things do not stop there. What actually happens within the CLR is that the MSIL is loaded via a Class Loader into the CLR's environment. This is then passed to the JIT Compiler.

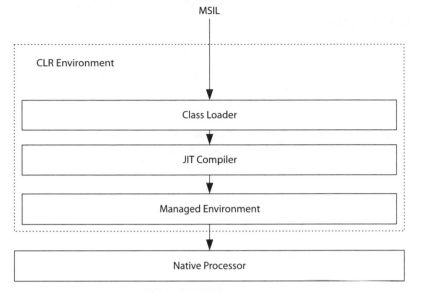

Figure 37.2 The CLR environment.

The JIT compiler verifies that code and the compiles it into native code. The native code is then executed on the actual processor. However, it is not left to run on its own: it is "managed" by the CLR environment. What does "managed" mean in this context? Well, the CLR is the part of the system that handles memory management and garbage collection, as well as handling exceptions and providing security controls etc. This is illustrated in Figure 37.2.

As all the languages in the .NET framework compile into MSIL and run within the CLR, these languages have the potential to interoperate. To simplify such interoperation the CLR specifies and enforces a common type system. Because all languages targeting the runtime follow the common type system rules for defining and using types, the usage of types is consistent across languages. In addition, metadata that describes the classes and their public interfaces enables language interoperability by defining a uniform mechanism for storing and retrieving information about types. The metadata itself is created by the various language compilers. The CLR uses metadata to locate and load classes, lay out instances in memory, resolve method invocations, generate native code, enforce security, and set run-time context boundaries

37.3.2 Framework Class Library

You have already made extensive use of the .NET Framework class library throughout this book. This is because the library provides a collection of reusable classes that you can use in your own applications. Examples of some of these classes are `System.Collections.ArrayList`, `System.Console` and `System.Text.RegularExpressions.Regex`. That is, all the classes, interfaces, structs and enumerated types you have used from the C# class libraries are part of the .NET Framework classes. Note that the classes, interfaces, structs and enums collectively define the types in the Common Language Runtime.

37.4 .NET My Services

.NET My Services is a Web service hosting initiative from Microsoft that is incorporated into .NET. It is proposed that it will use the Passport single sign-on mechanism to handle security and user identification. The basic idea behind .NET My Services is that companies can develop Web services and publish them to .NET My Services via SOAP (Simple Object Access Protocol). Once published to .NET My Services, potential users of the Web service can register with a Web service to obtain access to it. The communication between the client and the server will then be in XML, allowing for independence of language or indeed platform. At the time of writing, the exact structure and future of .NET My Services is unclear. However, some form of service is likely to be provided as part of .NET.

37.5 Language Interoperability

One of the features of the CLR is that many different languages can compile to it. Thus classes written in C#, Visual Basic, JScript and C++ all compile to the same intermediate format and all run in the same runtime environment. This means that we can write code in C# that is called by code written in any other of the .NET languages (and vice versa). In fact, it also means that any existing classes available for inheritance etc. could be written in any of the .NET languages. These classes could then be used as the parent class for a new class in say C#. In other words it does not matter what language a class was written in nor what language it is used in; the CLR hides the details and we can just use those classes as necessary. For example, you may have looked at the .NET Framework SDK Documentation. In this documentation you will find that there are descriptions of how to use a class and its methods from a variety of different languages. This is illustrated in Figure 37.3.

In Figure 37.3 the class ArrayList is presented for the languages VisualBasic, C#, C++ and JScript. As you are now familiar with C# you should be able to see what the VisualBasic, C++ and JScript versions mean. Also note that in the example section is a Visual Basic example (and in fact a C# example follows it). This shows that the class ArrayList can be used (in the appropriate manner) from any one of these languages. Indeed, we don't actually know which language ArrayList was defined in! It could have been C# or it could have been one of the other languages).

At this point you may be asking the question "How is all this possible?". After all, the language we have just mentioned, i.e. Visual Basic, C# and C++, all have very different features. For example, C++ supports pointers, Visual Basic does not, and C# only supports then in unsafe mode!. The answer is that if you wish to interoperate between languages in .NET you do need to keep a few things in mind. Not least of these is that you should not use features in the API of a class that are not supported in the other languages that will need to use that class. In general, what can and can't be done is specified in the Common Language Specification (CLS). This describes what features can be visible in the public interface of the class. Remember that this is the public interface: any feature supported by the implementing language can be used internally within the class.

To simplify this process and to help developers determine whether they are producing CLS-compliant code, it is possible to mark code as such. Then when the code is compiled it is

Figure 37.3 Multi-language SDK documentation.

possible to turn on CLS compliance checking that will report any problems. This is done by specifying the ClsCompliant assembly attribute in the source file.

In general the restrictions on CLS compliance are:

- Unsigned types can't be exposed as part of the public interface of a class or interface.
- Unsafe types (such as pointers) can't be exposed as part of the public interface of a class or interface.
- Identifiers (such as class names, method names and variable names) can't differ only in case.

Part 7

Object-Oriented Design

Chapter 38

Object-Oriented Analysis and Design

38.1 Introduction

This chapter surveys the most significant object-oriented design and analysis methods to emerge since the late 1980s. It concentrates primarily on OOA (Coad and Yourdon, 1991) and Booch (Booch, 1991, 1994), Object Modeling Technique (Rumbaugh *et al.*, 1991), Objectory (Jacobson, 1992) and Fusion (Coleman *et al.*, 1994). It also introduces the Unified Modeling Language (Rational, 2001; Jacobson *et al.*, 1998).

This chapter does not aim to deal comprehensively with either the range of methods available or the fine details of each approach. Rather, it provides an overview of the design process, and the strengths and weaknesses of some important and reasonably representative methods.

38.2 Object-Oriented Design Methods

The object-oriented design methods that we consider are all architecture-driven, incremental and iterative. They do not adopt the more traditional waterfall software development model; instead, they adopt an approach which is more akin to the spiral model of Boehm (1988). This reflects developers' experiences when creating object-oriented systems – the object-oriented development process is more incremental than that for procedural systems, with less distinct barriers between analysis, design and implementation. Some organizations take this process to the extreme and adopt an evolutionary development approach. This approach delivers system functions to users in very small steps and revises project plans in the light of experience and user feedback. This philosophy has proved very successful for organizations which have fully embraced it and has led to earlier business benefits and successful end products from large development projects.

38.3 Object-Oriented Analysis

We first consider the Object-Oriented Analysis approach (OOA) of Coad and Yourdon (1991). The identification of objects and classes is a crucial task in object-oriented analysis and design, but many techniques ignore this issue. For example, both the Booch method and OMT do not deal with it at all. They indicate that it is a highly creative process which can be based on the identification of nouns and verbs in an informal verbal description of the problem domain. A different approach is to use a method such as OOA as the first part of the design process and then to use another object-oriented design method for the later parts of the process.

OOA helps designers identify the detailed requirements of their software, rather than how the software should be structured or implemented. It aims to describe the existing system and how it operates, and how the software system should interact with it. One of the claims of OOA is that it helps the designer to package the requirements of the system in an appropriate manner (for object-oriented systems?) and to reduce the risk of the software failing to meet the customer's requirements. In effect, OOA helps to build the Object Model, which we look at in more detail when we look at OMT.

There are five activities within OOA which direct the analyst during the analysis process:

- Finding classes and objects in the domain.
- Identifying structures (amongst those classes and objects). Structures are relationships such as *is a* and *part of*.
- Identifying subjects (related objects).
- Defining attributes (the data elements of the objects).
- Defining services (the active parts of objects that indicate what the object does).

These are not sequential steps: as information becomes available, the analyst performs the appropriate activity. The intention is that the analyst can work in whatever way the domain expert finds it easiest to express their knowledge. Thus the analyst may go deeper into one activity than the others as the domain expert provides greater information in that area. Equally, the analyst may jump around between activities identifying classes one minute and services the next.

38.4 The Booch Method

The Booch method (also known as Booch and Object-Oriented Development, or OOD) is one of the earliest recognizable object-oriented design methods. It was first described in a paper published in 1986 and has become widely adopted since the publication of a book describing the method (Booch, 1991; Booch, 1994).

The Booch method provides a step-by-step guide to the design of an object-oriented system. Although Booch's books discuss the analysis phase, they do so in too little detail compared with the design phase.

38.4.1 The Steps in the Booch Method

Identification of classes and objects involves analyzing the problem domain and the system requirements to identify the set of classes required. This is not trivial and relies on a suitable requirements analysis.

Identification of the semantics of classes and objects involves identifying the services offered by an object and required by an object. A service is a function performed by an object and, during this step, the overall system functionality is devolved among the objects. This is another non-trivial step and it may result in modifications to the classes and objects identified in the last step.

Identification of the relationships between classes and objects involves identifying links between objects as well as inheritance between classes. This step may identify new services required of objects.

Implementation of classes and objects attempts to consider how to implement the classes and objects and how to define the attributes and provide services. This involves considering algorithms. This process may lead to modifications in the deliverables of all of the above steps and may force the designer to return to some or all of the above steps.

During these steps, the designer produces

- Class diagrams which illustrate the classes in the system and their relationships.
- Object diagrams which illustrate the actual objects in the system and their relationships.
- Module diagrams which package the classes and objects into modules. These modules illustrate the influence that Ada had on the development of the Booch method (Booch, 1987).
- Process diagrams which package processes and processors.
- State transition diagrams and timing diagrams which describe the dynamic behaviour of the system (the other diagrams describe the static structure of the system).

Booch recommends an incremental and iterative development of a system through the refinement of different yet consistent logical and physical views of that system.

38.4.2 Strengths and Weaknesses

The biggest problem for a designer approaching the Booch method for the first time is that the plethora of different notations is supported by a poorly defined and loose process (although the revision to the method described in Booch (1994) addresses this to some extent). It does not give step-by-step guidance and possesses very few mechanisms for determining the system's requirements. Its main strengths are its (mainly graphical) notations, which cover most aspects of the design of an object-oriented system, and its greatest weakness is the lack of sufficient guidance in the generation of these diagrams.

38.5 The Object Modeling Technique

The Object Modeling Technique (OMT) is an object-oriented design method which aims to construct a series of models which refine the system design until the final model is suitable for implementation. The design process is divided into three phases:

- The Analysis Phase attempts to model the problem domain.
- The Design Phase structures the results of the analysis phase in an appropriate manner.
- The Implementation Phase takes into account target language constructs.

38.5.1 The Analysis Phase

Three types of model are produced by the analysis phase:

- *The object model* represents the static structure of the domain. It describes the objects, their classes and the relationships between the objects. For example, the object model might represent the fact that a department object possesses a single manager (object) but many employees (objects). The notation is based on an extension of the basic entity–relationship notation.
- *The dynamic model* represents the behaviour of the system. It expresses what happens in the domain, when it occurs and what effect it has. It does not represent how the behaviour is achieved. The formalism used to express the dynamic model is based on a variation of finite state machines called statecharts. These were developed by Harel and others (1987, 1988) to represent dynamic behaviour in real-time avionic control systems. Statecharts indicate the states of the system, the transitions between states, their sequence and the events which cause the state change.
- *The functional model* describes how system functions are performed. It uses data flow diagrams which illustrate the sources and sinks of data as well as the data being exchanged. They contain no sequencing information or control structures.

The relationship between these three models is important, as each model adds to the designer's understanding of the domain:

- The object model defines the objects which hold the state variables referenced in the dynamic model and are the sources and sinks referenced in the functional model.
- The dynamic model indicates when the behaviour in the functional model occurs and what triggers it.
- The functional model explains why an event transition leads from one state to another in the dynamic model.

You do not build these models sequentially; changes to any one of the models may have a knock-on effect in the other models. Typically, the designer starts with the object model, then considers the dynamic model and finally the functional model, but the process is iterative.

The analysis process is described in considerable detail and provides by step-by-step guidance. This ensures that the developer knows what to do at any time to advance the three models.

38.5.2 The Design Phase

The design phase of OMT builds upon the models produced during the analysis phase:

- *The system design step* breaks the system down into subsystems and determines the overall architecture to be used.

- *The object design step* decides on the algorithms to be used for the methods. The methods are identified by examining the three analysis models for each class etc.

Each of the steps gives some guidelines for their respective tasks; however, far less support is provided for the designer than in the analysis phase. For example, there is no systematic guidance for the identification of subsystems, although the issues involved are discussed (resource management, batch versus interactive modes etc.). This means that it can be difficult to identify where to start, how to proceed and what to do next.

38.5.3 The Implementation Phase

The implementation phase codifies the system and object designs into the target language. This phase provides some very useful information on how to implement features used in the model-based design process used, but it lacks the step-by-step guidance which would be useful for those new to object orientation.

38.5.4 Strengths and Weaknesses

OMT's greatest strength is the level of step-by-step support that it provides during the analysis phase. However, it is much weaker in its guidance during the design and implementation phases, where it provides general guidelines (and some heuristics).

38.6 The Objectory Method

The driving force behind the Objectory method (Jacobson, 1991) is the concept of a *use case*. A use case is a particular interaction between the system and a user of that system (an actor) for a particular purpose (or function). The users of the system may be human or machine. A complete set of use cases therefore describes a system's functionality based around what actors should be able to do with the system. The Objectory method has three phases which produce a set of models.

38.6.1 The Requirements Phase

The requirements phase uses a natural language description of what the system should do to build three models.

- *The use case model* describes the interactions between actors and the system. Each use case specifies the actions which are performed and their sequence. Any alternatives are also documented. This can be done in natural language or using state transition diagrams.
- *The domain model* describes the objects, classes and associations between objects in the domain. It uses a modified entity–relationship model.
- *The user interface descriptions* contain mock-ups of the various interfaces between actors and the system. User interfaces are represented as pictures of windows while other interfaces are described by protocols.

38.6.2 The Analysis Phase

The analysis phase produces the analysis model and a set of subsystem descriptions. The analysis model is a refinement of the domain object model produced in the requirements phase. It contains behavioural information as well as control objects which are linked to use cases. The analysis model also possesses entity objects (which exist beyond a single use case) and interface objects (which handle system–actor interaction). The subsystem descriptions partition the system around objects which are involved in similar activities and which are closely coupled. This organization structures the rest of the design process.

38.6.3 The Construction Phase

The construction phase refines the models produced in the analysis phase. For example, inter-object communication is refined and facilities provided by the target language are considered. This phase produces three models:

- Block models represent the functional modules of the system.
- Block interfaces specify the public operations performed by blocks.
- Block specifications are optional descriptions of block behaviour in the form of finite state machines.

The final stage is to implement the blocks in the target language.

38.6.4 Strengths and Weaknesses

The most significant aspect of Objectory is its use of use cases, which join the building blocks of the method. Objectory is unique among the methods considered here, as it provides a unifying framework for the design process. However, it still lacks the step-by-step support which would simplify the whole design process.

38.7 The Fusion Method

The majority of object-oriented design methods currently available, including those described in this chapter, take a systematic approach to the design process. However, in almost all cases this process is rather weak, providing insufficient direction or support to the developer. In addition, methods such as OMT rely on a "bottom up" approach. This means that the developer must focus on the identification of appropriate classes and their interfaces without necessarily having the information to enable them to do this in an appropriate manner for the overall system. Little reference is made to the system's overall functionality when determining class functionality etc. Indeed, some methods provide little more than some vague guidelines and anecdotal heuristics.

In contrast, Fusion explicitly attempts to provide a systematic approach to object-oriented software development. In many ways, the Fusion method is a mixture of a range of other approaches (indeed, the authors of the method acknowledge that there is little new in the approach, other than that they have put it all together in a single method; see Figure 38.1).

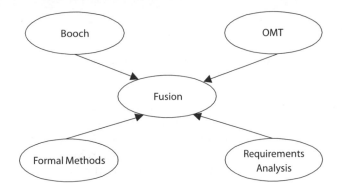

Figure 38.1 Some of the influences on Fusion.

As with other object-oriented design methods, Fusion is based around the construction of appropriate models that capture different elements of the system and different knowledge. These models are built up during three distinct phases:

- *The analysis phase* produces models that describe the high-level constraints from which the design models are developed.
- *The design phase* produces a set of models that describe how the system behaves in terms of a collection of interacting objects.
- *The implementation phase* describes how to map the design models onto implementation language constructs.

Within each phase a set of detailed steps attempts to guide the developer through the Fusion process. These steps include checks to ensure the consistency and completeness of the emerging design. In addition, the output of one step acts as the input for the next.

Fusion's greatest weakness is its complexity – it really requires a sophisticated CASE tool. Without such a tool, it is almost impossible to produce a consistent and complete design.

38.8 The Unified Modeling Language

The Unified Modeling Language (UML) is an attempt by Grady Booch, Ivar Jacobson and James Rumbaugh to build on the experiences of the Booch, Object Modeling Technique (OMT) and Objectory methods. Their aim is to produce a single, common, and widely useable modelling language for these methods and, working with other methodologists, for other methods. This means that UML focuses on a standard language and not a standard process, which reflects what happens in reality: a particular notation is adopted as the means of communication on a specific project and between projects. However, between projects (and sometimes within projects), different design methods are adopted as appropriate. For example, a design method intended for the domain of real-time avionics systems may not be suitable for designing a small payroll system. The UML is an attempt to develop a common meta-model which unifies semantics and from which a common notation can be built.

38.9 Summary

In this chapter, we have reviewed a number of object-oriented analysis and design methods and the Unified Modeling Language. We have briefly considered the features, strengths and weaknesses of each method.

In all these systems, during the design process it is often difficult to identify commonalities between classes at the implementation level. This means that during the implementation phase, experienced object-oriented technicians should look for situations in which they can move implementation-level components up the class hierarchy. This can greatly increase the amount of reuse within a software system and may lead to the introduction of abstract classes which contain the common code.

The problem with this is that the implemented class hierarchy no longer reflects the design class hierarchy. It is therefore necessary to have a free flow of information between the implementation and design phases in an object-oriented project.

Chapter 39

The Unified Modeling Language

39.1 Introduction

The Unified Modeling Language (UML) is part of a development to merge (unify) the concepts in the Booch, Objectory and OMT methods (Jacobson *et al.*, 1998; Rational, 2001). The method is still under development (and has taken a low profile recently); however, the notation underlying this method is nearing completion. This notation is now the focus of the current work of Booch, Rumbaugh and Jacobson and is receiving a great deal of interest. Microsoft, Hewlett-Packard, Oracle and Texas Instruments have all endorsed the UML.

The UML is a third generation object-oriented modeling language (Rational, 2001) which adapts and extends the published notations used in the works of Booch, Rumbaugh and Jacobson (Booch, 1994; Rumbaugh *et al.*, 1991; Jacobson, 1992) and is influenced by many others such as Fusion (Coleman *et al.*, 1994), Harel's statecharts (Harel *et al.*, 1987; Harel, 1988) and CORBA (Ben-Natan, 1995), as illustrated in Figure 39.1.

The UML is intended to form a single, common, widely useable modelling language for a range of object-oriented design methods (including Booch, Objectory and OMT). It is also intended that it should be applicable in a wide range of applications and domains. It should be equally applicable to client–server applications and to real-time control applications.

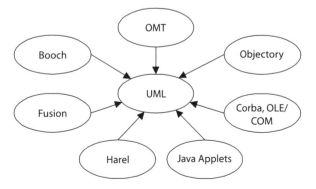

Figure 39.1 The influences on the UML notation.

429

The justification for UML is that different organizations, applications and domains require (and use) different design methods. An organization may develop its own methods or modify other methods through experience. Different parts of the same organization may use different methods. The notation that they use acts as a language to communicate the ideas represented in part (or all) of the design.

For example, the production of shrink-wrapped, off-the-shelf software, is different from the creation of one-off bespoke software. However, both activities may be carried out by a software company. Such an organization may well wish to exchange ideas, designs or parts of a design among its departments or operational units. This kind of exchange relies on the availability of a common language; UML provides such a language.

At present, the UML is in draft form (Booch *et al.*, 1996); however, it is being presented to the Object Management Group (OMG), in the hope that it will be accepted as a standard (this is an ongoing process and is part of the OMG's call for information on object-oriented methods). For the latest information on the UML (and other developments on the unification front) see the Rational Software Corporation's Web site (http://www.rational.com/).

This chapter provides a brief introduction to the UML. It considers how the UML represents the classes, objects, relationships and attributes in an object-oriented system. It also considers sequence and collaboration diagrams, state diagrams and deployment diagrams.

For further information, see version 1.0 of the UML documentation set. There is also a series of books on the UML, including a Reference Manual and a User Guide (Booch *et al.*, 1997). Other books are becoming available, for example a Process Book (which, at the time of writing, is still in the pipeline) and Fowler and Scott (1997).

39.2 The Meta-Model

The UML is built upon a common meta-model which defines the semantics of the language. On top of this, there is a common notation which interprets these semantics in an easily (human) comprehensible manner.

A meta-model describes the constituents of a model and its relationships. It is a model which documents how another model can be defined. Such models are important because they provide a single, common and unambiguous statement of the syntax and semantics of a model. A meta-model allows CASE tool builders to do more than provide diagramming tools. The meta-model serves several purposes:

- defining the syntax and describing the semantics of the UML's concepts
- providing a (reasonably) formal basis for the UML
- providing a description of the elements of the UML
- providing the basis for the interchange of models between vendors' tools

In the normal course of events, a user of the UML (or indeed of a tool which supports the UML) need not know about the meta-model. However, for the developers of the UML and for tool vendors in general the meta-model is a valuable, indeed essential, feature.

At present, the UML meta-model is defined in terms of the UML and textual annotations (although this may appear infinitely recursive, it is possible). Work on the meta-model is still progressing; the authors of the UML are attempting to make it more formal and simpler.

39.3 The Models

The UML defines a number of models and their notations:

- *Use case diagrams* organize the use cases that encompass a system's behaviour (they are based on the use case diagrams of Objectory).
- *Class diagrams* express the static structure of the system (they derive from the Booch and OMT methods), for example the *part-of* and *is-a* relationships between classes and objects. The class diagrams also encompass the object diagrams. Therefore, in this book, we refer to them as the Object Model (as in OMT).
- *Sequence diagrams* (known as message-trace diagrams in version 0.8 of the Unified Method draft) deal with the time ordered sequence of transactions between objects.
- *Collaboration diagrams* (previously known as object-message diagrams) indicate the order of messages between specified objects. They complement sequence diagrams as they illustrate the same information. Sequence diagrams highlight the actual sequence, while collaboration diagrams highlight the structure required to support the message sequence.
- *State machine diagrams* are based on statecharts, like those in OMT. They capture the dynamic behaviour of the system.
- *Component diagrams* (known as module diagrams in version 0.8 of the Unified Method draft) represent the development view of the system; that is, how the system should be developed into software modules. You can also use them to represent concepts such as dynamic libraries.
- *Deployment diagrams* (previously known as platform diagrams) attempt to capture the topology of the system once it is deployed. They reflect the physical topology upon which the software system is to execute.

39.4 Use Case Diagrams

Use case diagrams explain how a system (or subsystem) is used. The elements which interact with the system can be humans, other computers or dumb devices which process or produce data. The diagrams thus present a collection of use cases which illustrate what the system is expected to do in terms of its external services or interfaces. Such diagrams are very important for illustrating the overall system functionality (to both technical and non-technical personnel). They can act as the context within which the rest of the system is defined.

The large rectangle in Figure 39.2 indicates the boundaries of the system (a telephone help desk adviser). The rectangles on either side of the system indicate external actors (in this case, a Service Engineer and a Telephonist) which interact with the system. The ovals inside the system box indicate the actual use cases themselves. For example, both the actors need to be able to "load a casebase".

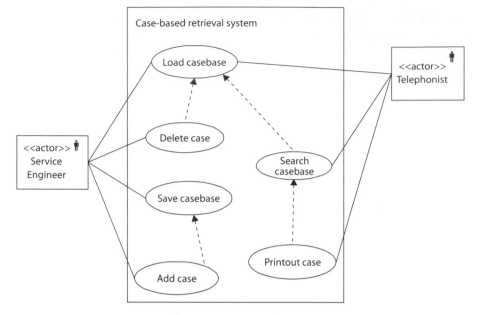

Figure 39.2 Use case diagram.

The notation for actors is based on "stereotypes" (which are discussed in more detail later). An actor is a class with a stereotype: <actor> indicates the actor stereotype and the stick figure is the actor stereotype icon. Although we have used the class icon (a box) as well as the stereotype icon (the stick man), we could have used only one of them if we had so wished.

Each individual use case can have a name, a description explaining what it does, and a list of its responsibilities, attributes and operations. It may also describe its behaviour in the form of a statechart. The most appropriate form of description for a use case differs from one domain to another and thus the format should be chosen as appropriate. This illustrates the flexibility of the UML; it does not prescribe the actual format of a use case.

You can use sequence diagrams and collaboration diagrams with use case diagrams to illustrate the sequence of interactions between the system and the actors. You should also annotate use cases with a statement of purpose to place the use case in context.

Finally, the relationship between use case diagrams and class diagrams is that use cases are peers of classes. Depending on the size of the system, they can be grouped with the object model in a package or remain totally independent.

39.5 The Object Model

The object model is the key element of the UML. The constituent diagrams illustrate the static structure of a system via the important classes and objects in the system and how they relate to each other. The UML documentation currently talks about class diagrams (and within this about object diagrams) stating that "class diagrams show generic descriptions of possible systems and object diagrams show particular instantiations of systems and their behaviour". It goes on to state that class diagrams contain classes, while object diagrams contain objects, but that it is possible to mix the two. However, it discusses both under the title *class diagrams*. To avoid confusion, we adopt the term Object Model to cover both sets of diagrams (following the approach adopted in both the Booch and OMT methods).

39.5.1 Representing Classes

A class is drawn as a solid-outline rectangle with three components. The class name (in bold type) is in the top part, a list of attributes is in the middle part and a list of operations is in the bottom part. Figure 39.3 illustrates two classes: Car and File. The Car class possesses three attributes (name, age and fuel are string, integer and string types, respectively) and four operations (start, lock and brake take no parameters, while accelerate takes a single parameter, to, which is an integer that represents the new speed).

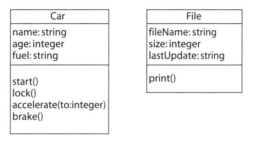

Figure 39.3 Classes with attributes and operations.

An attribute has a name and a type specified in the following format:

    name: type = initialValue

The name and type are strings that are ultimately language-dependent. The initial value is a string representing an expression in the target language.

An operation has a name and may take one or more parameters and return a value. It is specified in the following format:

    name (parameter : type = defaultValue, ...): resultType

The constituent parts are language-dependent strings.

You can hide the attribute and operation compartments from view to reduce the detail shown in a diagram. If you omit a compartment, it says nothing about that part of the class definition. However, if you leave the compartment blank, there are no definitions for that part of the class. Additional language-dependent and user-defined information can also be included in each compartment in a textual format. The intention of such additions is to clarify any element of the design in a similar manner to a comment in source code.

A class *stereotype* tells the reader what "kind" of class it is (for example, exceptions, controllers, interfaces, etc.). You show the stereotype as a normal font text string between < > centred above the class name (see Figure 39.4).

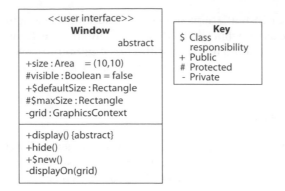

Figure 39.4 Class with additional annotations.

However, UML makes no assumptions about the range of stereotypes which exist and designers are free to develop their own. Other (language-specific) class properties can also be indicated in the class name compartment. For example, in Figure 39.4 the Window class is an abstract class.

You can also indicate the intended scope of attributes and operations in the class definition. This can be useful even for languages, such as Smalltalk, which do not support concepts such as public, private and protected attributes and operations. The absence of any symbol in front of an attribute or operation indicates that the element is public for that class. The significance of this depends on the language. The symbols currently supported are shown in Figure 39.4. You can combine symbols to indicate, for example, that an operation is a class-side public method (such as +$new()).

39.5.2 Representing Objects

An object is drawn as a hexagon with straight sides and slight peaks at the top and bottom (see Figure 39.5). If you are familiar with Booch clouds, you can think of it as a structured cloud.[1]

The object symbol is divided into two sections. The top section indicates the name of the object and its class in the format objectName : className. In Figure 39.5, the object is repMobile1 and the class is Car (see Figure 39.3 for the definition of the Car class). The object name is optional, but the class name is compulsory. You can also indicate how many objects of a particular class are anticipated by entering the maximum value, range etc. in the top compartment. The lack of any number indicates that a single object is intended. The lower compartment contains a list of attributes and their values in the format name type = value (although the type is usually omitted). You can suppress the bottom compartment for clarity.

---

1 From September 1996, the 0.91 addendum to the UML states that an object is now drawn as a rectangle, with the objectName : className underlined. This is a major notational change which the UML authors made so that they do not have to invent a different symbol every time they have a type–instance relationship. However, it means that the distinction between objects and classes in diagrams is minimal and can easily lead to confusion. In an attempt to make objects clearly distinguishable, we continue to use the structured cloud symbol.

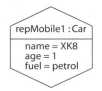

Figure 39.5 An object.

39.5.3 Representing Relationships

A relationship between classes or objects is represented by an association drawn as a solid line (see Figure 39.6). An association between classes may have a name and an optional direction arrowhead that shows which way it is to be read. For example, in Figure 39.6 the relationship called hasEngine is read from the Car class to the Engine class. In addition, each end of an association is a *role*. A role may have a name that illustrates how its class is viewed by the other class. In Figure 39.6, the engine sees the car as a name and the car sees the engine as a specified type (e.g. Petrol, Diesel, Electric).

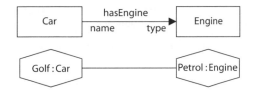

Figure 39.6 Association between classes and links between objects.

Each role (i.e. each end of the association) indicates the multiplicity of its class; that is, how many instances of the class can be associated with one instance of the other class. This is indicated by a text expression on the role: * (indicating zero or more), a number or a range (e.g. 0..3). If there is no expression, there is exactly one association (see Figure 39.7). You can

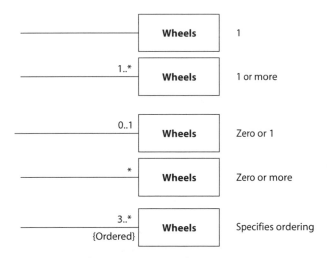

Figure 39.7 Annotated associations.

specify that the multiple objects should be ordered using the text {Ordered}. You can also annotate the association with additional text (such as {Sorted}), but this is primarily for the reader's benefit and has no meaning in UML.

In some situations, an association needs attributes. This means that you need to treat the association as a class (see Figure 39.8). These associations have a dashed line from the association line to the association class. This class is just like any other class and can have a name, attributes and operations. In Figure 39.8, the associations show an access permissions attribute which indicates the type of access allowed for each user for each file.

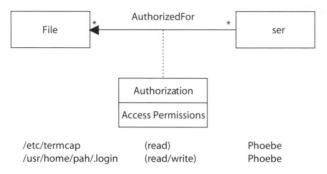

Figure 39.8 Associations with attributes.

Aggregation indicates that one or more objects are dependent on another object for their existence (*part–whole* relationships). For example, in Figure 39.9, the Microcomputer is formed from the Monitor, the System box, the Mouse and the Keyboard. They are all needed for the fully functioning Microcomputer. Aggregation is shown by an empty diamond on the role attached to the whole object.

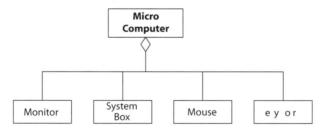

Figure 39.9 Aggregation tree notation.

It is sometimes useful to differentiate between by-value and by-reference references (see Figure 39.10). If the aggregation symbol is not filled, it indicates a by-reference implementation (i.e. a pointer or other reference); if the aggregation symbol is filled, it indicates a by-value implementation (i.e. a class that is embedded within another class).

A qualified association is an association which requires both the object and the qualifier to identify uniquely the other object involved in the association. It is shown as a box between the association and the class. For example, in Figure 39.11, you need the catalogue and the part number to identify a unique part. Notice that the qualifier is part of the association, not the class.

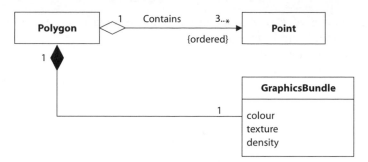

Figure 39.10 Reference implementation.

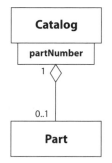

Figure 39.11 Qualified associations.

A ternary (or higher order) association is drawn as a diamond with one line path to each of the participating classes (see Figure 39.12). This is the traditional entity–relationship model symbol for an association (the diamond is omitted from the binary association to save space).

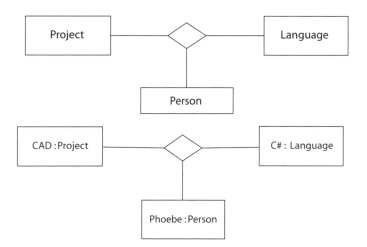

Figure 39.12 Ternary associations.

Ternary associations are very rare and higher order associations are almost non-existent. However, you can model them if necessary.

Inheritance of one class by a subclass is indicated by a solid line drawn from the subclass to the superclass with a large (unfilled) triangular arrowhead at the superclass end (see Figure 39.13). For compactness, you can use a tree structure to show multiple subclasses inheriting from a single superclass.

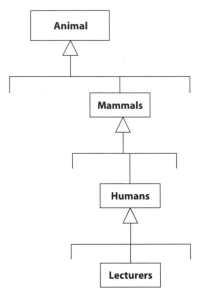

Figure 39.13 Inheritance hierarchy.

You can also model multiple inheritance, as languages such as the Common Lisp Object System (CLOS) and C++ support it. Multiple inheritance is represented by inheritance lines from a single subclass to two or more superclasses as in Figure 39.14. In this figure, the class *Motor powered water vehicle* inherits from both *Motor powered* and *Water vehicle*.

A derived value can be represented by a slash ("/") before the name of the derived attribute (see Figure 39.15). Such an attribute requires an additional textual constraint defining how it is generated; you indicate this by a textual annotation below the class between curly brackets ({}).

A class may define a pattern of objects and links that exist whenever it is instantiated. Such a class is called a composite, and its class diagram contains an object diagram. You may think of it as an extended form of aggregation where the relationships among the parts are valid only within the composite. A composite is a kind of *pattern* or *template* that represents a conceptual clustering for a given purpose. Composition is shown by drawing a class box around the embedded components (see Figure 39.16) which are prototypical objects and links. That is, a composite defines a context in which references to classes and associations, defined elsewhere, can be used.

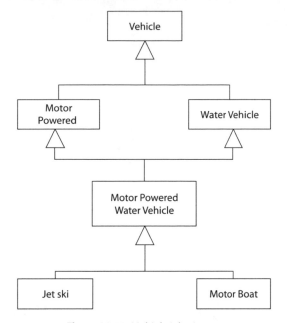

Figure 39.14　Multiple inheritance.

{age = currentDate − birthdate}

Figure 39.15　Derived values.

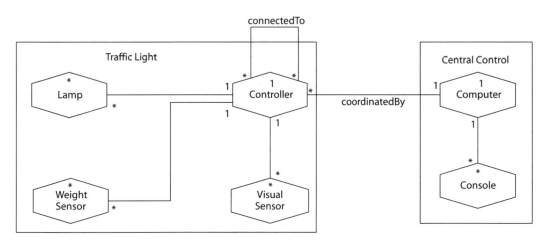

Figure 39.16　Composite classes.

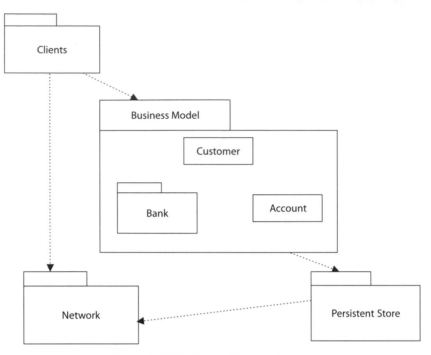

Figure 39.17 Packages with dependencies.

39.6 Packages

Packages group associated modelling elements such as classes in the object model (or subsystems in component diagrams). They are drawn as tabbed folders.

Figure 39.17 illustrates five packages called Clients, Business Model, Persistent Store, Bank and Network. In this diagram, the contents of Clients, Persistent Store, Bank and Network have been suppressed (by convention, the package names are in the body) and only Business Model is shown in detail (with its name in the top tab). Business Model possesses two classes, Customer and Account, and a nested package, Bank. The broken lines illustrate dependencies between the packages. For example, the package Clients directly depends on the packages Business Model and Network (i.e. at least one element in the Clients package relies on at least one element in the other two packages).

A class may belong to exactly one package but make reference to classes in other packages. Such references have the following format:

packageName :: *className*
Business Model :: Customer

Packages allow you to structure models hierarchically; they organize the model and control its overall complexity. Indeed, you may use a package to enable top-down design of a system (rather than the bottom-up design typical of many object-oriented design methods) by allowing designers to specify high-level system functionality in terms of packages which are "filled out" as and when appropriate.

39.7 Sequence Diagrams

A *scenario* shows a particular series of interactions among objects in a single execution of a system. That is, it is a history of how the system behaves between one start state and a single termination state. This differs from an *envisionment*, which describes all system behaviours from all start states to all end states. Envisionments thus contain all possible histories (although they may also contain paths which the system is never intended to take).

Scenarios can be presented in two different ways: *sequence diagrams* and *collaboration diagrams*. Both these diagrams present the same information although they stress different aspects of this information. For example, sequence diagrams stress the timing aspects of the interactions between the objects, whereas collaboration diagrams stress the structure between these objects (which helps in understanding the requirements of the underlying software structure).

Figure 39.18 illustrates the basic structure of a sequence diagram. The objects involved in the exchange of messages are represented as vertical lines (which are labelled with the object's name). Caller, Phone Line and Callee are all objects involved in the scenario of dialling the Emergency services. The horizontal arrows indicate an event or message sent from one object to another. The arrow indicates the direction in which the event or message is sent. That is, the receiver is indicated by the head of the arrow. Normally return values are not shown on these diagrams. However, if they are significant, you can illustrate them by annotated return events.

Time proceeds vertically down the diagram, as indicated by the broken line arrow, and can be made more explicit by additional timing marks. These timing marks indicate how long the

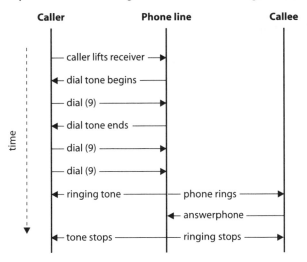

Figure 39.18 A sequence diagram.

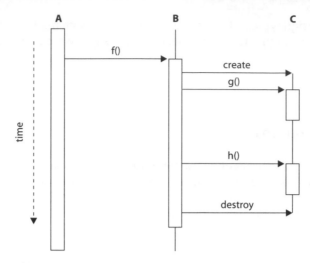

Figure 39.19 Sequence diagram with focus-of-control regions.

gap between messages should be or how long a message or event should take to get from the sender to the receiver.

A variation of the basic sequence diagram (called a focus-of-control diagram) illustrates which object has the thread of control at any one time. This is shown by a fatter line during the period when the object has control (see Figure 39.19). Notice that the bar representing the object C only starts when it is created and terminates when it is destroyed.

39.8 Collaboration Diagrams

As stated above, collaboration diagrams illustrate the sequence of messages between objects based around the object structure (rather than the temporal aspects of sequence diagrams). A collaboration diagram is formed from the objects involved in the collaboration, the links (permanent or temporary) between the objects and the messages (numbered in sequence) that are exchanged between the objects. An example collaboration diagram is presented in Figure 39.20.

Objects which are created during the collaboration are indicated by the label *new* before the object name (e.g. the Line object in Figure 39.20). Links between objects are annotated to indicate their type, permanent or temporary, existing for this particular collaboration. These annotations are placed in boxes on the ends of the links and can have the following values:

A   Association (or permanent) link
F   Object field (the target object is part of the source object)
G   Global variable
L   Local variable
P   Procedure parameter
S   Self reference

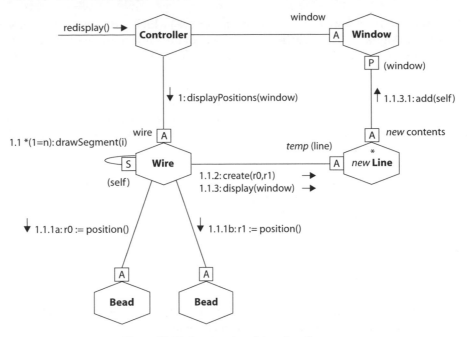

Figure 39.20 An example collaboration diagram.

You can add role names to distinguish links (e.g. self, wire and window in Figure 39.20). Role names in brackets indicate a temporary link, i.e. one that is not an association.

The messages which are sent along links are indicated by labels next to the links. One or more messages can be sent along a link in either or both directions. The format of the messages is defined by the following (some of which are optional):

1. *A comma-separated list of sequence numbers in brackets, e.g.* [seqno, seqno] which indicate messages from other threads of control that must occur before the current message. This element is only needed with concurrency.
2. *A list of sequence elements separated by full stops, "."*, which represent the nested procedural calling sequence of the message in the overall transaction. Each element has the following parts:
   - A letter (or name) indicating a concurrent thread. All letters at the same level of nesting represent threads that execute concurrently i.e. 1.2a and 1.2b are concurrent. If there is no letter, it usually indicates the main sequence.
   - An integer showing the sequential position of the current message within its thread. For example, message 2.1.4 is part of the procedure invoked by message 2.1 and follows message 2.1.3 within that procedure.
   - An iteration indicator (*), optionally followed by an iteration expression in parentheses, which indicates that several messages of the same form are sent either sequentially (to a single target) or concurrently (to the elements of a set). If there is an iteration expression, it shows the values that the iterator assumes, such as (i=1..n); otherwise, the details of the iteration must be specified in text or simply deferred to the code.
   - A conditional indicator (?), optionally followed by a Boolean expression in parentheses. The iteration and conditional indicators are mutually exclusive.

3. *A return value name followed by an assignment sign* (:=) which indicates that the procedure returns a value designated by the given name. The use of the same name elsewhere in the diagram designates the same value. If no return value is specified, then the procedure operates by side-effects.
4. *The name of the message* which is an event or operation name. It is unnecessary to specify the class of an operation since this is implicit in the target object.
5. *The argument list of the message* which is made up of expressions defined in terms of input values of the nesting procedure, local return values of other procedures and attribute values of the object sending the message.

You may show argument values and return values for messages graphically using small data flow tokens near a message. Each token is a small circle, with an arrow showing the direction of the data flow, labelled with the name of the argument or result.

39.9 State Machine Diagrams

Scenarios are used to help understand how the objects within the system collaborate, whereas state diagrams illustrate how these objects behave internally. State diagrams relate events to state transitions and states. The transitions change the state of the system and are triggered by events. The notation used to document state diagrams is based on *statecharts*, developed by Harel (Harel *et al.*, 1987; Harel, 1988).

Statecharts are a variant of the finite state machine formalism, which reduces the apparent complexity of a graphical representation of a finite state machine. This is accomplished through the addition of a simple graphical representation of certain common patterns of finite state machine usage. As a result, a complex sub-graph in a "basic" finite state machine is replaced by a single graphical construct.

Statecharts are referred to as state diagrams in UML. Each state diagram has a start point at which the state is entered and may have an exit point at which the state is terminated. The state may also contain concurrency and synchronization of concurrent activities.

Figure 39.21 illustrates a typical state diagram. This state diagram describes a simplified remote control locking system. The chart indicates that the system first checks the identification code of the handheld transmitter. If it is the same as that held in the memory, it allows the car to be locked or unlocked. When the car is locked, the windows are also closed and the car is alarmed.

A state diagram consists of a start point, events, a set of transitions, a set of variables, a set of states and a set of exit points.

39.9.1 Start Points

A start point is the point at which the state diagram is initialized. In Figure 39.21, there are four start points indicated (Start, lock, close and unlock). The Start start point is the initial entry point for the whole diagram, while the other start points are for substate diagrams.

Any preconditions required by the state diagram can be specified on the transition from the start point (for example, the transmittedID must be the same as the memoryID). It is the initial

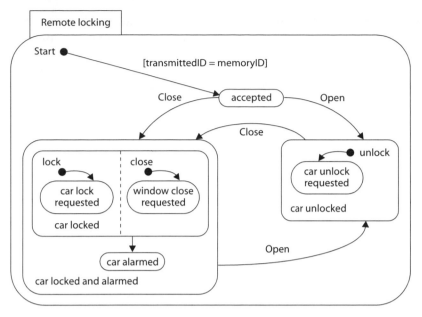

Figure 39.21 An example state diagram.

transition from which all other transitions emanate. This transition is automatically taken when the state diagram is executed. Notice that the initial Start point is not equivalent to a state.

39.9.2 Events

Events are one-way asynchronous transmissions of information from one object to another. The general format of an event is as follows:

eventName (parameter:type, ...)

Of course, many events do not have any associated parameters.

39.9.3 A Set of Transitions

These are the statements which move the system from one state to another. In a state diagram, each transition is formed of four (optional) parts:

1. An event (e.g. lock).
2. A condition (e.g. transmittedID = memoryID)
3. The initiated event (e.g. ^EngineManagementUnit.locked)
4. An operation (e.g. /setDoorToLock)

The event is what triggers the transition; however, the transition only occurs if the condition is met. If the event occurs and the conditions are met, then the associated operation is performed. An operation is a segment of code (equivalent to a statement or program or method) which causes the system state to be altered. Some transitions can also trigger an event which should be sent to a specified object. The above example sends an event `locked` to the `EngineManagementUnit`. The process of sending a global event is a special case of sending an event to a specified object. The syntax of an event is as follows:

```
event(arguments) [condition] ^target.sendEvent(arguments) /
operation(arguments)
```

39.9.4 A Set of State Variables

These are variables referred to in a state diagram, for example, `memoryID`. They have the following format:

```
name: type = value
```

39.9.5 A Set of States

A state represents a period of time during which an object is waiting for an event to occur. It is an abstraction of the attribute values and links of an object. A state is drawn as a rounded box containing the (optional) name of the state. A state may often be composed of other states (the combination of which represents the higher level state). A state has duration; that is, it occupies an interval of time.

A state box can contain two additional sections: a list of state variables and a list of triggered operations (see Figure 39.22).

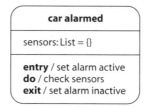

Figure 39.22 State box with state variables and triggered operations.

An operation can be of the following types:

- *entry* operations are executed when the state is entered. They are the same as specifying an operation on a transition. They are useful if all transitions into a state perform the same operation (rather than specifying the same operation on each transition). Such operations are considered to be instantaneous.
- *exit* operations are executed when the state is exited. They are less common than entry actions and indicate an operation performed before any transition from the state.
- *do* operations are executed while the state is active. They start on entry to the state and terminate when the state is exited.

- *events* can trigger operations while within a particular state. For example, the event *help* could trigger the *help* operation while in the state *active*.

Each operation is separated from its type by a forward slash (/). The ordering of operations is:

1. Operations on incoming transitions
2. Entry operations
3. Do operations
4. Exit operations
5. Operations on outgoing transitions

State diagrams allow a state to be a single state variable, or a set of substates. This allows for complex hierarchical models to be developed gradually as a series of nested behaviour patterns. This means that a state can be a state diagram in its own right. For example, *car alarmed* is a single state and *car locked* is another state diagram. Notice that the transition from *car alarmed* to *accepted* jumps from an inner state to an outer state.

The broken line down the middle of the *car locked* state indicates that the two halves of that state run concurrently. That is, the car is locked as the windows are closed.

A special type of state, called a history state, represents a state which must be remembered and used the next time the (outer) state is entered. The symbol for a history state is an H in a circle.

39.9.6 A Set of Exit Points

Exit points specify the result of the state diagram. They also terminate the execution of the state diagram.

39.10 Deployment Diagrams

The elements in Figure 39.23 are called nodes. They represent processors (PCs and Server) and devices (Printer and Fax). A node is thus a resource in the real world upon which we can distribute and execute elements of the (logical) design model. A node is drawn as a three-dimensional rectangular solid with no shadows. The <device> stereotype designation of the Fax and Printer indicates that these nodes are not processors. That is, they do not have any processing ability (from the point of view of the model being constructed). You can also show how many nodes are likely to be involved in the system. Thus the Order Entry PC is of order * (0 or more), but there is exactly one server, printer, fax etc. Finally, the diagram also shows the roles of the associations between nodes and their stereotype. For example, the *Receiving* association on one PC uses a type of ISDN connection (which has yet to be specified).

39.11 Summary

This chapter has presented an overview of the Unified Modeling Language. The UML is an attempt to develop a third generation object-oriented modelling language for use with a variety of object-

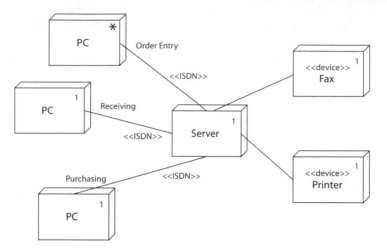

Figure 39.23 Nodes in a deployment diagram.

oriented design methods. It can be used for documenting the design of client–server, real-time, distributed and batch applications. It captures the best elements of the notations used by a number of existing design methods, including Booch, OMT and Objectory while attempting to remain extensible, simple, clear and (relatively) concise. Many CASE tool vendors are already committed to supporting the UML and it is being presented to the OMG by a consortium of organizations as the basis of a standard notation for object-oriented systems development.

Chapter 40

The Unified Process

40.1 Introduction

This chapter provides an overview of the Unified Process (for more details on this design process see Hunt (2000) and Jacobson *et al.* (1998)).

40.2 The Unified Process

The Unified Process is a design framework that guides the tasks, people and products of the design process. It is a framework because it provides the inputs and outputs of each activity, but does not restrict how each activity must be performed. Different activities can be used in different situations, some being left out, others being replaced or augmented. The Unified Process comprises a number of different hierarchical elements (see Figure 40.1).

The Unified Process actually comprises low-level activities (such as finding classes), which are combined together into workflows (which describe how one activity feeds into another). These workflows are organized into iterations. Each iteration identifies some aspect of the system to be considered. How this is done is considered in more detail later. Iterations themselves are organized into phases. Phases focus on different aspects of the design process, for

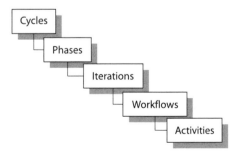

Figure 40.1 Key building blocks of the Unified Process.

449

example requirements, analysis, design and implementation. In turn phases can be grouped into cycles. Cycles focus on the generation of successive releases of a system (for example, version 1.0, version 1.1 etc.).

40.2.1 Overview of the Unified Process

There are four key elements to the philosophy behind the Unified Process. These four elements are:

- iterative and incremental
- use case-driven
- architecture-centric
- acknowledges risk

Iterative and Incremental

The Unified Process is iterative and incremental as it does not try to complete the whole design task in one go. In contrast to the waterfall model, the Unified Process has an iterative and incremental model. That is, the design process is based on iterations which either address different aspects of the design process or move the design forward in some way (this is the incremental aspect of the model). The end result is that you incrementally produce the system being designed.

Use Case-Driven

The Unified Process is also use case-driven. This is because use cases help identify the primary requirements of the system. Use cases are then used to ensure that the evolving design is always relevant to what the user required. Indeed, the uses cases act as the one consistent thread through out the whole of the development process, as is illustrated in Figure 40.2. For example, at the beginning of the design phase one of the two primary inputs to this phase is the use case model. Then, explicitly within the design model, are use case realizations which illustrate how each use case is supported by the design. Any use case which does not have a use case realization is not currently supported by the design.

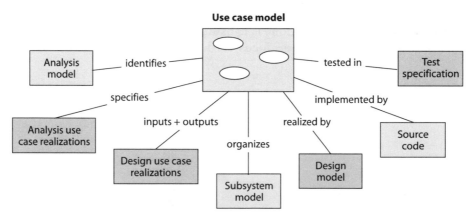

Figure 40.2 The role of use cases.

Architecture-Centric

One problem with having an iterative and incremental approach is that while one group may be working on part of the implementation another group may be working on part of the design. To ensure that all the various parts fit together there needs to be something. That something is an architecture. An architecture is the skeleton on which the muscles (functionality) and skin (the user interface) of the system will be hung. A good architecture will be resilient to change and to the evolving design. The Unified Process explicitly acknowledges the need for this architecture by being architecture centric. It describes how you identify what should be part of the architecture and how you go about designing and implementing the architecture. The remainder of the Unified Process then refers back to that architecture.

Obviously the generation of this architecture (Figure 40.3) is both critical and very hard. Therefore the Unified Process prescribes the successive refinement of the executable architecture, thereby attempting to ensure that the architecture remains relevant.

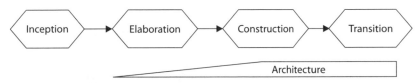

Figure 40.3 The development of the architecture.

Acknowledges Risk

Finally, the Unified Process explicitly acknowledges the risk inherent in software design and development. It does this by highlighting unknown aspects in the system being designed and other areas of concern. These areas are then targeted as either being critical to the system and therefore part of the architecture, or areas of risk that need to be addressed early on in the design process (when there is more time) rather than later on (when time tends to be short).

40.2.2 Life Cycle Phases

The Unified Process comprises four distinct phases. These four phases focus on different aspects of the design process. The four phases are Inception, Elaboration, Construction and Transition. The four phases and their roles are outlined below.

- *Inception* This phase define the scope of the project and develops the business case for the system. It also establishes the feasibility of the system to be built. Various prototypes may be developed during this phase to ensure the feasibility of the proposal.
- *Elaboration* This phase captures the functional requirements of the system. It should also specify any non-functional requirements to ensure that they are taken into account. The other primary task for this phase is the creation of the architecture to be used throughout the remainder of the Unified Process.
- *Construction* This phase concentrates on completing the analysis of the system, performing the majority of the design and the implementation of the system. That is, it essentially builds the product.

- *Transition* The transition phase moves the system into the users' environment. This involves activities such as deploying the system and maintaining it.

Each phase has a set of major milestones that are used to judge the progress of the overall Unified Process (of course with each phase there are numerous minor milestones to be achieved). The primary milestones (or products) of the four phases are illustrated in Figure 40.4.

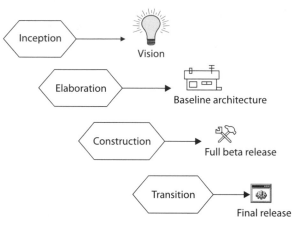

Figure 40.4 Major deliverables of each phase.

A milestone is the culmination of a phase and is comprised of a set of artefacts (such as specific models) which are the product of the workflows (and thus activities) in that phase. The primary milestones for each phase are:

- *Inception* The output of this phase is the vision for the system. This includes a very simplified use case model (to identify that the primary functionality of the system is), a very tentative architecture and the most important or significant risks are identified and the elaboration phase is planned.
- *Elaboration* The primary output of this phase is the architecture along with a detailed use case model and a set of plans for the construction phase.
- *Construction* The end result of this phase is the implemented product which includes the software as well as the design and associated models. The product may not be without defects, as some further work has yet to be completed in the transition phase.
- *Transition* The transition phase is the last phase of a cycle. The major milestone meet by this phase is the final production quality release of the system.

40.2.3 Phases, Iterations and Workflows

There can be confusion over the relationship between phases and workflows. Not least because a single workflow can cross (or be involved in) more than one phase (see Figure 40.5). One way to view the relationships is that the workflows are the steps you actually follow. However, at different times we can identify different major milestones that should be met.

For the majority of this chapter we will focus on the various workflows (not least because this is the emphasis which the designer typically sees).

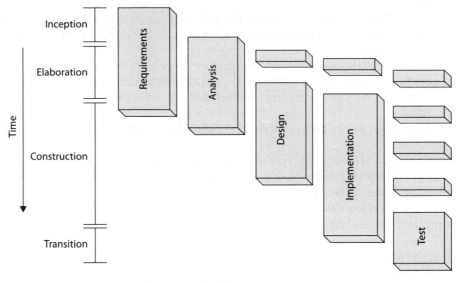

Figure 40.5 Workflows versus phases.

The five workflows in the Unified Process are Requirements, Analysis, Design, Implementation and Test (as indicated in Figure 40.5). Note that the Design, Implementation and Test workflows are broken Unified Processes. This is to indicate that elements of each workflow may take place earlier than the core parts of the workflow. In particular the design, implementation and testing of the architecture will happen early on (in the Elaboration phase). Thus part of each of the Design, Implementation and Test workflows must occur at this time.

The focus of each workflow is described below (their primary products are illustrated in Figure 40.6):

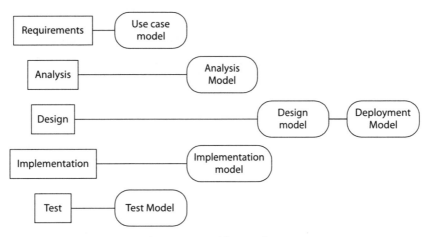

Figure 40.6 Workflow products.

- *Requirements* This workflow focuses on the activities which allow the functional and non-functional requirements of the system to be identified. The primary product of this workflow is the use case model.
- *Analysis* The aim of this workflow is to restructure the requirements identified in the requirements workflow in terms of the software to be built rather than in the users' less precise terms. It can be seen as a first cut at a design; however, that is to miss the point of what this workflow aims to achieve.
- *Design* The design workflow produces the detailed design which will be implemented in the next workflow.
- *Implementation* This workflow represents the coding of the design in an appropriate programming language (for this book that is C#) and the compilation, packaging, deployment and documenting of the software.
- *Test* The test workflow describes the activities to be carried out to test the software to ensure that it meets the users requirements, that it is reliable etc.

Notice that the workflows all have a period when they are running concurrently. This does not mean that one person is necessarily working on all the workflows at the same time. Instead, it acknowledges that in order to clarify some requirement, it may be necessary to design how that requirement might be implemented and even implement it to confirm that it is feasible.

40.2.4 Workflows and Activities

Having discussed workflows we should make mention of what workflows do and what they are comprised of. A workflow describes how a set of activities are related. Activities are the things that actually tell the designer what they should be doing. An activity takes inputs and produces outputs. These inputs and outputs are referred to as artefacts. An artefact that acts as an input to a particular activity could be a use case, while the output from that activity could be a class diagram etc. The actual activities that comprise each of the workflows will be discussed below; however, Figure 40.7 lists the primary activities for each of the workflows.

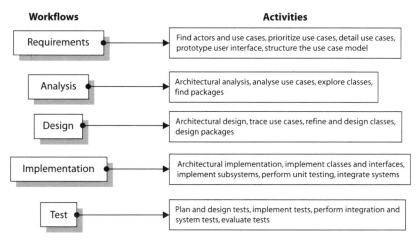

Figure 40.7 Workflows are comprised of activities.

40.3 Requirements Workflow

This section provides an introduction to requirements workflow of the Unified Process. The intention of the use case analysis is to identify how the system is to be used and what it is expected to do in response to this use. To help in identifying the use cases, you can ask the following questions (Jacobson, 1992):

- What are the main tasks of each actor?
- Will the actor have to read/write/change any of the system information?
- Will the actor have to inform the system about outside changes?
- Does the actor wish to be informed about unexpected changes?

Having identified the use cases, we can identify the steps performed within each use case.

40.3.1 Interface Descriptions

Having defined the actors in the system and the uses they make of the system, the next step is often to specify the interfaces between the actors and the system. For human users of the system, these interfaces may well be graphical user interfaces (GUIs). You can draw them with a drawing tool or develop a mock-up using some form of interface simulation software. For non-human interfaces any proposed communications protocols can be defined and checked (for example, that the interacting system is capable of sending and receiving the appropriate information).

40.4 Analysis Workflow

The aim of the analysis workflow is to analyse the requirements identified in the use case analysis (the requirements workflow) and to structure them in terms of the internals of the system. That is, the requirements are converted from the external user's view into "what the system needs to do to support the user's requirements". This does not mean how the system will do it, merely what it must do. For example, the user may be unaware that they have an internal *profile* which specifies what they can and cannot do, however an *internal* requirement on the system might be to check the users' actions against their profile.

Four primary activities comprise the analysis workflow. These activities are:

- generation of analysis classes
- generation of analysis packages
- analysis of use cases
- generation of use case realizations

Once again this process is not as sequential as this list might suggest, rather it is iterative. In addition each activity may effectively be carried out in parallel. Thus the results of one activity may impact on another.

The analysis model is the key element of the analysis workflow. It is the first step in the understanding of how the system should be formed. The analysis model is essentially comprised of the analysis class diagrams. These diagrams illustrate the static structure of a system via the important analysis classes in the system and how they relate to each other.

The information for the analysis model comes from:

- the problem statement (possibly written in natural language)
- a requirements analysis process
- the domain experts
- general knowledge of the real world
- and, in particular, the use case model

The analysis model should be viewed as elucidating the requirements as described in the use case model.

40.4.1 Analysis Model Classes

Analysis model classes represent an abstraction of one or more classes or subsystem (in the final design model). This is because the level of detail expected in the design model is explicitly not required nor appropriate for the analysis model. The focus here is on handling functional requirements at a high level of abstraction. Thus analysis classes are distinguished from design classes, as they:

- *Have responsibilities not operations.* These responsibilities should be documented in textual form. In addition a textual description of the purpose of the class should also be provided.
- *Have high-level attributes described in domain terms.* That is, an attribute in the analysis model may represent a complex concept which will need to be expanded in the design model. For example, an invoice can be treated as a simple attribute in the analysis but not in the design. Another example, would be that an amount in a bank account can be treated as currency without worrying about how currency should be represented.
- *Have relationships,* but these relationships are concept-oriented rather than implementation-oriented. They thus express the abstract relationship between two classes rather than how two classes should be linked in order to be implemented.
- All analysis classes should be *directly involved in one or more use case realizations.* No analysis classes should exist which are not directly used to explain how a use case could be implemented (in terms of the analysis model).
- *Are all of one of three types of class.* These classes are entity, boundary or control classes.

As analysis classes are quite distinct from design classes they have been given their own stereotype with a stereotype icon to illustrate them. These stereotypes are illustrated in Figure 40.8. The three types of analysis class are described below:

- *Entity classes.* Such classes represent data that tends to exist over a period of time (such as a customer's bank account), important concepts in the system, major components or significant elements in the system (such as a fundamental subsystem). If an entity class represents some data, then in many cases this information is persistent and may be stored in some form of long-term storage (such as a database). Entity classes most often model information, concepts or

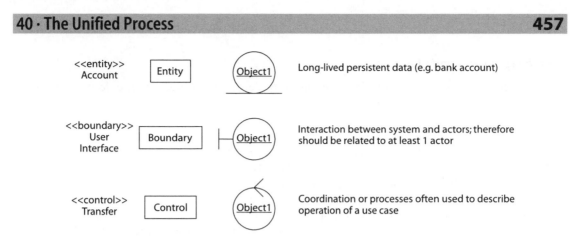

Figure 40.8 Types of analysis class.

real-life objects or events. In many cases, entity classes are an abstraction of some more complex concept that will need to be expanded on and explored in the design model. These are the real nuggets of gold which the analysis model is attempting to mine. It is these classes we need to identify in order to have a chance in creating a robust, reusable, stable architecture.

- *Boundary classes.* These are classes that are used to model the interaction with the actors (i.e. the users of the system). This interaction involves sending, receiving (or both) information. Thus boundary classes often represent abstractions of graphical user interfaces or external APIs or indeed protocols such as http or ftp.
- *Control classes.* A control class represents the functionality required to manage the interaction between the user via the boundary class and the data in the entity class (i.e. it is the set of events in the user case re-stated in the terminology of the system). That is, control classes encapsulate the coordination and sequencing of the interactions between other classes. Note that a single user-oriented event in a use case might map into a number of actions within the control class. Thus it is not necessarily a one-to-one mapping between the events in the use case and the actions described by the control class.

40.4.2 Constructing the Analysis Model

The analysis model may be constructed by following these steps:

- Identify objects and classes.
- Generate use case realizations.
- Prepare a data dictionary.
- Identify associations (including aggregations) between objects.
- Identify attributes of objects at an abstract (probably textual) level.
- Organize and simplify object classes using inheritance.
- Iterate and refine the model.
- Group classes into modules.

You should not take the sequence of these steps too strictly; analysis and design are rarely completed in a truly linear manner.

Identifying Objects and Classes

The first step in constructing the object model is to identify the objects in the domain and their classes. Such objects may include:

- physical entities such as petrol pumps, engines and locks
- logical entities such as employee records, purchases and speed
- soft entities such as tokens, expressions or data streams
- conceptual entities such as needs, requirements or constraints

As long as an item makes sense for the application and the domain, then it is a candidate object or class. The only things you should avoid are objects which relate to the proposed computer implementation.

Once you have a comprehensive list of candidate classes, you can discard any unnecessary or incorrect ones by using the following criteria:

- Are any of the classes redundant?
- Are any of the classes irrelevant?
- Are any of the classes vague?
- Are any of the classes really attributes of other classes?
- Are any of the classes really operations?
- Does the name of the class represent its intrinsic nature and not its role in the application? For example, the class `Person` might represent an object in a restaurant booking system, but the class `Customer` is a better representation of its role in the system.
- Is a class really an implementation construct?

Generate Use Case Realizations

In order to generate the analysis use case realizations it is necessary to examine each of the use cases in turn. For each use case you need to:

- Start by considering the event generated by the actor which triggers the use case realization. This should be sent to a boundary class and is the starting point for finding classes.
- Move through the flow of events identifying the classes involved in the flow of events and the messages and links between the classes.
- Identify all the analysis classes involved in the use case sequence of events.
  - Each time you need to find a class examine those already in the data dictionary to see if there is one which matches your requirement.
  - If new classes are found then they need to be added to the use case realization and to the data dictionary. Note that it is often very useful to appoint a librarian who will be responsible for the data dictionary, for maintaining it, for updating it and for managing the identification and acceptance of new classes.
- Distribute the use cases behaviour among the classes.
  - Record the responsibilities of the classes in the data dictionary (and with the class itself).
  - Classes can have more then one responsibility (as they are abstractions of what will be in the design model). However, the responsibilities should be related to keep the class consistent.

- Note any special requirements from the use cases or identified during the analysis workflow with the use case realization.
- Record interactions between classes.
- The basic path associated with all use cases should produce one collaboration diagram.
- Alternative paths may produce one or more collaboration diagrams. A useful rule of thumb is to break the alternative paths into multiple collaboration diagram if they become too complex to explain in one sentence.

Note that you are not expected to find all the classes first time, nor just by considering the use cases. Generating the use case realizations and the process of generating the analysis classes themselves is really a very iterative process in which many different techniques come into play.

Preparing a Data Dictionary

A data dictionary provides a definition for each of the terms or words used in the evolving analysis models. Each entry precisely describes each object class, its scope, any assumptions or restrictions on its use and its attributes and operations (once they are known).

Identifying Associations Between Objects

The next step is to identify any (and all) associations between two or more classes. In particular, look for the following types of relationships:

- physical location (next to, part of, contained in)
- directed actions (drives)
- communication (talks to)
- ownership (has, part of)
- satisfaction of some condition (works for, married to, manages)

You should consider which classes are likely to need to work with which other classes (e.g. the accounts clerk may need to work with the salaries clerk).

Once you have a set of candidate associations, you can refine them using the following criteria:

- Is the association between eliminated classes?
- Are any of the associations irrelevant or implementation associations?
- Are any associations transient?
- Are any of the associations ternary? It is a good idea to keep things simple and only have binary relationships.
- Are any of the associations derivable?
- Are any of the associations misnamed?
- Add role names where appropriate.
- Are there any qualified associations?
- Specify multiplicity on the associations.
- Are there any missing associations?

Identifying Attributes of Objects

An important point to note is that you should only be trying to identify application domain attributes. This means that attributes which are needed during the implementation of the system should not be included at this stage. Next you should refine the attributes:

- Should the attribute be an object?
- Is an attribute really a name?
- Is an attribute an identifier?
- Is an attribute really a link attribute?
- Does the attribute represent an internal state of the object which is not visible outside the object?
- Does the attribute represent fine detail?
- Are any of the attributes unlike the others in their class?

Using Inheritance

You can refine your classes using inheritance in both directions. That is, you can group common aspects of existing classes into a superclass, or you can specialize an existing class into a number of subclasses that serve specific purposes.

Testing Access Paths

This step involves checking that paths in the model make sense, are sufficient and are necessary.

Iterating and Refining the Model

To refine your model you can ask yourself the following questions:

- Are there any missing objects?
- Are there any unnecessary classes?
- Are there any missing associations (such as a missing access path for some operation)?
- Are there any unnecessary associations?
- Are all attributes in the correct class?
- Are all associations in the correct place?

Grouping Classes into Packages

The final step associated directly with the object model is to group classes into packages.

40.5 Design Workflow

The primary inputs to the design workflow come from the use case analysis and the analysis workflow. The design workflow differs from the analysis workflow as it is aimed at implementation abstraction, i.e. how the system should be built, rather than trying to rephrase the system requirements (at a high level of abstraction). There are four primary activities in the design workflow, these are:

- *Generation of design classes.* We are now interested in all the details required to design the system. Thus there will be many more classes required to support the use case realizations than was the case in the analysis workflow.
- *Identification of design interfaces.* To reduce the dependency between classes, we will also identify the key interfaces in the system.
- *Generation of design use case realizations.* We now need to consider how the design implements the use cases identified during the requirements workflow.
- *Generation of subsystems.* We are also interested in producing actual subsystems, rather than subsystems that help us understand the system.

Note that the design class notation does not use the three stereotype classes presented in the analysis workflow. This is because we are now interested in the classes which will actually form part of the system, rather than an abstraction of what the system needs to do. Thus we use the standard box notation with the attribute and operation compartments fully documented.

40.5.1 Identifying Classes

First look at the analysis classes in the analysis model:

- For *Boundary* classes you should "implement" then with appropriate interface classes. Or you may need to specify a design class that provides a particular protocol etc.
- For *Entity* classes you will need to determine what classes, files, database etc. will "implement" these classes. It is often the case that one entity class will result in multiple design elements, even to the extent of representing a design subsystem, and care needs to be taken with this analysis. Remember that the entity classes describe the key concepts in the system; thus whatever they evolve into in the design will be key elements in the design!
- *Control* classes. Essentially the behaviour encapsulated in the analysis control classes needs to be divided between the various design classes that will implement that behaviour.

It is also likely that you will need to consider additional support classes, above and beyond what might have been identified straight from the use cases and the analysis classes.

40.5.2 Refining the Set of Classes

Once you have an initial set of classes you will need to start refining them (just as you did in the analysis workflow). The issues you will need are essentially the same as in the analysis phase, with the addition of:

- Do any subsystem interfaces imply classes?
- Do any other interfaces need classes?
- Are any of the classes vague?
- Are any of the classes really operations?
- Do any of the classes map directly to C# classes?

- Is it too big – would it benefit from being broken down into a number of different classes?
- Instead of using inheritance, can you identify any component-based reuse which will allow you to modifying the class's behaviour by "plugging in" another class to provide that behaviour?

40.5.3 Identifying and Refining Attributes

As you are identifying your classes, you should also be thinking about the attributes they possess. This is important, as it will not only help you to identify other classes (when an attribute is a composite of a grouping of information) but also help you to identify classes that are really the same – just with different names.

Once you have an initial set of attributes for a class you are ready to refine them (this is really an iterative process of discovery and refinement). To refine the attributes you have identified for a design class you can apply essentially the same questions as were used in the analysis phase.

40.5.4 Identifying and Refining Operations

When searching for the operations that an object should perform, you should look for:

- Operations implied by the responsibilities documented on analysis classes.
- Operations implied by the steps performed by the analysis workflow control classes (and where they should be located).
- Operations implied by events and particularly interactions with actors.
- Operations implied by interaction diagrams such as collaboration or sequence diagrams. The messages in these diagrams usually map onto operations.
- Transitions implied by statecharts.
- Interfaces implemented by a class.
- Operations implied by state actions and activities.
- Application or domain operations.
- Special requirements on analysis classes.

Once you have identified an initial set of operations you can begin to refine them. Once again the process of discovering operations and refining them is an iterative and incremental one. The things to consider when refining the operations include:

- Look for simplifying operations. For example, view the description associated with the operation. Does the operation attempt to fulfil more than one role? If so, can it be broken down?
- Visibility of operations.
- Every operation should be traceable to a use case realization.
- Ensure all roles played by the class are supported by the operations.
- All operations should be documented with functionality performed, pre- and post-conditions, meaning of inputs, return value etc.
- Dependencies implied by parameters or return types.

40.5.5 Design Use Case Realizations

You should now consider the design equivalents of the use case realizations you produced for the analysis workflow. These are necessary so that you can be sure that all use cases are supported by your design. Of course, the classes in your design model are influenced by the use cases and the use case realizations, so these processes are likely to be iterative and incremental and tightly coupled. Design use case realizations are made up of:

- textual flow of events description
- class diagrams
- interaction diagrams
- subsystems and system interfaces involved in use cases

You may also wish to document any non-functional requirements that are either annotated on the use cases or analysis realizations or that are identified during the generation of the design use case realizations. It is also useful to include a list of implementation issues that should be dealt with during the implementation workflow.

40.5.6 Generating a Sequence Diagram

There are a variety of ways in which you could generate a sequence diagram. The following presents a series of steps which can act as a guideline relating to how to do this:

- Identify all the classes involves in a particular sequence. You may notice that this statement assumes that all the classes are already defined; however, as with much of the design process, this is really an iterative process in which, as the classes become clearer, so the sequence diagrams may evolve.
- Determine the life line of the objects; that is, when they are created and when they are destroyed. If the sequence diagram creates or destroys the object then you will need to make this clear.
- Identify the initiating event (you should look to the use cases for this).
- Determine the subsequent message(s), i.e. what does the "boundary" object do when the actor initiates the event? Then consider the behaviour of the receiving object and what messages it might send etc.
- Identify the focus of control for the object.
- Identify any returned messages (returned values)
- Identify any deviations (either annotate them on the sequence diagram or generate separate sequence diagrams for each deviation).

40.5.7 Building a Statechart Diagram

You should construct a state diagram for each object class with nontrivial dynamic behaviour. Every sequence diagram (and thus collaboration diagram) corresponds to a path through a state diagram. Each branch in control flow is represented by a state with more than one exit transition. The procedure for producing state diagrams is summarized by the following algorithm:

1. Pick a class.
2. Pick one sequence diagram involving that class.
3. Follow the events for the class; the gaps between the events are states. Give each state a name (if it is meaningful to do so).
4. Draw a set of states and the events that link them based on the sequence diagrams.
5. Find loops – repeated sequences of states – within the diagram.
6. Choose another sequence diagram for the class and produce the states and events for that diagram. Merge these states and events into the first diagram.
7. Repeat Step 6 for all sequence diagrams involving this class.
8. Repeat from Step 1 for all classes.

After considering all normal events, add boundary cases and special cases. You should now consider any conditions on the transitions between states and any events that are triggered off by these transitions.

40.5.8 Identifying and Refining Associations

To identify design associations between design classes:

*   Look at the analysis entity class associations.
*   Look at messages in interaction diagrams. Every time an event of operation is sent between two objects in an interaction diagram, there needs to be an association place.
*   Look at use of interfaces. If one class implements an interface and another class uses that same interface, then there is an implied association between the two.
*   Look at access paths. Make sure that any collaborations which are required to support all use cases are supported by appropriate associations.
*   Consider association multiplicity, role names, association classes, ordering etc.
*   Consider whether association is aggregation (i.e is an inner class required)?

Having identified an initial set of associations, it is still necessary to refine them. The questions you ask to refine associations are the same as those asked in the analysis phase.

40.5.9 Identifying Interfaces and Inheritance

As with the analysis phase you should now attempt to identify any inheritance and system (as well as core entity) interfaces. As noted although this chapter, this is more incremental than is implied here. The places to look for interfaces include:

*   Interfaces between subsystems, as these are considered architecturally significant
*   Dependencies between classes, classes and subsystems, subsystems and subsystems
*   Dependencies between layers

Places to look for inheritance include:

*   Common operations and attributes between classes (Generalization)
*   Special cases of classes (Specialization)

- Functionality provided by C# classes
- Common associations and dependencies – may imply a package
- Move functionality and attributes up the hierarchy as high as possible.

40.5.10 Remaining Steps

The remaining steps that you should consider in this phase are:

- Optimize the design by looking for redundant associations that will simplify the implementation or rearranging the computation for greater efficiency etc.
- Test all access paths.
- Design the form of control to be used in the application (for example determine how and where events will be triggered).
- Adjust the class structure in light of the evolving design.
- Determine how associations will be implemented.

40.6 Implementation Workflow

This section considers the implementation workflow of the Unified Process. This workflow is concerned with implementing the design produced by the design workflow (that is, in C# terms it concentrates on implementing classes and interfaces, creating packages and producing class files). It also deals with the remaining non-functional requirements and the deployment of the "executable" modules (in our case C# class files) onto nodes (such as specific processors etc.). It must therefore deal with any implementation issues that have been left as too specific during the design workflow.

You should treat the implementation of an object-oriented system in just the same way as you would treat the implementation of any software system. This means that it should be subject to, and controlled by, the same processes as any other implementation.

40.7 Testing Workflow

The aim of the test workflow is to ensure that the system provides the required functionality. As the required functionality was originally captured in the form of the use cases in the use case model, there is obviously some form of relationship between the two. Therefore the system as implemented should be tested against the use cases as originally identified. You should therefore start to build you test plan based on your use cases. However, you should not be blind to other sources of test information, as use cases are just one source of test information (albeit a very important one).

40.8 Summary

To conclude, the Unified Process is a design process framework that is hierarchical, as it is made from a Unified Process of cycles, comprised of phases, which are themselves made from a Unified Process from workflows that describe how activities are linked.

References

Alexander, C., Ishikawa, S. and Silverstein, M. (with Jacobson, M., Fiksdahl-King, I. and Angel, S.) (1977). *A Pattern Language: Towns, Buildings, Construction*. New York: Oxford University Press.

Alexander, C. (1979). *The Timeless Way of Building*. New York: Oxford University Press.

Arnold, K. and Gosling, J. (2000). *The Java Programming Language*. Reading, MA: Addison Wesley.

Beck, K. and Johnson, R. (1994) Patterns generate architectures. *Proceedings of ECOOP'94*, pp. 139–149.

Ben-Natan, R. (1995). *CORBA: A Guide to Common Object Request Broker Architecture*. New York: McGraw-Hill.

Binder, Robert V. (ed.) (1994). Special Issue of *Communications of the ACM: Object-Oriented Software Testing* **37**(9). ACM Press.

Binder, Robert V. (1994). Design for testability in object-oriented systems. *Special Issue of Communications of the ACM: Object-Oriented Software Testing*, **37**(9), 87–101.

Birrer, A. and Eggenschmiler, T. (1993). Frameworks in the financial engineering domain: an experience report. *Proceedings of ECOOP'93*, pp. 21–35.

Boehm, B. W. (1988) A spiral model of software development and enhancement. *IEEE Computer*, May, 61–72.

Booch, G. (1986). Object-oriented Development. *IEEE Transactions on Software Engineering*, February, **12**(2), 211–221.

Booch, G. (1987). *Software Components with Ada*. Menlo Park, CA: Benjamin Cummings.

Booch, G. (1991). *Object-Oriented Design with Applications*. Menlo Park, CA: Benjamin Cummings.

Booch, G. (1994). *Object-Oriented Analysis and Design with Applications*, 2nd edn. Redwood City, CA: Benjamin Cummings.

Booch, G. (1996). *Object Solutions: Managing the Object-Oriented Project*. Menlo Park, CA: Addison–Wesley.

Booch, G., Jacobson, I. and Rumbaugh, J. (1997). *The Unified Modeling Language User Guide*. Reading, MA: Addison–Wesley.

Brooks, F. (1987). No silver bullet: essence and accidents of software engineering, *IEEE Computer*, April.

Brown, A. L. (1989). *Persistent Object Stores*. Ph.D. Thesis, University of St Andrews, Scotland.

Budd, T. (1991). *An Introduction to Object-Oriented Programming*. Reading, MA: Addison–Wesley.

Budinsky, F. J. *et al.* (1996). Automatic code generation from design patterns. *IBM Systems Journal*, **35**(2).

Buschmann, F. *et al.* (1996). *Pattern-Oriented Software Architecture – A System of Patterns*. Chichester: Wiley.

Chan, P., Lee, R. and Kramer, D. (1997). *The Java Class Libraries*, Vol. 2. Reading, MA: Addison-Wesley.

Chan, P., Lee, R. and Kramer, D. (1998). *The Java Class Libraries*, Vol. 1. Reading, MA: Addison-Wesley.

Chan, P., Lee, R. and Kramer, D. (1999). *The Java Class Libraries*, 2nd edn, Vol. 1. Supplement for the Java 2 Platform, Standard Edition, v1.2. Reading, MA: Addison Wesley; ISBN: 0201485524

Coad, P. and Yourdon, E. (1991). *Object-Oriented Analysis*. Englewood Cliffs, NJ: Yourdon Press.

Coleman, D., Arnold P. *et al.* (1994). *Object-Oriented Development: The Fusion Method*. Englewood Cliffs, NJ: Prentice Hall.

Cook, S. and Daniels, J. (1994). *Designing Object-Oriented Systems: Object-Oriented modelling with Syntropy*. New York: Prentice Hall.

Coplien, J. O. and Schmidt, D. C. (eds.) (1995). *Pattern Languages of Program Design*. Reading, MA: Addison–Wesley.

Cornell, G. and Horstmann, C. S. (1997). *Core JAVA*, 2nd edn. Upper Saddle River, NJ: Prentice Hall.

Cox, B. J. (1990). There *is* a silver bullet. *BYTE*, October, pp. 209–218.

Cox, B. J. and Novobilski, A. (1991). *Object-Oriented Programming: An Evolutionary Approach*, 2nd edn. Reading, MA: Addison–Wesley.

Derr, K. W. (1995). *Applying OMT: A Practical Step-by-Step Guide to Using the Object Modeling Technique*. Upper Saddle River, NJ: Prentice Hall.

ECOOP'89, *Third European Conference on Object-Oriented Programming* (S. Cook ed.). The British Computer Society Workshop series. Cambridge: Cambridge University Press.

ECOOP'92, *European Conference on Object-Oriented Programming* (O. Lehrmann Madsen ed.). Lecture Notes in Computer Science series. Berlin: Springer-Verlag.

ECOOP'93, *European Conference on Object-Oriented Programming*. Lecture Notes in Computer Science 707. Berlin: Springer-Verlag.

ECOOP'94, *European Conference on Object-Oriented Programming*. Lecture Notes in Computer Science 821. Berlin: Springer-Verlag.

ECOOP'95, *Ninth European Conference on Object-Oriented Programming*. Lecture Notes in Computer Science 952. Berlin: Springer-Verlag.

Englander, R. (1997). *Developing JavaBeans*. Sebastopol, CA: O'Reilly.

Flanagan, D. (1996). *Java in a Nutshell*. Sebastopol, CA: O'Reilly.

Fowler, M. (1997). *Analysis Patterns: Reusable Object Models*. Reading, MA: Addison–Wesley.

Fowler, M. and Scott, K. (1997). *UML Distilled*. Reading, MA: Addison–Wesley.

Freedman, R. S. (1991). Testability of software components. *IEEE Trans. Softw. Eng.*, **17**(6), 553–564.

Gamma, E., Helm, R., Johnson, R. and Vlissides, J. (1993). Design patterns: abstraction and reuse of object-oriented design, *ECOOP'93* (Lecture Notes in Computer Science 707), pp. 406–431. Berlin: Springer-Verlag.

Gamma, E., Helm, R., Johnson, R. and Vlissides, J. (1995). *Design Patterns: Elements of Reusable Object-Oriented Software*. Reading, MA: Addison–Wesley.

Geary, D. M. and McClellan, A. L. (1997). *Graphic Java*. SunSoft Press.

Goldberg, A. (1984). *Smalltalk-80: The Interactive Programming Environment*. Reading, MA: Addison–Wesley.

Goldberg, A. and Robson, D. (1983). *Smalltalk-80: The Language and its Implementation*. Reading, MA: Addison–Wesley.

Goldberg, A. and Robson, D. (1989). *Smalltalk-80: The Language*. Reading, MA: Addison–Wesley.

Gosling, J. and Yellin, F. (1996). *The Java Application Programming Interface, Vol. 1: Core Packages*. Reading, MA: Addison–Wesley.

Gosling, J. and Yellin, F. (1996). *The Java Application Programming Interface, Vol. 2: Window Toolkit and Applets*. Reading, MA: Addison–Wesley.

Gosling, J., Joy, B. and Steele, G. (1996). *The Java Language Specification*. Reading, MA: Addison–Wesley.

Hamilton, G., Cattell, R. and Fisher, M. (1997). *JDBC Database Access With Java: A Tutorial and Annotated Reference*. Reading, MA: Addison-Wesley,.

Harel, D. (1988). On visual formalisms. *Communications of the ACM*, **31**(5), 514–530.

Harel, D., Pnueli, A., Schmidt, J. and Sherman, R. (1987). On the formal semantics of statecharts, *Proceedings of the 2nd IEEE Symposium on Logic in Computer Science*, Ithaca, NY, pp. 54–64.

Harmon, P. and Taylor, D. (1993). *Objects in Action: Commercial Applications of Object-Oriented Technologies*. Reading, MA: Addison–Wesley.

Hoffman, D. and Strooper, P. (1995). The testgraph methodology: automated testing of collection classes. *Journal of Object-Oriented Programming*, **8**(7), 35–41.

Hopkins, T. and Horan, B. (1995). *Smalltalk: An Introduction to Application Development Using VisualWorks*. Upper Saddle River, NJ: Prentice Hall.

Hunt, J. E. (1997). Constructing modular user interfaces in Java. *Java Report*, **2**(8), 25–32.

Hunt J. E. (2000). *The Unified Process for Practitioners*. London: Springer-Verlag.

ISO (1993). *Information Technology, Software Packages, Quality Requirements and Testing*. ISO Draft International Standard, ISO/IEC DIS 12119.

Jacobson, I. (1992). *Object-Oriented Software Engineering: A Use Case Driven Approach*. Reading, MA: Addison–Wesley.

Jacobson, I., Booch, G. and Rumbaugh, J. (1998). *The Unified Software Development Process*. Reading, MA: Addison-Wesley.

Jepson, B. (1997). *Java Database Programming*. Chichester: John Wiley.

Jepson, B. (1998). *Official Guide to Mini SQL 2.0* Chichester: John Wiley.

Johnson, R. E. (1992). Documenting Frameworks with Patterns. *Proceedings of OOPSLA'92, SIGPLAN Notices*, **27**(10), 63–76.

Kemerer, C. F. (1987). An Empirical validation of software cost estimation models. *Communications of the ACM*, **30**(5), 416–429.

Kernighan, B. W. and Ritchie, D. M. (1988). *The C Programming Language*, 2nd edn. Englewood Cliffs, NJ: Prentice Hall.

Krasner, G. E. and Pope, S. T. (1988). A cookbook for using the Model-View Controller user interface paradigm in Smalltalk-80. *Journal of Object-Oriented Programming*, **1**(3), 26–49.

Kuhn, T. (1962). *The Structure of Scientific Revolutions*. Chicago, IL: University of Chicago Press.

Lalonde, W. and Pugh, J. (1991). Subclassing /= subtyping /= Is-a. *Journal of Object-Oriented Programming*, January, 57–62.

Lindholm, T. and Yellin, F. (1996). *The Java Virtual Machine Specification*. Reading, MA: Addison–Wesley.

Love, T. (1993). *Object Lessons: Lessons Learned in Object-Oriented Development Projects*. New York: SIGS Books.

Meyer, B. and Nerson, J. (1993). *Object-Oriented Applications*. Englewood Cliffs, NJ: Prentice Hall.

Meyer, B. (1988). *Object-Oriented Software Construction*. Englewood Cliffs, NJ: Prentice Hall International.

Microsoft (1997). *Microsoft ODBC 3.0 Software Development Kit and Programmers Reference*. Redmond, WA: Microsoft Press.

Moser, S. and Nierstrasz, O. (1996). The effect of object-oriented frameworks on developer productivity. *IEEE Computer*, September, 45–51.

Moss, K. (1998). *Java Servlets*. New York: McGraw-Hill.

Myers, G. J. (1979). *The Art of Software Testing*. Chichester: John Wiley.

OOPSLA/ECOOP'90, *Joint Conference on Object-Oriented Programming: Systems, Languages and Applications* (N. Meyrowitz ed.). Reading, MA: Addison–Wesley.

OOPSLA'91, *Conference on Object-Oriented Programming Systems, Languages and Applications*; also as *ACM SIGPLAN Notices*, **26**(11) (A. Paepcke ed.). Reading, MA: Addison–Wesley.

OOPSLA'92, *Seventh Annual Conference on Object-Oriented Programming Systems, Languages and Applications*; also as *ACM SIGPLAN Notices*, **27**(10) (A. Paepcke ed.). Reading, MA: Addison–Wesley.

OOPSLA'93, *Conference on Object-Oriented Programming Systems, Languages and Applications*. Reading, MA: Addison–Wesley.

Orfali, R., Harkey, D. and Edwards, J. (1995). *The Essential Distributed Objects Survival Guide*. Chichester: John Wiley.

Ousterhout, J. K. (1994). *TCL and the TK Toolkit*. Reading, MA: Addison–Wesley.

Palmer, I. (2001) *Essential Java3D Fast*. London: Springer-Verlag.

Parker, T. (1994). *Teach yourself TCP/IP in 14 Days*. Indianapolis, IN: Sams Publishing.

Perry, D. E. and Kaiser, G. E. (1990). Adequate testing and object-oriented programming. *Journal of Object-Oriented Programming*, **2**(5), 13–19.

Rational (2001). *UML Resource Center*. Rational Software Corporation (http://www.rational.com/uml/).

Reese, G. (1997). *Database Programming with JDBC and Java*. Sebastopol, CA: O'Reilly.

Rumbaugh, J., Blaha, M., Premerlani, W., Eddy, F. and Lorensen, W. (1991). *Object-Oriented Modeling and Design*. Englewood Cliffs, NJ: Prentice Hall.

Scharf, D. (1995). *HTML Visual Quick Reference*. Indianapolis, IN: Que.

Sevareid, J. (1997). The JDK 1.1's new delegation event model. *Java Report*, **2**(4), 59–79.

Smith, D. N. (1994). *IBM Smalltalk: The Language*. New York: Benjamin Cummings.

Sparks, S., Benner, K. and Faris, C. (1996). Managing object-oriented framework reuse. *IEEE Computer*, September, 52–61.

Stephens, R. K. (1997). *Teach Yourself SQL in 21 Days*, 2nd edn. Indianapolis, IN: Sams.

Taylor, D. A. (1992). *Object-Oriented Information Systems: Planning and Implementation*. New York: John Wiley.

van der Linden, P. (2001). *Just Java 2*. SunSoft Press.

Vlissides, J. M., Coplien, J. O. and Kerth, N. L. (1996). *Pattern Languages of Program Design 2*. Reading, MA: Addison–Wesley.

Wirfs-Brock, R., Wilkerson, B. and Wiener, L. (1990). *Designing Object-Oriented Software*. Englewood Cliffs, NJ: Prentice Hall.

Yourdon, E. (1994). *Object-Oriented Systems Design*. Upper Saddle River, NJ: Prentice Hall.

Index